Lecture Notes in Artificial Intelligence   3505

Edited by J. G. Carbonell and J. Siekmann

Subseries of Lecture Notes in Computer Science

Vladimir Gorodetsky   Jiming Liu
Victor A. Skormin (Eds.)

Autonomous Intelligent Systems: Agents and Data Mining

International Workshop, AIS-ADM 2005
St. Petersburg, Russia, June 6-8, 2005
Proceedings

 Springer

Series Editors

Jaime G. Carbonell, Carnegie Mellon University, Pittsburgh, PA, USA
Jörg Siekmann, University of Saarland, Saarbrücken, Germany

Volume Editors

Vladimir Gorodetsky
St. Petersburg Institute for Informatics and Automation
39, 14-th Liniya, St. Petersburg, 199178, Russia
E-mail: gor@mail.iias.spb.su

Jiming Liu
Hong Kong Baptist University, Kowloon Tong, Hong Kong
E-mail: jiming@comp.hkbu.edu.hk

Victor A. Skormin
Binghamton University, Watson School of Engineering
Binghamton, NY 13902, USA
E-mail: vskormin@binghamton.edu

Library of Congress Control Number: 2005926661

CR Subject Classification (1998): I.2, H.2.8, H.4, H.3, C.2.4

ISSN   0302-9743
ISBN-10   3-540-26164-8 Springer Berlin Heidelberg New York
ISBN-13   978-3-540-26164-3 Springer Berlin Heidelberg New York

Springer is a part of Springer Science+Business Media

springeronline.com

© Springer-Verlag Berlin Heidelberg 2005
Printed in Germany

Typesetting: Camera-ready by author, data conversion by Scientific Publishing Services, Chennai, India
Printed on acid-free paper   SPIN: 11492870   06/3142   5 4 3 2 1 0

Preface

This volume contains the papers presented at the International Workshop "Autonomous Intelligent Systems: Agents and Data Mining" (AIS-ADM 2005) held in St. Petersburg, Russia, during June 6–8, 2005. The workshop was organized by the St. Petersburg Institute for Informatics and Automation of the Russian Academy of Sciences (SPIIRAS) in cooperation with Binghamton University (SUNY, USA) and the Web Intelligence Consortium.

Autonomous Intelligent Systems (AIS) constitute an emerging class of intelligent information systems integrating recent advances in various technologies of Artificial Intelligence. Modern AIS incorporate multi-agent and data mining systems providing a new dimension for further progress in intelligent information technology.

AIS-ADM 2005 provided an international forum to multi-agent and data mining researchers. A total of 29 papers from 15 countries relating to various aspects of both theory and applications of multi-agent systems, data mining and their joint area were submitted to AIS-ADM 2005. Out of them 17 were selected as regular presentations. Three technical sessions were organized, namely: Integration of Multi-agent and Data Mining Techniques; Ontology Issues and Web Mining; and Applications and Case Studies of the Integrated Technology. The panel discussion was devoted to the mutual enrichment and challenging problems emerging in the joint area of research. The AIS-ADM 2005 program was enriched by six distinguished invited speakers: Nick Jennings, Chengqi Zhang, Mircea Negoita, Pericles Mitkas, Hai Zhuge and Leonid Perlovsky.

The success of the workshop was assured by the team efforts of sponsors, organizers, reviewers and participants. We would like to acknowledge the contribution of the individual Program Committee members and thank the paper reviewers. Our sincere gratitude goes to the participants and all the authors of the submitted papers.

We are grateful to our sponsors, the European Office of Aerospace Research and Development (EOARD) of the US Air Force; the US Office of Naval Research Global (ONRGlobal); the U.S. Army International Technology Center-Atlantic, European Research Office; the Russian Foundation for Basic Research (RFBR); the Ministry of Science and Education of the Russian Federation; and AgentLink III- European Co-ordination Action for Agent-Based Computing, for their generous support.

We wish to express our gratitude to Springer's LNCS team, managed by Alfred Hofmann, for their help and co-operation.

June 2005

Vladimir Gorodetsky
Jiming Liu
Victor Skormin

Organization

Workshop Chairmen

General Chairmen

Rafael M. Yusupov   St. Petersburg Institute for Informatics and
Automation, Russia

John Tangney   Air Force Office of Scientific Research, USA

Program Committee Chairmen

Vladimir Gorodetsky   St. Petersburg Institute for Informatics and
Automation, Russia

Jiming Liu   Hong Kong Baptist University, Hong Kong, China

Victor Skormin   Binghamton University, SUNY, USA

Program Committee

Reviewers

Eduardo Alonso	(University of York, UK)
Shlomo Berkovsky	(University of Haifa, Israel)
Sviatoslav Braynov	(University of Illinois at Springfield, USA)
Cory Butz	(University of Regina, Canada)
William Cheung	(Hong Kong Baptist University, Hong Kong, China)
Vladimir Gorodetsky	(SPIIRAS, Russia)
Heikki Helin	(TeliaSonera, Finland)
Henry Hexmoor	(University of Arkansas, USA)
Nick Jennings	(University of Southampton, UK)
Xiaolong Jin	(Hong Kong Baptist University, Hong Kong, China)
Oleg Karsaev	(SPIIRAS, Russia)
Kristian Kersting	(University of Freiburg, Germany)
Daniel Kudenko	(University of York, UK)
Raymond Y.K. Lau	(Queensland University of Technology, Australia)
Michael Luck	(University of Southampton, UK)
Vladimir Marik	(Czech Technical University, Czech Republic)
John Mashford	(CSIRO, Australia)
Pericles A. Mitkas	(Information and Telematics Institute, Greece)
Mircea Negoita	(Wellington Institute of Technology, New Zealand)
Hung Son Nguyen	(Institute of Decision Process Support, Poland)
Eugenio Oliveira	(University of Porto, Portugal)
Zbigniew Ras	(University of North Carolina, USA)
Andrzej Skowron	(Institute of Decision Process Support, Poland)
Josenildo C. da Silva	(DFKI, Germany)
Zhong Zhi Shi	(Institute for Computer Technology, China)
Alexander Smirnov	(SPIIRAS, Russia)
Huaglory Tianfield	(Glasgow Caledonian University, UK)
Huaiqing Wang	(University of Technology, Sydney, Australia)
Philipp Yu	(IBM Thomas J. Watson Research Center, USA)
Ning Zhong	(Maebashi Institute of Technology, Japan)
Hai Zhuge	(Chinese Academy of Sciences, China)
Nikolay Zagoruiko	(Sobolev Institute of Mathematics, Russia)

Table of Contents

Ontology and Web Mining

Applications and Case Studies

Negotiation Technologies

Nick Jennings

University of Southampton, Highfield, Southampton SO17 1BJ, UK
nrj@ecs.soton.ac.uk

Abstract. Negotiation is a key form of interaction in a wide variety of areas (including multi-agent systems, the Grid, pervasive computing, and the Semantic Web). Given this ubiquity, automated negotiation technologies exist in many different forms, each of which has different characteristics and properties. Against this background, this talk discusses work on a variety of models, covering bi-lateral encounters, auctions and argumentation-based negotiation.

V. Gorodetsky, J. Liu, and V.A. Skormin (Eds.): AIS-ADM 2005, LNAI 3505, p. 1, 2005.
© Springer-Verlag Berlin Heidelberg 2005

Knowledge Discovery for Training Intelligent Agents: Methodology, Tools and Applications

Pericles Mitkas

Department of Electrical and Computer Engineering,
Aristotle University of Thessaloniki,
and Informatics & Telematics Institute, CERTH,
Thessaloniki, Greece
Tel.: +30-2310-99-6390, Fax: +30-2310-99-6447
mitkas@eng.auth.gr

Abstract. In this paper we address a relatively young but important area of re-search: the intersection of agent technology and data mining. This intersection can take two forms: a) the more mundane use of intelligent agents for improved knowledge discovery and b) the use of data mining techniques for producing smarter, more efficient agents. The paper focuses on the second approach. Knowledge, hidden in voluminous data repositories routinely created and main-tained by today's applications, can be extracted by data mining. The next step is to transform this knowledge into the inference mechanisms or simply the be-havior of agents in multi-agent systems. We call this procedure "agent train-ing." We define different levels of agent training and we present a software en-gineering methodology that combines the application of deductive logic for generating intelligence from data with a process for transferring this knowledge into agents. We introduce Agent Academy, an integrated open-source frame-work, which supports data mining techniques and agent development tools. We also provide several examples of multi-agent systems developed with this approach.

1 Introduction

The astonishing rates at which data are generated and collected by current applica-tions are difficult to handle even for the most powerful of data processing systems. This windfall of information often requires another level of distillation to produce *knowledge*. Knowledge is the essence of information and comes in many flavors. Expert systems, knowledge bases, decision support systems, machine learning, autonomous systems, and intelligent agents are some of the many packages research-ers have invented in order to describe applications that mimic part of the human men-tal capabilities. A highly successful and widely popular process to extract knowledge from data repositories is data mining.

The application domain of Data Mining (DM) and its related techniques and tech-nologies have been greatly expanded in the last few years. The continuous improve-ment of hardware along with the existence of supporting algorithms have enabled the

V. Gorodetsky, J. Liu, and V.A. Skormin (Eds.): AIS-ADM 2005, LNAI 3505, pp. 2 – 18, 2005.
© Springer-Verlag Berlin Heidelberg 2005

development and flourishing of sophisticated DM methodologies. Numerous approaches have been adopted for the realization of autonomous and versatile DM tools to support all the appropriate pre- and post-processing steps of the knowledge discovery process in databases.

Since DM systems encompass a number of discrete, nevertheless dependent tasks, they can be viewed as networks of autonomous, yet collaborating units, which regulate, control and organize all the, potentially distributed, activities involved in the knowledge discovery process. Software agents, considered by many the evolution of objects, are autonomous entities that can perform these activities.

Agent technology (AT) has introduced a wide range of novel services that promise to dramatically affect the way humans interact with computers. The use of agents may transform computers into personal collaborators that can provide active assistance and even take the initiative in decision-making processes on behalf of their masters. Agents participate routinely in electronic auctions and roam the web searching for knowledge nuggets. They can facilitate 'smart' solutions in small and medium enterprises in the areas of management, resource allocation, and remote administration.

Research on software agents has demonstrated that complex problems, which require the synergy of a number of distributed elements for their solution, can be efficiently implemented as a multi-agent system (MAS). As a result, multi-agent technology has been repeatedly adopted as a powerful paradigm for developing DM systems.

In a MAS realizing a DM system, all requirements collected by the user and all the appropriate tasks are perceived as distinguished roles of separate agents, acting in close collaboration. All agents participating in a MAS communicate with each other by exchanging messages, encoded in a specific agent communication language. Each agent in the MAS is designated to manipulate the content of the incoming messages and take specific actions/decisions that conform to the particular reasoning mechanism specified by DM primitives [1-2].

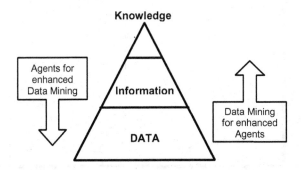

Fig. 1. Mining for intelligence

Considerable effort is expended to formulate improved knowledge models for data mining agents, which are expected to operate in a more efficient and intelligent way (see Fig. 1). Moving towards the opposite direction, we can envision the application of data mining techniques for the extraction of knowledge models that will be embedded into agents operating in diverse environments [1].

1.1   The Synergy of Data Mining and Agent Technology

A review of the literature reveals several attempts to couple DM and AT. Galitsky and Pampapathi in their work combine inductive and deductive reasoning, in order to model and process the claims of unsatisfied customers [3]. Deduction is used for describing the behaviors of agents (humans or companies), for which we have complete information, while induction is used to predict the behavior of agents, whose actions are uncertain to us. A more theoretical approach on the way DM-extracted knowledge can contribute to AT performance has been presented by Fernandes [4]. In this work, the notions of data, information, and knowledge are modeled in purely logical terms, in an effort to integrate inductive and deductive reasoning into one inference engine. Kero et al., finally, propose a DM model that utilizes both inductive and deductive components [5]. Within the context of their work, they model the discovery of knowledge as an iteration between high level, user-specified patterns and their elaboration to (deductive) database queries, whereas they define the notion of a meta-query that performs the (inductive) analysis of these queries and their transformation to modified, ready-to-use knowledge.

In rudimentary applications, agent intelligence is based on relatively simple rules, which can be easily deduced or induced, compensating for the higher development and maintenance costs. In more elaborate environments, however, where both requirements and agent behaviors need constant modification in real time, these

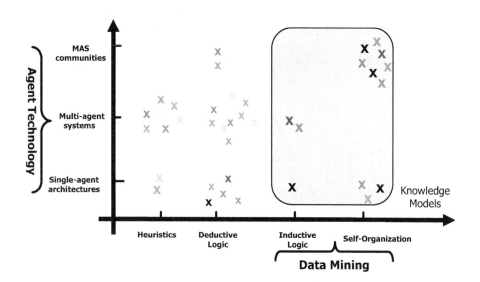

Fig. 2. Agent-based applications and inference mechanisms

approaches prove insufficient, since they cannot accommodate the dynamic transfer of DM results into the agents. To enable the incorporation of dynamic, complex, and reusable rules in multi-agent applications, a systematic approach must be adopted.

Existing agent-based solutions can be classified according to the granularity of the agent system and inference mechanism of the agents, as shown in Figure 2.

According to this qualitative representation of the MAS space, agent reasoning may fall under four major categories ranging from simple rule heuristics to self-organizing systems. Inductive logic and self-organization form two manifestations of data mining. Therefore, the shaded region delineates the scope of our approach.

The main thesis of this paper is that knowledge, hidden in voluminous data repositories, can be extracted by data mining and provide the logic for agents and multi-agent systems. In other words, these knowledge nuggets constitute the building blocks of agent intelligence. Here, intelligence is defined loosely so as to encompass a wide range of implementations from fully deterministic decision trees to self-organizing communities of autonomous agents. In many ways, intelligence manifests itself as efficiency. We argue that the two, otherwise diverse, technologies of data mining and intelligent agents can complement and benefit from each other, yielding more efficient solutions [1].

The dual process of knowledge discovery and intelligence infusion is equivalent to learning, better yet, teaching by experience. Indeed, existing application data (i.e., past transactions, decisions, data logs, agent actions, etc.) are filtered in an effort to distill the best, most successful, empirical rules and heuristics. The process can be applied initially to train 'dummy' agents and, as more data are gathered, it can be repeated periodically or on demand to further improve agent reasoning.

In this paper we describe a unified methodology for transferring DM-extracted knowledge into newly-created agents. As illustrated in Figure 3, data mining is used

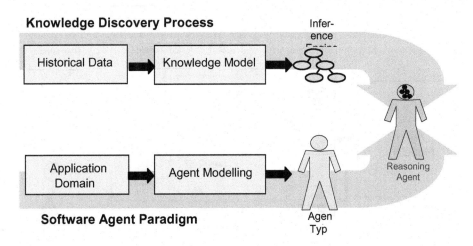

Fig. 3. Embedding DM-extracted knowledge into agents

to generate knowledge models which can be dynamically embedded into the agents.The process is suitable for either upgrading an existing, non agent-based application by adding agents to it, or for improving the already operating agents of an agent-based application. The methodology relies heavily on the inductive nature of data mining, while taking into account its limitations. Our perspective leans more towards agent-oriented software engineering (AOSE) than artificial intelligence (AI).

We have also developed an integrated platform, called *Agent Academy,* which consolidates the steps of our methodology and provides the user with access to a variety of software development tools in a single environment. *Agent Academy* (AA) is an open-source product, which combines data mining functionality with agent design and development capabilities [6,7]. We have used AA to implement a number of agent-based applications. Some of them are briefly described in this paper.

The remainder of the paper is organized as follows: Section 2 presents the methodology for agent training, while Section 3 describes the architecture and basic functionality of AA. Section 4 outlines a few multi-agent systems that were developed with AA and Section 5 contains a summary of this work and our conclusions.

2 Methodology

In this section, we present a unified methodology for MAS development, which relies on the ability of DM to generate knowledge models for agents. As shown in Figure 4,

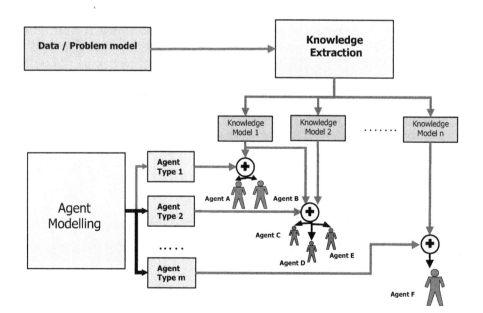

Fig. 4. Different agent types may receive one or more DM-extracted knowledge models

agent types, defined during the agent modelling phase, receive one or more knowledge models extracted through a separate process. Each agent type will give rise to one or more agent instances.

In our approach, we consider three distinct cases, which correspond to three types of knowledge extracted and to different data sources and mining techniques. These three types demarcate also three different modes of knowledge diffusion.

Case 1. Knowledge extracted by performing DM on historical datasets recording the business logic (at a macroscopic level) of a certain application

Case 2. Knowledge extracted by performing DM on log files recording the behavior of the agents (at a microscopic level) in an agent-based application, and

Case 3. Knowledge extracted by the use of evolutionary data DM techniques in agent communities.

The basic methodology encompasses a number of stages and is suitable for all three cases of knowledge diffusion. Most of the steps are common to all cases, while some require minor modifications to accommodate each case (see Figure 5).

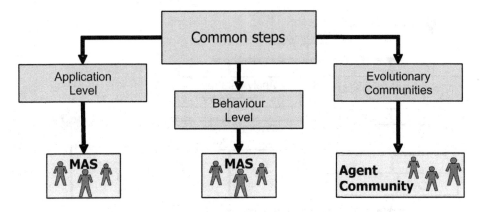

Fig. 5. Three cases of the methodology

The methodology pays special attention to two issues: a) the ability to dynamically embed the extracted knowledge models (KMs) into the agents and b) the ability to repeat the above process as many times as deemed necessary. Standard AOSE processes are followed, in order to specify the application ontology, the agent behaviors and agent types, the communication protocol between the agents, and their interactions. In parallel, DM techniques are applied for the extraction of appropriate KMs.

The ten steps of the methodology are listed below. They are also illustrated in the form of a flow diagram in Figure 6. It must be noted that steps 9 and 10 are optional and needed only when agent retraining is required. The interested reader may find a more detailed description of the methodology in Reference [1].

```
1.  Develop the application ontology
2.  Design and develop agent behaviours
3.  Develop agent types realizing the created behaviours
4.  Apply data mining techniques on the provided dataset
5.  Extract knowledge models for each agent type
6.  Create the agent instances for the application
7.  Dynamically incorporate the knowledge models to the
    corresponding agents
8.  Instantiate multi-agent application
9.  Monitor agent actions
10. Periodically retrain the agents of the system
```

Following this methodology, we can automate (or semi-automate) several of the processes involved in the development and instantiation of MAS. Taking an AOSE perspective, we can increase the adaptability, reusability, and flexibility of multi-agent applications, simply by re-applying DM on different datasets and incorporating the extracted KMs into the corresponding agents. Thus, MAS can be considered as efficient add-on components for the improvement of existing software architectures.

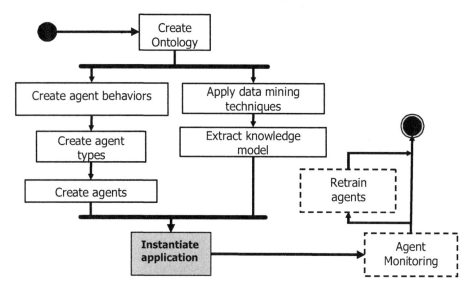

Fig. 6. The MAS development mechanism

Slight variations and/or additions may be needed to the presented methodology in order to adapt it to each one of the three cases. These differentiations may be either related to the agent behaviour creation phase (Cases 2 and 3 - e.g., model agent actions), the training phase (Cases 1, 2, and 3 - e.g., training set selection, knowledge model representation, retraining intervals), or the retraining phase (Cases 1,2, and 3 - e.g., retraining initiation).

Let us consider a company that would like to embrace agent technology and transform its processes from legacy software to a MAS. During the modelling phase, agent roles and interactions are specified. Then, agent behaviours and logic models have to be defined, a process extremely complicated, since the specification of an appropriate (sound) set of rules is not always straightforward.

In most cases, domain understanding is infused to the system in the form of static business rules, which aim to satisfy refractory, nevertheless suboptimal, MAS performance. In the case the rules are set by a domain expert, there is a high probability of ignoring interesting correlations between events that may occur during system operation. Moreover, the rigidity of the rules introduced, cannot capture the dynamism of the problem at hand (the problem the MAS is assigned to solve). The extraction of useful knowledge models from historical application data is, therefore, considered of great importance.

3   Agent Academy: A Platform for Developing and Training Agents

We have developed an integrated platform that automates most of the steps outlined in the previous section. Agent Academy is an open-source software platform available at http://www.source-forge.net/projects/AgentAcademy. AA has been implemented upon the JADE [8,10] infrastructure, ensuring a relatively high degree of FIPA compatibility, as defined in [9,10]. AA is itself a multi-agent system, whose architecture is based on the GAIA methodology [11]. It provides an integrated GUI-based environment that enables the design of single agents or multi-agent communities, using common drag-and-drop operations. Using AA, an agent developer can easily go into the details of the designated behaviours of agents and precisely regulate communication properties of agents. These include the type and number of the agent communication language (ACL) messages exchanged between agents, the performatives and structure of messages, with respect to FIPA specifications [12-14], as well as the semantics, which can be defined by constructing ontologies with Protégé-2000 [15].

AA also supports the extraction of decision models from data and the insertion of these models into newly created agents. Developing an agent application using AA involves the following activities from the developer's side:

a. the creation of new agents with limited initial reasoning capabilities;
b. the addition of these agents into a new MAS;
c. the determination of existing, or the creation of new behaviour types for each agent;
d. the importation of ontology-files from Protégé-2000;
e. the determination of message recipients for each agent.

In case the developer intends to create a reasoning engine for one or more agents of the designed MAS, four more operations are required for each of those agents:

f. the determination of an available data source of *agent decision attributes*;
g. the specification the parameters of the data mining mechanism;
h. the extraction of the decision/knowledge model;
i. the insertion of this model to the agent.

Figure 7 illustrates the Agent Academy functional diagram, which represents the main components and the interactions between them. In the remainder of this section, we discuss the AA architecture and outline its main functionality.

3.1 Architecture

The main architecture of AA is also shown in Figure 7. An application developer launches the AA platform in order to design a multi-agent application. The main GUI of the development environment is provided by the Agent Factory (AF), a specifically designed agent, whose role is to collect all required information from the agent application developer regarding the definition of the types of agents involved in the MAS, the types of behaviours of these agents, as well as the ontology they share with each other. For this purpose, Agent Academy provides a Protégé-2000 front-end. The initially created agents possess no referencing capabilities ("dummy" agents). The developer may request from the system to create rule-based reasoning for one or more agents of the new MAS. These agents interoparate with the *Agent-Training Module* (ATM), which is responsible for inserting a specific decision model into them. The latter is produced by performing DM on data entered into Agent Academy as XML documents or as datasets stored in a database. This task is performed by the *Data Mining Module* (DMM), another agent of AA, whose task is to read available data and extract decision models, expressed in PMML format [16].

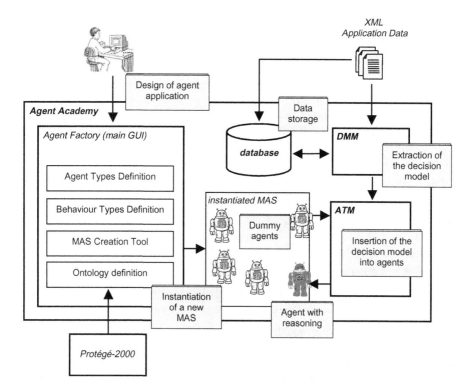

Fig. 7. Diagram of the Agent Academy development framework

AA hosts a database system for storing all information about the configuration of AA-created agents, their decision models, as well as data entered into the system for DM purposes. The whole AA platform was created as a MAS, executed on JADE.

3.2 Developing Multi-agent Applications

Agent Factory consists of a set of graphical tools, which enable the developer to carry out all required tasks for the design and creation of a MAS, without any effort for writing even a single line of source code. In particular, the Agent Factory comprises the Ontology Design Tool, the Behaviour Type Design Tool, the Agent Type Definition Tool, and the MAS Creation Tool.

a) Creating Agent Ontologies

A required process in the creation of a MAS, is the design of one or more ontologies, in order for the agents to interoperate adequately. The Agent Factory provides an *Ontology Design Tool*, which helps developers adopt ontologies defined with the Protégé-2000, a tool for designing ontologies. The RDF files that are created with Protégé are saved in the AA database for further use. Since AA employs JADE for agent development, ontologies need to be converted into special JADE ontology classes. For this purpose, our framework automatically compiles the RDF files into JADE ontology classes.

b) Creating Behaviour Types

The *Behaviour Type Design Tool* assists the developer in defining generic behaviour templates. Agent behaviours are modeled as workflows of basic building blocks, such as receiving/sending a message, executing an in-house application, and, if necessary, deriving decisions using inference engines. The data and control dependencies between these blocks are also handled. The behaviours can be modeled as *cyclic* or *one-shot* behaviours of the JADE platform. These behaviour types are generic templates that can be configured to behave in different ways; the structure of the flow is the only process defined, while the configurable parameters of the application inside the behaviour, as well as the contents of the messages can be specified using the MAS Creation Tool. It should be denoted that the behaviours are specialized according to the application domain.

The building blocks of the workflows, which are represented by nodes, can be of four types:

1. `Receive nodes`, which enable the agent to filter incoming FIPA-SL0 messages.
2. `Send nodes`, which enable the agent to compose and send FIPA-SL0 messages.
3. `Activity nodes`, which enable the developer to add predefined functions to the workflow of the behaviour, in order to permit the construction of multi-agent systems for existing distributed systems.
4. `Jess nodes`, which enable the agent to execute a particular reasoning engine, in order to deliberate about the way it will behave.

c) Creating Agent Types

After having defined certain behaviour types, the *Agent Type Definition Tool* is provided to create new agent types, in order for them to be used later in the MAS Creation Tool. An agent type is in fact an agent plus a set of behaviours assigned to it. New agent types can be constructed from scratch or by modifying existing ones. Agent types can be seen as templates for creating agent instances during the design of a MAS.

During the MAS instantiation phase, which is realized by the use of the MAS Creation Tool, several instances of already designed agent types will be instantiated, with different values for their parameters. Each agent instance of the same agent type can deliver data from different data sources, communicate with different types of agents, and even execute different reasoning engines.

d) Deploying a Multi Agent System

The design of the behaviour and agent types is followed by the deployment of the MAS. The *MAS Creation Tool* enables the instantiation of all defined agents running in the system from the designed agent templates. The receivers and senders of the ACL messages are set in the behaviours of each agent. After all the parameters are defined, the agent instances can be initialized. Agent Factory creates *default AA Agents*, which have the ability to communicate with AF and ATM. Then, the AF sends to each agent the necessary ontologies, behaviours, and decision structures.

3.3   Data Mining and Agent Training

The inference engine of an agent that needs to be trained is generated as the outcome of the application of DM techniques into available data. This operation takes place in the DMM. The mechanism for embedding rule-based reasoning capabilities into agents is realized through the ATM. Both modules are implemented as JADE agents, which act in close collaboration.

The flow of the agent training process is shown in Figure 8. At first, let us consider an available source of data formatted in XML. The DMM receives data from the XML document and executes certain DM algorithms (suitable for generating a decision model), determined by the agent-application developer. The output of the DM procedure is formatted as a PMML document.

PMML is an XML-based language, which provides a rapid and efficient way for companies to define predictive models and share models between compliant vendors' applications. It allows users to develop models within one vendor's application, and use other vendors' applications to visualize, analyze, evaluate or otherwise use the models. The fact that PMML is a data mining standard defined by DMG (Data Mining Group) [16] provides the AA platform with versatility and compatibility to other major data mining software vendors, such as Oracle, SAS, SPSS and MineIt.

The PMML document represents a KM for the agent we intend to train. This model is translated, through the ATM, to a set of facts executed by a rule engine. The implementation of the rule engine is provided by JESS [17], a robust mechanism for executing rule-based reasoning. Finally, the execution of the rule engine becomes part of the agent's behaviour.

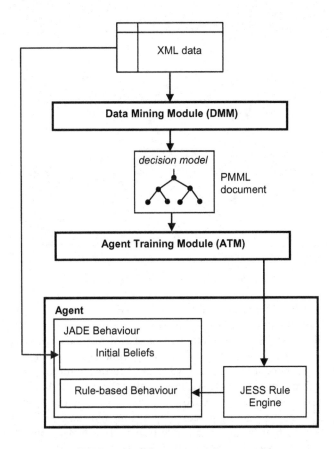

Fig. 8. Diagram of the agent training procedure

As shown in Figure 8, an agent that can be trained through the provided infrastructure encapsulates two types of behaviours. The first is the basic initial behaviour predefined by the AF module. This may include a set of class instances that inherit the
Behaviour class defined in JADE. The initial behaviour is created at the agent generation phase, using the Behaviour Design Tool, as described in the previous section.
This type of behaviour characterizes all agents designed by Agent Academy, even if
the developer intends to equip them with rule-based reasoning capabilities. This essential type of behaviour includes the set of initial agent beliefs.

The second supported type of behaviour is the rule-based behaviour, which is op-
tionally created, upon activation of the agent-training feature. This type of behaviour
is dynamic and implements the decision model.

In the remainder of this section, we take a closer look at the DMM. In the initial
phase of the DM procedure, the developer launches the GUI-based wizard depicted in
Figure 9 and specifies the data source to be loaded and the *agent decision attributes*
that will be represented as internal nodes of the extracted decision model. In subsequent steps, the developer selects the type of the DM technique from a set of available

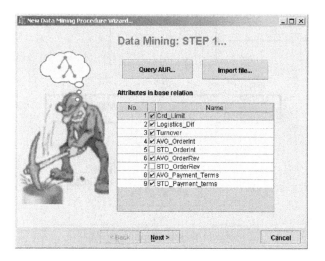

Fig. 9. The first step of the DMM wizard

options, which include classification, clustering, and association rule extraction. For each technique, a number of DM algorithms are at the user's disposal.

DMM was developed by incorporating a set of DM methods based on the WEKA [18] library and tools and by adding some new algorithms. We have also extended the WEKA API in order for it to support PMML. For further information on the developed DM algorithms and on the DMM functionality the interested reader may see [1, 21] or visit http://www.source-forge.net/projects/DataMiner.

The completion of the training process requires the translation of the DM resulted decision model into an agent-understandable format. This is performed by the ATM, which receives the PMML output as an ACL message sent by the DMM, as soon as the DM procedure is completed, and activates the rule engine. Actually, the ATM converts the PMML document into JESS rules and communicates, via appropriate messages, with the "trainee" agent, in order to insert the new decision model into it. After the completion of this process, our framework automatically generates Java source code and instantiates the new "trained" agent into the predefined MAS. The total configuration of the new agent is stored in the development framework, enabling future modifications of the training parameters, or even the retraining of the already "trained" agents.

4 Applications

The interesting, non-trivial, implicit and potentially useful knowledge extracted by the use of DM would be expected to find fast application on the development and realization of agent intelligence. The incorporation of knowledge based on previous observations may considerably improve agent infrastructures while also increasing reusability and minimizing customization costs.

In order to demonstrate the feasibility of our approach, we have developed several agent-based applications that cover all three cases of knowledge diffusion [1]. Using

AA we have built an agent-based recommendation engine situated on top of an operating ERP system and capable of tapping the wealth of data stored in the ERP's databases [19]. Such an approach can combine the decision support capabilities of more traditional approaches for supply chain management (SCM), customer relationship management (CRM), and supplier relationship management (SRM) [20]. This was clearly a system that implements Case 1 of knowledge diffusion, since data mining is performed on historical application data.

We have also applied the methodology for the development of an environmental monitoring system which falls into the class of applications called Environmental Monitoring Information Systems (EMIS). The primary function of EMIS is the continuous monitoring of several environmental indicators in an effort to produce sound and validated information. The architectures and functionalities of EMIS vary from naive configurations, focused on data collection and projection, to elaborate decision-support frameworks dealing with phenomena surveillance, data storage and manipulation, knowledge discovery and diffusion to the end users (government agencies, non-governmental organizations, and citizens). The presented synergy of AT and DM can provide to EMIS efficient solutions for the monitoring, management and distribution of environmental changes, while eliminating the time-overhead that often exists between data producers and data consumers. The MAS that we developed is situated upon a sensor network that monitors a number of air quality indicators and pollutants [22]. The MAS interweaves multiple data streams, validates and stores the information, decides whether an alarm must be issued, and, in the latter case, notifies the interested parties.

To demonstrate Case 2 of knowledge diffusion, we have implemented a MAS, which addresses the problem of predicting the future behaviour of agents based on their past actions/decisions. With this system we showed how data mining, performed on agent behaviour datasets, can yield usable behaviour profiles. We have introduced ! -profile, a DM process to produce recommendations based on aggregate action profiles [23]. The system in this case is a web navigation engine, which tracks user actions in corporate sites and suggests possibly interesting sites. This framework can be extended to cover a large variety of web services and/or intranet applications.

Another interesting area that is classified as Case 2, involves the improvement of the efficiency of agents in e-commerce and, more specifically, agents participating in e-auctions [24]. The goal here is to create both rational and efficient agent behaviours, to enable reliable agent-mediated transactions. In fact, through the presented methodology the improvement of agent behaviours in auctions is feasible (see Figure 10). Data mining can be performed on available historical data describing the bidding flow and the results can be used to improve the bidding mechanism of agents for e-auctions. Appropriate analysis of the data produced as an auction progresses (historical data) can lead to more accurate short-term forecasting. By the use of trend analysis techniques, an agent can comprehend the bidding policy of its rivals, and, thus, readjust its own in order to yield higher profits for buyers. In addition, the number of negotiations between interested parties is reduced (m instead of n, where $m<n$), since accurate forecasting implies more efficient bidding.

Finally, we have developed Biotope [25] as a typical example of knowledge diffusion in agent communities and evolutionary systems (Case 3). Biotope is an agent

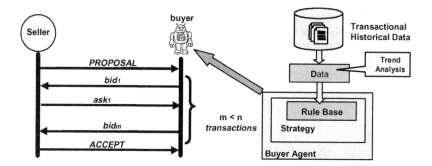

Fig. 10. Improving the behavior of agents participating in e-auctions

community used to simulate an ecosystem, where agents, representing living organisms, live, explore, feed, multiply, and eventually die in an environment with varying degrees of uncertainty. Genetic algorithms and agent communication primitives are exploited to implement knowledge transfer, which is essential for the survival of the community.

Multi-agent systems can also be exploited for the improvement of the software development process [1]. Software houses often develop frameworks for building end-user applications, following a standard methodology. Such frameworks interconnect different software modules and combine different software processes into workflows, in order to produce the desired outcome. Apart from the scheduling and planning, where agents collaborate and negotiate to reach the optimal solution, data mining techniques can be applied on workflow graphs, in order to discover correlations between certain workflow traverses. In addition, DM techniques can be applied to solve any kind of application-level problems, i.e., decision making capabilities.

5 Summary and Conclusions

In this paper we have presented the concept of combining the two, otherwise diverse areas, of data mining and agent technology. Limitations related to the nature of different types of logic adopted by DM and AT (inductive and deductive, respectively), hinder the unflustered application of knowledge to agent reasoning. We argue that our methodology can overcome these limitations and make the coupling of DM and AT feasible. Nevertheless, for a fruitful coupling, either historical data (application or agent-behaviour) must be available, or the knowledge mechanisms of agents must allow self-organization.

Agent Academy is a multi-agent development framework for constructing MAS, or single agents. AA combines a GUI-based, high-level MAS authoring tool with a facility for extracting rule-based reasoning from available data and inserting it into agents. The produced knowledge is expressed as PMML formatted documents. We have presented the functional architecture of our framework and outlined the agent training process.

Through our experience with Agent Academy, we are convinced that this development environment significantly reduces the programming effort for building agent applications, both in terms of time and code efficiency, especially for those MAS developers who use JADE. For instance, one MAS, that requires the writing of almost 6,000 lines of Java code, using JADE, requires less than one hour to be developed with Agent Academy. This test indicates that AA meets the requirement for making agent programs in a quicker and easier manner. On the other hand, our experiments with the DMM have shown that the completion of the decision model generated for agent reasoning is highly dependant on the amount of available data. In particular, a dataset of more than 10,000 records is adequate enough for producing high-confidence DM results, while datasets with fewer than 3,000 records have yielded non-consistent arbitrary output.

Acknowledgements

Work presented in this paper was partially funded by the European Commission, under the IST initiative as a research and development project (contract number IST-2000-31050, "Agent Academy: A Data Mining Framework for Training Intelligent Agents"). The author would like to thank all members of the Agent Academy consortium for their remarkable efforts in the development of such a large project.

References

1. Symeonidis, A., Mitkas, P.A.: Agent Intelligence Through Data Mining, Springer, (2005)
2. Lind J.: Issues in Agent-Oriented Software Engineering. In: First International Workshop on Agent-Oriented Software Engineering (AOSE-2000), Limerick, Ireland (2000)
3. Galitsky, B. and Pampapathi, R.: Deductive and inductive reasoning for processing the claims of unsatisfied customers. Proc. of the 16th IEA/AIE Conference. Springer-Verlag. (2003) 21–30
4. Fernandes, A. A. A.: Combining inductive and deductive inference in knowledge management tasks. Proc. of the 11th International Workshop on Database and Expert Systems Applications. IEEE Computer Society (2000) 1109–1114
5. Kero, B., Russell, L., Tsur, S., Shen, W. M.: An overview of data mining technologies. Proc. of the KDD Workshop in the 4th International Conference on Deductive and Object-Oriented Databases (1995)
6. Agent Academy: http://www.source-forge.net/projects/AgentAcademy and http://agentacademy.iti.gr/
7. Mitkas, P. A., Kehagias, D., Symeonidis, A. L., Athanasiadis, I.: A framework for constructing multi-agent applications and training intelligent agents. Proc. of the 4th International Workshop on Agent-Oriented Software Engineering. Springer-Verlag. (2003) 1–16
8. Bellifemine F., Poggi A., Rimassa G., Turci P.: An Object-Oriented Framework to realize Agent Systems. In: Proceedings of WOA 2000 Workshop, Parma, Italy (2000) 52–57
9. Foundation for Intelligent Physical Agents, the: FIPA Developer's Guide (2001) available at: http://www.fipa.org/specs/fipa00021/
10. Bellifemine F., Caire G., Trucco T., Rimassa G.: JADE Programmer's Guide. (2001) available at: http://sharon.cselt.it/
11. Wooldridge, M, Jennings, N.R., Kinny, D.: The Gaia Methodology for Agent-Oriented Analysis and Design. In: Journal of Autonomous Agents and Multi-Agent Systems. Vol. 3, No. 3. (2000) 285–312

12. Foundation for Intelligent Physical Agents, the: FIPA Communicative Act Library Specification. (2001) available at: http://www.fipa.org/specs/fipa00037/
13. Foundation for Intelligent Physical Agents, the: FIPA SL Content Language Specification (2002) available at: http://www.fipa.org/specs/fipa00008/
14. Foundation for Intelligent Physical Agents, the: FIPA ACL Message Structure Specification (2002) available at http://www.fipa.org/specs/fipa00037/
15. Noy, N.F., Sintek, M., Decker S., Crubezy, M., Fergerson, R.W., & Musen, M.A.: Creating Semantic Web Contents with Protégé-2000. In: IEEE Intelligent Systems 16 (2): (2001) 60–71
16. Data Mining Group, the: Predictive Model Markup Language Specifications (PMML), ver. 2.0 available at: http://www.dmg.org
17. Java Expert System Shell (JESS): http://herzberg.ca.sandia.gov/jess/
18. Witten, I.H., Frank, E.: Data Mining: Practical Machine Learning Tools and Techniques with Java Implementations. Morgan Kaufmann publishers, San Francisco, CA (2000)
19. Symeonidis, A. L., Kehagias, D., Mitkas, P. A.: Intelligent policy recommendations on enterprise resource planning by the use of agent technology and data mining techniques. Expert Systems with Applications, 25 (2003) 589–602
20. Symeonidis A.L, Kehagias D., Koumpis A., Vontas A.: Open Source Supply Chain. In: 10th International Conference on Concurrent Engineering (CE-2003), Workshop on intelligent agents and data mining: research and applications, Madeira, Portugal (2003)
21. Athanasiadis, I.N., Kaburlasos, V.G., Mitkas, P.A., and Petridis, V.: Applying Machine Learning Techniques on Air Quality Data for Real-Time Decision Support. In: First International NAISO Symposium on Information Technologies in Environmental Engineering (ITEE'2003), Gdansk, Poland (2003)
22. Athanasiadis, I.N., Mitkas, P.A.: An agent-based intelligent environmental monitoring system. Management of Environmental Quality. 15. (2004) 229–237
23. Symeonidis, A.L., Mitkas, P.A.: A methodology for predicting agent behaviour by the use of data mining techniques. Proc. of AIS-ADM '05 workshop. St. Petersberg, Russia. (2005)
24. Kehagias, D., Symeonidis, A.L., Mitkas, P.A.: Designing pricing mechanisms for autonomous agents based on bid-forecasting. Journal of Electronic Markets, 15. (2005)
25. Symeonidis, A. L., Seroglou, S., Valtos, E., Mitkas, P. A.: Biotope: An Integrated Simulation Tool for Multiagent Communities Residing in Hostile Environments. To appear in IEEE Transactions on Systems, Man, and Cybernetics (2005)

Artificial Immune Systems—An Emergent Technology for Autonomous Intelligent Systems and Data Mining

Mircea Negoita

Centre for Computational Intelligence, Wellington Institute of Technology,
Private Bag 39089, Wellington
Buick Street, Petone, New Zealand
mircea.negoita@weltec.ac.nz
http://www.weltec.ac.nz/schools/it/cci/index.html

Abstract. *Artificial Immune Systems (AIS)* are still considered with an attitude of reserve by most practitioners in *Computational Intelligence (CI),* much more some of them even considering this emergent computing paradigm in an infancy stage. This work aims to prove why *AIS* are of interest, starting from the real-world of applications that is asking for a radical change of the information systems framework. Namely, the component-based framework must be replaced with an agent-based one, where the system complexity requires that any agent to be clearly featured by its autonomy. The *AIS* methods build adaptive large-scale multi-agent systems that are open to the environment, systems that are not at all fixed just after the design phase, but are real-time adaptive to unpredictable situations and malicious defects. The *AIS* perform the defense of a complex system against malicious defects achieving its survival strategy by extension of the concept of organization of multicellular organisms to the information systems. The main behavioral features of AIS — as self-maintenance, distributed and adaptive computational systems — are defined and described in relation to the Immune System as an information system. A comparison of *AIS* methodology with other Intelligent Technologies is another point of the lecture. The overview of some actual *AIS* applications is made using a practical engineering design strategy that views AIS as the effective software with agent-based architecture.

1 Introduction

Any living organism is in fact a complex system typically featured by characteristics as evolution, adaptation and fault tolerance that cannot be implemented in real world systems using traditional engineering methodologies. The use of biologically inspired *CI* techniques play a crucial role in developing robust and effective applications where complex systems set their face successfully against the large diversity of unpredictable and dangerous events that exploit the weak points or systems holes. Two emerging and promising biologically inspired techniques, *Artificial Immune Systems (AIS)* and *DNA* computing, seem to be the impulse of the moment in developing the strategy of systems survival in the defence of actual information systems against malicious faults ([1], [2]). The collective effort of a large spectrum of

V. Gorodetsky, J. Liu, and V.A. Skormin (Eds.): AIS-ADM 2005, LNAI 3505, pp. 19–36, 2005.

high technology practitioners, mainly the computer scientists, engineers acting in different technical fields, biologists and natural environment specialists, led to the interdisciplinary development approach of *AIS* and *DNA* reliant hybridisation algorithms, techniques and application. A lot of interesting, reliable and high performance applications in critical environment conditions are reliant on *AIS* and/or *DNA* techniques despite the fact that these methods are still at their incipient stage [3].

1.1 Basic Considerations Related to the Natural Immune System

The natural immune system is a system of high complexity. Its physiology is featured by a bunch of spectacular and useful functions, among them being a highly effective defence mechanism for a given host against pathogenic organisms and infections. This defence strategy acts by performing two tasks: firstly, the recognition is achieved of all cells within the host body, namely whether they are self (belonging to the body) or nonself (not belonging to the body); secondly, the distinction between body own's cells and the foreign invader cells is followed by a classification of the nonself cells together with the induction of some appropriate defensive mechanisms for each of these dangerous foreign antigens that can be bacteria, viruses and so on. Details from different works in immunology science ([4], [5], [6]) converge to a unique simplified block diagram of how the defence mechanism of the natural immune system is structured; see Fig. 1 as from [2].

A lot of interesting aspects regarding basic immune recognition and activation mechanisms, more deep details in physiology of the immune system, innate immune system and adaptive immune system and other functional fundamentals as pattern recognition, the clonal selection principle, sel/nonself discrimination or immune network theory are to be mentioned when an overview is made on the basics of immunology. This paper is limited to just introduce the elements of immunology knowledge that are in connection with the defence mechanism of immune systems.

The defence activity of the natural immune system is achieved by the white blood cells, *leukocytes*, under a strategy of defence structured in a form of two distinctly implemented tasks of defence:

- the **Innate Immune System (IIM)** and
- the **Adaptive Immune System (AIS).**

The **Innate Immune System** *(IIM)* is implemented by two kinds of leukocytes, the *granulocytes* and *macrophages. IIM* combating responsibility consists of the fight against a wide range of bacteria without requiring previous exposure to them. Any is its body exposure to an antigen, the *IIS* response remains constant along the life time of an individual. A special combating strength features both the macrophages and the neutrophils: they are able of ingesting and digesting several microorganisms and/or antigenic particles; accordingly they are called together as phagocytes. But the macrophages are more powerful by having also the strength to present antigens to other cells, accordingly being additionally called also **a***ntigen-***p***resenting* **c***ells (APC)*. The the granulocytes are cells with multiglobule nuclei containing cytoplasmatic granules filled with chemical elements (enzymes). The following three kinds of the granulocytes are known, namely: the *neutrophils*, that are the most abundant IIS cells;

the *eosinophils*, with a main task in the fight against infection by parasites; the *basophiles* with their functional task still not well elucidated.

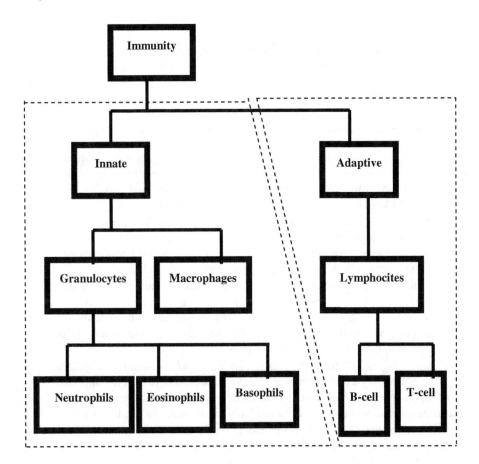

Fig. 1. A simplified block diagram of how the defence mechanism of the natural immune system is structured (after de Castro & Timmis [2])

The **Adaptive Immune System (AIS)** is implemented by one kind of leukocytes, the *lymphocytes* that are responsible both for the recognition and for suppression of a pathogenic agent. *AIS* combating responsibility is performed by producing antibodies just only in response to specific infections. This means that the presence of antibodies in an individual mirrors the history of all infections to which its body has already been exposed, either in case of a disease or a vaccination, and the practical action of AIS lymphocytes results in immunity against re-infection to the same infectious agent. This result proves the fact that *AIS* lymphocytes are capable of developing an immune memory. The lymphocytes are capable of recognizing the same antigenic stimulus at any time when it is presented again. The immune memory avoids the re-installation of the disease inside the body. Much more, *AIS* physiological mechanism improves the natural immune systems with each encounter of a given antigen.

There two main kinds of lymphocytes: *B-lymphocytes (B-cells)* and *T-lymphocytes (T-cells)*. The *AIS* is acquired through the lifetime of an individual and is not at all inherited by an offspring. *AIS* acronym stands for Adaptive Immune System just in this paragraph, this notation stands for Artificial Immune System for all next sections of the paper.

Two structural details of the natural immune system are crucial for both the terminology and comprehensibility of an *AIS :* the lueockocyte's receptor recognizing a particular molecular pattern is called an *antibody ;* the molecular part recognized by an antibody is called an *antigen.*

1.2   Why AIS Must Be of Interest for Information and Other Complex Systems

Different variants of defining the field of *AIS* are available in the literature, but the most complete is as from [2]: << *AIS*s are adaptive systems, inspired by theoretical immunology and observed immune functions, principles and models, which are applied to problem solving >>.

It would be absolutely wrong to limit us by thinking that *AIS* is just a methodology concerned only with the use of immune system components and processes as inspiration to construct computational systems. *AIS* means much more, namely it is a concept and framework that radically changes the design philosophy of any artificial systems and in the same time sensitively improves the system behavior in the adverse external environment of application. This affirmation is made by relying on some considerations of reliability design that are deeply related to the drawbacks of the artificial systems towards error and faults and also are technically justified in connection with the concept of malicious defects.

All kind of actual artificial systems not reliant on *AIS* are limited in their behavior regarding the wrong events, errors and faults namely. These systems are passive and event-driven because they usually wait for a specific wrong event and trigger a treatment specific to the event. Both the fault and its remedia can be apriori specified and enumerated and the system is dependent on the concept of redundancy: if a fault occurs that causes a loss of function, the function lost because of the faulty component is replaced by a redundant standby component [1].

AIS framework develops an attitude towards the errors and faults that is radically different; they are mainly relied on actively using the information from the application environment. They are ready to act and successfully annihilate any challenges posed by elements that are coming from a dynamic external environment involving a large range of unpredictable events. The high degree of complexity featuring the actual applications requirements and also the intrinsic systems architecture/functionality are difficult circumstances favoring an unexpected level of effect evolution of exogenous dangerous element on systems. These elements of real danger evolved so much that even can reproduce and spread. The concept of malicious fault is a reality, see for example the malicious software that causes serious damages and troubles, even more worse that ordinary hardware or software faults are doing. The malicious defects must be viewed as the viruses, parasites and /or predators are for the biological systems.

As a conclusion, the role of *AIS* concept and framework is essential in developing a crucial strategy for of systems survival —the intelligent defence of the information systems against malicious faults.

2   Elements of the AIS Concept and Framework

Some elements of *AIS* design are introduced starting from the conceptual philosophy of artificial immunity-based systems that revolutionizes the engineering of complex artificial intelligent systems. This section comprises also a comparative discussion of the *AIS* against other biologically inspired *Intelligent Technologies*. This is done because the rest of branches in *Computational Intelligence* influenced the framework to *AIS* design, especially but not at all exclusively through **N**eural **N**etworks *(NN)* and **E**volutionary **A**lgorithms *(EA)*.

2.1   General Design Consideration for an AIS

The artificial immunity-based systems are complete information systems featured by three main informational features ([1], [7], [8]):

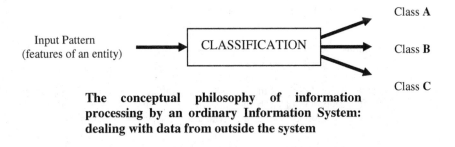

The conceptual philosophy of information processing by an ordinary Information System: dealing with data from outside the system

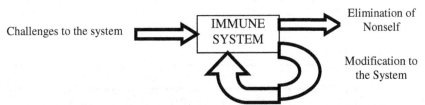

The conceptual philosophy of information processing by AIS relied Information System: a system dealing with the system itself

Fig. 2. The fundamental difference between an ordinary Artificial Information System and an AIS designed Information System (after Ishida [1])

STEP 1
Application Specification

1.1 Global Requirements Specification of the problem (task) to be solved

1.2 Detailed Specification of the Basic (Structural) Application Elements to be handled by the *AIS* (e.g., variables, constants, agents, functions, application specific parameters)

STEP 2
Selection of the AIS Model(s) and Algorithm(s) Fitting the application

(Sometimes even more than one *AIS* may be developed for simultaneously acting to solve an application)

STEP 3
AIS(s) model's Algorithmic implementation and run

3.1 Defining the Immune Components (the sets and types of antigens and antibodies)

3.2 Encoding (Representing) the Immune Components and selecting the corresponding type of Affinity Evaluation

3.3 AIS Algorithm Runs its appropriate dynamic behaviour (The concentration of antibodies must reflect a suitable match of the antigens with a set of antibodies associated with a set of appropriate behaviours)

3.4 AIS Metadynamics simultaneously related to Step 3.3 (insertion and elimination of antibodies from the network, possibly pre venting the alteration of *AIS* strength of action/creativity, by introdu cing a mechanism to generate candidate antibodies to enter the *AIS*)

STEP 4
Real world implementation of the AIS solution

4.1 Decoding the *AIS* solution

4.2 Downloading the decoded (interpreted) solution into the application for real world

Fig. 3. The main steps of AIS Engineering Design

- the *self-maintenance* property involving monitoring not only of the nonself but also of the self and this based on the self counterpart of the system

- the property of a *distributed system* structured by autonomous components having a capability of mutual evolution that results in forming an ad hoc network with specific recognition

- the property of *an adaptive system* featured by diversity and selection, based on selection as opposed to instruction

The fundamental differences in information processing that make the distinction between an *AIS* and a usual information system are illustrated in Fig.2 as from [1]. Fig. 2 gives us a double suggestion both on the pattern recognition and regarding the processed data. It suggests that an ordinary Information System is limited to just a pattern recognition by the simply classification with classes, a mapping to a number of classes, whilst *AIS* performs in fact another kind of operation called dichotomy, that runs qualitatively different at a metalevel, namely from classes captured at the same level. The second message suggests that *AIS* incorporate the self-system and its relation to the outer world, but not at all prepare or embed a part of the solution into the model. Regarding the processed data, an *AIS* deals with challenges affecting the system itself, not with data that can be defined without referring to the system.

The basic elements of the framework that implements both the *AIS* structure and methodology involve: a representation (encoding) of *AIS* components; the evaluation (affinity) functions measuring the interaction between *AIS* components; typical algorithms managing *AIS* dynamical behaviour. The encoding must not only comprise just suitable elements corresponding to the antibodies or to the antigens, but also must reflect the strength of binding between an antigen and an antibody, also including other refined details such as the fact that an antigen can be a foreign antigen or a portion of an antibody, this means a self-antigen. The main steps of *AIS* Engineering Design look as in Fig. 3 for most of the application developments.

2.2 AIS Versus Other Techniques of Computational Intelligence

The algorithms managing *AIS* dynamical behaviour can be applied to problem solving in different settings. But an essential detail of *AIS* engineering states that the pool of immune algorithms is mainly divided in two categories: *population-based (PB)* and *network-based (NB)* ones. We just limit ourselves here by mentioning the fundamental feature that divides *AIS* into the above mentioned two classes: the encoded components of *PB-AIS* interact exclusively with the external environment – represented by antigens, this is the case of bone marrow or thymus models; the encoded components of *NW-AIS* are more co-operative by interacting both with each other and with the antigens representing the external environment, this is the case of immune network models. This section will focus not so much on the similarities and differences among *AIS* and other biologically inspired *Intelligent Techniques*, see [12] for a comparison between *AIS* and the *GA*, or ([10], [11]) in case of *AIS* versus *NN*. It will be mainly a briefly overview of the possible *AIS* aggregation with the other

Computational Intelligence approaches in form of *Hybrid Intelligent Systems* that influenced both *AIS* design and their applications ([3], [9]).

The artificial immunity-based systems are hybrid information systems almost by their nature as from the three main informational features ([1], [7], [8]), so they offer an optimal technical frame of hybridization with all other *Computational Intelligence* paradigms both at the level of model and most important at an algorithmic level ([3], [9]).

An example of *AIS-NN* hybridization at the level of model may be found in [13] where a new *NN* learning algorithm was built. The learning is performed by strength variation of the input stimuli instead of varying the *NN* weights that are constant. Also the *NN* memory capacity was increased due to the *AIS* behaviour as a system with a large number of attractors.

The great potential of *AIS-EA* hybridization is illustrated by a large variety of technical improvements to most of the *EA* paradigms. Some bidirectional improvements featuring the *AIS-GA* hybridization were reported: *AIS* niches, species and diversity were controlled by a *GA* of the hybrid immunity-based algorithm in [14]; *GA* constraints handling was made by a simulated *AIS* where the antigens fight against the antibodies, so as the resulting antibodies are the constituents of an evolved population of constraint conditioned individuals [15]. Even an AIS-based *GP* variant that uses an *AIS* dynamic fitness function was reported in [16].

FS – *AIS* hybridization was strongly used in a wide range of real-world applications. Distributed Autonomous Robotic Systems may have a *FS* like modeling of the stimulation level of an antibody (individual robot strategy of action) while an *AIS* relying on clonal selection is used for transmitting high quality strategies of action (antibodies) among the robots. No central control exists and the role of antigens is played by elements of external environments [17].

Other advanced *AIS*-based *HIS* will be introduced in section 4 of this work, including *AIS* aggregation with the emergent *Intelligent Technologies* such as *Evolvable Hardware* (*EHW*) or *DNA Computing*.

3   Multiagent Framework—The Adequate Environment for AIS Engineering

The fundamental design philosophy for any complex information system must definitely escape from the *component-based framework* to the *agent-based framework* where each agent has its own intelligence and autonomy in order to attend the required complexity [1]. An agent is defined as any entity – human or software-capable of carrying out by itself an activity standalone.

Using the *CI* methods creates an agent-based framework where the own intelligence of each agent may even evolve to a behavioral one. A multi-agent approach using an arsenal of *CI* methods that is mainly relied on the *AIS* would perform the defense of a complex system against malicious defects and other unpredictable events, achieving its survival strategy by extension of the concept of organization of multicellular organisms to the information systems. The main reasons of using the agents for information processing and managing are as follows: the agents are proactive, they are cooperative, and they are able of learning and also of reasoning, as the case [42].

The agents are proactive, means they initiate by themselves the decision making for an action when they find it necessary to proceed in such a way. This task is crucial because the information may be generated by different sources and often from different places. The agent's ability of cooperation/information interchange means their availability of knowledge sharing among them or benefiting from the other agents' experience by asking for their advice. By learning agents we mean just agents that can learn from their own previous experience, comprising both mistakes and successes. Finally, each agent in the *CI* multi-agent framework may utilize any sophisticated *CI* technology of reasoning.

The infrastructure of a multi-agent system includes: agents, agent platforms, agent management and an agent communication language [43]. The multi-agent approach to complex systems enables the separation of social behavior (problem solving, decision making and reasoning) at social communication level from individual behavior (routine and knowledge processing, and problem solving) at autonomy level. The two distinct communication levels, the social one and the autonomy level, along with the dynamic agent-task association, frame the multi-agent infrastructure.

The *AIS* main informational features — the *self-maintenance* property, the property of a *distributed system* and the property of *an adaptive system* as from ([1], [7], [8]) – justify a continuous elaboration work of different variants of AIS agent-based architecture [1], [24], [33], [44], [46].

The so-called "most naïve immune algorithm" was introduced in [33] as proceeding to implement an adaptive *AIS* running in three steps: step 1 — Generation of Diversity; step 2 — Establishment of Self-Tolerance and step 3 — Memory of Non-Self. The algorithm views the system as the "self" and the external environment as the "non-self". Both the self and the non-self are unknown or cannot be modelled. Step 1 generates the recognizers' diversity in its specificity. A developmental phase drives structural changes during Step 2 on the recognizers aimed of becoming insensitive to known patterns (self). Parameter changes are driven during Step3 on the recognizers aimed to be more sensitive to unknown patterns (the non-self). The recognizer is an *AIS* unit featured by only recognizing and communication capabilities.

The corresponding Agent-based architecture handles high performance intelligent and autonomous units called *agents* that beside the recognizing and communication capability are able of adaptation and self-replication. The main three steps of the agent – based *AIS* have similar functional meanings: Step1 – diversity generation; Step 2 performs the activation of the recognizing agents by an encounter with the antigens; During Step 3, the activated recognizing agent will reproduce its clone to enhance the ability of elimination of the antigen. Mutation operators to increase the affinity with the antigen perform this reproduction.

An interesting fault tolerant *AIS*-based multi-agent architecture of a distributed system was proposed that performs self-repairing [44]. The performances of this architecture were proved by a distributed computer network system consisting of *N* host computers each of them being able of sending mobile agents to adjacent hosts. The abnormal units, either host computers or mobile agents are identified by an *AIS* strategy. Some units try to self-repair; by this means these units replace their data with data received from other units.

4 AIS Applications

This section is not supposed to be an absolutely complete review of *AIS* application fields with detailed descriptions, but mainly focus on some *AIS* applications in context with the *HIS* framework that progressed toward some spectacular and effective combinations envisaging even the emergent *CI* paradigms such as *DNA Computing* and *EHW* [3].

4.1 A Survey of Some Applications of the AIS

A *DNA-AIS* intelligent hybrid system was reported in [18] where *DNA Computing* was proved as an alternative to implement AIS. In this work, an *AIS* negative selection algorithm was implemented in a *DNA* computing framework. Using *DNA* single strands under denaturation, renaturation and splicing operators, was implemented the censoring and monitoring parts of this selection algorithm was successfully implemented.

A recent intelligent hybridization of *AIS* is applied in case of one of the most revolutionary technology nowadays, namely in case of E*volvable* H*ardware (EHW)*. A main reason for *EHW – AIS* hybridization was reliant on two *AIS* features, healing and learning, that were applied to design *EHW* fault – tolerant *FPGA* systems [19]. An additional layer that imitates the action of antibody cells was incorporated to the previously elaborated embryonic architecture by the same team [21] Two variants of this new *EHW* architecture use an interactive network of antibody cells featured by 3 independent types of communication channels: the data channels of the embryonic array of cells, the data channels of antibody array of cells and the inter-layer communication channels ensuring that antibody cells can monitor the embryonic cells. The antibody array of cells performs monitoring and checking of the embryonic array of cells, so that the correct functionality of any particular *EHW* configuration can be achieved at any time.

Another *AIS* inspired variant of *EHW* hardware fault detection was reported in [20]. They used an advanced *FPGA* hardware- Virtex XCV300 - to implement a hardware negative clonal selection *AIS* attached to a F*inite* S*tate* M*achine (FSM)*. This is very important because any hardware system can be represented by either a stand-alone or an interconnected array of *FSMs*.

The main *AIS* applications have been developed in areas such as: autonomous navigation/robotics, computer network security, job-shop scheduling, (fault) diagnosis, data analysis and optimisation [2]. Some of these applications are reliant on the idea of combining *AIS* with different other *CI* techniques (*FS, NN, EA, KBES, DNA* computing) with the aim of creating *HIS* that are collecting the individual strength of each *CI* component [3]. *AIS* are a new *CI* approach that has not only applications involved in the *HIS* framework but also has its own standalone applications.

Refined details of behavior arbitration for autonomous mobile robots were solved in [30] through new *AIS* based decentralized consensus-making system. The adaptation mechanism for an appropriate arbitration uses reinforcement signals that were used for evolving the proposed *AIS*: current situations detected by sensors work as multiple antigens, the prepared (desired) competence modules work as antibodies, the interaction between modules is represented by stimulation and suppression between antibodies.

But *AIS* applications have evolved so far that they are able to improve the lives of human beings even in the most unexpected aspects. *AIS* are also applied to improve the comfort in our daily real life at a micro level. The *AIS*-based smart home technology is aimed to improve the technical facilities, including the security of a home not only against the burglars but against other external dangers too. Such an *AIS* was modeled as a multi-agent system where the sensors and actuators are taken as agents that prove to behave as the human immune system with respect to self organization and flexible reaction, with gradation, on dangerous events outside [31].

But the *AIS* may act for improving our daily comfort even at a macro level. Potential applications of the *AIS* in some selected areas of physical infrastructure assessment and modeling at the national level, in particular for surface transportation (highways, railroads, air transportation facilities) are suggested in [32]. For example, an *AIS* relied on negative selection is proposed for condition assessment by analyzing the instances of a more general problem distinguishing itself (normal condition data not below a threshold value) from other (deteriorated data below the threshold). Also an AIS network model may implement the fault states diagnosis of infrastructure systems where each infrastructure subsystem is regarded as a distinct antibody, and the information about the state of the global infrastructure system is treated as an antigen. An *AIS*-based robotic system for infrastructure assessment may be applied for the maintenance activity in pavement infrastructure systems: the maintenance-actions are acting as antibodies, whilst the infrastructure conditions behave as antigens.

Most application areas in the major field of pattern recognition actually make use of *AIS*-based methods. Among them is the feature extraction in recognition of complex characters, such the Chinese characters [22]. An *AIS* model relies on the effect of diffusion of antibodies, namely the amount of diffused antibodies is calculated by adopting the (spatial) distribution of antibodies centroids as the virtual points where antibodies were concentrated and redistribution of antibodies is performed accordingly [22]. *AIS* based on the partial template method are effective for the personal identification with finger vein patterns [45].

A very interesting **M**ultilevel **I**mmune **A**lgorithm (*MILA*) was proposed for novel pattern recognition and was tested with anomalous pattern problems [23]. This algorithm has four phases: Initialization phase, Recognition phase, Evolutionary phase and Response phase. Real-valued strings represent both antibodies and antigens, which is different to the Negative and Clonal selection. The antigen/antibody recognition is modelled by using a Euclidian distance measure as the degree of matching.

Security systems for computers and the Internet work environment are another productive application area of *AIS*. Intrusion detection on the Internet – for internal masqueraders mainly, but for external ones too – is reported in [24]. The method was inspired by the diversity and specificity of an immune system, namely each immune cell has a unique receptor featured by a high degree of matching a specific antigen. So each of the agents that are used in this approach has its unique profile and computes a high score against the sequential (command) set typed by the specific user matching this profile. By evaluating all the scores (for all the profiles), one of the agents determines whether a particular user is an intruder (masquerader) or not. *AIS* self-monitoring approach has applicability also in solving specific problems to distributed intrusion detection systems [25].

Usually computer protection is referring to anti-virus protection and to intruders' detection, but [26] applied *AIS* for immunity to unsolicited e-mail (spam or junk mail) where regular expressions, patterns that match a variety of strings, are used as antibodies. These regular expressions are grouped in a library of gene sequences and in their turn the regular expressions are combined to randomly produce other regular expressions to produce antibodies that match more general patterns.

The *AIS*s were proved to be superior to hybrid *GA* in function optimization [27]. Here the *AIS* algorithm inspired by clonal selection and called *BCA* (**B-c**ell **a**lgorithm) got a high quality optimisation solution by performing significantly fewer evaluations than a *GA*. A unique mutation operator was used – contiguous somatic hyper mutation – that operates by subjecting the contiguous region of the operative element (vector) to mutation. The random length utilised by this mutation operator confer to the BCA individual the ability to explore a much wider region of the affinity (fitness) landscape than just the immediate neighbourhood of an individual.

A hybrid clonal selection *AIS* was used more successfully than the evolutionary algorithms for solving a combinatorial optimisation application, the Graph colouring problem [28]. Here the use of a crossover operator was avoided by using a particular mutation operator combined with a local search strategy. In this way there was no embedding specific domain knowledge.

*AIS*s that are based on clonal selection have proven to be effective both for combinatorial optimisation and for machine learning problems. An AIS modelled as a noisy channel has applicability in adaptive noise neutralization [29], where the signal is the population of B-cells, the channel is the global *AIS*, the noise source is the antigen and the received signal E is the antibody. Regarding the machine learning methods that are used in implementing classification algorithms for "hard" applications as the gene expression of cancerous tissues, *AIS* proved to be superior to *SVM* and *NN* by a better error rate of the algorithm, despite of a longer amount of computational time [40].

4.2   AIS Applications in Optimization of ITS Multi-agent Environment

A recent but promising area of *HIS* applications is focused on the Intelligent T*utoring* S*ystems* (*ITS*). These systems model instructional and teaching strategies, empowering educational programs with the ability to decide on "what" and "how" to teach students. A "stand alone" intelligent, HIS reliant, tutoring component is added to the usual learning environments, so the work that is done by lecturers and students is complemented ([34], [35]). Usually, learning systems require that the student change to fit the system, but the *ITS* radically differ by an added flexibility of performing an intelligent learning strategy, namely the learning system *"change to fit the students needs"*. A good description of the basic structure of an *ITS* was made in [38].

The *WITNeSS* (**W**ellington **I**nstitute *of* **T**echnology **N**eural **E**xpert **S**tudent **S**upport) is an original *HIS* using *Fuzzy-Neural-GA techniques* for optimising the presentation of learning material to a student [36]. *WITNeSS* works relied on the concept of a *"virtual student"*. This student model simulates the learning and forgetting that occurs when a human learning attempts to acquire knowledge. Its modelling was made by using fuzzy technologies so as to be useful for any *ITS*, by providing it with an optimal learning strategy for fitting the *ITS* itself to the unique needs of each individual student. More details giving a relevant image of *WITNeSS* working may be found in [3]. The *Student Model* is placed into a typical *ITS* system configuration [38] and a *GA*-based agent we call the *"Optimizer"* was added. The optimizer agent is used to "fine-tune" the linguistic variables of a fuzzy rule decision structure that is used by a *Tutor* model to decide on *"what"* should be presented next to a student and *"how"* it should be presented. There is a detailed description of how the concept of an *"optimizer"* works, see [39]. Here we just limit ourselves to represent the optimization methods as included into an ultra simplified hybridization flow of *the Intelligent Technologies* that works in *WITNeSS* as in Fig.4.

WITNeSS, as a whole, works in the following way:

– The *human student* interacts with *WITNeSS*, which presents a sequence of learning activities that result in the student learning the knowledge structure. The key to this learning sequence is the fuzzy rule decision structure used by the *Tutor* agent to decide on "**what**" to present and "**how**" to present it. However the "shape" of the linguistic variables held in these fuzzy rules doesn't guarantee optimal learning. Each student learns differently so what we need is the system to find the best "shape" for the linguistic variables, for that particular student. Hence our motivation is for an *"Optimizer"* agent.

– When the student first logs onto the system, the *Optimizer* agent makes its own copy of the main agents (*Student*, *Tutor* and *Knowledge*), including the current fuzzy rule structure. While the student is working with the main system, the *Optimizer* works in the background, trying different "shapes" to the linguistic variables in an effort to improve the current fuzzy rule structure. This would result in the *Tutor* deciding on a quicker, higher quality learning sequence.

The *Optimizer* sends its "shape refined" linguistic variables back to the main *Tutor*, replacing its fuzzy rule structure with a more efficient one. The *Optimizer* then starts over, taking the latest information about how the student is performing, and works to find an even better "shape" to the linguistic variables.

Our work regarding *AIS* involvement in *WITNeSS*, has an accurate aim. The actual task is to increase the optimization speed by using an *AIS*-based *Optimizer* agent that relies on the clonal selection process in performing significantly fewer evaluations than the *GA*-based agent does. Results are not presented in this paper. We actually are also encouraged in thinking to expand the *AIS*-based Optimization at the level of a *System Optimizer* that will produce learning complex cells implementing the dynamics of an *AIS* model at the global level of *WITNeSS*.

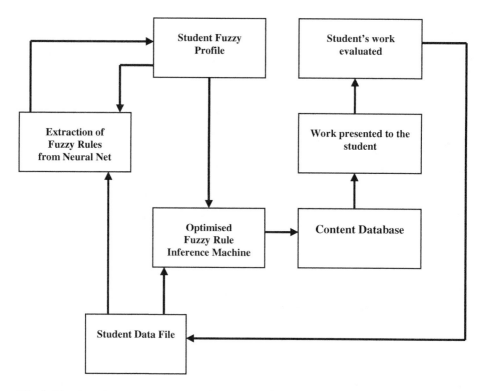

Fig. 4. The simplified hybridization flow of *the Intelligent Technologies* technologies as used in in *WITNeSS*

5   Concluding Remarks

This work try to convince that *AIS* conceptual philosophy revolutionizes the engineering of complex artificial intelligent systems indeed by extension of the concept of organization of multicellular organisms to the information systems: the *AIS*-based modern complex information systems are adaptive large-scale multi-agent ones that are open to the environment, they are not at all fixed just after the design phase, but are real-time adaptive to unpredictable situations and malicious defects. *AIS* offer the unique framework performing the defense of a complex system against malicious defects achieving its survival strategy.

AIS application area has become already traditional and accurate in fields such as: computer and data security, image and other pattern recognition (including signature verification), fault and anomaly detection and diagnosis, noise detection, autonomous navigation and control, scheduling, machine learning, machine monitoring. The *AIS* feature some very effective general-purpose engineering and science design methodologies with a large applicability for search and optimization strategies and also for design of the multi-agent based systems. *AIS* actually penetrate some totally new and unconventional application area of our social-economic life, such as the modern instructional and educational tools of ITS or the smart home technology. *AIS* proved to be an effective standalone *CI* paradigm for many engineering applications including computer science, but it strength is sensitively increased in aggregation with other *CI* paradigms in form of *HIS*. *AIS*-based *HIS* are applied in high tech areas as distribute autonomous robot systems, classification and prediction systems of high performance, or risk analysis evaluations featuring highly complex applications as the highway infrastructure deterioration at the national level.

References

1. Ishida, Y.: Immunity-Based Systems: A Design Perspective. Springer Verlag, Berlin, Heidelberg, New York (ISBN: 3-540-00896-9) (2004)
2. de Castro, L N, Timmis, J. I.: Artificial Immune Systems: A New Computational Approach. Springer Verlag, London (ISBN: 1-85233-594-7) (2002)
3. Negoita, M. Gh, Neagu, C. D., Palade, V.: Computational Intelligence – Engineering of Hybrid Systems. Springer Verlag , Berlin, Heidelberg, New York (ISBN: 3-540-23219-2) (2005)
4. Jerne, N.K.: The Immune System. In *Scientific American*, **229** (1) (1973)52–60
5. Jerne, N.K.: The Generative Grammar of the Immune System. In *The EMBO Jour nal*, 4(4) (1985) 847–852
6. Percus, J.K., Percus, O., Person, A.S.: Predicting the Size of the Antibody Combining Region from Consideration of Efficient Self/Nonself Discrimination. In Proceedings of The National Academy of Science, 60, (1993) 1691–1695
7. Ishida, Y.: The Immune System as a Self-Identification Process: a Survey and a Pro posal. Workshop Notes-Workshop 4: Immunity-Based Systems, International Conference on Multiagent Systems/International Symposium on Models for Software Architecture, December, Keihanna Plaza, Tokyo, Japan (1996) 2–13
8. Dasgupta, D., Attoh-Okine, N.: Immunity-Based Systems: A Survey. Workshop Notes-Workshop 4: Immunity-Based Systems, International Conference on Multiagent Systems/International Symposium on Models for Software Architecture, December, Keihanna Plaza, Tokyo, Japan (1996) 13–25
9. Negoita, M.Gh.: Basics of Engineering the Hybrid Intelligent Systems — Not only Industrial Applications. In: Negoita M Gh, Reusch B (eds) Real World Applications of Computational Intelligence. Springer Verlag , Berlin, Heidelberg, New York (ISBN: 3-540-25006-9) (2005) 5–55
10. de Castro, L.N., Von Zuben, F.J.: Immune and Neural Networks Models: Theoretical and Empirical Comparisons. International Journal of Computational Intelligence and Applications (IJCIA) 1(3) (2001) 239–259
11. Dasgupta, D.: Artificial Neural Networks and Artificial Immune Systems: Simi arities and Differences. In: Proceedings of The IEEE Systems, Man and Cybernetics Conference, 1 (1997) 873–878
12. Forrest, S., Perelson, A.: Genetic Algorithms and the Immune Systems. In: Goos, C., Hartmanis, J. (eds) Proceedings of The Parallel Problem Solving from Nature. Springer Verlag, Berlin, Heidelberg, New York (1990) 320–325
13. Hoffman, G.W.: A Neural Network Model Based on the Analogy with the Immune System. Journal of Theoretical Biology 122 (1986) 33–67
14. Forrest, S., Javornik, B., Smith, R.E., Perelson, A.: Using Genetic Algorithms to Explore Pattern Recognition in the Immune System. Evolutionary Computation 1(3): (1993) 191–211

15. Yoo, J., Hajela, P.: Immune Network Simulations in Multicriterion Design. Structural Optimization **18** (2/3): (1999) 85–94
16. Nikolaev, N. I., Iba, H., Slavov, V.: Inductive Genetic Programming with Immune Network Dynamics. Advances in Genetic Programming , MIT Press (3): (1999) 355–376
17. Jun, J.-H., Lee, D.-W., Sim, K.-B.: Realization of Cooperative Behavior in Distributed Autonomous Robotic Systems Using Artificial Immune System. In: Proceedings of the IEEE of The IEEE System, Man, and Cybernetics. **4** (1999) 614–619
18. Deaton, R., Garzon, M., Rose, J.A., Murphy, R.C., Stevens, Jr.S.E., Franceschetti, D.R.: A DNA Based Artificial Immune System for Self-Nonself Discrimination, In: Proceedings of The IEEE System, Man, and Cybernetics I: (1997) 862–866
19. Bradley, D. W., Ortega-Sanchez, C., Tyrrell, A.: Embryonics + Immunotronics: A Bio-Inspired Approach to Fault Tolerance. In: Proceedings of the 2nd NASA/DoD Workshop on Evolvable Hardware. IEEE Computer Society, Los Alamitos, California (2000) 215–223
20. Bradley, D. W., Tyrrell, A.: The Architecture for a Hardware Immune System. In: Proceedings of the 3nd NASA/DoD Workshop on Evolvable Hardware. .IEEE Computer Society, Los Alamitos, California (2001) 193–200
21. Ortega, C., Mange, D., Smith, S., Tyrrell, A.: Embryonics: A Bio-Inspired Cellular Architecture with Fault-Tolerant Properties. In: J Genetic Programming and Evolvable Machines 1–3: (2000) 187–215
22. Shimooka, T., Shimizu, K.: Idiotypic Network Model for Feature Extraction in Pattern Recognition . In: Palade, V., Howlett, J.R., Jain, L. (eds) Knowledge-Based Intelligent Informa tion and Engineering Systems. Springer-Verlag, Berlin Heidelberg New York, Part I I (2003) 511–518
23. Dasgupta, D., Yu, S., Majmudar, N.S.: MILA – Multilevel Immune Learning Algorithm.In: Cantu-Paz, E., Foster, J., Kalaynmoy, D., Lawrence, D.D., Rajkumar, R., O'Reilly, U-M., Beyer, H-G., Standish, R., Kendall, G., Wilson, S., Harman, M., Wegner, J., Dasgupta, D., Potter, M., Schultz, A., Dowsland, K., Jonoska, N., Miller, J. (eds) Genetic and Evolutionary Computation – GECCO 2003, Springer Verlag Berlin Heidelberg New York, Part I (2003) 183–194
24. Okamoto, T., Watanabe, T., Ishida, Y.: Towards an Immunity-Based System for Detect ing Masqueraders. In: Palade V., Howlett J. R., Jain L. (eds) Knowledge-Based Intelligent Information and Engineering Systems. Springer-Verlag, Berlin Heidelberg New York, Part II (2003) 488–495
25. Watanabe, Y., Ishida, Y.: Immunity-Based Approaches for Self-Monitoring in Distrib uted Intrusion Detection System. In: Palade, V., Howlett, J.R., Jain, L. (eds) Knowledge-Based Intelligent Information and Engineering Systems. Springer-Verlag, Berlin Heidelberg New York, Part II (2003) 503–510
26. Oda, T., White, T.: Developing an Immunity to Spam. In: Cantu-Paz, E., Foster, J., Kalaynmoy, D., Lawrence, D.D., Rajkumar, R., O'Reilly, U-M., Beyer, H-G., Standish, R., Kendall, G., Wilson, S., Harman, M., Wegner, J., Dasgupta, D., Potter, M., Schultz, A., Dowsland, K., Jonoska, N., Miller, J. (eds) Genetic and Evolutionary Computation – GECCO 2003, Springer Verlag Berlin Heidelberg New York, Part I (2003) 207–242
27. Kelsey, J., Timmis, J.I.: Immune Inspired Somatic Contiguous Hypermutation for Function Optimization. In: Cantu-Paz, E., Foster, J., Kalaynmoy, D., Lawrence, D.D., Rajkumar, R., O'Reilly, U-M., Beyer, H-G., Standish, R., Kendall, G., Wilson, S., Harman, M., Wegner, J., Dasgupta, D., Potter, M., Schultz, A., Dowsland, K., Jonoska, N., Miller, J. (eds) Genetic and Evolutionary Computation – GECCO 2003, Springer Verlag Berlin Heidelberg New York, Part I (2003) 207–218

28. Cutello, V., Nicosia, G., Pavone, M.: A Hybrid Immune Algorithm with Information Gain for the Graph Coloring Problem. In: Cantu-Paz, E., Foster, J., Kalaynmoy, D., Lawrence, D.D., Rajkumar, R., O'Reilly, U-M., Beyer, H-G., Standish, R., Kendall, G., Wilson, S., Harman, M., Wegner, J., Dasgupta, D., Potter, M., Schultz, A., Dowsland, K., Jonoska, N., Miller, J. (eds) Genetic and Evolutionary Computation – GECCO 2003, Springer Verlag Berlin Heidelberg New York, Part I (2003) 171–183

29. Cutello, V., Nicosia, G.: Noisy Channel and Reaction-Diffusion Systems: Models for Artificial Immune Systems. In: Palade, V., Howlett, J.R., Jain, L. (eds) Knowledge-Based Intelligent Information and Engineering Systems. Springer-Verlag, Berlin Heidelberg New York, Part II (2003) 496–502

30. Ishiguro, A., Watanabe, Y., Kondo, T., Shirai, Y., Uchikawa, Y.: Immunoid: A Robot with a Decentralized Behavior Arbitration Mechanisms Based on the Immune System . Work shop Notes-Workshop 4: Immunity-Based Systems, International Conference on Multi agent Systems/International Symposium on Models for Software Architecture, December, Keihanna Plaza, Tokyo, Japan (1996) 82–92

31. Dilger, W.: The Immune System of the Smart Home. Workshop Notes-Workshop 4: Immunity-Based Systems, International Conference on Multiagent Systems/International Symposium on Models for Software Architecture, December, Keihanna Plaza, Tokyo, Japan (1996) 72–81

32. Attoh-Okine, N.: General Framework for Applying Artificial Immune Systems to a Highway Infrastructure Deterioration Modeling. Workshop Notes-Workshop 4: Immunity-Based Systems, International Conference on Multiagent Systems/International Symposium on Models for Software Architecture, December, Keihanna Plaza, Tokyo, Japan (1996) 25–37

33. Ishida, Y.: Agent-Based Architecture of Selection Principle in the Immune System. Workshop Notes-Workshop 4: Immunity- Based Systems, International Conference on Multiagent Systems/International Symposium on Models for Software Architecture, December, Keihanna Plaza, Tokyo, Japan (1996) 93–105

34. Negoita, M.Gh., Pritchard, D.: Testing Intelligent Tutoring Systems by Virtual Students. In: Arif Wani M (ed) Proc Int Conf on Machine-Learning and Applications (ICMLA'03). Los Angeles, USA (2003) 98–104

35. Negoita, M.Gh., Pritchard, D.: Some Test Problems Regarding Intelligent Tutoring Systems. In: Palade, V., Howlett, J.R., Jain, L. (eds) Knowledge-Based Intelligent Information and Engineering Systems. Springer-Verlag, Berlin Heidelberg New York, Part II (2003) 986–992

36. Negoita, M.Gh., Pritchard, D.: Using Virtual Student Model for Testing Intelligent Tutoring Systems. J Interactive Technology & Smart Education 1 (2004) 3–10

37. Negoita, M.Gh., Pritchard, D.: A "Virtual Student" Leads to the Possibility of Optimizer Agents in an ITS. In: Kantardzic M (ed) Proc. ICMLA'04, Louisville, KY, USA (2004)

38. Mc Taggart, J.: Intelligent Tutoring Systems and Education for the Future. In: 512X Literature Review April 30, http://www.drake.edu/mathcs/mctaggart/ C1512X/ LitReview. pdf (2001)

39. Pritchard, D., Negoita, Gh.M.: A Fuzzy – GA Hybrid Technique for Optimisation of Teaching Sequences Presented in ITSs. In: Reusch B (ed) Proc 8-th Fuzzy Days. LNCS, Springer Verlag , Berlin Heidelberg New York (2004)

40. Ando, S., Iba, H.: Artificial Immune System for Classification of Gene Expression Data. In: Cantu-Paz E, Foster J, Kalaynmoy D, Lawrence,D D, Rajkumar R, O'Reilly U-M, Beyer H-G, Standish R, Kendall G, Wilson S,Harman M, Wegner J, Dasgupta D, Potter M, Schultz A, Dowsland K, Jonoska N,Miller J (eds) Genetic and Evolutionary Computation – GECCO 2003, Springer Verlag Berlin Heidelberg New York, Part II (2003) 1926–1937

41. Oeda, S., Ichimura, T., Yamashita, T., Yoshida, K.: A Proposal of Immune Multi-agent Neural Networks and Its Application to Medical Diagnostic System for Hepatobiliary Disorders. In: Palade, V., Howlett, J.R., Jain, L. (eds) Knowledge-Based Intelligent Information and Engineering Systems. Springer-Verlag, Berlin Heidelberg New York, Part II (2003) 527–532

42. Vizcaino, A., Favela, J., Piattini, M. A Multi-agent System for Knowledge Management in Software Maintemance. In: Palade, V., Howlett, J.R., Jain, L. (eds) Knowledge-Based Intelli gent Information and Engineering Systems. Springer-Verlag, Berlin Heidelberg New York, Part I (2003) 413–421

43. Tianfield, H.: A Study on the Multi-agent Approach to Large Complex Systems. In: Palade, V., Howlett, J.R., Jain, L. (eds) Knowledge-Based Intelligent Information and Engineering Systems. Springer-Verlag, Berlin Heidelberg New York, Part I (2003) 438–444

44. Watanabe, Y., Sato, S., Ishida, Y.: An Approach for Self-repair in Distributed System Using Immunity-Based Diagnostic Mobile Agents. In: Negoita, M., Howlett, J.R., Jain, L. (eds) Knowledge-Based Intelligent Information and Engineering Systems. Springer-Verlag, Berlin Heidelberg New York, Part II (2004) 504–510

45. Shimooka, T., Shimizu, K.: Artificial Immune System for Personal Identification with Finger Vein Pattern . In: Negoita, M., Howlett, J.R., Jain, L. (eds) Knowledge-Based Intelligent Informa tion and Engineering Systems. Springer-Verlag, Berlin Heidelberg New York, Part I I (2004) 511–518

46. Okamoto, T., Watanabe, T., Ishida, Y.: Mechanism for Generating Immunity-Based Agents that Detect Masqeraders. In: Negoita, M., Howlett, J.R., Jain, L. (eds) Knowledge-Based Intelligent Information and Engineering Systems. Springer-Verlag, Berlin Heidelberg New York, Part I I (2004) 534–540

Evolving Agents: Communication and Cognition

Leonid Perlovsky

Air Force Research Lab., 80 Scott Rd., Hanscom AFB, MA 01731
Tel: 781-377-1728
Leonid.Perlovsky@hanscom.af.mil

Abstract. Computer programming of complex systems is a time consuming effort. Results are often brittle and inflexible. Evolving, self-learning flexible multi-agent systems remain a distant goal. This paper analyzes difficulties toward developing evolving systems and proposes new solutions. The new solutions are inspired by our knowledge of the human mind. The mind develops language and cognitive abilities jointly. Real-time sensor signals and language signals are integrated seamlessly, before signals are understood, at pre-conceptual level. Learning of conceptual contents of the surrounding world depends on language and vice versa. This ability for integrated communication and cognition is a foundation for evolving systems. The paper describes a mathematical technique for such integration: fuzzy dynamic logic and dual cognitive-language models. We briefly discuss relationships between the proposed mathematical technique, working of the mind, applications to understanding-based search engines and evolving multi-agent systems.

1 Cultural Evolution: Computers Versus Nature

Computer capabilities for communication and cognition currently are developed separately, usually in different organizations. The nature does it differently. A child develops both capabilities *jointly*. We do not know if it is possible to code computers to be 'cognitive' or 'language capable', one capability separately from the other. Current engineering approaches could be invalid in principle. These considerations are prime motivations for this paper. Let us examine them in some details. Evolution of the human mind from pre-human ancestors occurred in three stages: genetic evolution, cultural evolution, and learning along with ontological development of an individual child into an adult. Cultural evolution and cognitive learning are much faster than genetic evolution. This paper concentrates on the mechanisms of cultural evolution and learning.

As physical infrastructure for communication systems and the Internet matures, the *information* services are gaining in importance. Distributed integration of sensor signals with flexible communications, with data and text data bases would be necessary for the future Sensor web, an integrated operation of multiple users and agents using sensors and communications. However, computer systems today use inflexible models and ontologies. Communication systems use fixed protocols. Contents of communications are intended for human understanding, computers do not understand contents.

V. Gorodetsky, J. Liu, and V.A. Skormin (Eds.): AIS-ADM 2005, LNAI 3505, pp. 37–49, 2005.

Practical implementations of complex multi-agent systems with communication and cognitive abilities are based on detailed models and protocols. These systems lack the flexibility of human cognition and natural languages.They integrate signals from sensors and communication messages only at high cognitive levels of logical predicates. First, information has to be extracted from sensor signals and formulated as logical statements at the appropriately high level of abstraction. Similar language or communication messages have to be pre-processed, the relevant data extracted and formulated as logical statements at a similar level of abstraction. Integration rely on models, ontologies, and protocols, which assume shared knowledge and understanding [1]. In practice, structures of these models have to be fixed. This is also true for ontologies being developed for semantic web. They are not as flexible as "shared knowledge" necessary for understanding among people. Specific mathematical reason for this inflexibility we discuss in section 2. The resulting systems are brittle. As requirements and hardware are changing, they become obsolete.

Contrary to the brittleness of artificial fusion systems, the human mind improves with experience. We discuss in this paper that learning, adaptive, and self-evolving capabilities of the mind are closely related to the ability to integrate signals subliminally. For example, during everyday conversations, human eye gaze as well as visual processing stream and the type of conceptual information extracted from the surrounding world are affected by contents of speech, even before it is fully processed and conceptually analyzed. Similarly, speech perception is affected by concurrent cognitive processing. To some extent, we see, what we expect to see; verbal preconditioning affects cognition, and vice versa. This close, pre-conceptual integration of language and cognition is important not only in real-time perception and cognition, but also in ontogenesis, during child growing up, as well as in evolution of culture and language. Concepts used by individual minds evolve over generations in interaction among multiple agent-minds. As we attempt to develop intelligent systems, these lessons from biological systems and their evolution should be taken into account.

Developing integrated systems with language and cognition abilities might seem premature. Even considered separately, these problems are very complex and far from being solved. Our systems for recognition, tracking, and fusion using sensor data often fall far short of human abilities. Similarly, our computer communication systems lack flexibility of language. Natural language understanding remains a distant goal. Let me repeat that the only way two computers can communicate at all, is due to fixed protocols. Communications among computers are intended for human users. Computers do not understand contents of communication messages, except within narrow domains. Everyone knows frustration of searching information on the Internet; Google and Yahoo do not understand our language. But, why should we hope to achieve progress in fusing two capabilities, neither of which is at hand?

The answer was given at the beginning of the paper. The only system that we know capable of human level cognition and communication is the human mind. An individual human mind develops both capabilities in ontogenesis, during childhood, *jointly*. This is opposite to current engineering approaches, which attempt to develop these capabilities separately, usually in different scientific and engineering organizations. It is quite possible that coding a computer to acquire language and cognitive abilities similarly to the human ways is an 'easier' task, possibly, the only way to go. We do not even know if it is possible to code computers to be 'cognitive' or 'language capable', one capability separately from the other. These current approaches could be invalid in principle.

A similar argument is applicable to the 'initial' computer code, which we would like to be similar to inborn child's capabilities, enabling joint learning of language and cognition. Human evolved this capability over at least two million years. It is possible, that simulating an accelerated evolution is an 'easier' scientific and engineering approach, than 'direct coding' into a computer of the current state of human baby mind. Moreover, we do not need to have to simulate evolution of culture; computers may learn from humans in collaborative human-computer environment. Therefore, along with smart heuristic solutions, we should try to uncover natural mechanisms of evolving language and culture, and to develop mathematical descriptions for these processes.

Scientific understanding of relationships between language and cognition in the past went through several reversals. Close relationships between language and cognition encouraged equating these abilities in the past. Rule-based systems and mathematics of logic implied significant similarities between the two: Thoughts, words, and phrases, all are logical statements. The situation has changed, in part due to the fact that logic-rule systems have not been sufficiently powerful to explain cognition, nor language abilities, and in part due to improved scientific understanding (psychological, cognitive, neural, linguistic) of the mechanisms involved. Many contemporary linguists consider language and cognition to be distinct and different abilities of the mind [see [2] for further references].

Language mechanisms of our mind include abilities to acquire a large vocabulary, rules of grammar, and to use the finite set of words and rules to generate virtually infinite number of phrases and sentences [3,4]. Cognition includes abilities to understand the surrounding world in terms of objects, their relationships (scenes and situations), relationships among relationships, and so on [5]. Researchers in computational linguistics, mathematics of intelligence and neural networks, cognitive science, neuro-physiology and psychology during the last twenty years significantly advanced understanding of the mechanisms of the mind involved in learning and using language, mechanisms of perception and cognition [3,4,5,6,7,8]. Much less advance was achieved toward deciphering mechanisms relating linguistic competence to cognition and understanding the world. Although it seems clear that language and cognition are closely related abilities, intertwined in evolution, ontogenesis, and everyday use, still the currently understood mechanisms of language are mainly limited to relations of words to other words and phrases, but not to the objects in the surrounding world, not to cognition and thinking. Possible mathematical approaches toward integrating language and cognition, words and objects, phrases and situations are discussed in this paper. This might be a foundation for cognitive learning and mechanisms of cultural evolution.

The paper starts with a mathematical description of cognition, which still is an issue of much controversy. Among researchers in mathematical intelligence it has become appreciated, especially during the last decades that cognition is not just a chain of logical inferences [5,8]. Yet, mathematical methods describing cognition as processes in human mind involving concepts, instincts, emotions, memory, imagination are not well known, although significant progress in this direction was achieved [5,8]. A brief historical overview of this area including difficulties and controversies is given in the next two sections from mathematical, psychological, and neural standpoints. It is followed by a mathematical description of cognitive processes, including image recognition, tracking, and fusion as variations of the same basic paradigm. Then the paper discusses the ways in which the mathematical description of cognition can be combined with language, taking advantage of recent progress in computational linguistics. It touches upon novel ideas of computational semiotics relating language and cognition through signs and symbols. Approaches to understanding-based web mining and building integrated multi-agent systems are discussed.

In conclusion, I briefly touch on relationships between mathematical, psychological, and neural descriptions of cognitive processes and language as parts of the mind. It turns out that, far from being esoteric abilities far removed from engineering applications, these abilities are inseparable from a mathematical description of even simplest cognition processes. Their understanding is helpful for developing integrated multi-agent systems.

2   Theories of the Mind and Combinatorial Complexity

Understanding signals coming from sensory organs involves associating subsets of signals corresponding to particular objects with internal representations of these objects. This leads to recognition of the objects. Developing mathematical descriptions of this very first *recognition* step was not easy; a number of difficulties were encountered during the past fifty years. These difficulties were summarized under the notion of combinatorial complexity (CC) [9]. CC refers to multiple combinations of various elements in a complex system; recognition of a scene often requires concurrent recognition of its multiple elements that could be encountered in various combinations. CC is prohibitive because the number of combinations is very large: for example, consider 100 elements (not too large a number); the number of combinations of 100 elements is 100^{100}, exceeding the number of elementary particles in a Universe; no computer would ever be able to compute that many combinations.

The problem was first identified in pattern recognition and classification research in the 1960s and was named "the curse of dimensionality" [10]. The following forty years of developing intelligent systems faced CC in various forms. Self-learning systems encountered *CC of learning requirements*. Logic-rule AI systems [11] and the first Chomsky ideas concerning mechanisms of language grammar related to deep structure [12] encountered *CC of rules*. Model-based systems were proposed to combine advantages of adaptivity and learning with rules by utilizing adaptive models. Along similar lines were *rules and parameters* ideas of Chomsky [13]. Model-based systems encountered *computational CC* (N and NP complete algorithms). The CC became a ubiquitous feature of intelligent algorithms and seemingly, a fundamental mathematical limitation.

CC was related to the type of logic, underlying various algorithms and neural networks [9]. CC of algorithms based on logic was related to the Gödel theory: It is a finite system manifestation of the incompleteness of logic [14]. Multivalued logic and fuzzy logic were proposed to overcome limitations related to the law of exeluded third [15]. Yet the mathematics of multivalued logic is no different in principle from formal logic. Fuzzy logic encountered a difficulty related to the degree of fuzziness: If too much fuzziness is specified, the solution does not achieve a needed accuracy, if too little, it becomes similar to formal logic.

Various approaches to signal and communication integration are related to mathematical methods considered above. For example, an influential and general method of Multiple Hypothesis Testing (MHT) is a model-based method. Its combinatorial complexity is widely appreciated. Combinatorial complexity prevents these mathematical methods from achieving human-like flexibility and adaptivity. In section 4 we discuss a biologically inspired mathematical technique, which overcomes CC. The biological inspirations for this approach are briefly summarized in the next section 3.

3   Mind: Instincts, Concepts, and Emotions

Among fundamental mechanisms of the mind are instincts, concepts, emotions, and control of behavior. Instincts operate like internal sensors: for example, when a sugar level in blood goes below a certain level an instinct "tells us" to eat. Concepts are like internal models of the objects and situations; this analogy is quite literal, e.g., during visual perception of an object, an internal concept-model projects an image onto the visual cortex, which is matched there to an image projected from retina (this simplified description will be refined later). Emotions are neural signals connecting instinctual and conceptual brain regions. Whereas in colloquial usage, emotions are often understood as facial expressions, higher voice pitch, exaggerated gesticulation, these are the outward signs of emotions, serving for communication. A more fundamental role of emotions within the mind system is that emotional signals evaluate concepts for the purpose of instinct satisfaction [16]. This emotional mechanism described in the next section is crucial for breaking out of the "vicious circle" of combinatorial complexity. Conceptual-emotional understanding of the world leads to actions (or behavior) in the outside world or within the mind. In this paper we describe only one type of behavior, the behavior of learning that is improving understanding and knowledge of the language and world.

4   Modeling Field Theory (MFT)

The mind involves a hierarchy of multiple levels of concept-models, from simple perceptual elements (like edges, or moving dots), to concept-models of objects, to complex scenes, etc. Modeling field theory (MFT) [5], summarized below, associates lower-level signals with higher-level concept-models; a result is an understanding of signals as concepts. The difficulties of CC described in Section 2 are avoided. It is achieved by a new type of logic, the fuzzy dynamic logic. MFT is a multi-level, hetero-hierarchical system. We start with a basic mechanism of interaction at a single level.

At each level, the output signals are concepts recognized (or formed) in input signals. Input signals are associated with concepts according to the representations-models and similarity measures at this level. In the process of association-recognition, models are adapted for better representation of the input signals; and similarity measures are adapted so that their fuzziness is matched to the model uncertainty. The initial uncertainty of models is high and so is the fuzziness of the similarity measure; in the process of learning models become more accurate and the similarity more crisp, the value of the similarity measure increases. This is a mechanism of fuzzy dynamic logic.

Input signals $\{X(n)\}$ are enumerated by $n = 1,...$ N; concept-models $h = 1,...$ H, are characterized by the models (representations) $\{M_h(n)\}$ of the signals $X(n)$; each model depends on its parameters $\{S_h\}$, $M_h(S_h,n)$. In a highly simplified description of a visual cortex, n enumerates the visual cortex neurons, $X(n)$ are the "bottom-up" activation levels of these neurons coming from the retina through visual nerve, and $M_h(n)$ are the "top-down" activation levels (or priming) of the visual cortex neurons from previously learned object-models [17]. Cognition process attempts to "match" top-down and bottom-up activations by selecting "best" models and their parameters. Computationally, it increases a similarity measure between the sets of models and signals, $L(\{X(n)\},\{M_h(n)\})$ [5].

$$L(\{X\},\{M\}) = \prod_{n \in N} \sum_{h \in H} r(h) \, l(X(n) \mid M_h(n)); \qquad (1)$$

here, $l(X(n)|M_h(n))$ (or simply $l(n|h)$) is a conditional partial similarity between one signal $X(n)$ and one model $M_h(n)$; (1) accounts for all possible combinations of signals and models. Parameters $r(h)$ are proportional to the number of signals $\{n\}$ associated with the model h. Maximization of similarity has the following psychological and neurobiological interpretation: it is an instinctual behavior that evolved with the purpose of understanding the world, it is *instinct for knowledge.*

Note, that (1) contains a large number of combinations of models and signals, a total of H^N items; this was a cause for the combinatorial complexity of the past algorithms discussed in section 2. MFT solves this problem using the mechanism of fuzzy dynamic logic (DL) [5,18]. The DL iteration's consist of two steps: first compute fuzzy association variables $f(h|n)$, then improve parameters

$$f(h|n) = r(h) \, l(n|h) \, / \sum_{h' \in H} r(h') \, l(n|h'). \qquad (2)$$

$$S_h = (1-\alpha) \, S_h + \alpha \sum_n f(h|n)[\partial lnl(n|h)/\partial M_h]\partial M_h'/\partial S_h, \qquad (3)$$

$$r(h) = N_h \, / \, N; \qquad N_h = \sum_n f(h|n); \qquad (4)$$

Here, parameter α determines the iteration step and speed of convergence of the MF system; N_h can be interpreted as a number of signals $X(n)$ associated with or coming from a concept-model n. After step (3, 4) the iterations returns to step (2) and continues until changes in parameters become negligible and similarity (1) stop increasing). The following theorem was proven [5].

Theorem. Equations (2) through (6) define a convergent dynamic system MF with stationary states given by $max_{\{S_h\}}L$.

In plain language this means that the above equations indeed result in concept-models in the "mind" of the MFT system, which are most similar [in terms of similarity (1)] to the sensory data. Despite a combinatorially large number of items in (1), a computational complexity of the MF method is relatively low, it is linear in N. This theorem is proved by demonstrating that similarity (1) increases at each iteration [5]. Psychological and neurobiological interpretation of this fact is that instinct for knowledge is satisfied with each iteration; MFT system 'enjoys' the process of convergence to better knowledge.

Summary of the MF convergence: during an adaptation process, initial fuzzy and uncertain models are associated with structures in the input signals, fuzzy models are getting more definite and crisp. The type, shape and number of models are selected so that the internal representation within the system is similar to input signals: the MF

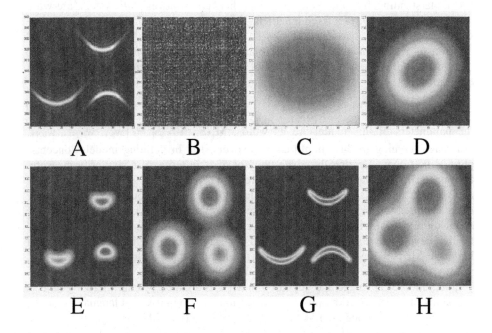

Fig. 1. Finding 'smile' and 'frown' patterns in noise, an example of dynamic logic operation: (a) true 'smile' and 'frown' patterns shown without noise; (b) actual image available for recognition (signal is below noise, signal-to-noise ratio is between –2dB and –0.7dB); (c) an initial fuzzy model, the fuzziness corresponds to uncertainty of knowledge; (d) through (h) show improved models at various iteration stages (total of 22 iterations). At stage (d) the algorithm tried to fit the data with more than one model and decided, that it needs three models to 'understand' the content of the data. There are three types of models: one uniform model describing noise (it is not shown) and a variable number of blob-models and parabolic models, which number, location and curvature are estimated from the data. Until about stage (g) the algorithm 'thought' in terms of simple blob models, at (g) and beyond, the algorithm decided that it needs more complex parabolic models to describe the data. Iterations stopped at (h), when similarity (1) stopped increasing. This example is discussed in more details in [19]

concept-models represent structure-objects in the signals. Computations describing this process are given by fuzzy dynamic logic eqs. (2, 3, 4). It is illustrated in Fig. 1 for recognition of 'smiles' and 'frowns' in the background of a strong noise. In terms of the mind, it describes an elementary cognition process involving instincts, imagination, emotions and concepts, but before discussing this cognitive-psychological interpretations, lets us briefly look into integrating this process with language.

By using concept-models with multiple sensor modalities, a MFT system can integrate signals from multiple sensors, while adapting and improving internal concept-models. Similarly, MFT can be used to integrate all sources of information, in particular, cognition and language. This requires linguistic MFT models, which can be developed using known linguistic structures [3,4,6,7,20]. Here, I briefly outline an approach to the development of MFT linguistic models.

Let us discuss the development of models of phrases from words for the purpose of text understanding. The input data, $\mathbf{X}(n)$, in this "phrase-level" MF system, are word strings, for simplicity, of a fixed length, S, $\mathbf{X}(n) = \{ w_{n+1}, w_{n+2} \ldots w_{n+S} \}$. Here w_n are words from a given dictionary of size K, $W = \{w_1, w_2 \ldots w_K\}$, and n is the word position in a body of texts. A simple phrase model is a subset of words from the dictionary, without any order or rules of grammar (computational linguists call it 'bag' model),

$$\mathbf{M}_h(\mathbf{S}_h,n) = \{ w_{h,1}, w_{h,2} \ldots w_{h,S} \}; \tag{6}$$

the parameters of this model are its words, $\mathbf{M}_h(\mathbf{S}_h,n) = \mathbf{S}_h = \{w_{h,1}, w_{h,2} \ldots w_{h,S}\}$. Language learning in this simplified context consists in defining models-concepts-phrases best characterizing the given body of texts in terms of a similarity measure. Extension of DL to language was considered in [21]. It can be applied to bag models and to other known structures of natural languages, such as noun and verb phrases, tree structures, etc. [3,4,6,7,20,22,23]. This accomplishes the goal of the language acquisition project without combinatorial complexity. This technique can be applied to the development of understanding-based web search engines. A hierarchical language-MFT is developed with higher levels of the hierarchy extending 'above' phrases to learning the contents of paragraphs, pages, documents.

Integration of language and cognition in MFT is attained by characterizing objects and situations in the world with two types of models, cognitive and language models; so that in eqs. (1) through (4) $\mathbf{M}_h(n) = \{\mathbf{M1}_{h1}(n), \mathbf{M2}_{h2}(n)\}$, $\mathbf{M1}$ for cognitive and $\mathbf{M2}$ for language models. Indexes h1 and h2 innumerate cognitive and language models; but it is not necessary to consider combinations of h1 and h2, because initially all models are same, fuzzy blobs, just placeholders for future knowledge. The above equations describe a single agent with a MFT-mind.

A MFT agent can be used in a particular application alone or as a part of collaborative multi-agent environment. A single MFT agent can utilize complex adaptive models, and can learn from data and signals. Several applications of this type were developed [5,22]. The more specific the models are, the less data will be required for learning. A different evolutionary approach can start with simple models and develop complex models and abilities as a result of evolution of a multi-agent MFT system. Multiple agents can learn from their environment along with communicating among themselves or within a collaborative environment with human.

First steps toward the development of evolving systems with cognitive and communicating multiple agents with a MFT mind are described in [24,25].

An integrated MFT system learns similarly to human, in parallel in three realms: (1) language and cognitive models are learned jointly, when language data are present in association with perception signals, like during mother talking to a baby: "this is a car" (perception-models and word-models), and like during more complicated conversations: "Look at Peter and Ann, they are in love" (cognitive-models and phrase-models); (2) language models are learned independently from cognition, when language data are encountered for the first time with no association with perception and cognition (most of language learning during the age 2 to 7); (3) similarly, cognitive models are learned independently from language, when perception signal data are encountered for the first time without association with linguistic data. In (2) and (3) above it is important to emphasize that cognitive and language learning enhance each other. The original, inborn models are fuzzy structures equally and poorly matching any sensory or language data. In the process of learning fuzziness decreases, crisp models get associated with specific situations and phrases, and cognitive models always remain associated with language models. Due to the integrated (cognitive, language)-model structures, association between language and cognition begins at a "pre-conceptual" fuzzy level, inaccessible to consciousness. Similarly a child learns a large number of language models, which association with real life is very fuzzy; throughout later life they facilitate learning of corresponding cognitive models; similarly, cognitive (say visual) models facilitate learning of language models; eventually h1 and h2, cognitive and language models are properly associated (that is similar across the system, so that people and computers understand each other).

5   Conclusion

At the beginning of this paper I summarized some justifications for following biological examples in engineering system design. Still, often one can hear a question: Why does an engineer need to know about concepts and emotions? After mathematical equations are derived, why not just use them for developing computer code, why should an engineer be concerned with interpretations of these equations in terms of instincts and emotions? This question is profound and an answer can be found in history of science and engineering. Newtonian laws can be written in few lines, but an engineering manager cannot hand these few lines to a young engineer and ask to design an airplane or rocket. Similarly, Maxwell's equations contain the main principles of radar and communication, but radars and communication systems cannot be built without knowledge of electromagnetic phenomenology. For the same reason, MFT and dynamic logic equations need to be supplemented by understanding phenomenology of the mind signal processing to be efficiently applied to design of high level fusion systems. For this reason in conclusion of this paper we summarize the main aspects of working of the mind as described by the equations given in this paper.

Equations in section 4 describe elementary processes of perception or cognition, in which a number of model-concepts compete for incoming signals, model-concepts are modified and new ones are formed, and eventually, more or less definite connections [high values of f(h|n), close to 1] are established among signal subsets on the one hand and some model-concepts on the other, accomplishing perception and cognition.

A salient mathematical property of this process is the correspondence between uncertainty in models and fuzziness in associations f(h|n). In perception, as long as model parameters do not correspond to actual objects, there is no match between models and signals; many models poorly match many objects, and associations remain fuzzy (between 0 and 1). Eventually, one model (h') wins a competition for a subset {n'} of input signals $\mathbf{X}$(n). In other words, a subset of data is recognized as a specific object (concept). Upon convergence, the entire set of input signals {n} is divided into subsets, each associated with one model-object, uncertainties become small, and fuzzy concept-models become crisp concepts. The general mathematical laws of cognition and perception are similar and constitute a basic principle of the mind organization. Kant was the first one to propose that the mind functioning involves three basic abilities: Pure Reason (concept-models), Judgment (emotional measure of correspondence between models and input signals), and Practical Reason (behavior; we only considered here the behavior of adaptation and learning) [26,27,28]. We now briefly discuss relationships between the MFT theory and concepts of mind originated in psychology, philosophy, linguistics, aesthetics, neuro-physiology, neural networks, artificial intelligence, pattern recognition, and intelligent systems.

A thought-process or cognition involves a number of sub-processes and attributes, including internal representations and their manipulation, attention, memory, concept formation, knowledge, generalization, recognition, understanding, meaning, prediction, imagination, intuition, emotion, decisions, reasoning, goals, behavior, conscious and unconscious [5,8]. We discuss how these processes are described by MFT.

A "minimal" subset of these processes, *an elementary thought-process*, has to involve mechanisms for afferent and efferent signals [8], in other words, bottom-up and top-down signals. According to Carpenter and Grossberg [29] every recognition and concept formation process involves a "resonance" between these two types of signals. In MFT, at every level in a hierarchy the afferent signals are represented by the input signal field $\mathbf{X}$, and the efferent signals are represented by the modeling fields $\mathbf{M}_h$; resonances correspond to high similarity values l(n|h) for some subsets of {n} that are "recognized" as concepts (or objects). The mechanism leading to the resonances between incoming signals and internal representations is given by equations in section 4.

A description of the workings of the mind as given by the MFT dynamics was first provided by Aristotle [30], describing cognition as a learning process in which an a priori form-as-potentiality (fuzzy model) meets matter (sensory signals) and becomes a form-as-actuality (a logical concept). Jung suggested that conscious concepts are developed by the mind based on genetically inherited structures, archetypes, which are inaccessible to consciousness [31] and Grossberg [8] suggested that only signals and models attaining a resonant state (that is, signals matching models) reach consciousness. Fuzzy uncertain models are less accessible to consciousness, whereas more crisp and certain models are better accessible to consciousness.

Recognizing objects in the environment and understanding their meaning is so important for human evolutionary success that an instinct has evolved for learning and improving concept-models. This instinct (for knowledge and learning) is described in MFT by maximization of similarity between the models and the world, eq. (1). Emotions related to satisfaction-dissatisfaction of this instinct we perceive as harmony-disharmony (between our understanding of how things ought to be and how they actually are in the surrounding world). Since Kant [27], emotions that are not related directly to bodily needs are called aesthetic emotions. Aesthetic emotions in MFT correspond to changes in the knowledge instinct (1). The mathematical basis for the theorem in section 4 can be interpreted psychologically: during dynamic logic iterations the aesthetic emotion is always positive. MFT system 'enjoys' learning.

Signs and symbols are essential for the workings of the human mind, as well as for accumulation and transmission of knowledge in human culture. They are also used extensively in intelligent and multi-level fusion systems. Scientific theories of signs and symbols, however, are not well developed, and even the exact meaning of these words is often confused. According to [32], "symbol" is the most misused word. We use this word in trivial cases referring, say, to traffic signs and in the most profound cases of cultural and religious symbols. In mathematics and in "Symbolic AI" there is no difference between signs and symbols. Both are considered to be notations, arbitrary non-adaptive entities with axiomatically fixed meaning. This non-differentiation is a "hangover" from an old superstition that logic describes mind, a direction in mathematics and logical philosophy that can be traced through the works of Frege, Hilbert, Russell, to its bitter end in Gödel theory, and its revival during the 1960s and 1970s in artificial intelligence. Profound use of the word "symbol" in general culture, according to Jung, is related to symbols being psychological processes of sign interpretation. Jung emphasized that symbol-processes connect the conscious and unconscious [31]. Pribram wrote of symbols as adaptive, context-sensitive signals in the brain, whereas signs he identified with less adaptive and relatively context-insensitive neural signals [33]. Deacon [32] thought that the essence of the human symbolic ability is two interacting parallel hierarchies, like described in section 4 hierarchy of cognitive models and a hierarchy of sign (language) models; he called it symbolic reference.

Combining mathematical developments in sections 4 with the above discussion, we reach the following conclusion for consistent meanings of signs and symbols. The essence of a sign is that it is an arbitrary notation, which can be interpreted by our mind or by an intelligent system to refer to something else, to an object or situation. Symbols are psychological processes of sign interpretation, they are equivalent to elementary thought processes, and they integrate unconscious (fuzzy models) with conscious (crisp models). A simple symbol process is mathematically described by a single MFT level, like in section 4. A complex symbol-process of cognition of culturally important concepts may take hundreds of years in human societies and many generations of MFT agents; it may involve multiple levels of MFT or the mind hierarchy. Future sensor-webs will be designed using this biological knowledge. They will participate in human-computer collaborative networks. They will evolve through generations of agents. They will integrate the learning of language with the learning of complex cognitive concepts. They will integrate communication with sensor signal processing, and instead of quick obsolescence, their performance will improve with time and experience by accumulating knowledge similar to human cultures.

Acknowledgments

The author is thankful to Ross Deming and Robert Linnehan for their contributions.

References

1. Boury-Brisset, A-C.: Ontology-based Approach for Information Fusion (2005)
2. Pinker, S.: The Language Instinct: How the Mind Creates Language. Harper Perennial (2000)
3. Jackendoff, R.: Foundations of Language: Brain, Meaning, Grammar, Evolution. Oxford University Press, New York, NY (2002)
4. Pinker, S.: Words and Rules: The Ingredients of Language Harper Perennial (2000)
5. Perlovsky, L.I.: Neural Networks and Intellect: using model-based concepts. Oxford University Press, New York, NY (2001)
6. Rieger, B.B., ed. Empirical Semantics II. A Collection of New Approaches in the Field. Quantitative Linguistics, v. 13, Brockmeyer, Bochum, Germany (1981)
7. Mehler,A.: Components of a Model of Context-Sensitive Hypertexts. In: Journal of Universal Computer Science (J.UCS) **8**(10) (2002) 924–943
8. For the discussions and further references see: Grossberg, S. (1988). *Neural Networks and Natural Intelligence.* MIT Press, Cambridge, MA. Meystel, A.M., Albus, J.S. (2001). *Intelligent Systems: Architecture, Design, and Control.* Wiley, New York; also.
9. Perlovsky, L.I.: Conundrum of Combinatorial Complexity. IEEE Trans. PAMI, **20**(6) (1998) 666–670
10. Bellman, R.E.: *Adaptive Control Processes.* Princeton University Press, Princeton, NJ (1961)
11. Minsky, M.L.: *Semantic Information Processing.* The MIT Press, Cambridge, MA (1968)
12. Chomsky, N.: *Language and Mind.* Harcourt Brace Javanovich, New York, NY (1972)
13. Chomsky, N.: *Principles and Parameters in Syntactic Theory.* In N.Hornstein and D.Lightfoot (eds), 1981, *Explanation in Linguistics. The Logical Problem of Language Acquisition,* Longman, London (1981)
14. Perlovsky, L.I.: *Gödel Theorem and Semiotics.* Proceedings of the Conference on Intelligent Systems and Semiotics '96. Gaithersburg, MD, **2** (1996) 14–18
15. Jang,J.-S.R., Sun,C.-T., and Mizutani, E.: Neuro-Fuzzy and Soft Computing: A Computational Approach to Learning and Machine Intelligence. Prentice Hall, Upper Saddle River, NJ (1996)
16. Grossberg, S. & Levine, D.S.: Neural dynamics of attentionally modulated Pavlovian conditioning: blocking, inter-stimulus interval, and secondary reinforcement. *Psychobiology,* **15**(3) (1987) 195–240
17. In fact there are many levels between the retina, visual cortex, and object-models; Zeki, S. (1993). *A Vision of the Brain.* Blackwell, Oxford, England; L. M. Chalupa, J. S. Werner, 2003, *The Visual Neurosciences,* MIT Press
18. Perlovsky, L.I.: *Mathematical Concepts of Intellect.* Proc. World Congress on Neural Networks, San Diego, CA; Lawrence Erlbaum Associates, NJ, pp.1013-16; Perlovsky, L.I.(1997). *Physical Concepts of Intellect.* Proc. Russian Academy of Sciences, **354**(3) (1996) 320–323

19. Linnehan, R., Mutz, Perlovsky, L.I., C., Weijers, B., Schindler, J., Brockett, R.: *Detection of Patterns Below Clutter in Images*. Int. Conf. On Integration of Knowledge Intensive Multi-Agent Systems, Cambridge, MA Oct.1-3, 2003 (2003)

20. Mehler, A.: Hierarchical Orderings of Textual Units. Proceedings of the 19th International Conference on Computational Linguistics, COLING 2002, Taipei. San Francisco: Morgan Kaufmann (2002) 646–652

21. Perlovsky, L.I.: Integrating Language and Cognition. IEEE Connections, Feature Article, **2**(2) (2004) 8–12

22. Perlovsky, L.I.: *Integration of Information in Human Brain*. Int. Conf. On Integration of Knowledge Intensive Multi-Agent Systems, Cambridge, MA Oct.1-3, 2003 (2003)

23. Rieger, B.B.: Tree-like dispositinal dependency structures for non-propositional semantic inferencing: n a SCIP upproachto natural language understanding by machine. In Bouchon-Meunier and Yager, eds., *Proc. 7th Int. Conf. On Information Processing and Management of Uncertainty in Knowledge-based Systems (IPMU-198)*, Paris, (1998) 351–358

24. Fontanari, J.F. and Perlovsky, L.I.: *Evolution of communication in a community of simple-minded agents*. IEEE Int. Conf. On Integration of Knowledge Intensive Multi-Agent Sys., Waltham, MA (2005)

25. Fontanari, J.F. and Perlovsky, L.I.: *Meaning Creation and Modeling Field Theory*. IEEE Int. Conf. On Integration of Knowledge Intensive Multi-Agent Sys., Waltham, MA (2005)

26. Kant, I.: (1781). *Critique of Pure Reason*. Tr. J.M.D. Meiklejohn, 1943. Willey Book, New York, NY

27. Kant, I.: (1790). *Critique of Judgment*. Tr. J.H. Bernard, 1914, 2nd ed., Macmillan & Co., London

28. Kant, I.: (1788). *Critique of Practical Reason*. Tr. J.H Bernard, 1986, Hafner

29. Carpenter, G.A. & Grossberg, S.: A massively parallel architecture for a self-organizing neural pattern recognition machine, Computer Vision, Graphics and Image Processing, 37 (1987) 54-115

30. Aristotle, IV BC, *Metaphysics,* tr. W.D.Ross, Complete Works of Aristotle, Ed.J.Barnes, Princeton, NJ 1995

31. Jung, C.G.: *Archetypes of the Collective Unconscious*. In the Collected Works, v.9,II, Bollingen Series XX, 1969, Princeton University Press, Princeton, NJ (1934)

32. Deacon, T.W. The Symbolic Species: The Co-Evolution of Language and the Brain. W.W. Norton & Company (1998)

33. Pribram, K.: Languages of the Brain. Prentice Hall (1971)

Agents and Data Mining:
Mutual Enhancement by Integration

Chengqi Zhang[1], Zili Zhang[2,3], and Longbing Cao[1]

[1] Faculty of Information Technology,
University of Technology, Sydney,
PO Box 123, Broadway NSW 2007, Australia
{chengqi, lbcao}@it.uts.edu.au
[2] Faculty of Computer and Information Science,
Southwest China Normal University, Chongqing 400715, China
zhangzl@swnu.edu.cn
[3] School of Information Technology,
Deakin University, Geelong, VIC 3217, Australia
zzhang@deakin.edu.au

Abstract. This paper tells a story of synergism of two cutting edge technologies — agents and data mining. By integrating these two technologies, the power for each of them is enhanced. Integrating agents into data mining systems, or constructing data mining systems from agent perspectives, the flexibility of data mining systems can be greatly improved. New data mining techniques can add to the systems dynamically in the form of agents, while the out-of-date ones can also be deleted from systems at run-time. Equipping agents with data mining capabilities, the agents are much smarter and more adaptable. In this way, the performance of these agent systems can be improved. A new way to integrate these two techniques –ontology-based integration is also discussed. Case studies will be given to demonstrate such mutual enhancement.

1 Introduction

Agents (adaptive or intelligent agents and multi-agent systems) constitute one of the most prominent and attractive technologies in Computer Science at the beginning of this new century. Agent and multi-agent system technologies, methods, and theories are currently contributing to many diverse domains. These include information retrieval, user interface design, robotics, electronic commerce, computer mediated collaboration, computer games, education and training, smart environments, ubiquitous computers, and social simulation.

This is not only a very promising technology, it is emerging as a new way of thinking, a conceptual paradigm for analyzing problems and for designing systems, for dealing with complexity, distribution and interactivity, and perhaps a new perspective on computing and intelligence.

Agent-based computing has been a source of technologies to a number of research areas, both theoretical and applied. These include distributed planning

V. Gorodetsky, J. Liu, and V.A. Skormin (Eds.): AIS-ADM 2005, LNAI 3505, pp. 50–61, 2005.
© Springer-Verlag Berlin Heidelberg 2005

and decision-making, automated auction mechanisms and learning mechanisms. Moreover, agent technologies have drawn from, and contributed to, a diverse range of academic disciplines, in the humanities, the sciences and social sciences. The fundamental research issues in agent technologies include multi-agent planning, agent communication languages, coordination mechanisms, matchmaking architectures and algorithms, information agents and basic ontologies, sophisticated auction mechanism design, negotiation strategies, and learning [8].

Agent technologies are a natural extension of current component-based approaches, and have the potential to greatly impact the lives and work of all of us and, accordingly, this area is one of the most dynamic and exciting in computer science today [9].

Data mining (also known as Knowledge Discovery in Databases - KDD) has been defined as "The nontrivial extraction of implicit, previously unknown, and potentially useful information from data." [10]. Using a combination of machine learning, statistical analysis, modeling techniques and database technology, data mining finds patterns and subtle relationships in data and infers rules that allow the prediction of future results. Typical applications include market segmentation, customer profiling, fraud detection, evaluation of retail promotions, and credit risk analysis.

Data mining is a powerful new technology with great potential to help companies focus on the most important information in their data warehouses. Data mining tools predict future trends and behaviors, allowing businesses to make proactive, knowledge-driven decisions. The automated, prospective analyses offered by data mining move beyond the analyses of past events provided by retrospective tools typical of decision support systems. Data mining tools can answer business questions that traditionally were too time consuming to resolve. They scour databases for hidden patterns, finding predictive information that experts may miss because it lies outside their expectations.

The large variety of data mining techniques which have been developed over the past decade includes methods for pattern-based similarity search, cluster analysis, decision-tree based classification, generalization taking the data cube or attribute-oriented induction approach, and mining of association rules [11].

Recent years saw a new trend in the combination of the multi-agent system approach, data mining and KDD. It could be observed that recent research areas in multi-agent systems (agent behavior adaptation and reinforcement learning, collective behavior learning, e.g., through modification of collective behavior protocols, etc.) utilize data mining and KDD as a source of innovative ideas. In return, multi-agent technology is used to address architectural and implementation issues in engineering and software implementation of data mining and KDD systems.

In this paper, we will tell a story of synergism of agent and data mining technologies based on our research as well as other peer colleagues. In Section 2, how agent technology can be used to facilitate the construction data mining systems is discussed. Section 3 presents how to enhance the capabilities of agents by equipping data mining ability. Section 4 demonstrates ontology-based integration of agents and data mining – a new way to integrate these two cutting edge technologies. Finally, Section 5 concludes this paper.

2   Agent-Based Data Mining

Most of the existing data mining techniques were originally developed for centralized data and need to be modified for handling the distributed case. This motivated the development of parallel and distributed data mining. However, current techniques developed for parallel/distributed data mining failed to meet the requirements of the problems. The inherent feature of agents of being autonomous, capable of adaptive and deliberative reasoning seems to fit quite well with the requirements of coping with the challenges of distributed data mining. Agent techniques play an important role in distributed data mining. Some typical work in this area is summarized in Section 2.1.

On the other hand, data mining systems are typical complex systems and difficult to construct due to many techniques and iterative steps involved in the process [12][13][14]. An agent is a computer system capable of flexible autonomous action in a dynamic, unpredictable and open environment. Agents offer a new and often more appropriate route to the development of complex systems, especially in open and dynamic environments [9]. Thus agent approach is particularly well-suited for data mining construction. Our work related to this topic is reported in Section 2.2.

2.1   Agents in Distributed Data Mining

Autonomous data mining agents as a special kind of information agents may perform various kinds of mining operations on behalf of its user(s) or in collaboration with other agents. Systems of cooperative information agents for data mining tasks in distributed, heterogeneous and massive data environments appear to be quite a natural vision for the near future to be realized. In [1], Klusch et al. discussed the advantages by using agents for distributed data mining. They argued that employing agent techniques to build distributed data mining systems can bring the following benefits:

- *Remaining the autonomy of data sources.* A data mining agent can be considered as a modular extension of a data management system to deliberatively handle the access to the underlying data source in accordance with given constraints on the required autonomy of the system, data, and model. This is in full compliance with the paradigm of cooperative information systems.
- *Facilitating interactive distributed data mining.* Pro-actively assisting agents can drastically limit the amount a user has to supervise and interfere with the running data mining process. For example, data mining agents can anticipate the individual limits of the potentially large search space and proper intermediate results particularly driven by their individual users' preferences with respect to the particular type of data mining task at hand.
- *Improving dynamic selection of sources and data gathering.* One challenge for data mining systems used in open distributed data environments is to discover and select relevant sources. In such settings data mining agents can be applied to adaptively select data sources according to given criteria such as the expected amount, type and quality of data at the considered source,

actual network and data mining server load. Such data mining agents can be used, for example, to dynamically control and manage the process of data gathering to support any online analytical processing and business data warehouse application.

- *Having high scalability to massive distributed data.* One option to reduce network and data mining application server load is to let data mining agents migrate to each of the local data sites in a distributed data mining system on which they can perform mining tasks locally, and then either return with or send relevant pre-selected data to their originating server for further processing.
- *Stimulating multi-strategy distributed data mining.* For some complex application settings and appropriate combination of multiple data mining techniques can be more beneficial than applying just one particular one. Data mining agents can learn in due course of their deliberative actions which one to choose depending on the type of data retrieved from different sites and mining tasks to be pursued.
- *Enabling collaborative data mining.* Data mining agents can operate independently on data they have gathered at local sites, and then combine their respective models. Or they can agree to share potential knowledge as it is discovered, in order to benefit from additional opinions of other data mining agents.

Recently agent techniques have been applied to distributed data mining. The most prominent and representative agent-based distributed data mining systems include BODHI, PADMA, JAM, and Papyrus.

In [16] and [17], the authors describe a parallel/distributed data mining system PADMA (PArallel Data Mining Agents) that uses software agents for local data accessing and analysis and a Web based interface for interactive data visualization. PADMA has been used in medical applications. In [18], an agent-based meta-learning system for large-scale data mining applications, which is called JAM (Java Agents for Meta-learning), is described. JAM was empirically evaluated against real credit card transaction data where the target data mining application was to compute predictive models that detect fraudulent transactions. However, these works are focusing on one of the many steps in data mining. Papyrus [19] is a Java-based system addressing wide-area distributed data mining over clusters of heterogeneous data sites and meta-clusters. It supports different task and predictive model strategies including C4.5. Mobile data mining agents move data, intermediate results, and models between clusters to perform all computation locally and reduce network load, or from local sites to a central root which produces the final result. Each cluster has one distinguished node which acts as its cluster access and control point for the agents. Coordination of the overall clustering task is either done by a central root site or distributed to the (peer-to-peer) network of cluster access points. Papyrus supports various methods for combining and exchanging the locally mined predictive models and metadata required to describe them by using a special markup language. Klusch et al. also proposed a kernel density estimation based clustering scheme for agent-based distributed data clustering [1].

2.2   Building Data Mining Systems from Agent Perspectives

It is well known that there are variety of methods related to different main tasks in data mining, and outputs of different data mining methods also have different forms. However, a single data mining technique has not been proven appropriate for every domain and data set. Instead, several techniques may need to be integrated into hybrid systems and used cooperatively during a particular data mining operation. Therefore, hybrid intelligent systems are required for data mining tasks. For further justifying this statement, a simple example is now provided.

The example is about how to identify a set of "promising" securities to be included in an investment portfolio based on the historical fundamental and technical data about securities. This is a very appropriate domain for data mining for two reasons. First, because the number of available securities being traded in the various exchanges is very large. Identifying appropriate securities for the goals of a particular portfolio is based on the close examination of the performance of these securities. Without the use of data mining techniques, analysts can only closely examine small amounts of such data. Second, analysts are able to state criteria for identifying securities that can potentially meet a set of investment goals. However, they cannot identify all the necessary criteria. Furthermore, even after a set of securities is identified, large volumes of data relating to these securities still has to be examined in order to fine-tune the stated performance criteria, as well as identify others not previously considered by the analyst. For this simple task, no single data mining technique is adequate. Methods to formulate a pattern (hypothesis) and test its validity on the target databases are needed. Methods to discover other relevant patterns from target databases are also required. Some other methods including classification method to classify each security, inductive learning methods, and visualization techniques are also helpful for this task. If we construct a computer system to perform this task, it is evident that this system is a hybrid system integrated different techniques.

Once again, data mining is iterative sequence of many steps, while many techniques are involved in each step. These techniques need to be integrated into hybrid systems and used cooperatively for data mining tasks.

We have argued that agent perspectives are well-suited to hybrid intelligent systems construction, and proposed an agent-based framework for complex problem solving [20]. This framework was successfully applied to build a hybrid intelligent system for data mining [4]. The data mining systems built from agent perspectives have the following crucial characteristics that differentiate from others:

- New data mining techniques can be added to the system and out-of-date techniques can be deleted from the system dynamically;
- Data mining related agents and other agents can interact at run-time with ease under this framework, but in other non-agent based systems, these interactions must be determined at design-time.

For demonstration purpose, we show the Weka system [15] re-implemented from agent perspectives. The main focus of Weka is on classifier and filter algorithms. It also includes implementations of algorithms for learning association rules and for clustering data for which no class value is specified.

To re-implement the programs in Weka from agent perspectives, the programs in Weka (written in Java) were compiled into .DLLs (dynamic link library) first. The Java Native methods and JATLite KQML layer templates were then employed to wrap these programs in .DLL. In this way, all the programs in Weka were equipped with KQML communication capability and are ready to add to the agent system.

In this agent-based data mining experimental system, in addition to the supporting agents (interface agent, planning agent, middle agent, and so on) there are 7 attribute selection related agents, 25 classifier related agents, 9 filter related agents, and 2 cluster related agents.

Figure 1 shows the user interface of the system, which can start from any Internet Browser or appletviewer.

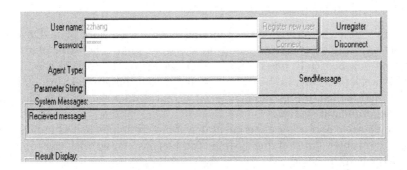

Fig. 1. User Interface of the System

To use the system, the user needs to type the user name and the password he likes in the corresponding fields and click "register new user" to register for the first time. Thereafter, just input the registered user name and password and click "connect". If the user wants to leave the system, click "disconnect" and "unregister".

The system can work in two modes. In one mode, all the data mining related agents can run individually, which is similar to execute the original Weka programs from the command line. In this mode, the user provides the system with the "agent type" and corresponding "parameter string" information in the corresponding input fields, and then click "SendMessage" button. The system will activate the given agent and display the results in the "result display" window. For example, if we type in "weke.classifiers.m5.M5Prime" in the "agent type" field, and "-t data\cpu.arff" in the "parameter string" field ("data\" was added before the data file as all data files in the system is in the "data" subdirectory), the system will display the following results (Figure 2), which are the same as running this program from the command line in Weka.

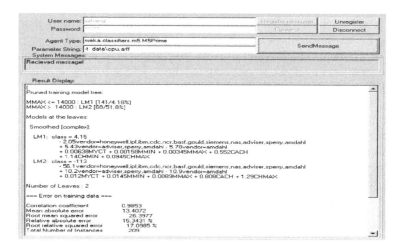

Fig. 2. Output from the M5 agent for numeric prediction

Another mode is to provide the planning agent with a work plan. The system then activates different agents based on the work plan. The work plan can be generated automatically based on meta-knowledge of the task in the planning agent. A work plan can also be edited manually according to the work plan specification and loaded into planning agent. Currently, only the latter implemented in the experimental system.

This example and other experimental systems we implemented indicate that flexible and robust data mining systems can be constructed with ease under the unified agent framework.

3   Agent Systems with Data Mining Capabilities

In this section we present an example to demonstrate that equipping agent systems with data mining abilities, the performance of agent systems can be improved. In the agent-based system for portfolio selection [7], data mining techniques were integrated.

Before we discuss the integration, we describe the process of analyzing large set of security data to discover the "promising" securities.

Assume the target database the analysis based contains monthly data of 2000 securities over a period of ten years.

Our goal is trying to create a "promising" security set of 15 − 20 securities which the portfolio selection models will use (and also the investor will subsequently trade). Such data may be purchased from stock exchange Inc. such as Australian Stock Exchange Limited or downloaded from the corresponding Websites. Suppose we are interested in stocks with high earnings-per-share growth and high dividend growth, where "high" in both instances means greater than 50%. We define the concept of *strong security* as one whose *earning-per-share-growth* and *dividend-growth* is greater than 50%. We define "promising" security as one its *return on investment* two quarters later will be greater than 5%.

Next, we need to formulate a pattern (hypothesis) and test its validity on the target database. The hypothesis states that "IF a security is *strong* at time t, THEN its *return on investment* two quarters later will be greater than 5%." In addition to selecting the concepts that will be included in this pattern, we must also specify the bindings between the attributes of the selected concepts.

Once we instruct the system to validate the hypothesis, the system returns two sets of answers based on randomly selected sample data set: the records (securities) that support the hypothesis and those that refute it.

We then test the discovered patterns by applying them to another data set, called the *test set*, that was not originally used to discover the patterns. With each security to be classified the system returns its prediction, along with the confidence level associated with the prediction, as well as the actual return on investment.

By examining the evidence for incorrect predictions, we can identify rules that are suspect. We may iteratively apply top-down and bottom-up data mining to obtain more correct and complete models and higher prediction accuracy.

The collection of patterns created through the pattern validation and data exploration operations forms the rule-based model. This model is then applied on the set of securities that are targeted. The top 20 of the securities whose return on investment is predicted by the model to be "high", i.e., greater than 5% over a six month period are included in the "promising" security set.

In the whole process to determine the "promising" security set from large volumes of data, different data mining techniques such supervised symbolic inductive learning etc. are used.

By incorporating data mining techniques into the system, such a system can closely examine far more securities than manual approaches when creating "promising" security set. This laid a sound foundations for finding good portfolios.

Combining agent and data mining these two cutting edge technologies together can improve the performance of portfolio selection. Such agent-based portfolio selection system with data mining ability is very promising to find portfolios which best meet the objectives of the investors.

4   Ontology-Based Integration of Agents and Data Mining

From the discussions of previous two sections, it is evident that agent technology and data mining technology need each other. These two cutting edge technologies can enhance each other significantly by integration. In this section, we discuss an effective and efficient way to integrate agent and data mining, which is called *ontology-based integration.*

The key point in ontology-based integration is a view of ontological engineering in agent-based system analysis and design. The ontological engineering normally deals with the following processes [21]:

- building ontology profiles for the domain problem,
- defining ontological semantic relationships,
- representing ontologies, and
- aggregating and transforming ontologies in one or cross-domains. This actually is the foundation for system analysis, design and implementation.

The application process of ontological engineering is as follows.

- Understanding business ontology and user personalization in terms of business and user profiles.
- Extracting domain ontologies and problem-solving ontologies in terms of business processes, work flow, requirements engineering, and agent-oriented methodology.
- Abstracting semantic relationships among ontology concepts for different ontological domains.
- Representing ontologies visually and formally in terms of semantic relationships, ontological domains, and implementation techniques.
- Defining aggregation and transformation rules for ontology concepts, which support semantic aggregation, transformation and mapping between ontology concepts and key words, from one ontological item to another, or cross ontological domains.

According to the above process, an agent-based data mining infrastructure called F-TRADE (Financial Trading Rules Automated Development and Evaluation) was developed. F-TRADE is a web-based automated enterprise infrastructure for evaluation of trading strategies and data mining algorithms with online connection to huge amount of stock data. The current version F-TRADE 2.0 can be accessed at *http://datamining.it.uts.edu.au:8080/tsap*.

F-TRADE can provide financial traders and researchers, and miners on financial data with a practically flexible and automatic infrastructure. With this infrastructure, they can plug their algorithms into it easily, and concentrate on improving the performance of their algorithms with iterative evaluation on a large amount of real stock data from international markets. All other work, including user interface implementation, data preparation, and result output etc. is maintained by this platform. For financial traders, for instance, brokers and retailers, the F-TRADE presents them a real test bed, which can help them evaluate their favorite trading strategies iteratively without risk before they put money into the real markets. On the other hand, the F-TRADE presents a large amount of real stock data in multiple international markets, which can be used for both realistic back-testing of trading strategies and mining algorithms.

The F-TRADE looks also like an online service provider. As a systematic infrastructure for supporting data mining, trading evaluation, and finance-oriented applications, the F-TRADE encompasses comprehensive functions and services. They can be divided into the following groups: trading service support, mining services support, data services support, algorithm services support, and system services support. From the ontological engineering perspective, there are two key functions in F-TRADE that support all these services. One is soft plug-and-play [22], the other is ontology transformation in cross-domains [23].

Soft plug-and-play is essential in F-TRADE. It gets involved in plug in of data sources, data requests, trading or mining algorithms, system functional components, and the like. As a matter of fact, it has been a significant feature which supports the evolution of the F-TRADE and the application add-ons on top of the F-TRADE. The analysis, design, and implementation of soft plug-and-play are mainly supported by the agent service-oriented technique, which includes the analysis and design of the role model and the agent services for the plug-and-play. Refer to [22] for the details.

There are multiple heterogeneous ontological domains existing in F-TRADE. Flexible and efficient transformation, mapping and discovery of ontologies from multiple heterogeneous ontological domains are essential for the success of such systems.

The ontology processing engine in F-TRADE semantically aggregates and transforms user-defined business-oriented (or domain-oriented) special terms to internal standard items used by the problem-solving system. Three aspects must be followed in order to do the semantic aggregation and ontological transformation from user-defined keywords to ontological elements in problem-solving ontological domain. They are (i) semantic aggregation between semantic relationships, (ii) semantic aggregation of ontological items, and (iii) transformation from one ontology domain to another. All the above three types of transformations can happen in either one ontological domain or multiple domains.

Semantic Aggregation of relationships is to study whether there are rules for transitivity, additivity and anti-symmetry which can be performed between ontological semantic relationships. The aggregation of multiple semantic relationships can simplify the combination of semantic relationships, and supports to find the final reduced semantic relationships. This will reduce the problem-solving sample space, and speed up the work of the engine.

Another situation of semantic aggregation is to aggregate ontological items which are linked by logic connectors associated with some semantic relationships. The objective of aggregating ontological items is to reduce items, and generate the resulting ontological items.

Transformation from ontological item to another in one or many domains could be a mapping from an arbitrary keyword in the business ontological domain to its relevant items in the problem-solving domain. The basic idea for transformation of ontological items is as follows: given an input item, checking candidate ontological items by semantic relationships, and finding the suitable candidate as the output item.

The rules for the three types of transformations are discussed in [23].

5   Concluding Remarks

This paper told a story how agents and data mining can enhance each other, and how these two cutting edge technologies can be integrated through an ontological engineering point of view.

Integrating agents into data mining systems, the flexibility of data mining systems can be greatly improved. New data mining techniques can add to the systems dynamically, while the out-of-date ones can also be deleted from systems at run-time. It is a real plug-and-play. Equipping agents with data mining capabilities, the agents are much smarter and more adaptable. In this way, the performance of these agent systems can be improved.

This paper is a brief summary of what we have done in the practice of combining agents and data mining techniques. Obviously, more efforts are required to explore this new trend of research.

Acknowledgement

This paper is partially supported by the Ministry of Education of China Key Project 104160 and Deakin University CRGS grant.

References

1. Klusch, M., Lodi, S. and Moro, G.: The Role of Agents in Distributed Data Mining: Issues and Benefits, *Proceedings of the IEEE/WIC International Conference on Intelligent Agent Technology*, IEEE CS Press (2003) 211–217
2. Ouali, A., Ramdane-Cherif, Z., Ramdane-Cherif, A., Levy, N. and Krebs, M.:A gent Paradigm in Clinical Large-Scale Data Mining Environment, *Proceedings of the 2nd IEEE International Conference on Cognitive Informatics*, IEEE CS Press (2003) 143–150
3. Klusch, M., Lodi, S. and Moro, G.: Agent-Based Distributed Data Mining: The KDEC Scheme, in: M. Klusch, S. Bergamaschi, P. Edwards, P. Petta (Eds.), *Intelligent Information Agents: The AgentLink Perspective, LNCS 2586*, Springer (2003) 104–122
4. Zhang, Z. and Zhang, C.: Constructing Hybrid Intelligent Systems for Data Mining from Agent Perspectives, in: N. Zhong and J. Liu (Eds.), *Intelligent Technologies for Information Analysis*, Springer (2004) 327–353
5. Zhang, Z., Zhang, C. and Zhang, S.: An Agent-Based Hybrid Framework for Database Mining, *Applied Artificial Intelligence* 17 No. 5–6 (2003) 383–398
6. Ong, K., Zhang, Z. et al.: Agents and Stream Data Mining: A New Perspective, *IEEE Intelligent Systems*, IEEE Press (2005) (forthcoming)
7. Zhang, Z. and Zhang, C.: Agent-Based Portfolio Selection with Data Mining Ability, *Proceedings of 8th International Conference on Neural Information Processing*, Shanghai, China (2001) 553–558
8. Jennings, N. R., Sycara, K. and Wooldridge, M.: A Roadmap of Agent Research and Development, *Autonomous Agents and Multi-Agent Systems* 1 (1998) 7–38
9. Luck, M., Mcburney, P. and Preist, C.: A Manifesto for Agent Technology: Towards Next Generation Computing, *Autonomous Agents and Multi-Agent Systems* 9 (2004) 203–252
10. Frawley, W., Piatetsky-Shapiro, G. and Matheus, C.: Knowledge Discovery in Databases: An Overview, *AI Magazine*, Fall (1992) 213–228
11. Chen, M.-S., Han, J. and Yu, P. S.: Data mining: an overview from a database perspective, *IEEE Trans. On Knowledge And Data Engineering* 8 (1996) 866–883

12. Dunham, M. H.: *Data Mining-Introductory and Advanced Topics*, Prentice Hall, NJ (2003)
13. Fayyad, U., Piatetsky-Shapiro, G. and Smyth, P.: From Data Mining to Knowledge Discovery: An Overview, in: U. Fayyad, G. Piatetsky-Shapiro, P. Smyth, and R. Uthurusamy (Eds.), *Advances in Knowledge Discovery and Data Mining*, MIT Press, Cambridge, MA (1996) 1–34
14. Dzeroski, S.: Data Mining in a Nutshell, in: S. Dzeroski and N. Lavrac (Eds.), *Relational Data Mining*, Springer (2001) 3–27
15. Witten, I. and Frank, E.: *Data Mining: Practical machine learning Tools and Techniques with Java Implementations*, Morgan Kaufmann publishers (2000)
16. Kargupta, H., Stafford, B. and Hamzaoglu, I.: Web Based Parallel/Distributed Medical Data Mining Using Software Agents, *Proceedings of 1997 Fall Symposium*, American Informatics Association (1997) *http://www.eecs.wsu.edu/~hillol/pubs.html*
17. Kargupta, H., Hamzaoglu, I. and Stafford, B.: Scalable, Distributed Data Mining Using an Agent Based Architecture, *Proceedings of Knowledge Discovery and Data Mining*, AAAI Press (1997) 211–214
18. Prodromidis, A., Chan, P. and Stolfo, S.: Meta-learning in Distributed Data Mining Systems: Issues and Approaches, in: H. Kargupta and P.Chan (Eds.), *Advances in Distributed and Parallel Knowledge Discovery*, AAAI/MIT Press (1999)
19. Bailey, S., Grossman, R., Sivakumar, H. and Turinsky, A.: Papyrus: A System for Data Mining over Local and Wide Area Clusters and Super-Clusters, *Proc. International Conference on Supercomputing*, ACM Press (1999) 63
20. Zhang, Z. and Zhang, C.: *Agent-Based Hybrid Intelligent Systems: An Agent-Based Framework for Complex Problem Solving*, LNAI 2938, Springer (2004)
21. Cao, L.: *Agent Service-Oriented Analysis and Design*, PhD Thesis, University of Technology, Sydney, Australia (2005)
22. Cao, L., Ni, J., Wang, J. and Zhang, C.: Agent-Services-Driven Plug-and-Play in F-TRADE, *Proceedings of 17th Australian Joint Conference on Artificial Intelligence, LNAI 3339*, Springer (2004) 917–922
23. Cao, L., Luo, D., Luo, C. and Liu, L.: Ontology Transformation in Multiple Domains, *Proceedings of 17th Australian Joint Conference on Artificial Intelligence, LNAI 3339*, Springer (2004) 985–990

Soft-Device Inheritance in the Knowledge Grid

Hai Zhuge

China Knowledge Grid Research Group, Institute of Computing Technology,
Chinese Academy of Sciences, Beijing, China
zhuge@ict.ac.cn

Abstract. Soft-devices are configurable and adaptive software virtual mechanism, representing distributed network software and devices. Soft-devices and human users constitute a cyber-world in the Knowledge Grid environment—an intelligent interconnection environment that enables people and machines to work in cooperation. The cyber world determines its social evolution mode according to the development of nature, science, technology and human society. New soft-devices are generated by fusing or inheriting from existing ones. Soft-devices evolve according to the optimization and effectiveness principles. Interactions of different types in this cyber world form the self-organization structure. This keynote presents the framework of the soft-device world, the method for soft-device inheritance in the environment, and demonstrates the application in culture heritage exhibition.

1 Introduction

The future interconnection environment will be a cyber world where human society and the machinery interconnection world will interact each other, co-exist, and co-evolve [18].

The Knowledge Grid is a future intelligent interconnection environment. It enables people and machines to effectively capture, publish, share and manage knowledge resources. It also provides appropriate on-demand services for scientific research, technological innovation, cooperative teamwork, problem-solving, and decision making [17].

The Knowledge Grid involves in the following three basic scientific issues:

- *Interconnection semantics*—the study of the semantics in the interconnection environment for supporting intelligent applications by meaningfully interconnecting resources in semantic spaces where machines and human can understand each other.
- *Normalized Resource Organization*—the study of organizing resources in semantic normal forms to eliminate redundant, disorder and useless resources so as to ensure the correctness and accuracy of resource operations, and to realize complete and effective resource sharing.
- *Intelligent clustering and fusing*—the study of self-organization and optimization of complex systems.

V. Gorodetsky, J. Liu, and V.A. Skormin (Eds.): AIS-ADM 2005, LNAI 3505, pp. 62 – 78, 2005.
© Springer-Verlag Berlin Heidelberg 2005

This paper intends to answer the following fundamental questions:

What are the individual and community, and their structure in the Knowledge Grid environment? And, how the individuals are generated? How they evolve? And how they are organized to perform tasks?

To simplify complex systems is a task of science. Object-oriented methodology and programming languages use the notions of object and class to simplify the conceptualization of complex objective existence [3, 4]. The only way to generate a new object is by inheritance. But the object is too passive to represent active and adaptive organisms in real world.

Along with the simplicity, the Knowledge Grid environment also needs the diversity and effectiveness. On one hand, we need to ensure the simplicity by uniformly structuring the versatile resources. But on the other hand, we also need to guarantee the diversity of individuals by enabling adaptation and inheritance. To uniformly specify versatile passive and active resources in the Knowledge Grid environment, the framework of soft-device mechanism is proposed [16]. Soft-devices interact with each other and with human to form an evolving cyber world. Establishing competition mechanism in the world helps improve the effectiveness of the cyber world.

Inheritance is a natural phenomenon in the biological world. The heredity information keeps the evolution of species, and the mutation of the hereditary information makes the diversity of species.

Human society assigns inheritance social characteristics. For example, law and morals set the condition for marriage and inheritance. An individual is assigned the right to own the heritage of his/her parents. These social characteristics of inheritance differentiate human society from the animal world.

The rapid development of Internet applications challenges traditional software structure and development methodology. Previous inheritance mechanism is only suitable for stable and local environment [9]. How to realize inheritance mechanism in dynamic and distributed Knowledge Grid environment challenges software engineering in the global networking age.

2 Related Work on Inheritance

Inheritance in biology is about the principles that govern the inheritance of genes on sex chromosomes. Males and females differ in their sex chromosomes. Inheritance patterns for X-chromosome linked genes vary between sexes. Evolutionary computing borrowed this idea in finding solutions to problems of optimization. As a special relationship, inheritance was investigated in artificial intelligence and relevant areas [7, 10, 11, 12].

In object-oriented programming, inheritance mechanism is mainly for software reuse. Inheritance relationship forms class hierarchy, in which a subclass can inherit the states (variable declarations) and methods from the super-class. Subclasses can add variables and methods to the classes they inherit from the super-class. Subclasses can also override the inherited methods and provide specialized implementations for those methods. Inheritance enables programmers to reuse the code in the super-class and implement subclasses by specializing the super-class. Such inheritance mechanism could raise the efficiency in software development.

From the viewpoint of interface management, inheritance was regarded as a combination operation $R=P\oplus\Delta R$ on record structures P and ΔR with possibly overlapping identifiers [13]. The combination operation $\oplus$ relates the interface of descendant R to the interface of parent P. Computer memory only has two relationships: references or contiguity. Therefore, two elementary strategies for implementing inheritance can be distinguished: *delegation* and *concatenation*. Delegation is a form of inheritance that implements interface combination by sharing the interface of the parent, i.e., using references. Concatenation achieves the same effect by copying the interface of the parent into the interface of the descendant. So, the descendant's interface will be contiguous. Due to different implementation, the way of message sending is different. In delegation, those messages that are not accepted by the most specialized part of the object must be delegated to parents. In concatenation, the interface of every object is self-contained, and thus no forwarding is needed.

There are different views on inheritance in object-oriented programming. One is that inheritance can only take place between classes. Object-oriented systems are built on classes. A class holds the similarities among a group of objects, dictating the structure and behavior of its instances, whereas instances hold the local data representing the state of the object. To add a new kind of object to a class-based system, a class describing the properties of that object type must be defined first.

Another alternative for traditional class inheritance is prototype inheritance, or object inheritance [3]. A prototype represents the default behavior for some concepts. There are no classes in prototype-based systems. Therefore, there is no notion of instantiation either. New object types are formed directly by constructing concrete, full-fledged objects (prototypes or exemplars). The distinction between the two types of inheritance reflects the philosophical dispute concerning the representation of abstractions. Some object-oriented languages like Smalltalk use classes to represent similarity among collections of objects. Prototype-based approaches view the world by exploiting alikeness rather than classification.

A characteristic of inheritance is sharing. There are two fundamental forms of sharing: *life-time sharing* and *creation-time sharing* [5]. Life-time sharing refers to physical sharing between parents and children. Once the sharing relationship between parent and child has been established, the child remains sharing the properties of its parent until the relationship is removed. Any change to the parent is implicitly reflected to the child. The creation-time sharing implies that sharing occurs only while the receiving process is in progress. It is characterized by the independent evolution of the parent and the child. Delegation discussed above results in life-time sharing, whereas concatenation results in creation-time sharing.

3 Soft-Device World

A soft-device is a network software virtual mechanism that can be configured for different purpose, can actively provide with services by automatically seeking requirements, and can adapt to change [16]. The configurable feature develops early special-purpose computer as general-purpose computer that can run software of different types. The process of configuring a soft-device is similar to installing software in computer, which contains multi-step human-computer interactions.

The soft-device takes the advantages of the active and intelligent features of the intelligent agents, the semantic-based features of the semantic web, the advantages of the Knowledge Grid, and the configurable feature of general-purpose computers. Soft-devices hide versatile forms of resources like text, image, services etc, and could actively provide services according to the content of the resources specified inside and the configure information related to the resources.

A soft-device world consists of the self-organized soft-device society and the requirement space, and two roles: producer and consumer. The producer could add the resources to a soft-device and then configuring it. The consumers could enjoy the service provided by any soft-device in two ways: push and subscribe. Soft-devices could actively push services to the consumers, and can also accept subscription from consumers to provide long-term services. People could either play the role of producer to produce soft-devices by putting in the contents of relevant resources, or could play the role of consumer to enjoy the proper services by just posting their requirement or selecting and using an operable browser (soft-device) to get the required services. A soft-device could play the roles of both the producer and the consumer. A soft-device could accept content definition from multiple providers and provide services for multiple consumers with the consideration of a certain economic cost.

There are no central controls in the soft-device world, so the soft-device world is completely peer-to-peer [1]. Any hard device accessible across the Internet is regarded as a soft-device that provides the same service. The operation of a hard device is implemented by a corresponding soft-device.

A soft-device consists of the following components:

- *The detector* detects the requirements in the requirement space, processes the informal requirements and transforms them into formal, and then seeks solutions in resource spaces.
- *The interface* supports interaction between soft-devices and between components. It also supports the producer in defining resources' content and offers services to others by appropriate means. A browser is a kind of interface for conveying the output of the explainer to the consumer.
- *The explainer* explains requirements, information, knowledge and services.
- *The multiple built-in workflows* enable the soft-device to work according to requirements. The workflow should be time sensitive and adaptive. A control flow operates the soft-device by coordinating the execution of components.
- The reasoning mechanism inferences according to the knowledge specified in the knowledge space, a specialization of the resource space. The explainer interprets the reasoning result and submits it to the interface.
- *The coordinator* coordinates and adapts above components.

- *The Resource Space*. It specifies versatile resources represented in a machine-understandable way, which could be realized by markup languages and ontology mechanisms [18]. *The knowledge space* supports the operation of the explainer, the detector, and the coordinator. It also contains meta-knowledge for adapting the processes according to the changing situation. The meta-knowledge is specific to the type of soft-device.

The resource space in a soft-device (i.e., local resource space) has two parts: a private resource space and a sharable resource space where resources are accessible to other soft-devices. All the sharable resource space constitutes a peer-to-peer global resource space. The local sharable resources can be shared in the following two ways:

- Merge or join relevant local resource spaces to get the entire view where resources are uniformly classified.
- Establish semantic links between resources, and then locate the required resources by using peer-to-peer locating algorithms.

Fig. 1 shows the reference structure of soft-devices.

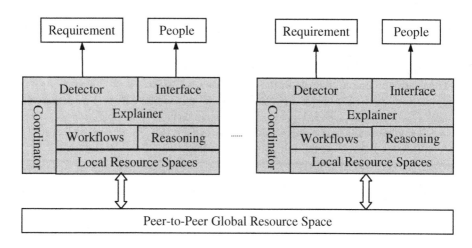

Fig. 1. The reference structure of soft-device

At the abstraction level, a soft-device can be defined as the encapsulation of processes (programs) on resource spaces, represented as *Soft-Device=<Resource-Space, Processes, Constraints>* and as *Soft-Device=<Resource-Space, Operations, Detector, Interface, Explainer, Workflows, Reasoning, Coordinator, Constraints>* in detail. The operations manage resources in the resource space under integrity constraints. The processes realize the functions of the soft-device by operating the detector, explainer, interface, coordinator, workflows, and reasoning mechanism. The resource spaces specify and organize information, knowledge and other resources in a normalized form [18]. Database and knowledge base are the instance of the resource space. The processes defined in the soft-device should satisfy the constraints to ensure the process integrity [18]: a process output its result either to another process or to the resource space, and ensure that the input of a process is either from another resource or the resource space.

The soft-device world is a society that contains a market mechanism for pricing, exchanging, evaluating and rewarding the services that the soft-devices provided. Soft-devices organize themselves according to their relationships and interactions during service process. The society evolves with the addition of new soft-devices and the removal of the soft-devices that have never served for others. Soft-devices compete each other in the market to contribute service and to obtain reward (increase its rank) through the service evaluation and reward mechanism. Our experiment shows that the distribution of the ranks of soft-devices in the society is close to the power-law [2, 18], but the highest ranks will be blocked and average out under the limitation of social regulations.

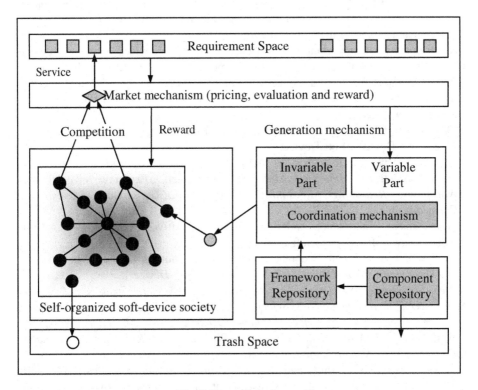

Fig. 2. The soft-device world

The soft-device world has a generation mechanism. New soft-devices are generated by getting a framework from the soft-device framework repository and then adding the variable part according to the request from the market mechanism.

4 Soft-Device Fusion and Inheritance

Two soft-devices can be loosely and tightly fused into a new one for a definite purpose by operations $\oplus$ and $\otimes$ as follows:

Soft-Device$\oplus$Soft-Device'=<Resource-Space$\otimes$Resource-Space', Operation $\cup$Operation', Processes$\cup$Processes', Constraints$\vee$Constraints'>, where $\otimes$ is the join or merge operations of two resource spaces [18]; $\cup$ is the union of two operation sets; $\cup$ also represents the merge of two processes such that *processes(ξ)=processes$\cup$processes'(ξ)* for any input ξ in the input field of the *process*; and, *Constraints$\vee$Constraints'* is the logic "or" of two constraints.

Similarly, *Soft-Device$\otimes$Soft-Device'=<Resource-Space$\otimes$Resource-Space', Operation $\cap$Operation', Processes$\cap$Processes', Constraints$\wedge$Constraints'>*.

A soft-device can be minimized under certain conditions, represented as *Soft-Device/Condition=<Resource-Space/Condition, Operation/Condition, Processes/ Condition, Constraints$\wedge$Condition>*, where *Resource-Space/Condition, Operation/ Condition* and *Processes/Condition* are the minimization of the *Resource-Space, Operation* and *Processes* under the *Condition*.

Inheritance is an important way to generate new soft-devices in the soft-device world. Different from previous inheritance mechanisms, soft-device inheritance is dynamic in nature due to continuous evolution of soft-devices. The children inherited from the same soft-device at different time could be different and they will keep evolving after generated.

A new soft-device is generated by inheriting from an existing soft-device denoted as: New.Soft-Device$\rightarrow$Soft-Device.

New.Soft-Device= <Resource-Space$\otimes\Delta$Resource-Space, Operation$\cup\Delta$Operation, Detector$\cup\Delta$Detector, Interface$\cup\Delta$Interface, Explainer$\cup\Delta$Explainer, Workflows$\cup$ ΔWorkflows, Reasoning$\cup\Delta$Reasoning, Coordinator$\cup\Delta$Coordinator, Constraints $\wedge$Constraints'>.

The above inheritance relationship is transitive, i.e., New.New.Soft-Device$\rightarrow$New.Soft-Device$\rightarrow$Soft-Device$\Rightarrow$ New.New.Soft-Device$\rightarrow$Soft-Device.

A new soft-device can also inherit from two or more soft-devices denoted as: *New.(Soft-Device'$\otimes$Soft-Device'')* $\rightarrow$ *Soft-Device'$\otimes$Soft-Device''*.

New.(Soft-Device'$\otimes$Soft-Device'')= <Resource-Space'$\otimes$Resource-Space''$\otimes$ ΔResource-Space, Operation'$\cup$Operation''$\cup\Delta$Operation, Detector'$\cup$Detector'' $\cup$ ΔDetector, Interface'$\cup$Interface'' $\cup$ ΔInterface, Explainer'$\cup$ Explainer'' $\cup$ ΔExplainer, Workflows' $\cup$Workflows'' $\cup$ ΔWorkflows, Reasoning'$\cup$ Reasoning''$\cup$ ΔReasoning, Coordinator' $\cup$Coordinator'' $\cup$ ΔCoordinator, Constraints'$\wedge$Constraints'' $\wedge$ ΔConstraints>.

A soft-device evolves with three dimensions: *time, inheritance,* and *variety*. A soft-device can have a hierarchy of varies descendants, and changes itself with time due to the change of requirement and its status. The change of a soft-device automatically induces the upgrading of its children. The changed soft-device could also have new children. Fig 3 depicts the evolution of a soft-device in the three dimensional space.

Soft-device inheritance can take different forms:

1. *Time-sensitive inheritance. New.Soft-Device(t+Δt)= <Resource-Space(t) $\otimes\Delta$Resource-Space(t+Δt), Detector(t)$\cup$ ΔDetector(t+Δt), Interface(t)$\cup$*

Δ*Interface*(t+Δt), *Explainer*(t)$\cup$ Δ*Explainer*(t+Δt), *Workflows*(t)$\cup$ Δ*Workflows* (t+Δt), *Reasoning*(t)$\cup$ Δ*Reasoning*(t+Δt), *Coordinator*(t)$\cup$ Δ*Coordinator*(t+Δt), *Constraints*(t)$\wedge$*Constraint*(t+Δt)>.

2. *Partial inheritance*. The ancestor can only allow its descendent to inherit a part of it, or the descendent only need to select a part of its ancestor to inherit, by using the minimization operation with given conditions. Inheritance rules can be derived to support advanced features based on the definition of the partial inheritance [14]. The constraint here is the selected part and the newly added part should satisfy the integrity constraints within a soft-device.

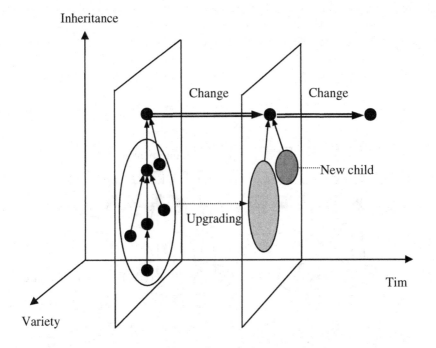

Fig. 3. Evolution of soft-devices

A soft-device society evolves with its social and market rules, which can be made with the reference to human society, as they need to harmoniously co-exist and evolve [18]. In the market mechanism, soft-device inheritance has the following social features:

– An evolving soft-device always tends to raise its rank (or reputation) in the society.
– The higher rank soft-devices tend to own higher rank descendents.
– A soft-device always intents to maximize its profit from the market if the soft-device society selects the free competition mechanism to organize themselves.

5 Self-organization and Self-adaptation of Soft-Devices

Self-organization has been investigated in Web structure, Web Services, and agent coalition formation [2, 8]. Soft-devices are self-organized through the dynamically evolved service spaces and the requirement space as well as the inheritance, knowledge and information flows as shown in Fig.4. The arrows in the soft-device space represent information and knowledge flows [15], the dashed arrows represent the operations for posting requirements, and the bi-arrows represent the matching between requirements and services. Applications initialize and add requirements in the requirement space. The person who posts a requirement needs to pay in the market and determines the initial price of the requirement. The fulfilled requirements will be removed from the requirement space. The requirement space evolves with the addition of new resources and removal of old requirements.

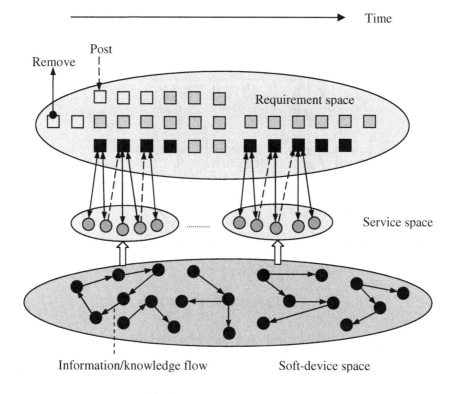

Fig. 4. Self-organization of soft-devices

Soft-devices will actively compete for providing services for the detected requirements and then get the reward. To ensure the justification in competition, a market mechanism selects soft-devices and logically organizes them together to fulfill the requirement. A selected soft-device can also post requirements in the requirement space to acquire services from other soft-devices.

Information and knowledge flow through soft-devices to enhance behaviors [15]. Competition in a large-scale soft-device world leads to unequal rank distribution among soft-devices [2]. Knowing the distribution law helps make routing strategy to enhance the efficiency of information and knowledge flows. The driving force of information and knowledge flows is the common interest in the involved soft-devices. The impact of the soft-devices in information and knowledge flow networks provide a reference evidence for them to make decisions to participate the market competition.

A soft-device will make decisions to survive during its life cycle under the regulations in the soft-device world. Decisions should benefit itself and the community it involved. To maximize the benefit, a soft-device should adapt its functions to meet the change of the society. It needs to consider the following factors when making decisions:

- *Adaptation cost*. Adaptation takes time for providing service to get profit. To own some necessary functions, the soft-device needs the cost for posting requirement and rewarding the services provided by others.
- *Market share and trend*. According to the market information and the competition, the soft-device will make the market share and trend analysis to determine the time for adaptation.
- *Profit*. The soft-device makes profit estimation according to the possible market shares and the adaptation cost.

The outcome of the decision is the adaptation target—the specification of new function. The coordinator mechanism will re-organize its functions according to the adaptation target.

6   Implementation

Since soft-device inheritance would carry out in a dynamic and distributed environment, using the delegation approach can facilitate the implementation because

- the parent and child can be loosely coupled (some object-oriented languages adopt the concatenation inheritance, but it is bounded so tight that any change on parent and child is not allowed), and,
- dynamic change of the parent can be facilitated.

A real example of the delegation approach is the proxy, which is a server that works between a client application and a real server. It intercepts all requests to the real server to see if it can fulfill the requests before it forwards the request to the real server. Proxy servers can filter requests and improve performance for groups of users because it saves the results of all the requests for a certain amount of time. The proxy server is often on the same network as with the user, so it can offer a much faster operation. Real proxy servers support hundreds or thousands of users. Some major online services such as America Online uses an array of proxy servers.

Since the services of a soft-device are offered through the interface, we can realize the proxy for soft-device interface. The interface services can be realized by using the

Remote Method Invocation (RMI), which allows the definition and the implementation to remain separately and to run on separate Java virtual machine. It processes as follows:

- The RMI server contains the implementation and interface of the remote soft-device.
- The RMI registers the remote soft-device.
- The RMI client finds the appropriate remote soft-device.
- The interface of the remote soft-device dynamically loads into local machine as a proxy.
- The RMI client uses the remote soft-device like local soft-device through the proxy.

The soft-device inheritance carries out as follows:

- The owner posts the static description of his/her soft-device in the requirement space.
- The child searches in the requirement space, and finds the required soft-device.
- According to the static description of the parent, add incremental part, and then form the static description of the child.
- The static description of the child is parsed to form a dynamic instance. The parent and child establish the message pipe in the meanwhile.

The changing of parent can be realized by changing the proxy with the consideration of two situations: the updated parent soft-device informs children, and the child changes its parent actively. In either situation, the child just needs to repeat the former two steps for updating itself. All operations can be done dynamically without recompiling and redeploying. But the children need to check the compatibility because some former services would still be used by its child even if they do not exist at present.

7 Application in Culture Heritage Exhibition

7.1 Using Soft-Devices to Animate Artifacts

The proposed approach is applying to animate Dunhuang cave culture—the precious world culture heritage. The artifact soft-device is a framework that can be configured to host programs for animating artifacts. A new artifact soft-device can be defined by inheriting from existing one. Fig.5 shows the effect of animating a wall-painting in Dunhuang cave (the up-left-hand image is the original). Fig. 6 shows another example of animating another Dunhuang wall-painting. The angels in the painting are animated by soft-devices, which can fly with different postures to form different meaningful patterns and interact with users upon pointed and clicked. The advantages of using soft-device technology include the following three aspects:

- The roles (e.g., angels) in the painting can actively and intelligently find clues among different roles in the same cave and in different caves made in different dynasty by querying each other and the sharable resource spaces. The advanced features of the resource space model support the effectiveness of information and knowledge shared among soft-devices.

- The roles can be generated by inheriting from one predefined artifact soft-device. Such dynamic inheritance relationship structures the soft-device society, establishes the basis for culture evolution, and can raise the efficiency of animation.
- The artifact soft-devices provide applications and designers with components to create the animation. For example, the implementation of the posture of the same types of roles can adopt similar operations.

In the soft-device society, we have used the market selection mechanism (i.e., the utility) to measure the fitness in the competition environment. The problem is how to interpret the fitness in culture selection during the evolution of culture. Considering the features of the artifacts in the distributed caves, we use the amount of occurrence of culture features with the development of dynasties as the selection criteria based on the following two basic assumptions of evolutionary game theory (http://plato.stanford.edu/entries/game-evolutionary/):

- *Individuals always want more rather than less*, and
- *Interpersonal comparisons are meaningful.*

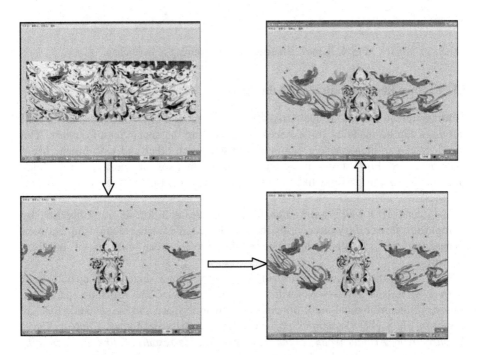

Fig. 5. Demo 1: animation of wall-paintings of Dunhuang

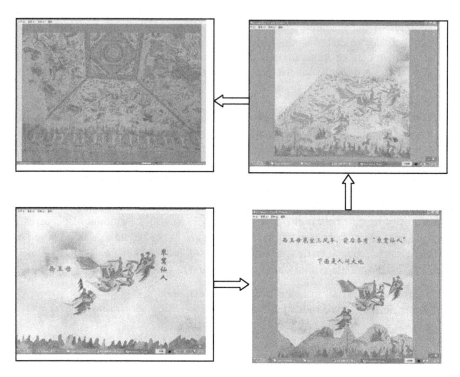

Fig. 6. Demo2: animation of wall-painting of Dunhuang

7.2 Culture Representation and Inheritance

Paintings tell stories and reflect artists' idea, feeling, and emotion. The roles in wall paintings can be made as soft-devices encapsulating the semantics of authors. The soft-devices can then actively communicate with each other and with human users when activated. Fig.7 shows an example of the artifact soft-devices, where the roles in the painting can perform like actors and explain themselves upon being clicked by users.

The scene of a wall painting can be also made as a soft-device composed by multiple soft-devices. By discovering the soft-device inheritance relationship between scenes, we can find the inheritance relationship between cultures of different dynasties.

A scene soft-device can be described by a semantic space and a set of operations as follows: *Scene-soft-device=<Semantic-Space, Operations>*. The semantic space here consists of the orthogonal multi-dimensional semantic space and the semantic links as shown in Fig.8 [17]: *Semantic-Space=<{<Author, Dynasty, Actors, Content, Cave, Resource-type, Artifact-type>, <Link-to-scenes, Link-to-resources, link-to-story, link-to-reality, link-to-knowledge, Semantic-relationship>}*, where the resource type refers to the text, image and sound. The artifact type refers to the building, color statue, and wall painting. The operations include {*<Move*(from *<x, y>* to *<x', y'>*)*>*,

Explanation(resource), *rotate-at*(<x, y>), *zoom-in*(<x, y>), *zoom-out*(<x, y>),
focus(<x, y, Radius>)}>.

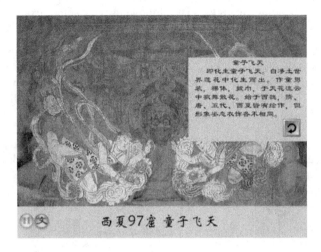

Fig. 7. Demo 3: Artifact soft-devices

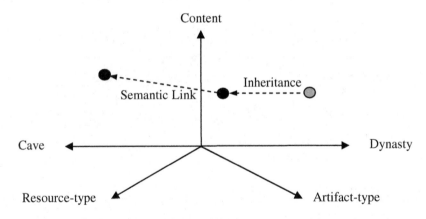

Fig. 8. Semantic Resource Space for Dunhuang Cave

Culture is represented by features like color, layout and architecture. Culture inheritance focuses on these features.

Cultural Inheritance. For two sets of features that describe scenes *A* and *A'*: *A*=<{*Color, Style, Layout, Architecture*}, *Time*> and *A'*=<{*Color', Style', Layout', Architecture'*}, *Time'*>. If the *Color, Style, Layout,* and *Architecture* is similar to *Color', Style', Layout',* and *Architecture'* respectively, and *A'* is created after *A* (i.e.,

Time'>Time), then we can say that *A'* is cultural inheritance from *A*. Fig. 9 shows an example of cultural inheritance.

The key to determine the culture inheritance relationship is to find similarities between corresponding features. The following are some examples that help determination:

–   Color *X* appears in *A* for describing *Y* also appears in *B* for describing *Y*.
–   Shape *X* is similar to *Y* if they are geometrically similar to each other.
–   Structure *X* is similar to *Y* if there exists an isomorphism between them.
–   Layout *X* is similar to *Y* if there exists an isomorphism between them.

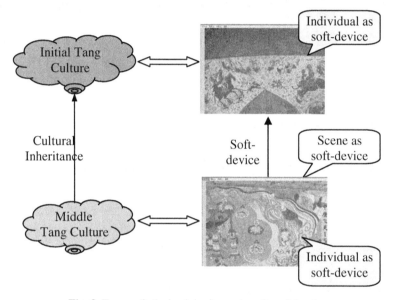

Fig. 9. From soft-device inheritance to culture inheritance

8   Conclusion

Soft-devices are configurable and adaptive, and can organize themselves to effectively perform tasks. Different from passive objects and active agents, soft-devices represent both passive and active resources in network environments. They can be as hard as hardware, as soft as software, and can even be a knowledge model that can actively detect problems and can fuse with and inherit from other knowledge to solve problems. The soft-device world obeys social and economical principles to ensure its simplicity, diversity and effectiveness. Soft-device inheritance is dynamic in nature. It enables the generation of new soft-devices in an evolving environment.

Research on soft-device will challenge current software structure and methodology. Incorporating domain features, soft-devices can be used to model any content-rich object. The cultural inheritance relationship can be automatically discovered by finding the inheritance relationship between artifact soft-devices. This keynote also demonstrates the real application of the proposed soft-device approach in the animation of Dunhuang cave culture.

Acknowledgement

This work is supported by National Basic Research and Development Program (973, No. 2003CB317001) and National Science Foundation (Grant No. 60273020 and 70271007) of China. The author also thanks all the team members of China Knowledge Grid Research Group (http://kg.ict.ac.cn) for their help and cooperation, especially the members of the Knowledge Grid Center and the Dunhuang Knowledge Grid Laboratory (http://www.knowledgegrid.net).

References

1. Balakrishnan, H. et al.: Looking Up Data in P2P Systems. Communications of the ACM, 46 (2) (2003) 43–48
2. Barabási, A.L., Albert, R.: Emergence of Scaling in Random Networks. Science, 286, (1999) 509–512
3. Blaschek, G.: Object-Oriented Programming with Prototypes. Springer-Verlag (1994)
4. Booch, G.: Object Oriented Design with Applications. Redwood City, Calif.: Benjamin/Cummings Pub. Co. (1991)
5. Dony, C., Malenfant, J., Cointe, P.: Prototype-based Languages: From a New Taxonomy to Constructive Proposals and Their Validation. ACM SIGPLAN Not. 27, 10 (1992) 201–217
6. Foster, I.: Internet Computing and the Emerging Grid. Nature, 408, 6815 (2000) www.nature.com/nature/webmatters/grid/grid.html
7. Horty, J.F., Thomason, R.H., Touretzky, D.S.: A Skeptical Theory of Inheritance in Nonmonotonic Semantic Networks. Artificial Intelligence, 42 (1990) 311–348
8. Iamnitchi, A., Ripeanu, M., and Foster, I.: Small-world file-sharing communities. In Proceedings of the IEEE Infocom 2004, Hong Kong
9. Taivalsaari, A.: On the Notion of Inheritance. ACM Computing Surveys, 28, 3 (1996) 438–479
10. Tamma, V.A.M. and Bench-Capon, T.J.M.: Supporting Inheritance Mechanisms in Ontology Representation, EKAW 2000, LNAI, 1937 (2000) 140–155
11. Morgenstern, L.: Inheritance Comes of Age: Applying Non-monotonic Techniques to Problems in Industry. Artificial Intelligence. 103 (1998) 1–34
12. Nillson, N.: Principles of Artificial Intelligence. Tioga, Palo Alto (1980)
13. Wegner, P., Zdonik, S.B.: Inheritance as an Incremental Modification Mechanism or What Like Is and Isn't Like. ECOOP '88 (European Conference on Object-Oriented Programming)
14. Zhuge, H.: Inheritance Rules for Flexible Model Retrieval. Decision Support Systems, 22 (4) (1998) 379–390
15. Zhuge, H.: A Knowledge Flow Model for Peer-to-Peer Team Knowledge Sharing and Management. Expert Systems with Applications, 23, 1 (2002) 23–30

16. Zhuge, H. Clustering Soft-Devices in Semantic Grid. IEEE Computing in Science and Engineering, 4 (6) (2002) 60–62
17. Zhuge, H.: The Knowledge Grid. World Scientific Publishing Co. Singapore (2004)
18. Zhuge, H.: Toward the Eco-Grid: A Harmoniously Evolved Interconnection Environment. Communications of the ACM, 47, 9 (2004) 79–83

Towards the Adaptive Organization: Formation and Conservative Reconfiguration of Agents Coalitions

Krzysztof Ciesielski

Institute Of Computer Science, Polish Academy Of Sciences,
ul. 21 Ordona, 01-237 Warszawa, Poland
K.Ciesielski@ipipan.waw.pl

Abstract. This research paper gives an overview of several clustering methods and presents their application in formation and reconfiguration of coalitions of agents cooperating in dynamically evolving environment. Our experimental generator of coalitional structures takes into account both the stability of resulting coalitions and efficiency of computations. It focuses on providing average-case optimal solution and generates coherent stable groups with respect to agents beliefs, intentions, capabilities as well as the current environmental state. Clustering based approach leads to a robust adaptation of existing structure in response to changing environmental conditions, even in case of complex, high-dimensional models. Among numerous future research challenges listed in the last section, an adaptive approach based on evolutionary models is outlined.

Keywords: adaptation and self-organization, agents coalitions, reconfiguration, hierarchical clustering.

1 Introduction

A coalition formation process, in which a number of independent, autonomous agents come together to act as a collective, is an important form of interaction in multiagent systems. Cooperation in an effective coalitional structure can improve the performance of the individual agents and the system as a whole can reach goals which are beyond individual capabilities. There are numerous real-life applications in which efficient formation and re-formation of coalitional structures in dynamically changing environment is needed (to mention only e-business [Tsvetovat00] or grid computing [Foster01]). However, the main problem is the computational complexity of coalitional structure generation. The problem of partitioning a group of agents in order to maximize the social payoff has been shown to be NP-hard [Sandholm98] and even finding a suboptimal solution (that can establish a worst-case bound from the optimal) requires searching the exponential number of solutions [Sandholm99, Shehory98, Klusch02]. Our approach focuses rather on providing efficient solution for coalitional structure generation which is average-case optimal and generates coherent stable groups with respect

V. Gorodetsky, J. Liu, and V.A. Skormin (Eds.): AIS-ADM 2005, LNAI 3505, pp. 79–92, 2005.

to agents beliefs, intentions, capabilities and the current environmental state [Keplicz02, Keplicz03a, Keplicz03b]. Another important issue here is to provide methods for a fast and conservative reconfiguration of existing structure in case of collective task execution failure [Keplicz01]. Conservativeness means to change an existing structure as little as possible with respect to context-dependent similarity measure between teams and agents.

2   Our Approach to Coalitions Management

The main goal of this project is to apply clustering methods to discover relationships and patterns of agents beliefs, intentions and capabilities and to find coalitional structure which is close to optimal (at present state). This structure is computed by adapted BIRCH algorithm [Zhang97], supplemented by heuristics establishing optimal algorithm parameters values. From the algorithmic point of view, coalition formation is construction of CF-tree of agents characteristics (represented as vectors of attributes). Next, a global grouping of CF-tree leaves [Alsabati98] is performed and coalitions are assigned to active tasks in a way that minimizes distance measure between coalition capabilities (as a whole) and given task specification.

The latter problem (so called *optimal assignment problem*) is solved by randomized greedy algorithm, but it is planned to adapt different methods, especially required when we permit agents to participate in more then one coalition at the same time *(fuzzy coalitions* [Alsabati98]). Informational (*beliefs*) as well as motivational (*intentions*) factors are taken into account during coalition formation to assure cohesion of coalition behavior as a whole. During task assignment phase only capabilities of individual coalitions (which are product of capabilities of agents constituting given coalition) are considered.

BIRCH is an incremental algorithm, which means that it is possible to add or remove agents to existing coalitional structure and dynamically modify it, if needed. Having the coalitional structure built, we take advantage of some specific features of PAM and Clarans clustering algorithms [Ng94] to conservatively rebuild it in response to dynamically changing internal and external conditions.

2.1   Global Clustering

Global methods need access to the whole information about clustered objects during processing, which means they are not incremental and not directly applicable in multi-agent context. We would exploit some of their features, as discussed later, but global methods itself will not be suitable for grouping (and re-grouping) dynamic sets of agents.

2.1.1   K-MEANS

K-MEANS is a *direct* technique: the desired number of clusters K has to be given as an input parameter. Cluster is represented by geometrical center of gravity of object in a given subset (so called centroid) Another possibility (K-MEDOIDS algorithm) is to represent cluster by centrally placed object from a given subset. In the sequel we will treat terms *coalition* and *cluster* as synonyms and use it interchangeably.

Algorithm 1 K-MEANS

---

1. Select K random agents (objects) $\left\{\overrightarrow{X_j}\right\}_{j=1,2,...,K}$ from the MAS consisted of N agents and set them as initial *centroids*
2. Assign each agent in MAS to the cluster represented by the nearest of K centroids
3. Recompute new centroids as $X_j = \sum_{X \in C_j} \frac{X}{|C_j|}$
4. Calculate error measure of present partition $E = \sum_{j=1}^{K} \sum_{X \in C_j} |X - X_j|^2 = \sum_{i=1}^{N} MIN\left\{|X - X_j|^2 : j \in \{1,...,K\}\right\}$
5. Repeat steps 2-4 until the change of error value E is insignificant or the cluster structure is not changing

---

This method (Algorithm 1) is relatively tolerant of outliers (agents which should not be included in final coalitional structure; we will discuss this issue later), independent of *unfavorable* order of agents characteristics processing and invariant to translation and orthogonal transformations of data vectors. But the main disadvantage is complexity of a single iteration, which is in order of $O(N^2)$. As we can have many such iterations, it makes K-MEANS not directly applicable in clustering huge groups of agents.

However, we have applied some additional optimizations. In particular, making use of Fibonacci heaps enabled us to find the nearest cluster fast. Still, information calculated in previous iterations should be exploited (taking advantage of the fact the cluster membership in a single iteration changes insignificantly). The latter is included in PAM algorithm.

2.1.2   PAM

K-MEANS is ignoring the information calculated in single iteration step and repeating clustering process almost from the beginning. Next three algorithms are free of this drawback. Assuming that one has initial (random) partition of N agents into K coalitions (represented by cluster centroids), it is modified by moving single agents between clusters to improve coalitions quality (Algorithm 2).

If we treat search space as a graph where each node is a K-element subset of the agent set (possible configurations of coalition groups partitions) and edges connects configurations which differ exactly one element (i.e. one agent changes its allocation) then PAM is *hill-climbing search* algorithm in such graph.

Main drawbacks of PAM algorithm are:

1. complexity of search space: PAM works well for moderate size systems (about 100 agents divided into 5 groups)

Algorithm 2 PAM (*Partitioning Around Medoids*)

---

1. Select K random agents (objects) from MAS and assign each agent to one of such initial *medoids*
2. Calculate the cost function of this configuration $TC_{ih} = \sum_j C_{jih}$ for every pair of agents such that A_i is one of medoids and A_h is not
3. Find pair $\langle A_i, A_h \rangle$ which minimizes value of the cost function TC_{ih} . If this minimum is negative, replace medoid A_i with A_h and go to step 2
4. If no cost function lowering is possible stop and assign agents to one of the previously found medoids

---

2. very high graph branching factor: second step of algorithm have to dispose of $K * (N - K)$ pairs of objects. So the complexity of single iteration is $O(K * (N - K)^2)$
3. algorithm converges only to local minimum of cost function, which - in general case - can be arbitrary distant from optimal partition

2.1.3   CLARA

CLARA [Ng94] is a modification of PAM, which tries to overcome first of PAM drawbacks. It randomly selects subgroup of agents (sub-graph) and runs PAM on such sample. Repeating this procedure several times we expect to find minimum. Resulting configuration is the one which minimizes the cost over the original agent set (i.e. in original space of agents attribute vectors).

CLARA is a trade-off: it significantly reduces the complexity [to $O(n)$], but it is also unlikely that it will find real optimum in original search space. Another difficulty is a choice of proper sample size. Authors suggest values proportional to the number of expected clusters (e.g. $40 + 2 * K$).

2.1.4   CLARANS

Basic idea of CLARANS is to combine the best features of PAM (finding the true minimum at the expense of searching in the full space) and CLARA (being fast while searching only randomly sampled subspaces). Idea of CLARANS is to search only *dynamically* chosen subset of neighbors starting from a given configuration (a set of potential medoids). It has two input parameters:

1. *maxneighbor*: the number of randomly chosen neighbors in a single iteration. The bigger this value is the more similar CLARANS is to original PAM approach (empirically estimated optimum is $maxneighbor = max(250, 1.25\% * K(N - K))$)
2. *numlocal*: the number of algorithm iterations. The lower *maxneighbor* value is, the higher should be the number of algorithm iterations to increase the probability of finding the global minimum. For above-given *maxneighbor* value it is enough to set *numlocal* to 2.

In each step it considers *maxneighbor* random neighbors of *current* node and evaluate the reduction of cost function value that would be obtained by moving to configuration represented by these nodes. If moving to any of them would reduce the cost then the best node found becomes the current node. This process is repeated until no further coalitional structure improvement can be made. In such case it is restarted (*numlocal* times) from randomly chosen node.

Above-mentioned algorithm can be reinforced by introducing some kind of system's memory (in a manner similar to evolutionary strategies approach) and switching between heuristically chosen node from a memory in case of encountering poorly evaluated path. It can also be computed in parallel, making use of distributed environment.

2.1.5   Conclusions

Although all the above described algorithms stand significant progress comparing with original K-MEANS approach, they still have many disadvantages:

1. they are very sensible to initial partition (configuration) and order in which agents data is processed
2. they find only local minimum (Clarans not always), searching in exponential complexity solutions space
3. they are not incremental: appearance of a new agent (or disappearance of one) requires starting the whole clustering from the very beginning
4. they treat all agents equally, in particular they don't cope with outliers
5. they are global: every decision requires complete information (impractical in MAS context)

In problem of searching for optimal agents coalitional structure and reconfiguring this structure conservatively (with respect to the appropriate distance or similarity measure, guiding local changes), most troubling drawbacks are the last three. Hierarchical approach presented below and based on BIRCH algorithm is free of these drawbacks.

2.2   Hierarchical Clustering

In order to avoid previously mentioned flat (single-level) methods deficiencies, numerous hierarchical solutions have been proposed: agglomerative techniques (clustered objects are gradually joined), divisive techniques (gradually splitting bigger clusters into smaller ones) and a direct techniques (the number of clusters is given a priori). BIRCH is a hybrid approach, combining direct, agglomerative and divisive features.

2.2.1   Algorithm Properties

BIRCH [Zhang97] (Balanced Iterative Reducing & Clustering using Hierarchies) algorithm has the following features:

1. the ability to operate on huge agents characteristics data (numerous and high-dimensional attribute vectors)

2. the ability to operate on summary of agents data, not only on single object (and, in particular, taking care of outliers)

3. optimization of I/O operations cost $[O(n)]$: algorithm exploits data structures similar to widely-known B-trees

4. low sensibility to *unfavorable (skewed)* order of agents characteristics processing

5. incrementality - algorithm allows to include or exclude agent and then modify clusters configuration, if needed

6. possibility of distributed and parallel execution

In our project hierarchical approach has an additional advantage, since we plan to integrate it with hierarchical contract net, which explicitly represents hierarchy of task bidders and their subcontractor groups.

2.2.2   Clustering-Feature Trees

The conception of CF-tree is based on widely used B-trees, which is balanced search-tree minimizing the cost of I/O operations [search, insertion and deletion of an object (agent) requires $O(h(T)) = O(log_t(N))$ disk access operations and $O(T * h(T)) = O(T * log_t(N))$ processor time; T - node capacity, N - tree size (the number of agents)]. A single inner CF-node consists of B-tuple in the form of B $[CFentry(i), childnode(i)]$ entries. The whole CF-tree defines hierarchy of clusters, which, in turn, defines hierarchy of agents coalitions.

CF-entry is a triplet $\left\langle N, \overrightarrow{LS}, \overrightarrow{SS} \right\rangle$, where N is the number of object in cluster, LS - vector sum of these objects (represented as points in Euclidean space), SS - square sum of these points. It is straightforward conclusion, that all basic clustering measures can be effectively computed solely on the basis of CF-entries representing individual clusters. Moreover, it can be shown that if CF1 and CF2 are CF-entries representing two disjoint clusters, then CF1+CF2 represents merged cluster.

CF-tree is parameterized by two parameters: branching factor B (defining maximum size of CF-entry) and threshold value T, which defines maximum cluster diameter. If cluster diameter exceeds T, then it has to be splitted. It can be easily shown that if $T1 \le T2$ are threshold values of trees C1 and C2 respectively (having the same branching factor B) then $height(T1) \ge_* height(T2)$. The higher threshold value is, the smaller input data have to be clustered and the less computation is required. On the other hand, lower threshold value leads to higher clustering accuracy. We will briefly discuss this issue later.

2.2.3   BIRCH

BIRCH algorithm is executed in four stages:
    Detailed reference on BIRCH algorithm can be found in [Zhang97].

Algorithm 3 BIRCH

1. CF-tree build: insert objects (representing agents) one by one into the tree, descending on path from root to leaf. On each level choose entry most similar (with respect to a certain similarity or distance measure) to a given object, in manner similar to B-tree insertion algorithm [Zhang97]. One should note that further computations operate solely on summary of agents data instead of original dataset, so we can expect smaller impact of agents insertion order on clusters structure. It also facilitates identification of possible outliers during coalition formation.
2. Optional CF-tree condensation: shrink CF-tree (via CF-tree rebuild algorithm [Zhang97], which increases threshold value T and then successively, one by one, in dictionary order, copies all paths to a newly created tree) to a size, which is adequate for global clustering algorithm, applied in third stage (e.g. 5000 objects in case of Clarans)
3. Global clustering: apply global clustering algorithm to all leaf entries. Complexity is this step is in the order of $O(m^2)$, m - the number of CF-entries
4. Optional partition refinement: redistribute (re-cluster) original agents characteristics (vectors of attributes) using centroids of clusters found in previous step as seeds. The purpose of this step is to avoid anomalies, where the same object agents to CF-tree twice (during different phases of insertion procedure) can be included in different clusters. It also allows to get rid of remaining outliers: agents too distant from the nearest seed will not be included in final structure.

2.3   Coalitional Structure Management

Our application is designed to work as a part of multi-agent system (in particular real-time MAS), incorporating all above described methods of efficient coalitional structure reconfiguration into a mechanism coordinating agents cooperation. A suitable solution here is a contract net [Smith80, Ferber99, Weiss99].

2.3.1   Cooperation via Contract Nets

Contract net is a mechanism utilizing principles of real-world auctions and tenders market. Communication between the client (manager) and the suppliers (bidders) consists of interleaved phases of requests for bids, proposals submissions and evaluations of proposals. Cooperation between manager and agent (or a coalition) is based on bilateral agreement, which makes possible to take account of a large number of parameters, such as agents capabilities, its current workload, the type of task to be carried out, the description of operations, the type of data and resources to be supplied, expected task execution time and cost etc.

Initiating agents, working inside contract net module, exploit their beliefs about current state of environment as well as up-to-date models of agents beliefs, intentions (desires) and capabilities and collects alternative solutions of optimal coalitional structure. Next, optimal coalition is created and agents are collectively committed to solve presented tasks. Collective commitment [Keplicz03a, Keplicz03b] is the basis of motivational attitude of a group of agents and reflects the way in which a social plan will be executed.

Contact net module copes with multiple, concurrent reconfiguration demands and allows to run many parallel grouping processes with different parameters and on different subsets (or subspaces) of agents characteristics. It is naturally designed for a distributed architecture so there is no need to create any additional, separate control mechanism.

The request for bids has four stages:

1. the manager broadcasts a description of the task which has to be carried out to all agents considered as potential bidders (i.e. potentially capable and willing to carry out particular task)
2. on the basis of this descriptions the bidders (that *in fact* had intention to execute the task) draw up proposals and submit it to the manager
3. the manager collects and evaluates submitted proposals and commissions best bidder to execute the task
4. contracting party sends a message to the manager to indicate that it is still prepared to carry out the required task and that it is committing itself to do it. If not, the protocol backtracks to one of previous stages (*broadcast, retry, announcement revision, alternative decomposition* [Weiss99]).

Taking into consideration all above features, contract net (and a hierarchical one in particular) seem to be adequate control mechanism to complement it with our own approach to problem of creation and reconfiguration of optimal (with respect to agents cooperation) coalitions of agents. Since we consider generalization of the presented approach to tasks decomposition, allocation and reallocation issues, all the most important cooperation coordination tasks could be included in one MAS control module.

2.3.2   Coalitional Protocol

State of environment, agent models and the dynamics of environmental changes are all described by scripts defining so-called coalitional protocol. Complete protocol specification can be found in [Ciesielski03]. Here we describe only the most important RECONFIGURE command, triggering actual reconfiguration in present environmental state.

Present state is defined by the execution of a sequence of commands and their combined influence on the initial environment state. From the algorithmic point of view reconfiguration is a construction (or modification) of CF-tree of CF-entries representing subgroups of agents and performing a global grouping (or regrouping, in case of Clarans algorithm) of CF-tree leaves. Next, coalitions are assigned to active (pending) tasks in a way that minimizes distance measure (e.g. weighted average) between coalition capabilities (as a whole) and given task parameters. The latter problem (so called *optimal assignment problem*) is solved by randomized greedy algorithm, but it is planned to apply different approaches (maximum net flow and maximum bipartite graph match), especially required when we permit agents to participate in more then one coalition at the same time (so called overlapping or fuzzy coalitions).

Informational (*beliefs*) as well as motivational (*desires*) factors are taken into account only during coalition formation (with appropriate weights, defined by WEIGHTS command) to assure cohesion of coalition behavior as a whole. During task assignment phase only individual coalitions capabilities (which are product result of capabilities of agents constituting given coalition) are considered.

The whole procedure is executed in the following cycle:

1. coordination module (contract net) passes on coalitional script to the agents that are capable of recognizing of potential for cooperation [Keplicz01] and will initiate coalition formation procedure
2. initiators verify script syntactic and semantic correctness and prepare (or update, in case of reconfiguration) data structures required by clustering process (maps of tasks descriptions and agents models); these structures are prepared on the basis of initialization section of the script
3. clustering parameters are determined (by user or by execution of heuristic) on the basis of current reconfiguration requirements (e.g. resource and time limitations)
4. executional section of the script (modelling dynamic changes in environmental state) is parsed and corresponding grouping or regrouping processes are triggered
5. if the coalition formation procedure succeeded, initiator returns optimal coalitional structure to the coordination module (contract-net); at this stage all necessary collective commitments [Keplicz03a, Keplicz03b] should already be established.

2.3.3   Additional Remarks

It should be stressed that not every agent in a given situation is interested (with respect to his desires or intentions) or should be taken into consideration (with respect to his capabilities) to be a member of any coalition [Keplicz02]. These agents should be identified as outliers and excluded from final structure. Not taking care of outliers and forcing agents which are not capable or not willing to cooperate (under present environmental conditions) within any coalition can negatively impact stability of resulting coalitional structure. Identification and management of such cases is important and not trivial problem.

A constructed CF-tree is gradually compressed (by CF-tree rebuild algorithm), when available time or space resources turn out to be insufficient. A priori knowledge of proper threshold value can essentially reduce running time. Threshold value should be estimated carefully: too high values lead to inaccurate partitions, whereas too low increase required computation time and space. Estimation of optimal value of new threshold T_{t+1} requires heuristic approach. There is not enough room to describe possible solutions in details; briefly, we search for T_{t+1} which is proportional to the portion of agents data processed so far, to the average CF-leaf cluster radius series in the former iterations and to minimum distance between two closest entries in most dense CF-leaf (found by greedy tree search). By approximation of radius growth rate we can extrapolate value of r_{t+1} as well as T_{t+1} using weighted regression methods. Application of such heuristics can be iteratively repeated, in order to find optimal, with respect to available time or resources, value of T_{t+1}.

Also further I/O optimization heuristics are possible. Outlier can be temporarily saved in external memory; periodically heuristic is started to check if agent classified as potential outlier is still outlier (with respect to appearing cooperation opportunities). If it is not, we incorporate agent into existing CF-tree. After clustering we can check it again and eventually remove from final structure. Similarly, we can delay threshold value change and CF-tree condensation.

Formed coalitions are often sub-optimal; typically to determine the coalition that best approximates the optimal, multiple sub-optimal coalitions can be formed in parallel (running clustering processes with different set of parameters and heuristics, or on different subsets of agents). Having partition similarity and evaluation measures, one can choose the best structure from proposed alternatives. It is particularly important in multi-agent applications context, where reconfigurations are frequent and can appear simultaneously (which means that a single agent can be a manager and a "bidder" at the same time, for a different tasks). Moreover, requests for bids can be carried out recursively, leading to a hierarchical structure of sub-contractors (sub-coalitions) and a hierarchical structure of tasks.

3   Experimental Results

Experiments have been divided into two separate groups: qualitative and computational tests.

3.1   Qualitative Tests

The aim of qualitative tests was to determine whether system behaves rationally (i.e. consistently with theory-based intuitions). As a test data we created small groups of agents (10-20) and several tasks specification, such that capabilities of each agent in unambiguous (but different for individual agents) way corresponded to the specification of one of the task. The purpose was to assert whether at the beginning of coalitional protocol execution agents will form expected initial coalitional structure.

Subsequently, multiple variants of coalitional protocol were executed, varying in dynamic change of environmental conditions (i.e. tasks settings) and agents parameters (i.e. their motivational attitudes, as well as capabilities). As we assumed, reconfigurations of coalitional structure were executed in conservative manner and at the same time it tended to find solutions near optimal under present environmental conditions.

Important observation is ability to exploit specific feature of PAM and Clarans algorithms, i.e. transition of configuration graph edges connecting *similar* coalitional structures, to model situations in which neither environmental conditions nor agents parameters have not changed, but nevertheless collective task realization has failed. This means a conservative reconfiguration in face of objective failure of collective task execution [Keplicz01].

Test were also diversified with respect to mutual importance levels (priorities) of informational factors (agent beliefs), motivational factors (agent goals) and agent capabilities. The aim was to verify our hypothesis that increasing (during coalition formation step) role of agent beliefs and desires at the cost of decreasing importance of their capabilities can be treated as an analogy and model for different possible mutual commitment strategies (*blindly-committed*, *single-minded* and *open-minded* [Rao91]).

As expected, decreasing importance of the fact that agents capabilities unambiguously correspond to demands reported by environment (i.e. appearance, disappearance or modification of tasks to be executed) and, at the same time, increasing role of their individual beliefs and desires caused reduction of system behavior conservativeness and more dramatic reconfigurations of coalitional structure during coalitional script execution.

Detailed results of various qualitative experiments can be found in [Ciesielski03].

3.2   Performance Tests

Also performance tests, examining execution time of implemented algorithms, heuristics and optimizations under various input parameters, gave good results. Application of very effective clustering methods to heuristic search of suboptimal coalition structure is fast even in case of complex, high-dimensional models. Crucial to reconfiguration execution time was the model size value (S), which is a product of agents group quantity (*sizeN*) and attribute space dimension (*dimD*); the hybrid BIRCH + K-MEANS approach (using in its 3rd phase optimized K-MEANS algorithm) complexity is $O(S * log(S))$. For instance, for model size in order of 50000 (and initial CF-tree threshold value *tresT* equal to 0, which means the highest computation precision), average computation time is about 8 seconds [AMD Athlon 1.8GHz, 256Mb RAM]. Such results let us to think of future applications to real-time multi-agent systems reconfiguration.

Exploitation of other global clustering algorithms (PAM, Clara, Clarans) led to execution times over 50% longer than optimized K-MEANS. It is planned to implement additional, optimized data structures, analogous to those implemented in K-MEANS (Fibonacci heaps), so we can expect to decrease differences between the algorithm and even a change in favor of Clarans. It would be especially useful for the sake of its previously mentioned advantages in application to conservative reconfiguration.

4   Conclusions and Future Research

Our application is implemented as an open module, allowing future development. After few modifications, in particular formalizing protocol for produced results (at present, results are first of all oriented towards readability for application user) it will be possible to integrate it with a real multi-agent system. It will enable us to verify first experimental results and full evaluation of effectiveness and flexibility of our approach in various domains. It would also suggest further requirements with respect to coalitional protocol syntax extensions, such as dynamically changing commitment strategies or externalities [Ferber99] modelling.

We put emphasis on system flexibility, which enables (by algorithm parameterizations) to control time and precision of computation, depending on particular application, needs, available resources etc. Attention should be paid to ability of finding optimal (for a particular application) value of *tresT* parameter, defining maximal diameter of CF-cluster in CF-tree leaves and influencing size of the tree on one hand and computation accuracy on the other. It should also be noted that for a fixed hardware configuration, given model size (i.e. quantity of agents set and dimension of attribute space) and distance measure function threshold value is constant, so it has to be computed only once.

We haven't yet examined impact of various agents attributes encoding strategies on application performance. Necessity to map attributes into real-valued vector space is a deficiency of presented method, nevertheless any coalition building approach needs to utilize some variant of evaluation function, which enables comparison of *similarities* and *dissimilarities* among different groups of agents. Presented heuristic approach, based on hierarchical clustering, allows to do even quite *wasteful* encoding (i.e. high-dimensional attribute spaces, taking into account diverse aspects of internal [agent] and external [environment] features), while retaining operation effectiveness. However, research on encoding techniques, analogous to some evolutionary algorithms approaches [Goldberg95, Wierzchon01], is one of major future research directions.

Other important future challenges include:

1. realization of *continuity* postulate [Keplicz01] by taking advantage of specific features of PAM and Clarans algorithm (transition of configuration graph edges connecting *similar* coalitional structures)
2. research into possibility of generalization of the presented solution to issues of *conservative adaptation* of existing collective plans, coping with task decomposition, allocation and reallocation (Partial Global Planning) as well as means-end analysis [Weiss99, Jennings98]
3. integration with hierarchical contract nets (i.e. explicitly representing hierarchy of task bidders and subcontractor coalitions) and research into influence of various possible commitment strategies (*early commitment, late commitment, commitment by hiring* [Ferber99])
4. extension of model specification to dynamically changing agent commitment strategies (by means of heuristically adjusted weights) and simulation of external events influence on a work of group of cooperating agents [Ferber99]
5. further optimization of Clarans algorithm by exploiting data structures enabling effective computation and search of cost matrix (binomial heaps or AVL/red-black trees)
6. modification of algorithm finding optimal task allocation: at present it is realized by randomized greedy search, but alternatively it could be done by application of maximum flow algorithms (e.g. Fulkerson-Ford algorithm), adaptation of algorithms solving problem of maximum matching in bipartite graphs or application of simplex algorithm and linear programming methods

7. design of context-dependent outliers identification and management algorithms.

Currently we are working on the extension of clustering methods to similarity-based (versus measure-based) techniques such as self-organizing maps [Kohonen01], growing neural gas (GNG) [Fritzke98][1] and artificial immune-based networks [Wierzchon01].

All three models have numerous advantages:

1. possibility of visual introspection of coalitional structure reconfiguration dynamics
2. straightforward adaptation to fuzzy (overlapping) coalitions reconfiguration and to model agents ability to participate in more than one coalition simultaneously
3. implicit representation of a social memory, enabling detection of agents behavioral and cooperational patterns and adaptation of coalitional structure based both on present environmental state and past experience.

The latter feature is particularly promising as it can take a priori problem-domain knowledge into account (including it in fit measure definition) and could constitute basis of previously mentioned context-dependent outliers identification method. Application of attractor-distractor fuzzy clustering algorithms allows to include the task specification directly in the clustering process, without dividing computations into two phases: group formation and task allocation. Another important (and common in multi-agent context) issue, which could be handled in this model is information incompleteness and uncertainty during coalition formation.

References

[Alsabati98]   Alsabti, K., Ranka, S., Singh, V.: Efficient K-Means Clustering Algorithm. In: Proceedings of First Workshop on High-Performance Data Mining (1998)
[Ciesielski03] Ciesielski, K.: Data mining applications in multi-agent system reconfiguration. MSc. Thesis, Institute of Informatics, Warsaw University (2003)
[Ciesielski05] Ciesielski, K., Draminski, M., Klopotek, M.A., Kujawiak, M., Wierzchon, S.T.: On Some Clustering Algorithms for Document Maps Creation, to appear in: Proceedings of Intelligent Infomation Systems 2005 Conference (IIS:IIPWM 2005), Gdansk, Poland (2005)
[Goldberg95]   Goldberg, D.E.: Genetic Algorithms in Search, Optimisation and Machine Learning. Addison-Wesley, Reading, MA (1995)
[Keplicz01]   Dunin-Kęplicz, B., Verbrugge, R.: A reconfiguration algorithm for distributed problem solving. Engineering Simulation, 18 (2001)

---

[1] Which is expected to be very efficient - we have already obtained good results with GNG models with utility function; implementation is based solely on local computations [Ciesielski05].

[Keplicz02]   Dunin-Kęplicz, B., Verbrugge, R.: Collective intentions, Fundamenta
                 Informaticae, 51(3), IOS Press (2002)
[Keplicz03a]   Dunin-Kęplicz, B., Verbrugge, R.: Calibrating collective commitments.
                 In: Proceedings of the 3rd International Central and Eastern European
                 Conference on Multi-Agent Systems (CEEMAS 2003), LNAI 2691 (2003)
[Keplicz03b]   Dunin-Kęplicz, B., Verbrugge, R.: Evolution of collective commitments
                 during teamwork, Fundamenta Informaticae, 56(4), (2003)
[Ferber99]   Jacques Ferber: Multiagent Systems: An Introduction To Distributed
                 Artificial Intelligence, Addison-Wesley (1999)
[Foster01]   Foster, I., Kesselman, C., Tuecke, S.: The anatomy of the grid. The
                 International Journal of High Performance Computing Applications,
                 15(3) (2001)
[Fritzke98]   Fritzke, B.: A self-organizing network that can follow non-stationary
                 distributions. In: Proceeding of the International Conference on Artifi-
                 cial Neural Networks '97, Springer (1997)
[Jennings98]   Jennings, N.R., Sycara, K., Woolridge, M.: A Roadmap of Agent Re-
                 search and Development. Autonomous Agents and Multi-agent Systems,
                 1 (1998)
[Klusch02]   Klusch, M., Gerber, A.: Dynamic coalition formation among rational
                 agents. IEEE Intelligent Systems, 17(3) (2002)
[Kohonen01]   Kohonen, T.: Self-Organizing Maps. Springer Series in Information Sci-
                 ences. 30 Springer, Berlin, Heidelberg, New York (2001)
[Mares00]   Mares, M.: Fuzzy coalition structures. Fuzzy Sets and Systems, 114 (2000)
[Ng94]   Ng, R.T., Han, J.: Efficient and Effective Clustering Methods for Spatial
                 Data Mining. In: Proceedings of the 20th VLDB Conference (1994)
[Rao91]   Rao, A., Georgeff, M.: Modeling rational agents within a BDI architec-
                 ture. In: Proceedings of the 2nd Conference on Knowledge Representa-
                 tion and Reasoning (1991)
[Sandholm98]   Sandholm, T., Lesser, V.: Coalition formation among bounded rational
                 agents. Artificial Intelligence Journal, 101(1-2) (1998)
[Sandholm99]   Sandholm, T., Larson, K., Andersson, M., Shehory, O.: Coalition
                 structure generation with worst case guarantees. Artificial Intelligence,
                 111(12) (1999)
[Shehory98]   Shehory, O., Kraus, S.: Methods for task allocation via agent coalition
                 formationm Artificial Intelligence Journal, 101(12) (1998)
[Smith80]   Smith, R.G.: The contract net protocol: High-level communication and
                 control in a distributed problem solver. IEEE Transactions on Comput-
                 ers, C-29(12) (1980)
[Tsvetovat00]   Tsvetovat, M., Sycara K.: Customer coalitions in the electronic mar-
                 ketplace. In: Proceedings of the Fourth International Conference on
                 Autonomous Agents (2000)
[Weiss99]   Gerhard Weiss (Ed.), Multiagent Systems: A Modern Approach to Dis-
                 tributed Artificial Intelligence, MIT Press (1999)
[Wierzchon01]   Wierzchon, S.T.: Artificial immune systems. Theory and applications
                 (in Polish), IPI PAN Publishing House (2001)
[Zhang97]   Zhang, T., Ramakrishan, R., Livny, M.: BIRCH: Efficient Data Clus-
                 tering Method for Large Databases. In: Proceedings of ACM SIGMOD
                 International Conference on Data Management (1997)

A Cooperative Multi-agent Data Mining Model and Its Application to Medical Data on Diabetes

Jie Gao[1], Jörg Denzinger[1], and Robert C. James[2]

[1] Department of Computer Science, University of Calgary, AB, Canada
{gaoj, denzinge}@cpsc.ucalgary.ca
[2] Aechidna Health Informatics, Winnipeg, MB, Canada
rob@aetiologic.ca

Abstract. We present *CoLe*, a model for cooperative agents for mining knowledge from heterogeneous data. *CoLe* allows for the cooperation of different mining agents and the combination of the mined knowledge into knowledge structures that no individual mining agent can produce alone. *CoLe* organizes the work in rounds so that knowledge discovered by one mining agent can help others in the next round. We implemented a multi-agent system based on *CoLe* for mining diabetes data, including an agent using a genetic algorithm for mining event sequences, an agent with improvements to the *PART* algorithm for our problem and a combination agent with methods to produce hybrid rules containing conjunctive and sequence conditions. In our experiments, the *CoLe*-based system outperformed the individual mining algorithms, with better rules and more rules of a certain quality. From the medical perspective, our system confirmed hypertension has a tight relation to diabetes, and it also suggested connections new to medical doctors.

1 Introduction

In recent years, data mining has been a hot topic that attracts both database and machine learning researchers. With the rapid development of data storage capacity, data mining calls for methods to handle large quantities of data, which could be heterogeneous with various types of data. However, most of the existing data mining methods are only capable of processing homogeneous data. Even many large-scale distributed data mining methods do not consider much about the heterogeneity of data. Another problem in data mining is that methods are more and more specialized (as was indicated in [1]). They perform well on ideal data sets. But when applied to real-world data, they often cause unsatisfactory results. Quite often different parts of a same data set are heterogeneous in characteristics. And a particular method may need different tuning for those parts.

Therefore it is necessary to propose a data mining model that allows for multiple different methods (or differently tuned methods) to work on one data set to handle its heterogeneity. This model should be a multi-agent system model so that we can use multiple agents to employ the different methods and consider

V. Gorodetsky, J. Liu, and V.A. Skormin (Eds.): AIS-ADM 2005, LNAI 3505, pp. 93–107, 2005.

the interaction and cooperation of these mining agents to produce integrated results as the knowledge discovered from the whole heterogeneous data set.

In this paper, we present a cooperative multi-agent data mining model, in which the agents use different methods to handle different types or parts of information in heterogeneous data sets. The results are combined to get integrated results. Critically, this model implies that agents cooperate with each other, so that our multi-agent mining model is not merely applying multiple algorithms to a data set, but trying to gain synergetic effects through the cooperation.

The rest of this paper is organized as follows: Our cooperative multi-agent mining model is introduced in Sect. 2. A concept-proving implementation in mining medical data is described in Sect. 3 and experimental results are presented in Sect. 4. Section 5 compares our model with some related work in distributed data mining. Finally Sect. 6 concludes this paper and potential work is given.

2   *CoLe*: Our Model for Cooperative Data Mining

To describe *CoLe* — our generic model of cooperative data mining, we need some basic definitions. First of all, our model works on different types of data. We can take them altogether as a "super data set". This super data set is called a *heterogeneous data set* (denoted by $\mathcal{D}$). The individual single-type data sets are called *simplex data sets* (denoted by $\mathcal{D}_i$) in this heterogeneous data set. Two simplex data sets of a heterogeneous data set do not necessarily need to be different. They are mainly used for showing the miners' ownerships (for *miners*, see below) of the simplex data sets. It is quite possible that the same simplex data set is worked on by several different mining algorithms.

From the data set we expect to discover *knowledge*. Although *knowledge* is an abstract concept and in many cases the knowledge representations depend on the specific mining method, we can represent (or convert) the knowledge in the majority of cases into an "if...then..." rule form. So we take a piece of knowledge as a *rule*, in the format of condition $\Rightarrow$ conclusion.

In our model, we have several mining methods employed to discover different rules from a given heterogeneous data set. For each simplex data set in it, we can have one or more suitable mining methods to discover knowledge from it. Such a mining method implementation is called a *miner*. It resembles a function $m : \mathcal{D}_i^* \to \mathcal{K}_i^*$, where $\mathcal{K}_i$ is the set of possible rules (knowledge) to be discovered by the miner. The rules expected to be discovered from different miners should have some conclusions in common (i.e. describing the same concept), so that we can combine the rule sets learned by different miners. Otherwise, the rules never have any conclusion in common, which gives us no hope to combine the rules.

In our cooperative multi-agent mining system, there are two types of agents. One type are miners, which implement the mining methods. The other type of agents are agents that combine the different types of rules. We assume there is only one such agent in a system (multiple such agents can be taken as a super agent). We call this agent *combination agent* (Ag_{CBN}). It is at the core of the cooperation in our model.

Ag$_{\mathrm{CBN}}$ decides how the miners cooperate. Its main task is to receive the learned rule sets from individual miners, use some strategies to combine them, evaluate the combined rules against the whole heterogeneous data set and put the satisfactory ones into a final rule set, and at the same time extract helpful information from the rule sets and send it back to the miners so that each miner can utilize the discoveries from other miners.

The implementation of Ag$_{\mathrm{CBN}}$ can vary according to the different needs. It can be a simple agent that only validates the different combinations of the rule sets. It can also be a group of agents (forming a super Ag$_{\mathrm{CBN}}$) to achieve complex interaction and cooperation strategies with the miners.

Basically our cooperative mining model contains the following elements: A heterogeneous data set $\mathcal{D}$ (whose simplex data sets decide what miners to use), a set of miners $\mathcal{M}$, and the combination agent Ag$_{\mathrm{CBN}}$. And we name this model *CoLe* (*Cooperative Learning*):

$$CoLe =< \mathcal{D}, \mathcal{M}, \mathrm{Ag}_{\mathrm{CBN}} >$$

The agent interactions in *CoLe* are illustrated in Fig. 1: Given a heterogeneous data set $\mathcal{D}$, each miner m_i learns on the simplex data set ($\mathcal{D}_i$) it can handle. The mined set of rules ($\mathcal{R}_i$) are sent to Ag$_{\mathrm{CBN}}$, which combines the rules and considers their quality in the whole heterogeneous data set $\mathcal{D}$, and puts the combination results to the final rule set $\mathcal{R}$. At the same time, for each miner m_i, Ag$_{\mathrm{CBN}}$ extracts useful information from $\mathcal{R}_1, \cdots, \mathcal{R}_{i-1}, \mathcal{R}_{i+1}, \cdots, \mathcal{R}_n$ and sends this feedback to m_i to help its work. The feedback could be rule condition fragments to help form good rules, data set clusters to help concentrate on uncovered data cases, etc.. In this model, the miners are cooperating via the intermediate Ag$_{\mathrm{CBN}}$.

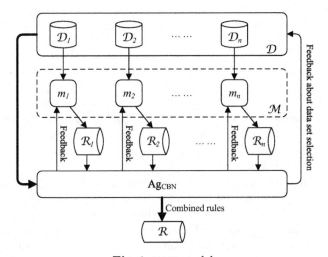

Fig. 1. C oLemodel

In the above description, we propose a mine-and-feedback way of cooperation. In this way, the miners are synchronized to send their partial results after an iteration ends. Ag$_{CBN}$ can then do its combination work and send feedbacks to help the miners' work in future iterations. The iterations continue until some end condition is met (e.g. an iteration number limit, or some rule quality threshold).

3   Application Problem and *CoLe* Solution

As a proof of concept for the *CoLe* model, a cooperative mining system was developed and implemented for mining diabetes patient data from the Calgary Health Region. This data set, originally used for public health insurance and billing purpose, contains very complete medical records. To identify the real disease cases from such data, the medical experts are not only interested in the diagnoses the individuals ever had, but, more over, they are also interested in the chronic development of the diseases. The *CoLe* mining model, with the ability to learn from different types of data, is very promising for their needs.

3.1   Problem Definition

In Sect. 2, the general *CoLe* model has already been discussed. When we fit the application problem — discover knowledge from medical history for identifying future diabetics — into the *CoLe* model, we have the instantiation as follows.

The *heterogeneous data set* in this problem is the public health data, which contains two different *simplex data sets*. One simplex data set $\mathcal{D}_s$ is the medical records of the individuals. These timestamped records can be interpreted as discrete temporal sequences. The other simplex data set $\mathcal{D}_c$ is the non-temporal version of these medical records (with only boolean fields for each possible diagnosis) and their annual statistics of the number of medical services, together with the personal information.

For $\mathcal{D}_s$, we have a *sequence miner* (Ag$_S$) to work on it. Ag$_S$ identifies key diagnosis sequences that are the indication of future diabetics. These key diagnoses are called *events*. We only care about the relative order of the events. Ag$_S$'s results are actually rules that use temporal sequences as conditions and the conclusion is always "diabetes". Such rules are called *sequence rules*.

For $\mathcal{D}_c$, the miner is called *conjunctive miner* (Ag$_C$) because its results are rules with conjunctions of predicates as conditions. The predicates are in the form "attribute *rel_op* value", where *rel_op* is a relation operator such as "=", ">", "<", and the order of these predicates in a rule is of no consequence. These rules are called *conjunctive rules*.

We use a single combination agent Ag$_{CBN}$ to combine the rules from Ag$_C$ and Ag$_S$ respectively. The combined rules may contain both sequence conditions and conjunctive conditions. Thus we call them *hybrid rules*.

In summary, in this problem of mining diabetes data, we have the data set $\mathcal{D} = \mathcal{D}_s \bowtie \mathcal{D}_c$, three types of rules: sequence rules, conjunctive rules and hybrid rules, the miner set $\mathcal{M} = \{Ag_S, Ag_C\}$, and the combination agent Ag$_{CBN}$.

3.2   System Design

As already stated, there are three major components, Ag$_S$, Ag$_C$ and Ag$_{CBN}$ in our system. Each miner receives its simplex data set, and learns rules from it. Both types of rules are sent to Ag$_{CBN}$, which combines them into hybrid rules and then validates them against the heterogeneous data set. The hybrid rules with higher quality than a pre-defined threshold are put into the hybrid rule set as the result of the combination. At the same time, Ag$_{CBN}$ also gives help to the two miners — generate the simplex data sets for the next iteration and send useful information extracted from Ag$_C$'s results to Ag$_S$ to help its future work. Such mining iterations will continue until our predefined iteration number limit has been reached.

Data Sets. The data set our system is going to work on is considerably large. To make the miners run efficiently, we do not let the miners run directly on the whole data set. Instead, we introduce *working data sets* with a smaller size for the miners to work on. In each of our mining iteration, Ag$_{CBN}$ generates working data sets for Ag$_S$ and Ag$_C$. The working data sets contain the same set of instances but different types of data, fitting the two miners respectively. The details of generating the working data sets are presented in Ag_{CBM}'s design.

Sequence Miner. The sequence miner (Ag$_S$) is the agent that does mining on the temporal simplex data set, and finds the sequence rules. Ag$_S$ uses a genetic algorithm to achieve temporal rule mining. We designed a Michigan-like approach (see [2]) with sequence rules as individuals. A Michigan-like approach has a smaller granularity and its average run time is shorter than that of Pittsburgh approaches. This is suitable for dividing the whole genetic algorithm process into many short runs — more suitable for cooperation as required by *CoLe*.

Besides the commonly used genetic operators crossover and mutation, we designed an "intelligent" genetic operator called *intellicut* to make the evolutionary process more targeted. In *intellicut*, each event in the middle of an individual is checked to see if the quality of the individual can be increased by cutting off the events after this point, i.e., it will cut off a bad "tail" in the sequence. In this way, even if an individual is not very good, the good parts of it are preserved.

The fitness of an individual is evaluated according to its *accuracy* — the ratio of true positives to all instances it matches, and *coverage* — the ratio of true positives to all cases in the data set. These two factors are both considered to make sure the individuals contain valid knowledge and they will not overfit the data. We propose the following equation to calculate the fitness:

$$fitness = 10 \times \left(\frac{tp}{tp + fp} \right)^x \times \frac{\ln(tp)}{\ln(case\_num)} \qquad (1)$$

In (1), *tp* and *fp* are the true positives (*cases* matched by this individual) and the false positives (*controls* matched by this individual) respectively, and *case_num* is the number of all *cases* in the data set. Here in the coverage calculation, the logarithm calculation makes the fitness less sensitive to coverage when the coverage is big enough. The fitness is the product of the two factors so that neither the accuracy nor the coverage can be low. The exponent x of the accuracy controls the weight of the two factors in the fitness. In fact, (1) is used as a global assessment of rule quality throughout the system. Different x values are chosen for specific situations based on our experiments with various x values in these situations.

Conjunctive Miner. The conjunctive miner (Ag_C) is the agent that mines on the non-temporal simplex data set to discover conjunctive rules.

The base mining algorithm used for Ag_C is the *PART* algorithm (see [3]). It forms rules from pruned partial decision trees built using *C4.5*'s learning method (for *C4.5*, see [4]). The resulting rules are in the form of conjunctive rules. *PART* has no global optimization and therefore can return a rule immediately after discovering it. This gives us the ability to interrupt it halfway with partial results, allowing run time limits for Ag_C and easy synchronization with other miners. In our system we use an implementation of *PART* directly from a machine learning package called *WEKA* (see [5]).

As *PART* is designed for creating rule sets for classification problems, it is necessary to do some pre- and post-mining work to make the results more suitable for our cooperative mining problem. The pre-mining tasks are mainly used for data reduction. We use a *relevance factor*:

$$RF(A) = \Pr(A) \times \log\left(\frac{\Pr(A|case)}{\Pr(A|control)}\right) \tag{2}$$

(inspired by [6]) to identify relevant possible diagnoses and eliminate irrelevant ones to reduce the number of attributes. The post-mining task is to generalize the results — generate simpler rules based on the results and use fitter (measured by (1)) ones in the simpler rules to replace the original ones.

Subrule Checking in Both Miners. Subrule checking is done in both Ag_S and Ag_C before sending their results to Ag_{CBN} to prepare more candidates for combination. A subrule is one whose condition is a subset of the original condition (and for sequence rules, the events should also appear in the same relative order as the original rule). For each rule, all the subrules of this rule will be checked against a fitness threshold over the entire data set $\mathcal{D}$. All qualified subrules are sent together with the original result set to Ag_{CBN} as the result of an individual miner. This brings more "materials" for the combination while the earlier tasks increase the overall rule quality.

Combination Agent. The cooperation is mainly achieved by Ag_{CBN} combining the results from the miners to produce hybrid rules.

In Ag_{CBN}, the combination inputs are *srules* and *crules*, which are the result rule sets of Ag_S and Ag_C, respectively. The combination is done in several stages:

1. Direct combination: Combine a sequence rule with a conjunctive rule (including subrules)

2. Crossing combination: Convert a predicate to an event (or vise versa) and combine with existing hybrid rules
3. Rule pruning: Remove duplicates and unnecessary parts
4. Working data set generation: Generate the working data set for the next iteration to the miners
5. Hints to Ags: Give hints to Ags according to Agc's results.

In these stages, a rule's quality is also measured by the fitness calculated by (1). A fitness threshold ft is set before hand. The combined rules with fitness greater than ft will be put into the hybrid rule set *hrules*. We assume all these rule sets contain only rules with a conclusion "diabetes", because the knowledge we intend to discover is "what a diabetes patient should be like" instead of "what a diabetes patient should not be like".

In direct combination, if a rule in *srules* or *crules* already has greater fitness than ft, it will be put to *hrules* directly. Then new hybrid rules are created by putting a sequence rule's condition and a conjunctive rule's together. The new hybrid rules with higher fitness than ft are put into *hrules* as well.

The second stage, crossing combination, uses the hybrid rules in *hrules* after the first stage, together with *srules* and *crules*, as the base. The basic idea of crossing combination is to convert some diagnostic predicates in conjunctive rules to events and put them into the sequence parts of a hybrid rule to see if the hybrid rule's fitness increases. A similar event-to-predicate combination is also done. The conversions can be made because both the diagnostic predicates and events are on the same set of possible diagnoses. For example, we can convert a predicate "Diagnosis_A = true" to an event "[Diagnosis_A]". In this way, the use of one miner's result to help the other is maximized. A hill-climbing method is used in the iterations to find the best results for each hybrid rule's combination.

After the combination stages, the resulting rule set *hrules* is pruned to eliminate duplicate rules and useless conditions. Single-event sequences are converted to a predicate since a single event cannot indicate any temporal order. A predicate that has a counterpart in the sequence part is erased because the condition in the sequence part is stronger than the conjunctive part. And finally duplicate rules are erased.

Ag_{CBN} then generates the working data sets for the two miners. The first working data set is generated randomly from the whole data set before the mining work starts. Later ones are generated according to the combination results, based on the previous working data set. We denote the previous working data set and the new (currently generating) one as W_o and W_n respectively. Ag_{CBN} first eliminates the correctly covered instances (true positives), as well as the true negatives covered by conjunctive rules predicting *controls*, from W_o. The remaining instances can take only up to 80% in W_n. The rest pending instances in W_n are randomly picked from the whole data set. By doing this, Ag_{CBN} can guide the miners to focus on the cases that have not been covered by existing rules without driving the miners into smaller and smaller corners.

The predicates of the conjunctive rules from Ag_C may contain some key indicators of diabetes. So they can act as domain specific knowledge to Ags.

After the combination, Ag_{CBN} will extract the predicate attributes from Ag_C's result, and make some candidate sequence segments from them in order to help Ag_S's work. These candidate segments can be used by the mutation operator in Ag_S's genetic algorithm. For example (shown in Fig. 2), we have conjunctive rules cr_1 and cr_2 coming from the conjunctive rule miner. Let $evt_1, \cdots, evt_5$ correspond to $pre_1, \cdots, pre_5$. We have sequence segments $ss_1, ss_2, \cdots, ss_8$ to be used as candidate individual parts in Ag_S. We do not have a counterpart for giving hints to Ag_C, because Ag_C is using an existing implementation and we have few ways to influence the *PART* algorithm directly.

$$cr_1:pre_1 \wedge pre_3 \Longrightarrow \text{disease} \quad cr_2:pre_2 \wedge pre_4 \wedge pre_5 \Longrightarrow \text{disease}$$

can generate sequence segments:

ss_1: $evt_1 \rightarrow evt_3$ ss_2: $evt_3 \rightarrow evt_1$ ss_3:$evt_2 \rightarrow evt_4 \rightarrow evt_5$

ss_4:$evt_2 \rightarrow evt_5 \rightarrow evt_4$ ss_5:$evt_4 \rightarrow evt_2 \rightarrow evt_5$ ss_6:$evt_4 \rightarrow evt_5 \rightarrow evt_2$

ss_7:$evt_5 \rightarrow evt_2 \rightarrow evt_4$ ss_8:$evt_5 \rightarrow evt_4 \rightarrow evt_2$

Fig. 2. Hints from Ag_C to Ag_S example

4   Experimental Evaluation

Our cooperative mining system has been tested with different experiments to show the advantage of cooperation.

4.1   Data Preparation

The diabetes medical control data for our mining system comes from the Calgary Health Region. The data contains population born before 1954 and have been living in Calgary continuously since 1994. We want to analyze the medical records 5 years prior to the identification of diabetes. So we keep only the individuals who have no diagnoses of diabetes before 2000 but have at least one diabetes diagnosis in 2000, i.e., first diagnosed as diabetes patients in 2000. They are the *cases* in our data. For each of the *cases*, we also give 2 *controls* who are in the same sex and similar age but have no diabetes diagnoses at all.

In the original data set, there are three tables. One is the registration table (REG table) containing ID, age, gender, and class (*case* or *control*). The other two are medical records, one for hospital (HOSP table) and the other for clinical services (MD table). The medical records are mainly the diagnostic codes given by the doctors, together with the date of service. In Table 1 the sample data tables are shown (some unused fields are omitted). We put the clinical and hospital medical records together and only extract the records from 1995 to 1999 — the 5-year period before diabetes diagnoses.

The diagnostic codes are defined by the International Classification of Diseases, 9th revision (ICD-9, see [7]). We use a higher-level abstraction, the ICD-9 Basic Tabulation List ([8]), to aggregate the diagnostic codes to 307 disease

Table 1. Sample data tables

REG				HOSP							
ID	CC	GENDER	YEAR	ADMIT	DX_1	DX_2	DX_3	DX_4	DX_5	...	ID
2	0	M	1921	1996-12-21	9975	5968	E8788	7140	36610	...	3
3	0	F	1922	1997-06-19	57420					...	3
5	0	F	1946	1997-06-30	57410	V1301				...	3
6	0	F	1930	1998-04-08	9962	E8781				...	7
7	1	M	1938	1999-04-16	99677	72709	2851	E8781		...	7
18	1	F	1950	1999-08-12	5409					...	7
19	1	M	1940	1998-04-27	9962	99813	E8781			...	7
		... ...				... ...					

MD					
...	SERV_SDATE	DIAG1	DIAG2	DIAG3	ID
...	2000-03-06				2
...	2000-03-25	595			2
...	1997-06-27	594.9	788.0		3
...	1995-12-07	466			5
...	1999-12-14	733	717.8	719.4	5
...	1999-10-08	174			5
...	2000-02-25	780.5			6
	... ...				

types in about 70 categories, to condense the data. Then we split the data set into sequence and conjunctive simplex data sets. For the sequence simplex data set, we order each instance's diagnoses, both hospital and clinical, by the date of service. For the conjunctive simplex data set, we put the basic information of the instances — age, gender, etc. — together with a boolean table for the diagnoses. If an instance ever had a diagnosis, the corresponding field has the value *true*, and vice versa.

There were two data sets prepared for the tests. A small data set contains 1800 instances, with 600 *cases* and 1200 *controls*. The corresponding working data set for the miners contains 900 instances. This small data set is used for most of the tests and comparisons in Sect. 4.2. We also prepared a large data set with all valid instances we have, containing 9450 instances (3150 *cases* and 6300 *controls*). The corresponding working data set size is 3150 instances. Test runs on this larger data set were made to get rules for evaluation of the knowledge discoveries in Sect. 4.3.

4.2 The Effect of Combination

Our first evaluation is the comparison of the single miners and the combinations so that we can show the effect of combination in our system. We had five test runs with different fitness thresholds in Ag_{CBN}. These fitness thresholds control how a rule is qualified (see Sect. 3.2). Other parameter values were decided by some experiments before hand so that their values used in the tests were reasonable and the same for all our tests here. Results of these tests are shown in Table 2. The run time for each of the tests was within 15 hours, which is quite acceptable. As our concentration is on the cooperation and combination, we do not put too much focus on the run time.

Table 2. Tests with different thresholds

Test No.		1	2	3	4	5
Fitness threshold		3.8	3.9	4.0	4.1	4.2
Rule origins	Ag_S	263	104	25	13	5
	Ag_C	0	0	3	0	0
	Combination	5745	1852	743	287	72
	Total	6008	1956	771	300	77
Fitness averages	Ag_S	3.973	4.089	4.162	4.282	4.251
	Ag_C	N/A	N/A	4.183	N/A	N/A
	Combination	4.054	4.117	4.258	4.312	4.344
	Overall	4.051	4.116	4.254	4.311	4.338
True positive averages	Ag_S	67.18	61.73	65.36	26.62	33.00
	Ag_C	N/A	N/A	46.333	N/A	N/A
	Combination	56.55	55.66	45.92	26.49	25.25
	Overall	57.02	55.98	46.55	26.49	25.75

The first comparison is the number of rules with different origins. Ag_S or Ag_C-origin rules include both qualified original rules from a miner and the qualified subrules in subrule checking. The rules with contributions from both miners take "Combination" as their origins. When our system records the origins, single-miner origins have higher priority, i.e. when a rule discovered by a single miner happens to be re-discovered by Ag_{CBN}, we give credit to the single miner instead of Ag_{CBN}. In Table 2 we can clearly see that the combined rules are much more than the ones with origins Ag_S or Ag_C. This is the first indication that the combination can produce more potential good rules according to our fitness measure.

The average fitness of the rules by origin are calculated as well. The averages differ as the thresholds are different. The average fitness of the combined rules is a bit higher than the ones from single miners. This again indicates the combination increases the quality of the discovered knowledge, or in another word, produce better knowledge from two types of materials.

In each test run the combined rules have comparable true positive coverage with the ones from single miners. This shows that our combination strategies are not overfitting the given data. Although the true positive coverages of combined rules are a bit lower than the ones of individual miners, this shows that the combined rules have higher accuracy, because our fitness measure in (1) is balanced between coverage and accuracy and the combined rules have higher fitness.

In addition to the summaries for the whole rule sets, summaries for the top 10 (by fitness) rules in each test are also presented here in Table 3. From this table we can see that most of the top 10 rules are combined rules. And in the only test with rules from Ag_S in the top 10, the combined rules have a higher average fitness than the ones from Ag_S. For the same reason indicated above, in Test No. 2 the true positive average of rules from Ag_S is a bit higher than that of the combined rules, indicating combined rules have higher accuracy.

Table 3. Tests with different thresholds (top 10 rules)

Test No.		1	2	3	4	5
Fitness threshold		3.8	3.9	4.0	4.1	4.2
Rule origins	Ag_S	0	2	0	0	0
	Ag_C	0	0	0	0	0
	Combination	10	8	10	10	10
	Total			Top 10		
Fitness averages	Ag_S	N/A	4.594	N/A	N/A	N/A
	Ag_C	N/A	N/A	N/A	N/A	N/A
	Combination	4.769	4.684	4.821	4.696	4.491
	Overall	4.769	4.666	4.821	4.696	4.491
True positive averages	Ag_S	N/A	24.50	N/A	N/A	N/A
	Ag_C	N/A	N/A	N/A	N/A	N/A
	Combination	23.80	23.38	24.40	23.20	25.60
	Overall	23.80	23.60	24.40	23.20	25.60

The use of hints to Ag_S was specially tested and evaluated to prove its contribution.

The tests were to run Ag_S's genetic algorithms with and without hints, to see if the results will be different in quality. To get some valid hints for the tests, the run log in test No. 3 in Table 2 was used and we extracted the hints and working data set in the tenth iteration from it. The tests made here all ran on this working data set, and the ones with hints used this hint set. To make sure we have a general result without the interference of random numbers, we repeat each test individually for five times. So totally we have 5 runs with hints, and 5 without hints. In each run, we use a generation size of 300, evolve the individuals for 50 generations, and finally filter out those individuals with fitness greater than 2.8.

Table 4 shows the qualified individual numbers for each test run. From the numbers and the averages, an obvious conclusion is that the runs with hints generate more qualified individuals. More detailed observations are made on the evolutionary process. In Fig. 3, average fitnesses of the first 10 generations in each test run's evolutionary process are presented in a line chart. We can see the average fitnessses for test runs with hints increase much faster than the ones without hints.

Table 4. Number of qualified individuals

Generation size	300					
Generation limit	50					
Fitness threshold	2.8					

Test No.	1	2	3	4	5	Average
With hints	13	33	33	51	63	38.60
Without hints	7	9	12	15	28	14.20

From the results shown in Table 4 and Fig. 3, we can conclude that Ag_S does benefit from hints so that it can start faster and get more out of the data.

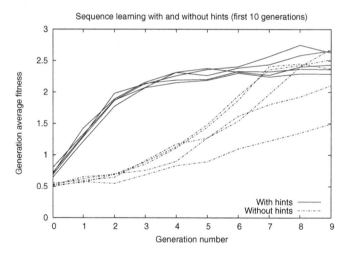

Fig. 3. Average fitness with and without hints (first 10 generations)

4.3   Knowledge Discovered

In this section the discoveries of our test runs on the full data set are examined and analyzed. We find in our results there are not only rules matching known facts about diabetes, but also promising and interesting discoveries that were new to the medical experts.

The most important discovery of our miner is the relation of hypertension and diabetes. In the medical field, it is already known that diabetes has a tight relation with hypertensive diseases. In our test runs, 100% of the discovered hybrid rules have either "hypertensive diseases" in the sequence part as an indicative event, or "hypertensive diseases=*true*" in the conjunctive part. With such high occurrences of hypertensive diseases diagnoses in our results, it is a very exciting result to the medical experts.

Another discovery is about a general diagnose "signs, symptoms and ill-defined conditions". This diagnosis also has high occurrences in our results. However, unlike the hypertension diagnoses, this diagnosis cannot tell us about any specific diseases or disorders, but only some indication in general that the patient does not feel well. In particular, many rules come in the form like Fig. 4, where the "signs, symptoms and ill-defined conditions" diagnoses appear repeatedly in the sequence part. This is an indication that the patients may have been feeling uncomfortable for long before diabetes related diagnoses are made. Among all our *cases* there are about 25% who match the rule in Fig. 4.

Part	Condition (ICD-9)	Description
Conjunctive	{466,480-519}=1	Other diseases of the respiratory system
Sequence	{780-799}	Signs, symptoms and ill-defined conditions
	{780-799}	Signs, symptoms and ill-defined conditions
	{780-799}	Signs, symptoms and ill-defined conditions
	{401-405}	Hypertensive disease

Fig. 4. A hybrid rule

Another frequent diagnosis, "other diseases of the respiratory system", has an average of over 80% to appear in all the final hybrid rules (the rule in Fig. 4 is one of them). In medical doctors' eyes, this discovery does not have an obvious explanation (according to the experts we have talked to so far). This should be an interesting topic for the medical experts.

5   Related Work

According to the categories for cooperative search problems discussed in [9] (knowledge-based search is essentially the core in data mining methods), the *CoLe* model has characteristics from both *dividing the problem into subproblems* — split of the heterogeneous data set into simplex data sets and use of multiple miners — and *improving on the competition approach* — result segments from different miners are competing to appear in the combined rules. Depending on the way the heterogeneous data set is split and the strategies for combination in Ag$_{CBN}$, the *CoLe* model's similarity to *dividing the problem into subproblems* and *improving on the competition approach* may vary.

Compared to existing applications, the *CoLe* model presents some new ideas and improvements.

In [10], a theorem proving system named *TECHS* is presented. Two types of provers are used, namely universal provers and specialized provers respectively. In the proving process, the provers exchange selected clauses periodically with each other and integrate received clauses into their own search states. Our *CoLe* model has some design similarities with *TECHS*. However, the major difference is that *CoLe*'s combination of rules is done in a central agent Ag_{CBN}, while in *TECHS* each agent is responsible for its own integration of others' results. The central combination agent in *CoLe* can have a global view on all the different types of results and thus has a better chance to gain good rules through combination.

Viktor et al. developed *CILT* (see [11]), in which several agents form the cooperative mining team. The agents are either *machine miners* or *human miners*. The machine miners each employ a different data mining technique to discover knowledge from data; and the human miners obtain knowledge from human experts. Although in *CILT* different algorithms and different types of miners are used, they all produce the same (compatible) type of results. This leads to few potentials of strengthening knowledge through combination, and knowledge cannot be represented in hybrid rule format, which fits the complex real world better. In *CoLe*, we consider the results from the miners to be heterogeneous. Combining these heterogeneous results can gain hybrid results that can not be achieved by any single miner.

Most importantly, the *CoLe* model emphasizes the combination of the different types of rules, which is not a key characteristic in any of the existing cooperative distributed methods. The combination is not only an effort to make the cooperation more thoroughly but it also enhances the knowledge that is discovered. This can lead to greater synergetic effects.

6   Conclusion and Future Work

We proposed a cooperative multi-agent mining model — *CoLe*. In *CoLe*, multiple miners use different algorithms to mine a heterogeneous data set. These results are sent to a combination agent to create hybrid results and extract useful information as feedbacks to the miners. *CoLe* highlights the interaction and cooperation of different algorithms and the combination of different-typed results from different algorithms, resulting in synergetic improvements against the single algorithms.

We implemented a mining system using our *CoLe* model, aimed at mining knowledge from diabetes data with both temporal and non-temporal information. We use a sequence miner and a conjunctive miner for mining. The combination agent in this system contains our strategies for combination and cooperation. Experiments showed clearly how our combined hybrid results enhance and strengthen the raw results from single miners. Additionally, in the medical field, these results not only confirmed known knowledge about diabetes, namely that hypertension has a tight relation with diabetes, but also found some observations new to the medical experts.

The implemented mining system is the first proof of concept for our *CoLe* model. While it shows good results in the experiments, we have a lot of potential work to do. First, more implementations of cooperative mining systems using *CoLe* should be made to show that our *CoLe* model is a general paradigm for various learning/mining problems. On the conceptual side, more ways are needed to provide feedback from one miner (or the combination agent) to others. On the medical data mining side, future work should include: making use of other information together with diagnoses; mining on data sets where the distribution of disease cases is more close to general population; and mining data on more diseases.

References

1. Fayyad, U., Uthurusamy, R.: Evolving Data into Mining Solutions for Insights. Communications of the ACM **45** (2002) 28–31
2. Goldberg, D.E.: Genetic Algorithms in Search, Optimization, and Machine Learning. Addison-Wesley Professional (1989)
3. Frank, E., Witten, I.H.: Generating Accurate Rule Sets Without Global Optimization. In: Proceedings of the 15th International Conference on Machine Learning, Morgan Kaufmann (1998) 144–151
4. Quinlan, J.R.: C4.5: Programs for Machine Learning. The Morgan Kaufmann Series in Machine Learning. Morgan Kaufmann (1993)
5. Witten, I.H., Frank, E.: Data Mining: Practical Machine Learning Tools and Techniques with Java Implementations. Morgan Kaufmann (1999)
6. Liu, H., Lu, H., Yao, J.: Toward Multidatabase Mining: Identifying Relevant Databases. IEEE Transactions on Knowledge and Data Engineering **13** (2001) 541–553
7. Karaffa, M.C.: International Classification of Diseases, 9th Revision, 4th Edition, Clinical Modification. Practice Management Information Corp., Los Angeles (1992)
8. World Health Organization: International Classification of Diseases, 9th Revision: Basic Tabulation List with Alphabetical Index. World Health Organization, Geneva (1978)
9. Denzinger, J.: Conflict Handling in Collaborative Search. In Tessier, Chaudron, Müller, eds.: Conflicting Agents: Conflict Management in Multi-agent Systems, Kluwer Academic Publishers (2000) 251–278
10. Denzinger, J., Fuchs, D.: Cooperation of Heterogeneous Provers. In: Proceedings of the 16th International Joint Conference on Artificial Intelligence (IJCAI'99), Stockholm, Sweden, Morgan Kaufmann (1999)
11. Viktor, H.L., Arndt, H.: Data Mining in Practice: From Data to Knowledge Using a Hybrid Mining Approach. The International Journal of Computers, Systems and Signals. **1** (2000) 139–153

Technology of Agent-Based Decision Making System Development

Oleg Karsaev

SPIIRAS, 39, 14-th Liniya, St.Petersburg, 199178, Russia
ok@mail.iias.spb.su

Abstract. The paper presents a technology for agent-based decision making system development using MASDK software tool implementing the well known and grounded Gaia methodology. An example of the software tool usage, and its mapping to the methodology are demonstrated via a case study from the area of computer network security. The principal attention is paid to consideration of the rule-based classifier that is a reusable component intended for classification problem solution. A specific feature of the methodology when applied to the decision making system development referring to training of rule-based classifiers and other problem-oriented reusable solutions are considered as well.

1 Introduction

Multi agent technologies due to their features are supposed to represent one of the most promising directions in the area of software engineering. For this, very substantial reasons could be listed, and here, it seems to be quite enough to just mention only some of them. Multi agent approach gives way to developing more tailored software systems for problem domains whose high complexity and the degree of the system's elements distribution are their main characteristics. Multi agent systems allow describing more naturally business processes, different schemes of negotiations, etc. The said above and some other reasons are the grounds for the growing interest and attention of scientific community to the multi agent technologies.

At present the three following trends of research and efforts in this area can be highlighted as the most actual from the practical point of view: *1) development of tools (environments, languages, specific components, etc), 2) development of methodologies,* and *3) search for and development of reusable solutions and components.* A full enough review of the results achieved in these directions can be found in [6]. At that, the most of them are viewed as not problem-oriented solutions. This paper focuses on how the specifics of any problem domain, more precisely, of the one for which decision making task is one of the primary importance, can enrich or somehow affect them. At that, MASDK (Multi Agent System Development Kit) [1] based on Gaia methodology [5] is considered to be the basis for this research.

The remainder of the paper is structured as follows. Section 2 provides survey of MASDK software tool structure, the methodology of multi agent system (MAS) development in it and the mapping of this methodology with Gaia one. The use of

V. Gorodetsky, J. Liu, and V.A. Skormin (Eds.): AIS-ADM 2005, LNAI 3505, pp. 108 – 122, 2005.

MASDK and methodology for development of MAS, aiming at anomaly detection in computer networks is described in section 3. Section 4 focuses on the reusable *Rule-based classifier* (RBC) component which is one of the main components used in decision making systems (DMS) and the life-cycle of its development, including its training stage. Section 5 describes possible specifics of DMS development methodology related to development and training of the RBC components.

2   General Description of MASDK and Methodology

MASDK 3.0 software tool consists of the following components (Fig.1): (1) *system kernel* that is a data structure for XML-based representation and for storing of MAS formal specification; (2) *integrated set* of the graphical *editors* supporting the user's activity aimed at formal specification of MAS being analyzed, designed and implemented; (3) library of C++ classes constituting what is usually called *Generic agent* corresponding to the common reusable components of the MAS agents; (4) the *communication platform* to be installed in the corresponding computers of a network, and (5) the *builder of software agent* instances, who generates the source code in C++ and the executable code for the software agents as well as deployment of the software agents within the earlier installed communication platform.

A MAS development process in MASDK can be technologically divided in to three stages. At the first stage a detailed design of the MAS is developed. In particular, this stage assumes the development of the models described in Gaia methodology [5], namely – role models, interaction model, agent models, service models, and acquaintance model. At that the service models of agent classes are described in greater detail than it is done with Gaia methodology. All activities at this stage are entirely carried out by the *integrated set of editors (ISE)* and the results (the detailed design of the MAS) are stored at the *system kernel* component in special XML-based language. The second stage consists in programming the particular components that can be derived from the detailed design of the MAS developed at the previous stage. A list of these components includes two groups: 1) a set of scripts comprising a specification of agent class services, and 2) a set of the activities to be carried out by

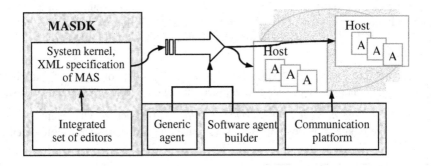

Fig. 1. MASDK software tool components and their interaction

the agent classes and described as external components in respect to the agent classes' specification.   The former are developed using a respective editor of the ISE component and stored in the *system kernel* component, the latter – in a usual programming environment, in our case in Visual C++. The third stage consists in compiling and building the software agents. It is executed automatically by the *software agent builder* component and 1) the detailed specification of the MAS in the system kernel, 2) generic agent component, and 3) external components developed at the second stage are used as inputs.

Thus, almost all development process is carried out based on the *ISE* component; so, let us discuss this component and the respective methodology of application systems development in detail. The set of editors comprising the *ISE* component can be divided into three categories (Fig.2): 1) the set of editors (*MAS meta-model, Protocol, Ontology* editors) aimed at describing abstract concepts and system organization, 2) the set of editors (*Agent class meta-model, State machine, State, Private ontology* editors) designed for description of concrete concepts and design of agent classes, and 3) the set of editors (*Agents' configuration and Agent mental model* editors) aimed at building and deployment of the agents.

The enumerated set of editors provides the following methodology for MASs development that starts from the two initial stages (*analysis* and *design*) which are parts of Gaia methodology [5].

1) *Analysis.* The development process is initiated with the requirements statement and the results of *role* and *interaction* models specification that comprise *an organizational model* of the MAS. The respective activities are supported by the *MAS meta-model* and the *Protocol* editors.

2) *Design.* According to Gaia methodology the objective of this stage assumes development of *agent, service* and *acquaintance* models. The agent model development assuming determination of agent classes and instances of each from them is carried out using the *MAS meta-model* and the *agents' configuration* editors. The service models are developed using the *agent class meta-model* editor and the acquaintance model with the aid of the *MAS meta-model* one.

3) *Ontology description.* Domain ontology description is specified by means of the *ontology* editor and initially[1] can be developed in parallel with stages 1 and 2. However there are relations between the models presupposes a certain sequence of their development. In particular, a detailed specification of communication acts of the protocols at later phases of development implies specifying of messages contents in terms of ontology notions. It means the respective notions of ontology have to be specified for doing it.

The first three stages are designed for describing abstract concepts of the application system. The concrete concepts are developed through the following sequence of stages.

4) *State machine development (Service development).* Each service identified at the design stage (stage 2) is developed as a state machine. At that, such a state machine is

---

[1] Development process in MASDK can have iterative character. It means each model developed in process of MAS development can be refined repeatedly.

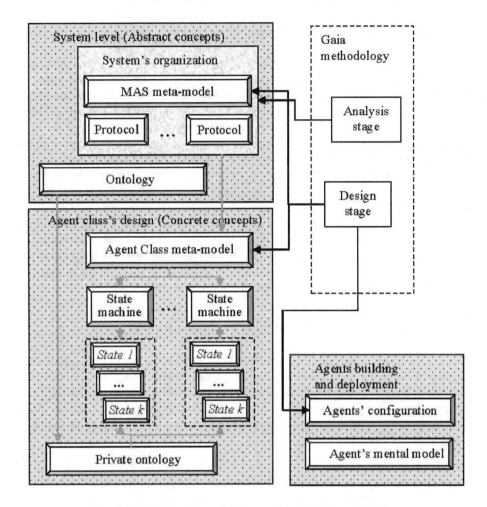

Fig. 2. MASDK models and their mapping with Gaia methodology

described at the level of states and transitions between them without minor details of states implementation.   A service is associated with respective protocols and activitiesand, consequently, development of a state machine assumes relating each state to either communication act of some protocol or one of the activities. One communication act is related to only one state, while one activity can be related to several states. Transitions between states describe the scenario of the service execution.

5) *Private ontology development*. Private ontology is required for specification of the notions used for describing the agent class mental model. At that, it involves private notions of the agent class and the notions inheriting ones from the shared ontology developed at stage 3. Private ontology development also assumes specifying a data storage scheme (or several storage schemes) of agent class.

6) *Agents initial mental model*. This stage consists in describing initial data and knowledge of the agents. It must be noted that at the previous stages (namely – 4, 5) the agent classes have been specified and the agents of each class have no specifics

except for their names. Therefore, the initial mental models of agents are their specifics that single out the agents of each class.

7) *Agent classes components programming*. Components of each agent class that have to be specified in the usual way (in case of MASDK environment it consists in developing a code in C++ language) are identified as a result of stage 3 execution. All of them are either scripts of agent classes' behavior in particular states of state machines or invoked from these scripts as external components.

8) *Agents code generating*. This function is executed automatically by *Software agent builder* component (Fig.1). Execution of it assumes the following sequence of activities. 1) XSLT-technology-based generation of a source code in C++ of components described at stage 4. 2) Compiling the executable agent class code that linking components: a) generated at stage 8.1, b) developed at stage 7, and c) *generic agent* component (Fig.1). 3) Automatic generation of agent classes' storages according to their schemes developed at stage 6.

9) *Agents configuration and deployment*. This stage assumes specifying the locations of agents, deploying of the agent according to the results, and filling in the storages of the agents with their initial mental models developed at stage 6.

3   Case Study: Anomaly Detection in Computer Network

This section briefly illustrates the use of MASDK for development of an agent-based decision making system in the area of computer network defence. The problem consists in what follows. Input data containing the logs of traffic and attacks, e.g. DARPA data set [7] are provided. It is required to develop an anomaly detection multi agent system (AD-MAS). For reason of brevity we will describe in detail only stages 1, 2, and 4 of development.

Analysis stage

Let us remember that the objective of the *analysis* stage is development of a system's organization that comprises development of role and interaction models. In many cases, there exist evident entities of the problem domain (such as departments, persons, etc) that can be regarded as the basis for role determination. Discovery of roles for the problem being solved has the following specifics. In the given case, the roles rather reflect the approach selected to development of the decision making system and respective activities related to it. The list of activities includes the following 8 ones.

➢ *Extractor* role extracts five different objects designated as *Cnc, W1, W2, W3, and W4* from the input traffic which comprise essential features and can be classified as either normal or abnormal objects. The *Cnc* objects comprise features of connection and other objects comprise different statistic data about the traffic.

➢ *BC_Cnc, BC_W1, BC_W2, BC_W3, BC_W4* roles classify respective objects as either normal or abnormal ones.

➢ *Meta_classifier* role is responsible for combining the decisions of the above base classifiers.

➢ *Assistant* role deals with current state representation of the host to the human expert.

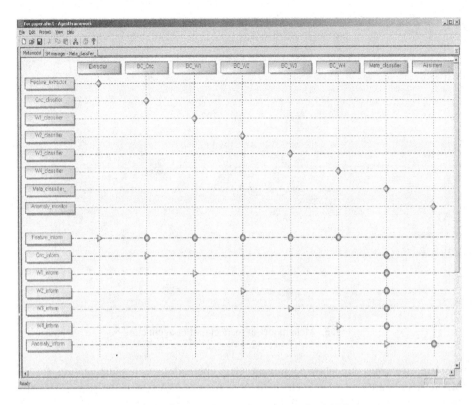

Fig. 3. Meta model of anomaly detection MAS

The list of the roles identified at this stage is depicted in the upper part of the *MAS meta-model* editor (Fig.3). The general diagram of the interaction model is shown in the lower part of the same editor. In the case it includes 7 protocols: *Feature_inform, Cnc_inform, W1_inform, W2_inform, W3_inform, W4_inform, Anomaly_inform*. Graphic representation of the interaction model structure in this editor allows for identifying participants and the initiator of each protocol. E.g., the participants of *Feature_inform* protocol are *Extractor, BC_Cnc, BC_W1, BC_W2, BC_W3* and *BC_W4* roles. At that, the *Extractor* role consists in initiating this protocol. Each of the protocols identified in the structure of the interaction model is specified in MASDK by means of a respective graphic editor that allows to specify all communication acts and a scenario of their execution. Fig.4 is an example of *Cnc_inform* protocol representation in this editor.

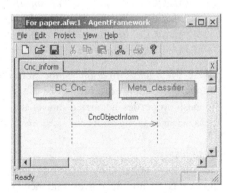

Fig. 4. Cnc_Inform protocol

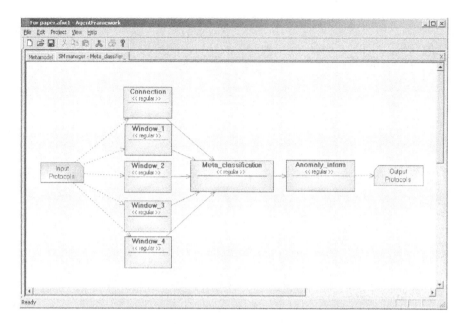

Fig. 5. Meta model of meta classifier agent class

Here, we must somehow comment Gaia methodology implementation for the MASDK software tool. One of the main objectives of MASDK is the graphic designer support, and accordingly, the environment comprises an integrated set of editors (ISE component, Fig.1). The main component of the role model that can be depicted graphically is the *liveness properties* [5]. While MASDK has no respective editor that could realize this possibility at the analysis stage, it is specified in the dialog describing roles as expression. E.g., the liveness properties of the meta-classifier role are specified as the following list of expressions:

$CncMetaClassification = (Cnc\_inform.$ *Meta_classification,* $Anomaly\_inform)^w,$
$W1MetaClassification = (W1\_inform.$ *Meta_classification,* $Anomaly\_inform)^w,$
$W2MetaClassification = (W2\_inform.$ *Meta_classification,* $Anomaly\_inform)^w,$
$W3MetaClassification = (W3\_inform.$ *Meta_classification,* $Anomaly\_inform)^w,$
$W4MetaClassification = (W4\_inform.$ *Meta_classification,* $Anomaly\_inform)^w,$

where *Meta_classification* is the activity being executed by this role and the rest atomic components are protocols. Nevertheless, the graphic representation of the role liveness properties is carried out, at the design stage during specification of the agent class services using an *Agent class meta-model* editor.

Design stage
Design stage consists in generating agents, services and acquaintance models. A set of agent classes[2] and the correspondence between them and roles are depicted in MASDK

---

[2] In Gaia methodology agent classes are named as agent types.

with the aid of *MAS meta-model* editor. E.g., Fig.3 illustrates such a model generated for AD-MAS. It comprises 8 agent classes, each of them one-to-one corresponding to respective role.

Service models are identified in terms of interacted state machines via *Agent class meta-model* editor. E.g., Fig.5 illustrates the services identified for *Meta_classifier* agent class. According to Gaia methodology they are derived from the liveness properties of the respective role. For a given case, the liveness properties of the *meta_classifier* role being played by a *meta_classifier* agent class are constructed using the five expressions given above. All of them and the respective services providing their execution are represented in this diagram in the following way. The services associated with the *Cnc_inform, W1_inform, W2_inform, W3_inform,* and *W4_inform* protocols are identified as *Connection, Window_1, Window_2, Window_3,* and *Window_4* state machines respectively. The service executing *meta_classification* activity is identified as a *meta_classification* state machine. The service associated with the *Anomaly_inform* protocol is identified as *Anomaly_inform* state machine.

State machine development (Service development)
At this stage each of the services identified for the agent classes is developed in more detail. Per se, it is reduced to development of all state machines identified for agent classes at the design stage. In MASDK this activity is executed with the aid of *State machine* editor. Fig.6 illustrates an example of the *Meta_classification* state machine specification in it. Inputs of the meta_classification state machine (service), derived from the *Cnc_inform, W1_inform, W2_inform, W3_inform* and *W4_inform* protocols are the decisions of based classifiers concerning the respective objects extracted from the traffic. Outputs of the state machine are decisions about the current state of

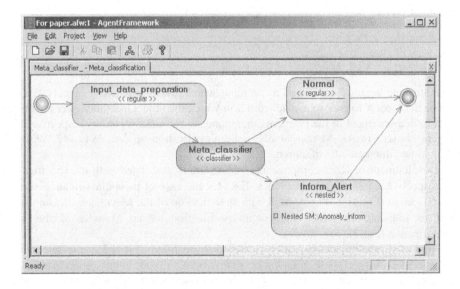

Fig. 6. Service specification in form of state machine

a host. The states comprising the state machine are designed for executing the following *functions*. *Input_data_preparation* state preprocesses the inputs and forms inputs for the meta classifier. In more detail this task is described in section 4. In *meta_vlassifier* state the meta classification procedure is executed. Depending on which decision (normal or abnormal) is made, the respective state (either *Normal* or *Inform_alert*) forms the message content for human expert.

Development of states in MASDK is supported by a set of different patterns that realizes reusable solutions for respective set of task classes. One of them used for specifying of classifiers is described in detail in the following section.

4   Rule-Based Classifier Development

In general case, a decision making system development in combination with creation of new solutions can deal with "standard" task statements and involve usage of reusable solutions (approaches, components, etc) for their realization. In the context of MAS development methodology this "standard" task statement can be associated with activities carried out by (tasks solved by) roles. These are found at the analysis stage and described in the role models. Examples of such task statements include *object classification, time-series classification,* etc. For solution of each of them there exist various approaches, methods, algorithms. Implement them in form of reusable solutions and software components can substantially support the process of agent-based decision making system development. The rest of this section contains an example of such a component – *Rule-based classifier (RBC)* developed in MASDK environment for this purpose.

The general statement of the problem that can be solved with the aid of RBC component looks as follows. There exist a class X of objects X that are specified by an attribute vector

$P = \{ P_1, ..., P_N \},$
and a set of alternative states
$S = \{ S_1, ..., S_M \}, M > 1.$

The attribute vector P is viewed as an input which allows to classify objects X, i.e. – for each object X to choose a state from S in which the object has failed. Let us remark that such a statement of the problem corresponds to the tasks solved by respective roles (agent classes) in AD-MAS, namely – the classification of Cnc, W1, W2, W3, W4 objects and the meta-classification.

Development of RBC components in MASDK is associated with the specification of respective states of state machines. E.g., for the case of meta-classification service specification (Fig.4) it is associated with specification of the Meta_classification state. Let us illustrate an RBC component specification by an example of this state specification (Fig.7).

First of all, the object class to be classified is identified. It is reduced to selection of a respective notion class (Fig.7, *Object of classification* field) in the *agent class context* that includes a set of notion classes (variables) for specifying of the agent class mental

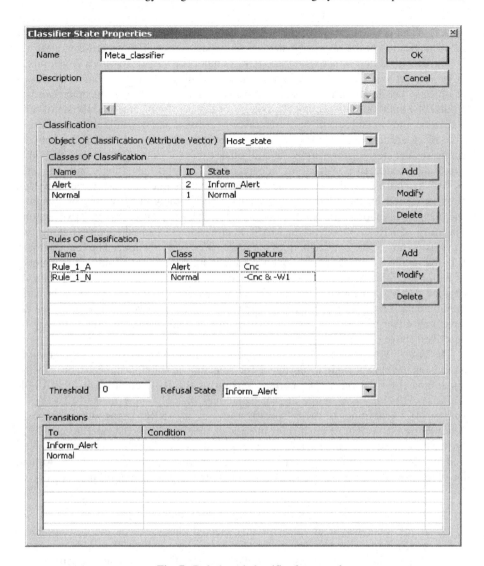

Fig. 7. Rule-based classifier framework

model. At that, the attributes of the selected notion class (the *Host_state* class) constitute the attribute vector **P**. In this case, the vector includes attributes that specify possible solutions of all based classifiers.

Then the possible classes of objects classification are identified in respective fields of the editor. In the case under consideration, these classes are *Normal* and *Alert* ones. The RBC components allow only to classify objects and are not aimed at specification of the agent class behavior for each possible solution. Such behavior is specified by means of other states of the state machine; so identification of classes implies identifying the respective states. At that, a set of these states has been determined earlier, at the previous stage of the state machine specification (Fig.6) and, therefore, the identification of the respective states is reduced to selecting the necessary ones.

The described bellow activity of the RBC component specification is a development of the rule set that can be divided into N subsets of rules, where N is number of classes of objects classification. Each subset of rules includes the rules (or in other words – arguments) in favor of respective class. E.g., for the case being analysed the set of rules is divided into two subsets of rules – in favor of *Normal* and *Alert* classes respectively. The rules are expressions for which the set of attributes of classifying objects comprises the atomic propositions, and all other expressions are formed with the aid of two logical connectives: "negation" (denoted by "-"symbol) and "logic and" (denoted by "&" symbol). E.g., the set of rules in Fig.7 includes one rule in favor of the *Alert* class (specified by the simplest expression *"Cnc"* composed of atomic proposition) and one rule in favor of the *Normal* class (specified by the *"-Cnc & -W1"* expression). The rules of RBC components in MASDK environment can be specified along two ways using one of the two techniques: *automatically,* or *by the user.* The first approach is based on the use of specific components realizing *GK2* [2] and *VAM* [3] techniques of automatic rules generating. This approach assumes generation of training data. In case of AD-MAS development the DARPA data set [7] is considered to be such training data. The second approach is supported by a respective editor that allows the developer either to describe new rules or to edit the rules generated automatically by described above components.

The last activity related to RBC component development consists in specification of a decision making technique designed for selecting a solution depends on specific inputs and the fired rules. The current version of the RBC component in MASDK realizes whilst only one of the known techniques, namely – the method of *weighed voting* [4]. According to it a specification of the RBC components supposes determining the weight of each rule. In case of training data existence the weight of each rule can be computed automatically and takes into account a) the volume of training data, b) the number of cases when a rule is fired rightly and c) falsely. At that, the object classification is computed according to the following algorithm.

1) The total weight of all fired rules referring to each class is computed.
2) The class with the largest total weight of fired rules is selected.
3) If the total weight of rules for the selected class exceeds the corresponding weight for each other class more then by the value of the *Threshold* parameter (Fig.7), it means that the selected class is the real result of object classification.

The RBC component examined in detail in this section is one of the reusable solutions that can essentially simplify the development process for different MASs in which decision making is considered as one of the main problems. Let us analyze an example of AD-MAS specification calling two more tasks that may need to be considered often enough in the problem domain and for which respective reusable components can be developed as well. These tasks are: 1) *attribute vector's computation,* and 2) *data stream's synchronization.* The first one is solved using the *Meta classifier* agent class, within the meta-model of which (Fig.6) this task corresponds to the *Input_data_preparation* state. The second task is treated as a part of each service described by *Connection, Window_1, Window_2, Window_3* and *Window_4* state machines.

The first task is connected to specific features of attribute vectors viewed as inputs for RBC components. Their attributes can only have values from the set – *{"true", "false", "not defined"}*. Evidently, these vectors do not allow to describe all variety of objects, related to which the classification problem is being solved. However, all of them can be transformed into attribute vectors. The general structure of this task can be explained by means of Table 1. According to it the transformation is reduced to development of expressions that are considered as predicates related to the objects being classified. At that, the values of these predicates are supposed to be the values of respective vector attributes.

Table 1

Attribute vector	
Attribute	Expression
A1	*Exp1*
A2	*Exp2*
...	...

The task having been outlined takes into consideration another specific feature of the classification problem. Object classification can be based on the data received from different data sources asynchrono- usly. It means that a value of each attribute can have time mark (Table 2). In the course of time passing values of the attributes can lose their validity and, therefore, before an RBC component operation they must be checked and if it is necessary some of them must be updated (e.g., take *"Not defined"* value).

Table 2

Attribute vector		
Attribute	Time stamp	Value
A1	*T1*	*V1*
A2	*T2*	*V2*
...	...	...

5   Particular Features of MAS Making Decision Development Methodology

The development methodology of MAS making decision, specifically – in case of using RBC components described in the previous section, can possess certain features related to *identification* and *training* of classifiers. Identification of classification problems is associated with the activities carried out by roles and therefore can be considered as a partial result of system organization, agents and service models development. In particular, in MASDK notations, achievement of such a result assumes specifying meta-models of all agent classes and all their state machines at the level of states and transitions between them. At that, several states in the state machines of different agent classes are associated with respective classifiers. Based on these models it is possible to represent the logic structure of a decision making system as a set of classifiers and a structure of their interaction. Such a representation of the AD-MAS system described above is illustrated in Fig.8. In fact, a decision making systems representation of this kind has also appeared at the analysis stage and can be used as an auxiliary model for system design.

Training of classifiers is implemented at stages 5 through 8 of the methodology (see section 2) and carried out at the same level as development of other functions of agents. However, training of classifiers has a specific feature that consists in the possibility of considering it as a partial problem. The classifiers are characterized by a *quality* parameter. At that, the process of training may have repetitive character if the initial training could not provide the necessary quality of classifier. Besides, in several cases at the stage of classifiers identification it is impossible to assess the quality of a classifier that can be achieved in the process of training. At that, if training of the identified classifiers could not provide the necessary quality level of some of them, it can

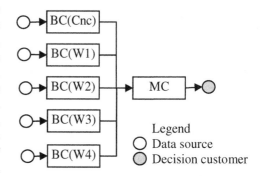

Fig. 8. Structure of classifiers

result in the necessity of modifying initial image of the decision making system and repeating the development process including the analysis and design stages. In particular, it can result in refining the system's organization, the agents and service models.

There exists another specific circumstance related to training of the classifiers that can affect the outcome of the analysis and design stages. The training process can be considered as a task of either the design-time or run-time stage of a system live cycle. It depends on how training data are formed. Indeed, training of classifiers can be carried out during the development of a system (agents) if the training data can be formed independently from both development and operation of the system. Development of AD-MAS is an example of such a case because the training data (DARPA data set) are considered to be the inputs for the development process.

Yet another case assumes that the data for classifiers training can be accumulated during the system operation. Let us consider an abstract example of such a case (Fig.9). Here, *Assistant*, *Classifier* and *Trainer* agents are elements of the system supporting solving of the decision making problem. The assistant agent is interfaced with the human expert solving classification task and provides the following services: *assistance, logging, testing, and decision making support.* The classifier agent provides *an object classification* service. This service has a pre-condition consisting in that the set of the classifier rules is not empty. The trainer agent provides the *training* and *reinforcement training of the classifier* services.

The function of the assistant agent includes receiving respective data, namely – the objects to be classified, and sending decisions (classification results) to consumers. At that, the human expert is responsible for decision making. The logging service sends the description of each decision making case at the address of the *trainer* agent. This agent solves the task of classifiers training (reinforcement training) and sends the results of training to the address of the *classifier* agent.

The testing service of the assistant agent checks the quality of classifier training. At that, it sends the object to be classified at the address of the classifier agent, receives the results of classification from it and compares the results of classification carried out by the classifier agent and the human expert. Due to repeating execution of this

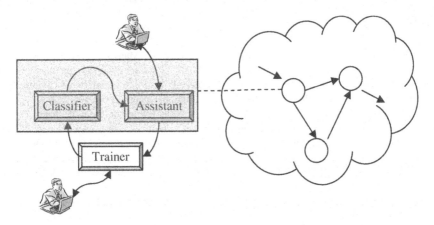

Fig. 9. Example of DMS-MAS assuming training classifiers during system operation

activity, the assistant agent accumulates necessary statistics and decides either to use the classifier or to continue training. After the decision about using the classifier is made, the decision making support service provides support for the human expert.

6 Conclusion

This paper presents the results of an attempt to consider a methodology of agent-based system development when applied to the decision making problem. It analyses the reusable not-problem-oriented solutions proposed by MASDK 3.0 multi-agent software tool based on well grounded Gaia methodology, and the reusable solutions that are viewed as problem-oriented ones for the decision making problem.

The primary goal of the paper has included analysis of the methodology specific features that must be taken into account during development of the systems in this problem domain and several problem-oriented reusable solutions one of them is rule-based classifier.

The proposed reusable solutions implemented within MASDK 3.0 software tool were practically used for development of a multi-agent system designed for anomaly detection in computer network. They are currently being used for development of flood monitoring and forecasting system, and as a component of an on-line target recognition system producing decisions based on infra red image fusion.

The objectives of the future work are: raising the number of reusable solutions that would support development of the decision making system as much as possible, and experimental assessment of the resulting software tool, based on development of various applications.

Acknowledgement

This research is supported by grant of European Office of Aerospace R&D (Project #1993P).

References

1. Gorodetski, V., Karsaev, O., Samoylov, V., Konushy, V., Mankov, E., and Malyshev, A.: Multi Agent System Development Kit: MAS Software Tool Implementing Gaia Methodology. In: Shi, Z., and He, O. (eds): Proceedings of the International Conference on Intelligent Information Processing (IIP2004), Beijing, Springer, (2004) 69–78
2. Gorodetsky, V., and Karsaev, O.: Algorithm of Rule Extraction from Learning Data. In Proceedings of the 8th International Conference (joint Europe-USA) "Expert Systems Application & Artificial Intelligence", IITT International, Paris, France, (1996) 133–138
3. Gorodetski, V., Skormin, V., Popyack, L.: Data Mining Technology for Failure Prognostics of Avionics. In: IEEE Transactions on Aerospace and Electronic Systems. Volume 38, # 2, (2002) 388–403
4. Dietterich,T.: Machine Learning Research: Four Current Directions. In: AI magazine. 18(4), (1997) 97–136
5. Wooldridge, M., Jennings, N.R., Kinny, D. The Gaia Methodology for Agent-Oriented Analysis and Design. Journal of Autonomous Agents and Multi-Agent Systems Vol.3. No. 3 (2000) 285–312
6. http://www.agentlink.org/resources/agent-software.php
7. http://www.ll.mit.edu/IST/ideval/data/1998

An Architecture for Distributed Agent-Based Data Preprocessing

Petteri Nurmi, Michael Przybilski, Greger Lindén, and Patrik Floréen

Helsinki Institute for Information Technology HIIT,
Basic Research Unit, Department of Computer Science,
P.O. Box 68, University of Helsinki, FI-00014 Finland
{firstname.lastname}@cs.helsinki.fi

Abstract. Advances in agent technologies have fueled interest towards combining agent-based techniques with tools from data mining. Furthermore, the advent of the ubiquitous computing paradigm has introduced a novel applications area, which offers new possibilities for further deepening this bond. Ubiquitous computing solutions are often designed for mobile environments, which poses additional requirements on practical solutions. Providing a distributed architecture enables the distribution of workload, while at the same time allowing the on-line processing of data. Such an architecture ensures the pervasiveness of privacy and security aspects in the overall design. In this paper we present an architecture for distributed data preprocessing in ubiquitous environments, which supports the full distribution of processing tasks and enables the encapsulation of privacy and security mechanisms within every component. As our second contribution we discuss more thoroughly the usefulness of the intelligent agent paradigm for context-aware systems.

Keywords: Agent technologies, distributed agents, software architectures, preprocessing, ubiquitous and context-aware computing, privacy and security.

1   Introduction

Advances in agent technologies have fueled interest towards combining agent-based techniques with tools from data mining. However, at the moment the true power of this combination has not been fully harnessed. Especially, the advent of the *ubiquitous computing paradigm* [1], i.e. availability of computing services anytime and anywhere, has introduced a novel applications area which offers various possibilities for further deepening the bond between the two approaches.

Another relevant computing paradigm is *context-aware computing*. According to Dey and Abowd [2], any information that can be used to characterize the situation of a person, place, or object that is considered relevant to the interaction between a user and an application is context. Respectively, a system is said to be context-aware, if it uses contextual information to modify its behavior. These kinds of context-aware systems are beginning to play an important

V. Gorodetsky, J. Liu, and V.A. Skormin (Eds.): AIS-ADM 2005, LNAI 3505, pp. 123–133, 2005.

role in software systems, especially in software for wireless information devices. As these devices are typically carried by users, they are a potential source for enormous amounts of contextual information, which can be further utilized by different applications. A major part of such applications deals with the task of interpreting (reasoning about) current contextual information, in order to provide a semantically flavored higher-level description of the context of an entity [3], as this is often more useful for applications. Even though this step is common to most applications, a standardized way for implementing this step has not yet been found and research in this field can still be considered to be in its infancy.

In order to design an architecture for context interpretation in ubiquitous environments, additional requirements arising from the environment need to be taken into account. Especially, ubiquitous computing solutions are usually designed for mobile environments and, in order to support mobility and the limited capabilities of the devices, the system architecture must allow specific software components to reside, at least potentially, on different devices. Another requirement is that, in contrast to traditional data mining, data is often processed in an online fashion. Furthermore, the distribution of processing tasks makes privacy and security aspects pervasive for the overall design.

According to Moran and Dourish [4] a possible way to implement context-aware systems is to use interacting agents which are distributed over a network. As practical implementations of context interpretation often require combining different reasoning paradigms (e.g. probabilistic and rule-based reasoning), distributed agent-based architectures for data mining seem to offer a promising basis for practical solutions. In this paper we follow this idea further and present a distributed agent-based architecture that provides support for implementing mechanisms for preprocessing contextual data. The architecture has been designed to meet the additional challenges discussed above and thus it allows potentially distributing processing tasks over the network. Furthermore, due to the pervasive nature of the tasks, security and privacy mechanisms have to be encapsulated within each component. Because the proposed architecture is only a part of a context-aware agent, as our second contribution we discuss the role of the intelligent agent paradigm in context-aware systems more thoroughly.

The rest of the paper is organized as follows. Section 2 discusses existing contributions to architectures of context-aware systems, while Section 3 introduces our proposed architecture. Section 4 discusses preprocessing more thoroughly and Section 5 introduces the overall framework, of which the proposed architecture is a central part. Finally, Section 6 concludes the paper and describes future work.

2   Related Work

As Winograd [5] recognizes, so far only very few suggestions towards the architecture of context-aware systems (see e.g. [6]) have been developed. In most cases, systems that support the study of context-awareness are built to support the specific study and it is usually very difficult to extend those systems for other purposes, or to integrate them with existing applications [4].

The approaches that have been taken to provide a common architecture for context-aware applications are very different. According to Moran and Dourish [4], current research focuses either on different versions of a blackboard-based approach, or on widget-based approaches. Usually these approaches are implemented in the form of middleware, or in the form of application frameworks. Another possibility that Moran and Dourish mention is the implementation using interacting agents, which are distributed over a network.

Examples of middleware approaches include, e.g., the *Reconfigurable Context-Sensitive Middleware* (RCSM) [7,8], and the *CORTEX* middleware [9]. RCSM is adaptive in the sense that, depending on the context-sensitive behavior of the applications, it adapts its object discovery and connection management mechanisms. CORTEX, on the other hand, introduces special entities, called *sentient objects*, which are responsible for receiving, processing, and providing context-related information. Sentient objects are defined as autonomous objects that are able to sense their environment and act accordingly [9]. The advantage of this approach is the possibility to re-organize them, e.g. depending on their primary task. However, the sentient object model has been designed to use only rule-based reasoning and, furthermore, the architecture offers no support for privacy mechanisms. Also Siegemund [10] has presented a very interesting approach of a communication platform for smart objects. Focusing on changing the communication mechanisms and the inter-object collaboration depending on the situation, the platform allows for the specification and implementation of context-aware communication services and adapts the networking structures according to the context of an object.

While these approaches are interesting, they are focused on the communication mechanisms and their context-based changes. While this influences systems built on such platforms, it is still very difficult for applications to gain access to context information and benefit from it.

Also some application frameworks that support context-awareness have been proposed. For example, Korpipää et al. [11] describe the implementation of a framework that supports management of context information on mobile terminals. The structure of this framework is centered around the blackboard paradigm for communication, which is handled by a context manager. Most components that use this framework, including the applications, act as clients for the context management system on the device itself. Other services can run not only on the device itself, but potentially also in a distributed environment. Unfortunately this approach seems to be rather limited, as extendind the framework with new context types is rather difficult. In addition, only little information is available about the approach.

Another framework approach, which cannot be neglected here, is the *Context Toolkit* [12]. Based on a widget approach, the framework separates acquisition and presentation of context information from the application that is using it. The focus of this work lays in the automatic inference of higher-level context information from lower-level sensory data. While the Context Toolkit provides a very flexible mechanism for the exchange of context information, the current implementation suffers from a large communication overhead between the different components of the system and a very high complexity.

3   System Architecture

According to Russel and Norvig [13, p.33] anything that can be viewed as perceiving its environment through sensors and acting upon that environment through actuators is considered to be an (intelligent) agent. This paradigm, especially in combination with the distribution of the different functionalities of sensing, recognition, decision making and acting, is also suitable for context-reasoning tasks, as will be shown in the paper. However, the distribution of functionalities requires additional support for, e.g., data management and storage. Furthermore, in ubiquitous environments also security and privacy issues must be taken into account at all design levels.

The motivation for distributing the implementation of logical components is that resources of mobile devices are rather limited. In particular, we are considering the processing power, which most of the reasoning mechanisms require, as well as the accessability of data. Also communication issues, such as availability, communication overhead, and delays, must be taken into account. However, these problems, as well as issues of costs (e.g. monetary, power, etc.) that arise from the distribution and the involved additional communication are not the focus of the paper.

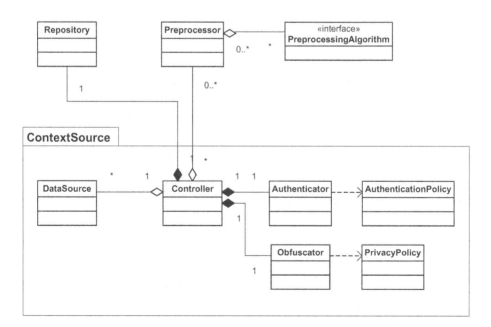

Fig. 1. UML class diagram of the architecture specification

The main focus of the remainder of this section is on the practical consider-ations regarding the implementation of the various supporting tasks and on the sensing mechanisms of the agents. The different logical components and their relationships are illustrated in Fig. 1 and a more thorough discussion about the functionalities of the different components is given in the following subsections. First, Subsection 3.1 discusses the sensing mechanisms. Subsection 3.2 discusses aspects related to the management of data, and Subsection 3.3 discusses how privacy and security issues are taken into account in the architecture. Finally, in Subsection 3.4 we discuss shortly other components of the architecture. A more thorough discussion about the preprocessing functionalities is presetned in Section 4.

3.1   Data Gathering (Sensing)

In our setting the sensing part of the agent corresponds to gathering context data. Typically the sources are very heterogeneous, which is why a flexible gathering mechanism is required. To this end, each *Context Source* component allows to encapsulate a combination of *data source* components, which are responsible for gathering the data from individual sources. The gathered data can be, e.g., raw context data (information from physical sensing-mechanisms such as tempera-ture sensor, GPS-location etc.), data gathered from applications (e.g. calendar entries, user-selected-profile etc.) or data gathered about the behavior of a user. A similar approach for data gathering has also been adopted in the Context Toolkit framework [12]. On the other hand, Mayrhofer [14] considers an alterna-tive approach, where a generic interface for accessing context data is provided only after preprocessing algorithms have been applied to the data.

3.2   Data Management

The responsibility of the *Controller* is to handle tasks related to data manage-ment. First of all, it is responsible for gathering data from the different sources and, furthermore, for distributing the data to different components that have reg-istered for specific context information. Secondly, the Controller must be able to provide other components information about the services it offers.

Different components can register their availabilit and their required services to the Controller, using a subscription interface, which allows to subscribe to a specific data source and a specific data-type. Besides the recipient's address, the interface also allows to specify additional parameters such as the quality of service (e.g. realtime requirement levels), or information regarding the transport mechanisms or protocols. Initially, the Controller is also responsible for provid-ing an interrogation interface, which allows other components to find specific Context Sources. Furthermore, the interface allows to inform the components about requirements that a particular Context Source might have. When new components subscribe to the controller, the security mechanisms are if necessary adapted.

The distribution of data is achieved by matching gathered data with requests made by different subscribed components. According to the subscription, and by using the privacy and security mechanisms, the context information is pushed to the subscribed components, such as the different preprocessors. Our approach, which is fully distributed to the different context sources, differs from the other framework approaches. Namely, the framework proposed by Korpipää et al. [11] uses a central data management structure, the blackboard. On the other hand, the *Context Toolkit* framework is based on polling the individual sensors and it does not offer any support for quality-of-service data publishing. Furthermore, the polling approach easily results in communications overhead. On the other hand, a similar kind of approach has been adopted within the CORTEX middleware [9].

3.3   Privacy and Security

Since gathered context data can often be linked to a particular user, it is necessary to ensure the confidentiality of the information. At the same time it is sometimes desirable to provide basic data to other components, while abstracting, e.g., syntactical information. Both of these tasks are supported by specific components that are linked to the Controller. The behavior of these components is determined by policies that are expressed using a suitable policy language, such as the Web-services policy language (WS-SecurityPolicy) [15] or REI [16].

The confidentiality of information is ensured using an *Authentication* mechanism, which match subscriptions and requests with existing *Authentication* policies. Furthermore, before data is being sent out to other components, the authentication mechanism is consulted and unauthorized requests are rejected.

Different security levels may allow the provisioning of some parts of the contextual information directly, while other parts of the contextual information need to be obfuscated. As an example, components that reside on the same device might be allowed to have access to the user's name and the user's location. On the other hand, components that are located on other devices may receive the user name only in an obfuscated form in order to ensure the user's privacy. The obfuscated data may then be converted back to the user's name, once it has been returned to the user's device. On another level, as described by the *Privacy Policy*, also the user's coordinates may be obfuscated, thus appearing to other components only as random data. A reasoning or preprocessing component however, may find a pattern in this kind of data and return it to the user's device, where it can be converted again to coordinates and used, for instance, by an application.

In most current implementations of context-aware systems, privacy and security aspects are not usually considered at the architectural level, but it is assumed that the used communications protocol and representation format (e.g. XMLDSIG [17] or XMLENC [18]) provide the required support for these tasks. However, although these mechanisms offer support for authentication, they do not support obfuscation of the data. Furthermore, communication protocol level authentication easily results in communication overhead for the devices.

3.4   Other Components

Similar to the Context Source, also other components of the overall framework contain a Controller, Authenticator and an Obfuscator. A preprocessing component, for instance, may use different algorithms to fulfill the task of cleaning different types of context data. The Controller in such a component would then be responsible not only for providing the cleaned, preprocessed data to other components, but it would be primarily responsible for subscribing to the specific Context Sources, to authenticate itself to the source, and match the different policies, transport mechanisms, etc.

In a similar way, a repository mechanism may connect to different sources and store different context information over a longer period of time, in order to provide it later on to different preprocessing, inference or learning mechanisms, or to applications and middleware services.

4   Preprocessing

After an agent has sensed its environment, it needs to form an internal representation. Furthermore, based on this representation, the agent selects which action to perform, i.e. how to react to the state of the environment. However, as in context-aware applications, the sensor measurements often contain errors and some measurements might be missing, the raw signals often need to be preprocessed before reliable inferences can be made.

In general, data preprocessing is defined as any type of processing that is performed on raw data as preparation for further processing. However, as different research fields analyze different kinds of data, also the methods that fall within the scope of this definition are rather different. We adopt a pattern recognition approach and refer to preprocessing as tasks that are done after sensing the data, but before feature extraction methods are applied [19]. Thus for us preprocessing includes, e.g., *outlier removal, normalization* and *handling missing values*. In this section we first discuss shortly the different categories of algorithms after which we discuss technical details about the preprocessor component of Fig. 1.

4.1   Preprocessing Algorithms

Outlier Removal. According to [19], an outlier is defined as a point that lies very far from the mean of the corresponding variable. This kind of points often correspond to erroneous measurements and can be removed from futher analysis. The simplest way to remove outliers is to assume that data is normally distributed and use hypothesis testing techniques to recognize the outliers. However, in general this method has been found not to be very robust.

In the context of time series data, the commonly used methods originate from signal processing. These methods include various filtering methods, such as mean and median filtering and wavelet denoising [20]. Also Bayesian methods have been developed for the task, but their effectiveness depends heavily on how well the used model family fits the data. For a more thorough overview of the different approaches we refer to Quinn and Tesar [20].

Normalization. Normalization is a technique which transforms a set of features to a similar range. Typically normalization is achieved by first estimating the mean $\overline{x}$ and the variance σ^2 of the data points x_i using the well-known Equations

$$\overline{x} = \frac{1}{N} \sum_{i=1}^{N} x_i \text{ and } \sigma^2 = \frac{1}{N-1} \sum_{i=1}^{N} (x_i - \overline{x}_i)^2 \ , \tag{1}$$

where N is the number of data points. Secondly, the original values are transformed using

$$z_{ik} = \frac{x_{ik} - \overline{x}_k}{\sigma_k}. \tag{2}$$

The motivation for this procedure is that according to laws of probability theory, the resulting random variable z_{ik} is approximately normally distributed with a mean value of 0 and a variance of 1. Thus, all the values will have identical mean and variance. If only the mean is subtracted (no division), the procedure is called *centering*.

A special case of normalization is scaling, which attempts to reduce the values to a predefined interval (typically either $[-1, 1]$ or $[0, 1]$). A widely used scaling technique is *sigmoid scaling*, which squashes all values to the interval $[0, 1]$ using a non-linear transformation

$$z_{ik} = \frac{1}{1 + \exp(-x_{ik})} \tag{3}$$

on the original variables. A further refinement is *data transformation* which, instead of trying to force the values to a predefined interval, simply uses some function $g(\cdot)$ on the data points. A common transformation is the logarithmic (scaling) function, which transforms the original variables to a logarithmic scale. The reason why this is commonly used is that the logarithm has certain nice mathematical properties and because small differences are easier to spot on a logarithmic scale.

Handling Missing Values. The most complicated task of preprocessing is how to handle missing values. Unfortunately, most of the techniques are rather heuristically motivated. However, some authors have also developed methods that attempt to discover statistical properties of the underlying distribution of data and infer likely figures for the missing values. A thorough discussion about the different methods can be found for instance in Hand et al. [21].

4.2   Preprocessor Component

As described in Subsection 3.4, the internal implementation of a *Preprocessor* component contains a Controller, Authenticator and an Obfuscator. In addition,

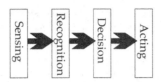

Fig. 2. The processing phases of an intelligent agent

several *Preprocessing Algorithm* components can attach themselves to the Controller of the preprocessor and thus the internal structure of the preprocessor is similar to that of the context source.

An important issue which often complicates the implementation of reusable context reasoning mechanisms is that the representation of data often varies across different domains. In addition, the nature of the data and the way it is handled usually vary, depending on the practical implementation. The architecture copes with the situation by requiring that each preprocessor supports a specific representation which is described in terms of a meta model. The meta model also defines the way data is fed to the preprocessing algorithms. To this end, the preprocessing algorithms are components that encapsulate a specific algorithm for data preprocessing, e.g. one of those mentioned earlier. Furthermore, the algorithms are required to implement a common interface which determines the way in which the data is represented. However, as the framework allows to use various preprocessors, there can also be different interfaces for the different preprocessors and thus for the algorithms.

5   The Overall Framework

In Section 3 we defined an agent as an entity which perceives its environment and acts on its changes through actuators. Thus far we have discussed in detail only the sensing mechanisms and preprocessing. Preprocessing is an intermediate step that takes place before the state of the environment is recognized and decisions are made. Due to page constraints, detailed descriptions about the other phases are out of the scope for the paper, but a short description of each remaining phase is given in this section.

In our setting, the recognition phase of the agent corresponds to interpreting the context of the user, i.e. giving semantically flavored higher-level descriptions about the situation of a user. Also this phase includes several subtasks such as feature extraction, feature (subset) selection, aggregation and classification. In our overall framework these tasks are implemented using entities which are called Context Providers. The internal structure of the components inside a Context Provider is basically very similar to what we have described here. However, the differences arise from the actual reasoning tasks that are performed, the representation of data after each phase and the chaining of the different reasoning tasks, i.e. the order in which they are performed.

In the decision making phase, the goal is to select which actions to perform in the recognized context. Depending on the used applications framework, the decision making phase can be implemented as part of the actual applications and services, or a separate personalization engine can be used. In either case the goal is to determine the most suitable actions to perform in a particular context. These actions include, e.g., the adaptation of a multi-modal user interface and the proactive launch of services.

Finally, the acting phase of the agent is realized by the applications that modify their behavior, based on the actions selected in the decision making phase. Thus in our setting the sensors used to gather data are the sensing mechanism of the agent and the personalized applications and services are the actuators of the agent. Since all these phases of the overall context-reasoning process are covered, we can see that the intelligent agent paradigm provides a suitable framework for implementing intelligent context-aware systems.

6   Conclusions and Future Work

In this paper we have shown the suitability of the intelligent agent paradigm for implementing intelligent context-aware systems. Furthermore, we have focused on a specific part of the overall architecture, which supports distributed preprocessing in ubiquitous environments. In addition, we have also included details about the sensing mechanisms of the agents.

While the interface definition is not yet finalized, a first, non-distributed version of this approach has been implemented, in order to verify the presented approach. Current work concentrates on the refinement of the different interfaces, as well as on the implementation of the presented structures in such a way that they can provide the framework for a distributed system.

References

1. Weiser, M.: The computer for the twenty-first century. Scientific American **265** (1991) 66–75
2. Dey, A.K., Abowd, G.D.: Towards a better understanding of context and context-awareness. Technical Report GIT-GVU-99-22, College of Computing, Georgia Institute of Technology (1999)
3. Nurmi, P., Floréen, P.:   Reasoning in context-aware systems.   http:// www.cs.helsinki.fi/u/ptnurmi/papers/contextreasoning.pdf (2004) HIIT position paper.
4. Moran, T.P., Dourish, P.: Introduction to special issue on context-aware computing. Human-Computer Interaction (HCI) **16** (2001) 87 – 96
5. Winograd, T.: Architectures for context. Human-Computer Interaction (HCI) **16** (2001) 401 – 419
6. Wallbaum, M., Dornbusch, P.: Design considerations for a platform supporting location-aware services. In: Proceedings of Multimedia, Internet Video Technologies (MIV). (2001)

7. Yau, S.S., Karim, F., Wang, Y., Wang, B., Gupta, S.K.: Reconfigurable context-sensitive middleware for pervasive computing. Pervasive Computing **1** (2002) 33–40
8. Yau, S.S., Karim, F.: An adaptive middleware for context-sensitive communications for real-time applications in ubiquitous computing environments. Real-Time Systems **26** (2004) 29–61
9. Duran-Limon, H.A., Blair, G.S., Friday, A., Grace, P., Samartzidis, G., Sivaharan, T., WU, M.: Context-aware middleware for pervasive and ad hoc environments. http://www.comp.lancs.ac.uk/computing/research/mpg/projects/cortex/archive/dmrg publications/cortexMiddleware.pdf (2003)
10. Siegemund, F.: A context-aware communication platform for smart objects. In Ferscha, A., Mattern, F., eds.: Proceedings of the 2nd International Conference on Pervasive Computing (PERVASIVE). Number 3001 in LNCS, Springer-Verlag, Berlin (2004) 69 – 86
11. Korpipää, P., Mäntyjärvi, J., Kela, J., Keränen, H., Malm, E.J.: Managing context information in mobile devices. Pervasive Computing **2** (2003) 42 – 51
12. Dey, A.K., Abowd, G.D., Salber, D.: A conceptual framework and a toolkit for supporting the rapid prototyping of context-aware applications. Human-Computer Interaction (HCI) **16** (2001) 97 – 166
13. Russel, S., Norvig, P.: Artificial Intelligence: A Modern Approach. First edn. Prentice Hall (1995)
14. Mayrhofer, R.: An Architecture for Context Prediction. PhD thesis, University of Linz (2004)
15. Della-Libera G. et al.: Web Services Security Policy. http://www-128.ibm.com/developerworks/webservices/library/ws-secpol/index.html (2002)
16. Kagal, L., Finin, T., Joshi, A.: A policy language for a pervasive computing environment. In: Proceedings of the IEEE 4th International Workshop on Policies for Distributed Systems and Networks. (2003) 63 – 76
17. World Wide Web Consortium: XML Digital Signature. http://www.w3.org/TR/xmldsig-core/ (2002)
18. World Wide Web Consortium: XML Encryption syntax and processing. http://www.w3.org/TR/2002/REC-xmlenc-core-20021210/ (2002)
19. Theodoridis, S., Koutroumbas, K.: Pattern Recognition. Academic Press (2004)
20. Quinn, A., Tesar, L.: A survey of techniques for preprocessing in high dimensional data clustering. In: Proceedings of the Cybernetic and Informatics Eurodays. (2000)
21. Hand, D., Mannila, H., Smyth, P.: Principles of Data Mining. MIT Press (2001)

Meta-reasoning Methods
for Agent's Intention Modelling

Michal Pěchouček, Jan Tožička, and Vladimír Mařík

Gerstner Laboratory, Agent Technology Group,
Czech Technical University in Prague
pechouc@labe.felk.cvut.cz

Abstract. Intention modelling in self-interested and adversarial communities of agents is a challenging issue. This contribution discusses the role of modelling and meta-reasoning in intention modelling. The formal model of deductive and inductive meta-reasoning is presented and supported by experimental implementations. This research has been motivated by the problem of intention detection in semi-collaborative multi-agent system for OOTW (Operation Other Than War).

1   Introduction

This paper presents a specific technology based on meta-agents and meta-reasoning for detecting agents private and semi-private knowledge, intentions and future commitments.

1.1   Domain Settings

This research has been motivated by a specific domain of the **war avoidance operations** such as peace-keeping, peace-enforcing, non-combat evacuation or disaster relief operations. Unlike in classical war operations, where the technology of decision making is strictly hierarchical, **operations other than war** (OOTW) are very likely to be based on cooperation of a number of different, quasi-volunteered, vaguely organized groups of people, non-governmental organizations (NGO's), institutions providing humanitarian aid, but also army troops and official governmental initiatives.

Collaborative, unlike hierarchical, approach to operation planning allows greater deal of flexibility and dynamics in grouping optimal parties playing an active role in the operation. New entities shall be free to join autonomously and involve themselves in planning with respect to their capabilities. Therefore any organization framework must be essentially "open". OOTW have, according to [1], multiple perspective on plan evaluation as there does not need to be one shared goal or a single metrics of the operation (such as political, economical, humanitarian). From the same reason, the goals of entities involved in a possible coalition may be in conflict. Even if the community members share the same goal, it can be easily misunderstood due to different cultural backgrounds.

The main reason why we can hardly plan operations involving different NGO's by a central authority results from their **reluctance to provide information** about their

V. Gorodetsky, J. Liu, and V.A. Skormin (Eds.): AIS-ADM 2005, LNAI 3505, pp. 134–148, 2005.

intentions, goals and resources. Consequently, besides difficulties related to planning and negotiation we have to face the problems how to assure sharing the detailed information. Many institutions will be ready to share resources and information within some well specified community, whereas they will refuse to register their full capabilities and plans with a central planning system and to follow centralized commands. They may agree to participate in executing a plan, in forming of which they played an active role. In our interpretation, an agent is a complex, organized entity (representing a NGO, humanitarian organization, army troop, etc.) playing an active role in the OOTW planning. A multi-agent system consists of a number of agents that group themselves in various, temporary coalitions (each solving a specific mission/part of the mission).

1.2   CPlanT

Within a specific AFOR research effort [2] there has been suggested a concept of a multi-agent system (we will refer to the system as CPlanT) that allows NGO actors to plan collaboration patterns autonomously, without any need to share their sensitive information centrally.

In CPlant, the key idea is based on structuring the agent community into **alliances** - sets of agents that agreed to share some of their private information and to cooperate eventually. Agents within a single alliance share *social knowledge*, that is stored in the *acquaintance models* [2] of the individual agents. As a result of a humanitarian conflict, the agents are trying to form a **coalition** that will fulfill the specific **mission**. Forming of alliances and coalitions is driven by agents private and semi-private knowledge. Agents are motivated to prevent disclosure of this knowledge. Our motivation was to disclose and detect the agents private and semi-private knowledge.

2   Decision Making in CPlanT

We will work with two key cooperation structures that will be explained below: alliance and coalitions.

Agents can create a **coalition** – $\chi(m)$, a set of agents, which agreed to cooperate on a single, well-specified mission – m. The coalition is temporary and dissolves upon completion of the mission. When forming a coalition agents need to propose collaboration, bid, and negotiate. During these activities substantial part of agents private knowledge discloses.

In order to optimize the amount of the disclosed private knowledge and to create an acceptably good coalition in a reasonable time, the community of object agents is partitioned into several disjoint groups called **alliances** – λ. All agents in an alliance agree to cooperate together, even if they can refuse to participate in a coalition allocated for a given mission.

In an ideal case, the alliance members solve the requested mission exclusively within the alliance. In cases when this is not possible, they need to subcontract part of the mission to alliance nonmembers (members of different alliances). All participating agents are still members of the coalition. Within the report we will refer the concept of **team** when we partition the coalition according to alliance membership. The coalition members from one alliance are regarded as members of the same team.

Agents' knowledge has been classified as (i)

- **private** – $K_{pr}(A)$, the piece of knowledge that is not accessible to any other agent
- **public** – $K_p(A)$, knowledge that is widely accessible to all agents and
- **semi-private** – $K_s(A)$, knowledge accessible reciprocally to alliance members only.

For formal definition of these classes of knowledge see [2]. This concept is very closely related to the concept of agent's neighborhood [3].

2.1 Forming a Coalition

In the CPlanT coalition planning system, the agents try to collaboratively form coalition that will work together on a specific mission. The **mission** specifies properties of a requested humanitarian operation in terms of a type of an operation (e.g. natural disaster, conflict, ...), severity, location, and primarily a list of requested services (food provision, shelters provision, ...).

$$m = \langle \texttt{id}, \texttt{type}, \texttt{degree}, \texttt{location}, \{\tau_i\} \rangle \tag{1}$$

For the mission – m to be accomplished the corresponding services – $\{\tau\}$ need to be implemented. The coalition is thus a collection of agents who commit themselves to participation in the mission by providing the requested services.

Once there is a request for mission operation, not all agents in the community are asked to form coalitions. Relevant agents subscribe the scenario map for notification about disasters and respective missions. Those agents, given the estimates of available resources of peer alliance members, construct **coalition proposal** – $\chi^*(m)$. The coalition proposal consist of the list of possible coalition members, the overall objective function of the coalition (e.g. price, delivery date, ...) and the list of required services that cannot be provided from within the alliance.

$$\chi^*(m) = \{A_i\}, \tag{2}$$

where an agent A_i is expected to provide a service τ_i of the mission m. Here we assume that a service is non-decomposable and can be implemented exclusively by a singular agent. Let us consider functions $\mathsf{leader}(\chi^*(m))$, $\mathsf{price}(\chi^*(m))$, $\mathsf{due}(\chi^*(m))$ and $\mathsf{to\_do}(\chi^*(m))$ for giving properties of the proposal. These properties give an objective function that optimizes the coalition proposal selection process.

After the coalition proposal is specified the members of $\chi^*(m)$ enter a rather complicated negotiation process (within and outside the alliance that the coalition leader is a member of) in order to fix a joint commitment that will ultimately form the coalition $\chi(m)$. The coalition that will cover a specific mission is constricted in three steps:

1. **Coalition Leader Selection.** Subscribed agents then inform each other about objective function of their proposals (a function of $\mathsf{price}(\chi^*(m))$, $\mathsf{due}(\chi^*(m))$ and $(|\mathsf{to\_do}(\chi^*(m))|)$ and compete one another. Under an assumption that the agents are true telling, they allocate (using a simple bidding strategy) a **coalition leader** – an agent who covers the most within its own alliance (the most preferred criterion) and with the shortest delivery time. In our experiment we have allowed only a limited number of agents to be subscribed for a single location in the map. As the bidding strategy is based on broadcasting we cannot easily scale this solution for higher number of agents.

2. **In-alliance Coalition Formation.** The coalition leader tries to form a part of the coalition from his alliance members. Given the knowledge about the peer alliance members, the coalition leader directly requests the agents for (i) participating in a mission that will take place in specific place and will be coordinated by the specific coalition leader and (ii) providing the required resources. While the coalition leader knows about resources availability, it is not aware of agents' private knowledge that may restrict it to work under certain agents' leadership (eg. army unit) or a specific place (e.g. place with major population of muslims).

3. **Inter-alliance Coalition Formation.** Coalition leader tries to subcontract – using the contract net protocol – other agents to contribute by services to the remaining requested services. In order to lower down the communication burden we will not want the coalition leader to do complete broadcasting. Instead only one member of each alliance (for simplicity we will refer in this report to this agent as a team-leader) is asked for the resources on behalf of the entire alliance. Team leader provides the coalition leader with a suggested service provider(s). Upon an approval from the coalition leader, the team leader is asked to request the resources from the suggested provider(s) in the same manner as above.

2.2   Goals of Meta-reasoning

When re-constructing agents decision-making models we are interested in (i) how a coalition proposal can be created and (ii) how the actual coalition can be negotiated. Therefore, we have to monitor and reason about a coalition formation process (forming $\chi^*(m)$, answering a question of a type '*what-coalition-will-be-proposed?*') and find out whether agents will eventually provide requested services (forming $\chi(m)$, answering a question of a type '*what-coalition-will-the-agents-finally-approve?*').

Semiprivate Knowledge: The coalition formation process is given by negotiation capabilities of the coalition leader (that takes care for what can be provided from within the alliance) and team leaders (who suggest service providers form outside of the alliance). In order to understand coalition/team leader decision making (how $\chi^*(m)$ can be constructed) we need to acquire knowledge that the coalition leader knows about the resources of the other agents. Provided that the meta-agent can access the copies of agent messages, this task is easy, as this information is maintained by means of the inter-alliance communication. Given the accessible semi-private knowledge the meta-agent can reconstruct easily the phase 1 (Coalition Leader Selection) and phase 2 (In-alliance Coalition Formation) of the coalition formation process.

Private Knowledge: For understanding the decision model of an alliance member (how we can arrive from $\chi^*(m)$ to $\chi(m)$, in other words to know whether the agent will provide the requested services) we need to identify its private knowledge that specifies primarily agents collaboration preferences and restrictions. This piece of knowledge cannot be simply re-constructed from the communication exchange. It need to be identified by the deductive or inductive meta-reasoning process.

Let us assume that we work with a multi-agent system where agents communicate using FIPA-like communication protocols. Detecting agents' private knowledge is based on observation of the REQUEST interaction protocol. An agent replies to a request message by an accept message if it agrees to provide the requested services for the mission while it replies with a refuse message if he does not like to be part of the proposed coalition.

3 Meta-reasoning and Meta-agents

We refer to meta-reasoning as an agent's capability to reason about the knowledge, mental states and reasoning processes of other members of the multi-agent community. We will refer to **object agents** which are subject of another agent's meta-reasoning process. We will refer to **meta-agent** as to any agent with the meta-reasoning ability.

There are different classes of meta-reasoning tasks we may need to solve in multi-agent system. In the case of **collaborative** environment the object agents are aware of being monitored, which is what they agree with and support. In **non-collaborative** environment the object-agents do not want to be monitored and do not support the meta-reasoning process. While in the former case the meta-agent may work with e.g. copies of communicated messages, in the latter case more speculative techniques need to be used (e.g. intruding agents [4]), monitoring the environment [5]).

Very often there is only one meta-agent that monitors the entire community. Alternatively we may have a **team of meta-agents** that monitor different group of agents (e.g. defined geographically), monitor the community behavior at different times, or monitor different aspect of agent's functionality. An appropriate mechanisms for knowledge fusion [6] need to be designed.

Even more complicated meta-reasoning process need to be designed if it is expected to be part of the **object agent's reasoning**. The algorithms need to be (i) light-weight so that they do not slow down the primary operation of the object agents and (ii) open to reasoning about mainly the community of agents where the meta-agent is a part of.

4 Abstract Meta-agent Architecture

The central point of the meta-agent's operation is maintenance and exploitation of the model of the community. This model has to be expressed in an appropriate language of adequate granularity. As any other high-level knowledge structure, the model can be represented **implicitly**, (e.g. piece of procedural program, characteristic function or set of rules) or **explicitly**, as a logical theory that consists of the true facts that the meta-agent knows about the object agents. In this work, we suppose that the behavior of agents is monotone, i.e. it does not change over the time. The model can be treated in two possible ways. It can be either maintained by

- **deductive reasoning** that maintains the model containing only formulae that logically follow from the monitored information (e.g. the model will be consistent with future possible events), or
- **inductive reasoning** techniques that may produce an *approximative model* that includes e.g. generalization formulae, that may prove to be in conflict with a future possible event.

The former type of reasoning produces an exact and 'safe' model of the community. The latter type of reasoning may provide more information while it can misclassify. In the following section we will be explaining the concept of deductive meta-reasoning using explicit representation.

4.1   Community Model

Our meta-agent works with the typed 1st order language with one of the types corresponding to agents. We say that a formula ϕ refers to an agent A if ϕ contains a predicate with an argument A. Any formula ϕ which refers to the agent A and which is true (from the point of view of the meta-agent) is our approximation of the meta-agent's belief about A - this property will be abbreviated $\beta_A(\varphi)$ in the rest of the paper. Similarly, if θ is a set of agents, let $\beta_\theta(\varphi)$ mean that ϕ is true and it refers to some agents from θ. All true formulas referring to any subset of the agents' community are denoted as belief formulas in our context. Obviously, the explicit model of the community maintained by the meta-agent A^m will be defined as a collection of such a belief-formulae:

$$\underline{m}(\mu^+(A^m)) = \left\{ \varphi \mid \exists\, \theta \subseteq \mu^+(A^m) : \beta_\theta(\varphi) \right\}, \tag{3}$$

where $\mu^+(A^m)$ specifies the set of object-agents (defined in [7]).

Generally we have three basic types of belief formulae in the explicit model of the community. For any reasonable manipulation with the model we need to specify the relevant default properties of the object-level community. We will assume default properties to be always true and to be known to all agents before any event in the community happens. Let us call these formulae **background-belief-formulae** and denote them by the predicate $gb(\varphi)$. The meta-agent A^m is expected to store all these formulae in the knowledge structure referred to as the **background-belief-base** – gbb, formally:

$$\forall\varphi : gb(\varphi) \Leftrightarrow \varphi \in gbb. \tag{4}$$

In the machine learning domain this knowledge is often referred to as the *background knowledge*. In the most transparent case, this is a theory in first order logic.

Besides, we have facts that were acquired by the meta-agent monitoring capabilities and they very often correspond to the events that happened in the community. Such a fact is referred to as a **event-belief-formulae**. Let us denote such a formula that represents an event happening in the time t by the predicate $eb_t(\varphi)$ stored in meta-agent's **event-belief-base** – $ebb_t(\mu^+(A^m))$, formally:

$$ebb_t(\mu^+(A^m)) = \{\varphi \mid \exists t_i \leq t : eb_{t_i}(\varphi)\} \tag{5}$$

In the following text, we will denote evn_t a formula φ such a $eb_t(\varphi)$.

Finally we have the **assumed-belief-formulae** (denoted as $ab_t(\varphi)$ that are products of the meta-reasoning process facts that happened in the community. In the same way, these are stored in the meta-agent **assumed-belief-base** – $abb_t(\mu^+(A^m))$, that is formalized similarly to equation 5.

Using the explicit representation we will want at any time instance the meta-agent's model of the object level community to consist of these three knowledge structures:

$$\underline{m}_t(\mu^+(A^m)) = gbb \cup ebb_t(\mu^+(A^m)) \cup abb_t(\mu^+(A^m)). \tag{6}$$

The meta-reasoning process in multi-agent system is built upon three mutually interconnected computational processes (figure 1):

1. **monitoring** – process that makes sure that the meta-agent knows the most it can get from monitoring the community of object agents. This process builds the base of the m – model of the community and implements the introspective integrity (in the sense of [8]).
2. **reasoning** – this process manipulates the model of the community so that true facts (other than monitored) may be revealed. Within the reasoning phase, the meta-agent tries to maintain validity of the model.
3. **community revision** – a mechanism for influencing operation of the object agents' community. In this phase, the meta-agent may also affect the operation of the community in order to improve the meta-reasoning process.

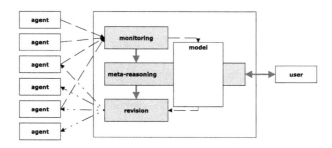

Fig. 1. Meta-Reasoning Architecture – A Process View

This architecture resembles similarities to the **information fusion architecture** [6] that has been developed within the support of AFRL. Monitoring corresponds to the level 1: *object identification*. The relevant data that can be acquired from the community shall be acquired first. The reasoning process implements levels 2 of the fusion architectures – *situation awareness*. The concept of meta-reasoning integrates various reasoning strategies that may be used, besides situation awareness for the aspects of the level 3 of the fusion architectures – *intent modelling*. The concept of revision phase is an analogy to the level 4 of the information fusion architecture – *process refinement*. In this phase we want to update or completely change the behavior of the agents according to the relevant findings of the reasoning process.

The meta-reasoning operation can be carried out in three different phases:

- **init***time*: initialization time when the meta-agent starts to reason about the system before it receives any event from the community,
- **revise***time*: the instance of the time when an event in the community happens and the community model is automatically revised and
- **inspect***time*: when the user (or other agent possibly) queries the model in order to find out about truthfulness of the goal hypotheses.

Balancing the amount of computational load in the **revise***time* and the **inspect***time* is really crucial. The proper design depends on the required meta-reasoning functionality. While for visualization and intrusion detection the most of computation is required in the **revise***time*, for explanation, simulation and prediction an important part of computational processes will be carried out in the **inspect***time* (for details see [7]).

4.2 Community Model Revision

Let us introduce the **community model revision** operator – ⊎, that is carried out in the **revise***time* exclusively. The community model revision represents the change of the model $\underline{m}_t$ in the time t with respect to the new formula evn_t that describes an event in the object-level community θ (we assume that $\theta = \mu^+(A^m)$):

$$\underline{m}_t(\theta) \uplus evn_t \rightarrow \underline{m}_{t+1}(\theta) \tag{7}$$

There are different types of events that initiate the community model revision process in the **revise***time*. We talk primarily about initiating a contract-net-protocol, team allocation request, accepting or rejection of the team allocation request, informing about actual resources, etc.

In the case of deductive meta-reasoning, we may distinguish between two marginal effects of the community revision operation – $\uplus^{max}$ and $\uplus^{min}$ as follows:

$$\underline{m}_t(\theta) \uplus^{max} evn_t = \{\varphi | \underline{m}_t(\theta) \cup \{evn_t\} \vdash \varphi\} \tag{8}$$

$$\underline{m}_t(\theta) \uplus^{min} evn_t = \underline{m}_t(\theta) \cup \{evn_t\}, \tag{9}$$

where φ is a formula.

The $\uplus^{max}$ operator revises the model so that it contains all possible true facts that logically follow from the original model – $\underline{m}_t(\theta)$ combined with the new event – evn_t. The $\uplus^{min}$ operator only appends the new formula to the model. In many cases, the $\uplus^{max}$ operator is hard to achieve as the resulting model may be infinite – we introduce such a model as an abstract marginal concept. The model that results from the $\uplus^{min}$ model revision is be always a subset of the model constructed by $\uplus^{max}$ operator.

When designing the community model revision process, we seek such an operation $\uplus$ that

$$\underline{m}_t(\theta) \uplus^{max} evn_t \supseteq \underline{m}_t(\theta) \uplus evn_t \supseteq \underline{m}_t(\theta) \uplus^{min} evn_t \tag{10}$$

The closer our operation gets to $\uplus^{min}$ the faster is the model revision process and more complex should be the computational process in the **inspect***time*. The closer we are to $\uplus^{max}$ the easier should be the query process while the revision process is getting really complex.

The background belief base gbb does not change in the time. Only the $ebb_t(\theta)$ changes if the community revision operator $\uplus^{min}$ is used, while both $ebb_t(\theta)$ and $abb_t(\theta)$ change in the time if another community revision operator is used.

4.3 Community Model Inspection

During the **inspect***time* (in any time t), the computational process of **community model inspection** provides the user (or other agent) the reply for a queried question. We introduce an operator ↬ for model inspection, which confirms the goal formula $goal_t$ if it is provable from the theory $\underline{m}_t(\theta)$, refutes the goal if $\neg goal_t$ can be proved. If the considered goal formula contains existentially quantified variables, the reply can also contain appropriate candidates for possible substitution.

In the case of deductive meta-reasoning, the **minimal** version of community model inspection process corresponds directly to checking occurrence of the goal formula within the model. The relevant formula can be retrieved from the model with no further reasoning.

$$\underline{m}_t(\theta) \leftadmin^{\min} goal \rightarrow \begin{cases} yes & \text{if } goal \in \underline{m}_t(\theta), \\ no & \text{if } \neg goal \in \underline{m}_t(\theta), \\ unsure & \text{otherwise.} \end{cases} \qquad (11)$$

In order to be able to use the minimal version of the model inspection in the **inspect**time, we need the maximal (or close to maximal) model revision ($\uplus^{\max}$) in the **revise**time of the meta-reasoning life-cycle.

If the reasoning triggered by the event (in **revise**time) has not produced the queried formula, the inspection process will be a more complex operation than simply parsing the existing model. The meta-agent is expected to employ reasoning in order to find out whether the requested goal formula logically follows from the model:

$$\underline{m}_t(\theta) \leftadmin goal \rightarrow \begin{cases} yes & \text{if } \underline{m}_t(\theta) \vdash goal \\ no & \text{if } \underline{m}_t(\theta) \vdash \neg goal \\ unsure & \text{otherwise.} \end{cases} \qquad (12)$$

4.4   Properties of the Model

The agents in the community can be represented not only as a collection of logical facts but also by an abstract decision making algorithm ψ_A which specifies how an agent will react to requests. Therefore, the model can be represented by an appropriate approximation ψ_A^* of the object agent's decision algorithm ψ_A.

The problem of revealing ψ_A^* can be transformed to the problem of learning unknown function, e.g. in the words of machine learning. Every event evn_t is decomposed into a pair containing the request for specific service τ_t and object agent's reaction: $evn_t = [\tau_t, \psi(\tau_t)]$, where τ_t also specifies question that can be answered by learned ψ_A^* algorithm. Therefore, we use the history of all prior events stored in the event belief base as a *training set*. It is stored in the following format:

$$ebb_t = \{[\tau_i, \psi(\tau_i)]\}_{0 \le i \le t} \qquad (13)$$

The ebb_t event belief base and gbb background belief base are stored in constructed model $\underline{m}_t$.

Model Decomposability. Let the community model be defined as in eqn. 3. Suppose, that it is possible to decompose the model $\underline{m}(\theta)$ of the community θ to the models of individual agents $A_i \in \theta$. We say that such model is **decomposable**:

$$\underline{m}(\theta) = \bigcup_{A_i \in \theta} \underline{m}(\{A_i\}), \qquad (14)$$

where $\underline{m}(A_i)$ denotes a meta-reasoning model of the singular agent A_i. If such a decomposition is not possible, we call the model **undecomposable**. This is the case of *emergent behavior* – collective behavior of agents that can not be intentionally initiated by a single agent. In both cases, the models contain the same information, but every type is suited to a different task of meta-reasoning.

Model Revision Operators. We shall distinguish between two basic types of model updating: $\uplus^T$ and $\uplus^G$. The $\uplus^T$ is implementing deductive meta-reasoning, i.e. it tries to generate all true facts about the object-level community and stores them in the model $\underline{m}^T(\theta)$. Then, when the goal formula is asked, the $\looparrowright$ operator tries to find out whether this formula or its negation is implied by the $\underline{m}^T(\theta)$ model. The $\uplus^G$ tries to find out more general rule which distinguishes positive and negative events, i.e. it implements inductive meta-reasoning. This rule is then evaluated for a given goal when the $\looparrowright$ operator is used. This rule can be found out by e.g. a machine learning algorithm.

In this work, the $\uplus^T$ operator is represented by the resolution principle and the $\uplus^G$ operator is implemented using inductive logic programming. The version space algorithm creates hypotheses in the form of $\underline{m}^G(\theta)$, but by working with all possible hypotheses it creates $\underline{m}^T(\theta)$ model.

5   Meta-reasoning Implementation

Three different meta-reasoning methods have been implemented:

Theorem Proving: Deductive meta-reasoning has been implemented by the resolution principle [9]. All the logical formulae, that describe the model $\underline{m}_t^{AR}$, are supposed to be encoded as a conjunction of clauses, where each is a disjunction of literals – CNF (conjunctive normal form). The explicitly represented model is divided at all times into two $\underline{m}_t^{min}(\theta)$ and $\underline{m}_t^S(\theta)$. The former part of the model is maintained using the $\uplus^{min}$ while the latter is maintained by $\uplus^{max}$. We have used the *shortening strategy* [4] for implementing $\uplus^{max}$. This strategy generates a new clause only if the length of the new clause (here the length equals to the number of the symbols in the clause) is smaller than one of its parents clauses. Forward and backward subsumption techniques [10] are included within the community revision process. We will refer to this process as $\uplus^n$ operator, where n determines the amount of clauses in the initial model maintained by the operation $\uplus^{max}$. The n paraments of the $\uplus^n$ abstractly characterize the completeness of revised model, and manipulates computational resources requirements in the **revise**time and **inspect**time respectively.

Version Space: One of the biggest problems in implementation of the explicit models is the representation of all created facts with a possibility to search trough them quickly, because the space of all facts logically following from the events could be large and even infinite. One possible solution is to work only with the implicit representation – representation of hypotheses about the object agent's decision making algorithm. Therefore, we are faced with an inverse task to the agent's decision making process described above (section 4.4): *Assuming the knowledge of gbb, identify ψ_A by observing agent A's decisions.* An inductive meta-reasoning have been implemented by the **version**

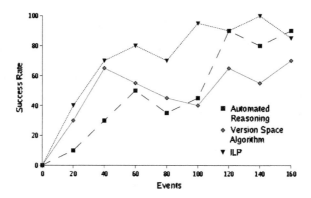

Fig. 2. Success of Prediction

space algorithm. During the community model revision phase (**revise***time*), we can create hypotheses ψ_A^* about the agent's A decision making algorithm ψ_A. A good way to manipulate the space of hypotheses is provided by a version space algorithm (VS) [11], where all consistent hypotheses are represented by two sets containing the most general and the most specific hypotheses.

Inductive Logic Programming: Implementation of inductive meta-reasoning can be also accomplished by means of an ILP system [12], whose input is actual object agent's model $\underline{\mathrm{m}}_t^{\mathsf{ILP}}$ in the time t: $\underline{\mathrm{m}}_t^{\mathsf{ILP}} = \mathrm{gbb} \cup \mathrm{ebb}_t$. The event belief base ebb_t contains history of A's decisions up to the instant t. Each item in the history is a pair $[\tau_t, \psi(\tau_t)]$. The output of the ILP algorithm is then a hypothesis ψ_A^*, which approximates the unknown correct ψ_A. Once, we have the hypothesis ψ_A^*, we can use it to predict A's decision during model inspection. The hypothesis is expressed in the programming language Prolog. In our implementation the community inspection phase has been implemented by $\biguplus^{\min}$. Before the $\underline{\mathrm{m}}_t^{\mathsf{ILP}}$ can reply given query, it is necessary to induce a hypothesis ψ_A^*. This is done in the in the **inspect***time*. The induced hypothesis ψ_A^* is used to answer the query goal_t by performing a resolution operation.

6   Experiments

By observing the inter-agent communication, the meta-agent was employed to identify agent's private knowledge (e.g. never work with partners form the specific country, always prefer coalitions under governmental coordination, etc.). A large number of experiments has been performed in order to verify used technologies, algorithms and proposed improvements.

A training set of the specific missions has been defined and sent to the CPlanT multi-agent system. The meta-agent tried to predict whether the object agent will accept or refuse a possible team allocation request.

See the graph in Figure 2 for studying how well the meta-reasoning methods performed at the time of learning. The y axis specifies the number of events predicted successfully. The complement to these numbers says how many times the method replied *unsure*. The exception is the ILP method, that gave also 3 % of incorrect prediction (i.e. replied *yes* instead of *no* or otherwise). The x axis gives the number of events that happened in the community (and the size of training set). ILP meta-reasoning operators outperform the classical theorem proving technique and version space algorithm. An interesting observation is that VS operates well with small number data – up to 60 events, and with time if performs much worse than ILP. Resolution based meta-reasoning operator does not perform very well with small number of data while with about 140 events it provides good performance.

The following table illustrates an average behavior of the meta-reasoning methods after the learning phase.

Resolution	Version Space	ILP
54 %	54 %	79 %

The inductive logic programming method seems to reach the best results due to the ability to generalize knowledge via the induction operation. On the other hand there ILP gave several incorrect predictions. There are no incorrect predictions if we use the automated reasoning method based on the deduction operation. The version space method does not generate incorrect predictions although the induction operation is used here, because it stores all possible hypothesis consistent with the previous events. The results of the automated reasoning (without the support of the reasoning simulation) and version space methods are similar. The version space method uses the same background knowledge as the automated reasoning method. While the automated reasoning method uses background knowledge in explicit form, version space method uses background knowledge in implicit form (see section 4).

6.1 Model Revision Operators

Using automated reasoning as meta-reasoning method we can implement full scale of $\uplus$ model revision operators as defined in equation 10. We will denote them as $\uplus^n$, where N indicates the number of ground belief formulae (from total of 249 formulae) in **revise***time* used to deduce all *relevant* consequences of new event evn_t. The choice of ground belief formulae is driven by a threshold of complexity – this process is described in details in [4]. There you can also find how we choose the *relevant consequences* in our domain. Having the scale of $\uplus^n$ operators we can choose the best one for our meta-agent. Generally, it holds that the more queries come per one event the closer should be the chosen $\uplus^n$ operator to $\uplus^{\max}$, and vice versa. Because more complex process in **revise***time* can reduce the time response in **inspect***time*.

In this experiment, we have compared following revision operators: $\uplus^{\min}$, $\uplus^7$, $\uplus^{73}$, $\uplus^{90}$, $\uplus^{235}$. The following table shows the number of generated clauses in the **revise***time* and in the **inspect***time*. This experiment shows that the choice of revision operator $\uplus^n$ can significantly reduce the process in **inspect***time*. But in the case, that the model contains large number of formulae, **inspect***time* can be negatively affected by searching and maintaining this model.

Model	Generated Clauses	
Revision	Model	Model
Operator	Revision	Inspection
$\uplus^{min}$	0	119498
$\uplus^7$	451	96451
$\uplus^{73}$	655	74927
$\uplus^{90}$	821	74864
$\uplus^{235}$	1553	12183

7   Analysis

As has been shown, all chosen methods can be used to support meta-reasoning in our domain. In this section, we will try to generalize our results and experiences gained during our research.

Uncertainty of Predictions. Generally, when we do not necessarily need correct replies and we prefer a prediction that is only expected to be good, we can use meta-agent using ILP that gave the best results even if, in several cases, the reply was incorrect. Otherwise, if the correctness of the prediction is a must, we can use either theorem proving or version space algorithm.

Background Knowledge. The choice of the appropriate meta-reasoning method depends also on the completeness of the background knowledge. For version space algorithm, it's almost necessary to know the whole background knowledge. When we use theorem proving methods, we get only replies logically following given knowledge, therefore all replies keep correct even if we reduce the completeness of background knowledge. ILP seems to be the less dependent on the background knowledge. This method need only minimal amount of background knowledge but the more knowledge is specified the more replies should be correct.

Scalability. With increasing complexity of the background knowledge and event belief formulae we can face several problems. Theorem proving methods can run out of computational resources and the method will more often reply *unsure*. The model in version space can reach memory resources limits. Time complexity of the model inspection phase will be also partially affected, but it should not be serious. The ILP method can be affected mainly during the model construction, while the time necessary for model inspection should be also partially affected only.

Meta-reasoning on Object-Agent Level. To be able to carry out the meta-reasoning process within every agent, we need to have some kind of light-weight meta-reasoning that will not very much affect efficiency of the agent primary decision making. The theorem proving method does not seem to be very appropriate due to its computational resources (time especially) requirements. Both ILP and version space algorithm can be used in this case. ILP can be further made light-weight by reduction of background theory.

There is another important requirement on such a meta-reasoning method – it should support agent's reflection, because a meta-agent using it has to reason about himself and his impact on the community.

Modalities of Object-Agent Level. Even though very simple behavior can be modelled by first order predicate logic (FOPL), in realistic scenarios the model needs to be extended by several types of modalities. The possibility of adding such modalities is explored mainly in automated reasoning domain: *modal logics* [?], *dynamic logics* [14], *temporal logics* [15]. While the theoretical background of these systems is well investigated, they have not been much used because of the complexity of prove searching process.

8   Conclusions

In this article, we have presented a formal model of the meta-agent and showed how three different AI methods are appropriate for the meta-reasoning process. Experiments showed that the ILP-based meta-reasoning combines advantages of both inductive and deductive reasoning.

Current meta-reasoning agent is based on several assumptions that are not met in many real domains. Firstly, the meta-agent has been asked to answer *yes-no* questions. But we might be interested in predicting a value from a more complex domain, e.g. real value function. In some cases, several different replies can be correct. Indeed, one can be more appropriate than the other, therefore we need some method to evaluate them and to choose the best one. We also intend to investigate possibilities how to importee the whole of the meta-reasoning process, e.g. by cooperation of different meta-reasoning methods. Quality of meta-reasoning (success rate) can be also increased by using e.g. default behavior (i.e. how the most of agents behave in similar situation). A lot of domains contains agents adapting their behavior over the time, reasoning about such agents should use e.g. truth maintenance system to overcome the conflicts in object agent's behavior. At the same time the language for meta-reasoning need to be extended by model operators (e.g. agent belief) for this purpose. Besides pure meta-reasoning we plan also to generalize the monitoring process. In current version it relies on sniffed messages only but we could use other accessible information sources based e.g. monitoring the environment.

Acknowledgement

The project work has been co-funded by European Office for Aerospace Research and Development (EORD) Air Force Research Laboratory (AFRL) – contract number: FA8655-02-M-4056, Office of Naval Research (ONR) – award number: N00014-03-1-0292 and by the Grant No. LN00B096 of the Ministry of Education, Youth and Sports of the Czech Republic.

References

1. Walker, E. C. T.: Coalition Planning for Operations Other Than War. Panel Report: Workshop at AIAI, Edinburgh (1999)
2. Pěchouček, M. and Mařík, V. and Bárta, J.: A Knowledge-Based Approach to Coalition Formation. IEEE Intelligent Systems **17** (2002) 17–25

3. Mařík, V., Pěchouček, M., Štěpánková, O." Social Knowledge in Multi-Agent Systems. In Luck, M., Mařík, V., Štěpánková, O., eds.: Multi-Agent Systems and Applications. LNAI, Springer-Verlag, Heidelberg (2001)
4. Bárta, J., Tožička, J., Pěchouček, M., Štěpánková, O.: Meta-Reasoning in CPlanT Multi-Agent System. Technical Report GL 166/03. 56 p. ISSN 1213-3000, http://agents.felk.cvut.cz/papers/MRinMAS.pdf, Gerstner Laboratory ©, Czech Techical University in Prague (2003)
5. Kaminka, G.A. and Pynadath, D. and Tambe, M.: Monitoring Deployed Agent Teams. In: Proceedings of the fifth international conference on Autonomous agents, Montreal, Quebec, Canada (2001)
6. Bell, B., Santos, E., Brown, S. M.: Making Adversary Decision Modeling Tractable with Intent Inference and Information Fusion. In: Proc. of the 11th Conf on Computer Generated Forces and Behavioral Representation, Orlando FL. (2002)
7. Pěchouček, M., Štěpánková, O., Mařík, V., Bárta, J.: Abstract Architecture for Meta-reasoning in Multi-Agent Systems. In Mařík, Muller, Pěchouček", eds.: Multi-Agent Systems and Applications III. Number 2691 in LNAI, Springer-Verlag, Heidelberg (2003)
8. Maes, P.: Computational Reflection. Technical Report 87-2, Free University of Brussels, AI Lab (1987)
9. Chang, Ch., Lee, Ch. R.: Symbolic Logic and Mechanical Theorem Proving. Academic Press New York and London (1973)
10. Loveland, D.: Automated Theorem Proving: A Logical Basis. North-Holland Publishing Company (1978)
11. Mitchell, T.: Generalization as Search. Artificial Intelligence **2** (1982) 203–226
12. Muggleton, S., Raedt, L. De: Inductive logic programming: Theory and methods. Journal of Logic Programming **19/20** (1994) 629–679
13. Singh, M. P., Rao, A. S., Georgeff, M. P.: Formal Methods in DAI: Logic Based Representation and Reasoning. In: Multiagent Systems A Modern Approach to Distributed Artificial Intelligence. MIT Press, Cambridge, MA. (1999) 201–258
14. Harel, D.: Dynamic Logic. In: Handbook of Philosophical Logic - Extension of Classical Logic. **II** D. Riedel Publishing Company, Dordrecht, The Netherlands (1984) 497–604
15. Fisher, M.: A survey of concurrent MetateM - the language and its applications. In Gabbay, D.M., Ohlbach, H. JK., eds.: Temporal Logic - Proceedings of the 1st International Conference. LNAI 827 Springer (1994) 480–505

Execution Engine of Meta-learning System for KDD in Multi-agent Environment

Ping Luo[1,2], Qing He[1], Rui Huang[1,3], Fen Lin[1,2],
and Zhongzhi Shi[1]

[1] Key Laboratory of Intelligent Information Processing, Institute of Computing Technology,
Chinese Academy of Sciences, 100080, Beijing, China
[2] Graduate School of the Chinese Academy of Sciences, 100080, Beijing, China
[3] Department of Information & Communication,
Nanjing University of Information Science & Technology, 210044, Nanjing, China
luop@ics.ict.ac.cn

Abstract. Meta-learning system for KDD is an open and evolving platform for efficient testing and intelligent recommendation of data mining process. Meta-learning is adopted to automate the selection and arrangement of algorithms in the mining process of a given application. Execution engine is the kernel of the system to provide mining strategies and services. An extensible architecture is presented for this engine based on mature multi-agent environment, which connects different computing hosts to support intensive computing and complex process control distributedly. Reuse of existing KDD algorithms is achieved by encapsulating them into agents. We also define a data mining workflow as the input of our engine and detail the coordination process of various agents to process it. To take full advantage of the distributed computing resources, an execution tree and a load balance model are designed too.

Keywords: execution engine, meta-learning, data mining workflow, multi-agent environment.

1 Introduction

Current data mining tools contain a plethora of algorithms, but lack the guidelines to appropriately select and arrange these algorithms according to the nature of the problem under analysis [1]. Thus, the data mining process (similar with KDD process) works either in a trial-and-error style or under the guidance of experts, and is largely an art rather than a science or system engineering. However, as data mining techniques have successfully walked out of the research laboratories the non-expert users call for more powerful data mining systems, which provide not only all kinds of algorithms, but also the best strategy to select and arrange algorithms for a given application. To address this problem, a number of researchers have suggested that meta-learning be introduced [1].

Meta-learning studies how a learning system can increase accuracy and efficiency through accumulating experience on the performance of multiple applications; the

V. Gorodetsky, J. Liu, and V.A. Skormin (Eds.): AIS-ADM 2005, LNAI 3505, pp. 149–160, 2005.

goal is to make the system flexible according to the domain or task under study [2]. In this paper, the meta-learning system for KDD means an open and evolving platform for efficient testing and effective recommendation of data mining process.

Such meta-learning system can offer services in four different levels. The higher the service level is, the more meta-knowledge it uses, the less computation it performs, and the more intelligent it works. The lowest level is exhaustive search, which tests all the mining plans in a batch mode and uses multi-criteria to rank the algorithms [3, 4]. The following level is selective and heuristic search, testing only some prospective algorithms, which may obtain better results. In these two levels, search is limited in the user-specified data mining plan, which is a great burden to end-users and may inevitably introduce personal biases to this impersonal process. In the third level, the meta-learning system can interactively and neutrally guide end-users to generate the mining plan according to specific applications and then test it. As for the last level, the ultimate goal is the thorough automation of the generation of the appropriate mining scheme for each real-world application. The meta-knowledge used in these services can be gained from ML/DM research of past theoretical and comparative study, and more importantly, through the use of inductive meta-learning on the cumulative meta-data of testing results. The update and augmentation of the meta-knowledge in such meta-learning system for KDD make it adaptive and evolving.

The central part of such a system should be a powerful execution engine, which supports all kinds of data mining algorithms, complex process control and efficient task assignment to test the mining plan as fast as possible. We organize this paper as follows. Section 2 presents the central position of execution engine in meta-learning system and articulates the reasons to implement it in multi-agent (MA) environment. Section 3 proposes the architecture of this engine and the features of its main components. Section 4 defines a multi-phase pipeline workflow to model the data mining process, and gives an execution tree as a simplified representative input of the engine to depict its executive semantics. Section 5 details the execution process of such a workflow, especially the cooperation and coordination of various agents in the MA environment. Related works are introduced with conclusions and future works in Section 6.

2   Execution Engine in Meta-learning System for KDD

The position of execution engine in meta-learning system can be expressed both externally and internally. On the external side, the execution engine is the provider and executor of data mining services, which works in on-line style to respond to real-time user requirements. On the internal side, it is the intelligent kernel of the system, which performs off-line computing to make the system more and more intelligent and efficient. This kind of computation involves meta-data and meta-knowledge update whenever possible or triggered by certain instances. In meta-data update scenario (Fig.1.A)), the execution engine exhaustively tests the mining plans in Plan Repository and outputs the mining results. Such results include not only the resultant models but also the meta-data of the application. In meta-knowledge update scenario (Fig.1.B)), the execution engine learns from the Mining Result Repository and increases its meta-knowledge. Therefore, due to its importance we pay careful consideration into it.

Fig. 1. A) Meta-data Update   B) Meta-knowledge Update

We implement this execution engine in MA environment, which consists of many computing resources such as PCs. Data mining plans can be executed on these resources through cooperation and coordination of various agents. The reason to adopt MA technology is that it fits to the characteristics and requirements of our execution engine.

- Computing intensive system. From the testing point of view, meta-learning itself is computing-intensive. A mining plan consists of several possible algorithms to be executed. Additionally, if the meta-learning system is web-enabled and accumulates lots of application data set and mining plans, the burden of on-line and off-line computing will be more and more great as this web service is more and more popular. It is necessary to streamline and scale up the computation. MA system is a natural distributed computing environment, allowing application agents running on different hosts simultaneously to achieve high availability. Moreover, MA middleware helps to form a unified computing interface and makes the distributed application easily-built.

- Open system. In an open system, the structure of the system itself is capable of dynamically changing. *Its components are not known in advance, can change over time, and may be highly heterogeneous (in that they are implemented by different people, at different times, using different software tools and techniques)* [5]. Meta-learning system is such a typical one, which must allow new data mining algorithms and techniques to be integrated into it. Agent technology provides multiple schemes of software reuse in different granularity [6]. To agentize the data mining algorithms improves the extensibility of our system.

- Computing distributed system. In modern applications, data are naturally stored on remote sites of a computer network, resulting in distributed data mining. Mobile agent can travel to remote site, process the data locally, and bring back only the necessary results. This feature alleviates network traffic when a large number of data from different repositories are to be processed. It also alleviates the computational bottlenecks by distributing the processing to multiple data sites.

- Complex system. Our system integrates meta-learning into the whole process of KDD. In this iterative process, the output of the early phase is the input of the following phase. Thus, we can not reach the final result until the whole process terminates, and distributed execution of this process involves more complex process control and management. To address the problem, we can develop a number of agents specializing at solving constituent sub-problem in autonomous way, and then coordinate these agents through efficient agent communication. MA environment well supports such message transportation by ACL (Agent Communication Language) and some communication protocol such as IMTP (Inner Message Transport Protocol).

- Intelligent system. Meta-knowledge should be increased and updated proactively and adaptively. When environment changes, intelligent agent can make suggestion and take some measures to meet new requirements rather than wait to be told what to do next.

Other technologies, such as thread computing, active objects, etc, may solve some of the above problems, but not all of them. Thus, we develop our execution engine on MA environment.

3 Architecture of the Execution Engine

The architecture of our engine is implemented on a MA environment MAGE [5]. It is designed so that more specialized data mining algorithms are compatible with lower-level MA mechanisms [7]. MAGE is a middleware that facilitates the development of MA systems. Each instance of the MAGE runtime environment for each computing host is called a container, as it can contain several agents. Each container on that host presents the corresponding computing resource. Several containers can connect with each other through networks to form a natural distributed computing environment. From the view of programmers, it seems that all the containers are running on the same computer. We encapsulate each algorithm into the behavior of different agents. Such an agent can be regarded as an algorithm entity that can run on any host. To initiate an agent on a host means to perform the behavior of that agent, and thus utilize the corresponding computing resource.

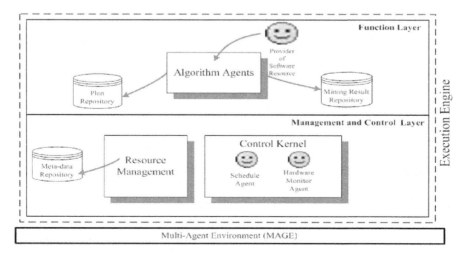

Fig. 2. System Architecture of Execution Engine

The execution engine is organized in two layers as shown in Fig. 2: Management and Control Layer (M&C Layer) and Function Layer (FL). The Interface Layer above FL, including plan generator and result visualizer, is excluded in this execution engine.

3.1 Function Layer

FL provides all kinds of operational software resource in the form of Agent. If a host has not the software copy of a certain agent and cannot instantiate it, it sends a request to the agent provider of software resources. Then the provider answers it with the required software copy and increases the computing capability of the host.

Different kinds of Algorithm Agents perform different operations in all phases of KDD process, including sampling, preprocessing, training, model combination and evaluation. Fig. 3 gives the hierarchy of Algorithm Agents and shows some of the data mining algorithms implemented in our engine. In Fig. 3, the frame without grid represents agent class, while the frame with gird represents single agent performing certain algorithm. For example, Ripper Agent, SVM Agent, and C4.5 Agent are three typical agents in the class of Training Agent.

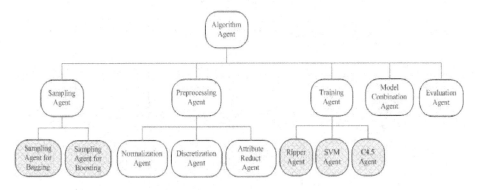

Fig. 3. Hierarchy of Algorithm Agents

3.2 Management and Control Layer

M&C layer offers the basic services for the control and execution of a distributed knowledge discovery computation in MA environment. One of its main goals is the management of all metadata describing features of resources in the engine. Moreover, this layer coordinates the *schedule agents* (SA) and *hardware monitor agents* (HMA) to complete the computation as quick as possible. It comprises two main subparts: Resource Management (RM) and Control Kernel (CK).

RM is responsible for maintaining a description of all resources used in the execution engine. Such resources include:

- The data to be mined. RM records the location of the data, type of the data and details of how to access the data.
- Data access agents and algorithm agents. RM describes the function and the input/output interface of these agents.

- Providers of software agents. RM describes the location of these providers and the responsibility of each provider.

CK is the core of execution engine. It is designed in thorough distributed manner so that SA and HMA are instantiated on each computing host. Its function is detailed in Section 5.

4   Data Mining Workflow of Execution Engine

Data mining process can be modeled as a multi-phase pipeline process, and in each phase, there are multiple methods to select. Fig. 4 depicts a simplified data mining workflow for the typical task of classification, consisting of preprocessing, training & testing and evaluation phase. The preprocessing phase can then be divided into sequential sub-phases of normalization, discretization, and attribute reduct. The mining steps within a phase are optional operations with the same function but different performances. For convenience and clarity, we give the following definitions.

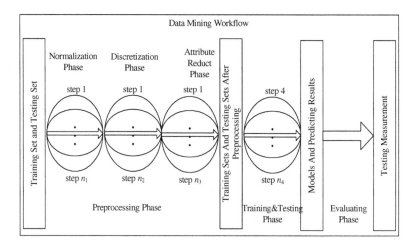

Fig. 4. The data mining workflow for classification

Definition 1 (Mining Step)
Each algorithm along with its parameters is a *mining step*. It is a running instance of Algorithm Agent. Only the mining step in each sub-phase of preprocessing can be null operation, which means do nothing in that sub-phase.

Definition 2 (Mining Path)
Any data mining plan with *one and only one* mining step for each mining phase is a *mining path*. It represents an intact mining scheme for certain application.

Definition 3 (Mining Workflow)
Any data mining plan with *at least* a mining step for each mining phase is a *mining workflow*. It is the set of several available mining paths.

In Fig. 4, a data mining path can be easily got when we select one mining step from each mining phase. If there are n_1, n_2, n_3, n_4 different mining algorithms in the four phases of normalization, discretization, attribute reduct and training & testing respectively, the number of all possible different mining paths amounts to $n_1 \times n_2 \times n_3 \times n_4$ according to Multiply Theorem. From the left to the right of a mining path, a mining step transforms its output to the immediate step as its input until the path terminates and gets the final result. Then, using the training and testing data sets as the inputs of the mining workflow, a measurement is extracted for each mining path according to a certain evaluation criterion. For classification problems, the evaluation measurements can be accuracy, weighted accuracy, etc. Our engine is designed to exhaustively or selectively test the mining workflow for different purposes.

The execution engine performs exhaustive testing in off-line style to accumulate meta-data, on which learning performs to update meta-knowledge. To get the $n_1 \times n_2 \times n_3 \times n_4$ measurements for the whole mining workflow, a normal way is to process every mining path one by one. However, there is no need in repeating a mining step with the same input data. The immediate result from a mining step can be shared by all of its following steps. An efficient execution way can be expressed by the execution tree in Fig. 5, corresponding to the mining workflow in Fig. 4. A link between two adjacent nodes represents a mining step which transforms the data in the father node to the resultant data in the child node. A node in the tree represents a status with its data. A path from the root node to any leaf represents a mining path. After a mining step, the ending node submits its resultant data to all the following mining steps as their inputs, and then these steps can start simultaneously. However, the steps along a path from the root to the leaf can only be processed sequentially. Thus, the execution process of the workflow is the growth process of its corresponding tree. The growth of each path is independent with each other while the growth of each link along a path is sequential. We call this execution style the mixture of parallel way among paths and sequential way along a path.

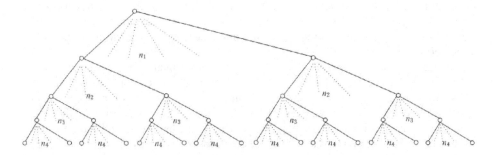

Fig. 5. Exhaustive Execution Tree for Mining Workflow

However, the execution engine performs selective testing in on-line style to respond to real-time user requirements through processing only the promising mining paths, which can be selected by the meta-knowledge in our execution engine. Meta-knowledge is formalized to be some execution conditions at certain nodes of the exhaustive execution tree. Then it can be pruned to a selective execution tree. Only the links, which satisfy the conditions at its father node, can continue to grow. The more knowledge we use, the smaller the corresponding selective execution tree is, and the less time it takes to compute.

For example, there are two pieces of meta-knowledge from theoretical study of data mining. One is that the data must be discretized before attribute reduct based on rough set. The other is that discretizing the data may decrease the predicting ability of SVM model. We infuse the former piece of knowledge into all the nodes in the third layer (the root is in the first layer) in Fig. 5 and the corresponding node terminates when the data without discretization as its input. The latter piece of knowledge can be injected into the nodes in the fourth layer and removes the computation of SVM training with discretized data. In this way, meta-knowledge from both theoretical and experimental study can be formalized to prune the exhaustive execution tree and gain computing efficiency without losing accuracy.

5   Execution Process of Data Mining Workflow

The design objective is to finish the execution process in Fig. 5 efficiently in our execution engine. The technical key is to share the computing resources of this distributed computing environment. In order to take full advantage of all computing resources, we must assign the data mining tasks to all hosts "equally", and all required data should be transformed to their related hosts respectively. Thus, load balance on these hosts and communication cost between them are two of the key problems. In this section, we first detail the load balance model used to assign tasks, and then describe the whole view of agent coordination in distributed manner to reduce data communication.

5.1   The Load Balance Model

This load balance model is the mathematical foundation of task assignment in our execution engine. When execute to an internal node of the execution tree, the sibling mining steps can run on different hosts simultaneously. The problem is to decide on which host each mining step will run.

The task amount of a mining step should be the assessment of its execution time on a certain host. Here, three factors are to be considered: 1) computing hardware; 2) amount of the input data; 3) computing complexity of the algorithm itself. In our execution engine, suppose that the computing hosts have more or less the same hardware configuration. The mining steps, which can be executed simultaneously, always have the same input data. Then, a simple assessment method is to empirically give each step a constant representing its task amount, according to the kind of data mining algorithm it performs. Such constants can be obtained from experiments on benchmarks and theoretical analysis. Thus, definition of this problem is:

Let $T = \{t_1, t_2, \cdots, t_n\}$ be the n corresponding task amounts of the mining steps, $L = \{l_1, l_2, \cdots, l_k\}$ be the k current load amounts of the k containers, and $\{T_1, T_2, \cdots, T_k\}$ be a partition of T while T_i is the set of mining steps assigned to container i. The objective is to find the best partition of T satisfying the following formula:

$$min \sum_{i=1}^{k} \left| \bar{l} - l_i' \right|$$

while $\quad \bar{l} = \dfrac{\displaystyle\sum_{j=1}^{n} t_j + \sum_{i=1}^{k} l_i}{k} \quad$ and $\quad l_i' = l_i + \displaystyle\sum_{t \in T_i} t$

(l_i' be the load amount of the ith container after task assignment.)

This is a problem of combinatorial optimization. There are k^n different partitions of T according to the definition above. To satisfy the optimal condition, all the partitions must be checked. Thus, it is a NP problem. However, our application has its own characteristics: 1) the concurrent mining steps are from the same mining phase with the same input data, and the algorithms within this mining phase always have the same time complexity. So their task amounts are almost the same. 2) After each task assignment, the load amount of each container is almost the same. Under these conditions we design a greedy algorithm with linear time complexity to find the suboptimal solution. By Algorithm 1, SA assigns concurrent mining steps to different hosts.

Algorithm 1: find the suboptimal assignment scheme
Input: $T = \{t_1, t_2, \cdots, t_n\}$ and $L = \{l_1, l_2, \cdots, l_k\}$
Output: $\{T_1, T_2, \cdots, T_k\}$ and $L' = \{l_1', l_2', \cdots, l_k'\}$
FOR each T_i **DO**
$\quad T_i = \Phi$
$\quad l_i' = l_i$
ENDFOR
FOR each $t_i \in T$ in ascending order **DO**
$\quad l_j'$ is the biggest element of $\{l_1', l_2', \cdots, l_k'\}$
$\quad T_j = T_j \cup \{t_i\}$
$\quad l_j' = l_j' + t_i$
ENDFOR

5.2   Coordination Process of Agents

To reduce communication cost and eliminate the bottleneck of centralized process control, the engine is designed to assign tasks in a distributed manner. For each container, SA and HMA are two never-ending agents. SA assigns the concurrent mining steps to different hosts and HMA records and answers the current computing load of the corresponding container. To execute a mining step on a host and then assign the following mining tasks, two components must be transported to that host: the input data for the current mining step, and the immediate sub-workflow describing all the following mining steps. When performing a certain mining step, an Algorithm Agent (AA) will be instantiated dynamically and terminate its execution after completing its task. Fig. 6 depicts a typical coordination process of these agents.

The process includes the following steps.

Step1: After an AA finishes its mining step, it sends the resultant data and the immediate sub-workflow to the SA in the same container.

Step2: As soon as the SA receives a valid message from an AA, it checks the corresponding execution conditions. If the conditions are not satisfied, the SA will do nothing. If the conditions satisfied, it parses the message to find out the n immediate mining steps and assesses their task amounts ($T = \{t_1, t_2, \cdots, t_n\}$). Then, the SA asks all the HMAs in the MA environment for the k current load amounts of each container ($L = \{l_1, l_2, \cdots, l_k\}$).

Step3: Each MA answers the question of the SA.

Step4: Using the Algorithm 1, the SA dynamically instantiates different AAs in its destination container. Then, each AA executes its corresponding mining step in its container.

Step5: Each AA follows the loop from Step1 to Step4 to continue the left process.

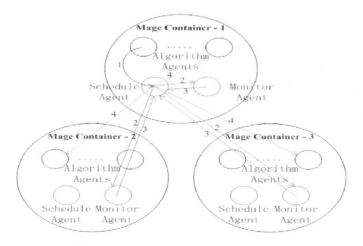

Fig. 6. Coordination Process of Multi-Agents

The whole picture of processing a mining workflow is: after receiving a new workflow, a *startup agent* is generated which sends the initial input data and the whole workflow to the SA in the same container. Then according to the process in Fig. 6, the loop from Step1 to Step4 continues until the left sub-workflow is NULL. At that time, each AA sends the measurement of the corresponding mining path to the *startup agent*. When the *startup agent* receives all those measurements, or no active agents initiated by this mining workflow are left, the computation terminates.

6   Conclusions, Related and Future Works

Our work focuses mainly on scalability and extendibility of the execution engine of meta-learning system for KDD using MA technology. The most similar project is METAL [8, 9], which is a web-enabled prototype assistant system, supports data mining guidance, and also uses agent technology. However, their work pays much emphasis on the technical details of distributed computation and implementation of MA middleware, such as agent registration and dynamic resource discovery. Our engine is built on mature MA environment, supporting powerful agent communication and distributed computing. This helps us to focus only on the development of higher level functions, not the lower level implementations of agents. And in METAL, the content of computation is dependent with the computing host, which means that certain data mining services can only be provided by certain hosts. It results in waste of computing resources if the requests for the services on that host are small, and computing bottleneck if the corresponding services are popular. In our system, the content of computation is independent with the computing host, which indicates that different agents can run on any computing host. The load balance model is also designed to make full use of all the computing resources.

To our best knowledge, all previous works in meta-learning concentrate on single data mining phase, especially on training and learning phase [10, 11, 12]. A recent meta-learning work [13] is done in preprocessing phase to reduce the number of samples during progressive sampling. The meta-knowledge from these works can only help the selection of single algorithm in the corresponding mining phase. Our system regards the whole KDD process as its meta-learning object, and output the "best" combination of several algorithms in sequential execution according to certain evaluation criterion. It is extremely helpful to accumulate meta-data to find the meta-knowledge about the combinatorial relationships between the algorithms from different KDD phases, which can indicate better or worse performances. We believe that "mining the data mining process" is our encouraging future work towards streamlined KDD.

In this paper, we first define the meta-learning system for KDD and its kernal execution engine. Then, we model the execution process by data mining workflow and implement this process by MA technology in distributed manner to gain system scalability. Our system is also a testing platform, which liberates data miners from tedious trial-and-error work and saves much experimentation time. Finally, we argue that such techniques can also be used to scale up any multi-phase pipeline process in other application domain.

Acknowledgement

This is the first published English paper of the first author. Special thanks for the comments and suggestions from the anonymous reviewers. Our work is supported by the National Science Foundation of China (No.60435010), Beijing Science Foundation (No.4052025), the 863 Project (No.2003AA115220) and China-Australia Special Fund for S&T Cooperation.

References

1. Vilalta, R., Giraud-Carrier, C., Brazdil, P., Soares, C.: Using Meta-Learning to Support Data Mining. International Journal of Computer Science Applications, Vol. I, No. 1 (2004) 31–45
2. Vilalta, R., Drissi, Y. A.: Perspective View and Survey of Meta-Learning. Journal of Artificial Intelligence Review, 18(2) (2002) 77–95
3. Nakhaeizadeh, G., Schnabel, A.: Development of Multi-criteria Metrics for Evaluation of Data-mining Algorithms. In Proceedings of the Third International Conference on Knowledge Discovery and Data Ming (1997)
4. Soares, C., Brazdil, P.: Zoomed Ranking: Selection of Classification Algorithms Based on Relevant Performance Information. In Proceedings of the Fourth European Conference on Principles and Practice of Knowledge Discovery in Databases (2000)
5. Nicholas R. Jennings, Michael J. Wooldridge: Applications Of Intelligent Agents. In Agent Technology Foundations, Applications and Markets, Springer-Verlag (1998)
6. Zhongzhi Shi, Haijun Zhang, Yong Cheng, Yuncheng Jiang, Qiujian Sheng, Zhikung Zhao: MAGE: An Agent-Oriented Programming Environment. In *Proc. IEEE-ICCI, (*2004) 250–257
7. Mario Cannataro, Domenico Talia, Paolo Trunfio: Distributed data mining on the grid. Future Generation Computer Systems 18(8) (2002) 1101–1112
8. Juan A. Botía, Antonio F. Gómez-Skarmeta, Juan R. Velasco, Mercedes Garijo: A Proposal for Meta-Learning Through a Multi-Agent System. Agents Workshop on Infrastructure for Multi-Agent Systems (2000) 226–233
9. Juan A. Botía, Antonio F. Gómez-Skarmeta, Mercedes Valdés, Antonio Padilla: METALA: A Meta-learning Architecture. Fuzzy Days (2001) 688–698
10. Chan P., Stolfo S.: On the Accuracy of Meta-Learning for Scalable Data Mining. Journal of Intelligent Integration of Information, Ed. L. Kerschberg (1998)
11. Friedman, J., Hastie, T., Tibshirani, R.: Additive Logistic Regression: A Statistical View of Boosting. Annals of Statistics **28** (2000) 337–387
12. Sohn, S.Y.: Meta Analysis of Classification Algorithms for Pattern Recognition. IEEE Transactions on Pattern Analysis and Machine Intelligence 21(11) (1999) 1137–1144
13. Leite R., Brazdil P.: Improving Progressive Sampling via Meta-learning on Learning Curves. In Proc. ECML (2004)

A Methodology for Predicting Agent Behavior by the Use of Data Mining Techniques

Andreas Symeonidis and Pericles Mitkas

Department of Electrical and Computer Engineering,
Aristotle University of Thessaloniki,
GR541 24 Thessaloniki, Greece
Tel.: +30-2310-996399, Fax: +30-2310-996398
asymeon@danae.ee.auth.gr, mitkas@eng.auth.gr

Abstract. One of the most interesting issues in agent technology has always been the modeling and enhancement of agent behavior. Numerous approaches exist, attempting to optimally reflect both the inner states, as well as the perceived environment of an agent, in order to provide it either with reactivity or proactivity. Within the context of this paper, an alternative methodology for enhancing agent behavior is presented. The core feature of this methodology is that it exploits knowledge extracted by the use of data mining techniques on historical data, data that describe the actions of agents within the MAS they reside. The main issues related to the design, development, and evaluation of such a methodology for predicting agent actions are discussed, while the basic concessions made to enable agent cooperation are outlined. We also present κ-Profile, a new data mining mechanism for discovering action profiles and for providing recommendations on agent actions. Finally, indicative experimental results are apposed and discussed.

1 Introduction

1.1 Web Personalization and Agent Behaviors

The core objective of agent action-based personalization is the discovery of a *recommendation set*, that will better predict the behavior of the agent "in action". Although such a topic is quite intriguing, going briefly through related bibliography, one can easily identify a lack of publications on agent action identification and prediction, since it is inherently complicated. However, this problem is very similar to web personalization, where a great number of research efforts have been published. By drawing an analogy to web personalization, agent behavior prediction may be feasible.

Rather popular approaches for web personalization include collaborative filtering [1],[2] and Web usage mining [3],[4],[5]. Advancing to more elaborate infrastructures, web usage mining systems have been built [6],[7] to discover interesting patterns in the navigational behavior of users [8]. Nevertheless, none of the above approaches had proven sufficient for providing successful personalization

V. Gorodetsky, J. Liu, and V.A. Skormin (Eds.): AIS-ADM 2005, LNAI 3505, pp. 161–174, 2005.

of users, and, correspondingly, of agents, until aggregation usage profiles were introduced. Several research groups [9],[10],[11] adopted this approach to identify association rules [12],[13], sequential patterns, pageview clusters and transaction clusters between users [9]. One of the most popular models for personalization and prediction, though, is the one proposed by Mobasher [14] and Mobasher, Cooley, & Srivastava [15],[16] and this is the model that has been adopted for the agent behavior prediction methodology to be built upon.

1.2   Agent Prediction System Prerequisites

The first task in such prediction systems is the collection of all necessary historical data. In order to predict the behavior of an agent, only information on its previous actions is needed. This is not necessarily the case, though, when creating behavior profiles. These profiles, which are extracted by the use of DM techniques, are the projection of "agent experience" on the data.

With respect to the dataset employed for predicting agent actions and for creating profiles, alternative architectures may occur for the prediction system. In a MAS, for example, each agent could maintain a history record for its own actions, in order to predict its own actions. In such a system, the predictions would be solely based on each agent's own "experience"; an agent with a no (limited) historical record, would, thus, produce no (poor) predictions. An alternative architecture could allow the historical records of all agents to be monitored by an appointed agent. Profiles would then be created on the whole of the agent action history, discarding nevertheless personalization. This is why we believe that a system for predicting agent actions should allow both personalization and collaboration between agents, in order to exploit other agents' experience, in case a agent specific cannot create good predictions.

In general, the main goal of a prediction system is the improvement of performance of a wider framework, which specifies the exact development principles and agent interactions of the prediction system.

Taking all these factors into account, a methodology for building a framework for predicting agent actions should comprise the following steps:

1. Model agent actions
2. Develop a mechanism for monitoring agent actions
3. Preprocess data, in order to incorporate domain understanding
4. Develop an appropriate DM algorithm for extracting agent action profiles
5. Develop a mechanism for storing and retrieving profiles
6. Develop an agent action recommendation interface

Figure 1 illustrates the functional architecture of such a system. It comprises two modules: a) an offline module, where action preprocessing, DM application, and profile creation takes place and, b) an online module, where the agent actions are recorded real-time and the recommendation interface is applied.

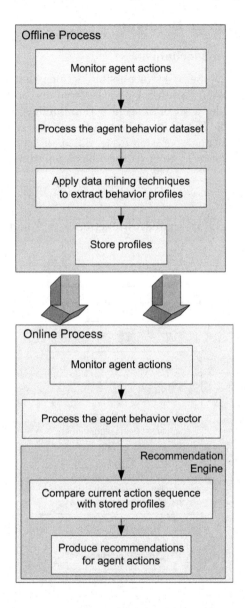

Fig. 1. The basic functionality of an agent prediction system

The rest of the paper is structured as follows: Section 2 deals with all issues related to the modeling of agent actions and presents the developed data mining mechanism. Section 3 presents the evaluation framework and the metrics used. Finally, section 4 provides indicative experimental results and concludes the paper.

2   Predicting Agent Behavior

2.1   The Prediction Mechanism

Let $P = \{p_1, p_2, \ldots, p_n\}$ be a set of possible actions that an agent may take during its execution phase. Parameter n varies from one operation cycle[1] to another. Let us also consider a set of m agent action bundles, $B = \{b_1, b_2, \ldots, b_m\}$, where each action bundle $b_i \in B$ is a subset of P, and describes the actions taken by an agent throughout one operation cycle. Since all agent action bundles are defined on the action space P, each vector b has a length n and is of the form:

$$b = < w(p_1, b), w(p_2, b), ..., w(p_n, b) > \tag{1}$$

where $w(p_i, b)$ is a weight associated with action $p_i \in P$ and $0 \leq w(p_i, b) \leq 1$.

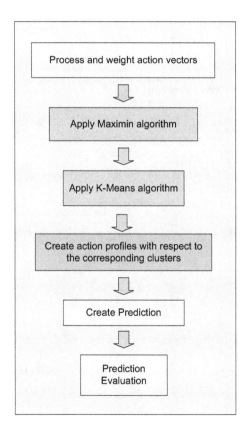

Fig. 2. The κ-Profile mechanism

---

[1] We define an operation cycle as the sequence of actions performed by an agent in its effort to accomplish the specific task it has been assigned to.

Let us consider a vector b that describes the actions taken by an agent within one operation cycle. The jth component $w(p_j, b)$ of this vector will be 0, if the agent has never taken action p_j, while $w(p_j, b) \neq 0$ when the agent has taken action p_j. In fact, the value of $w(p_j, b)$ increases if the action under consideration is of great importance. Let us now consider an operation cycle that has not yet terminated. Its corresponding vector has, in general, more null elements than a vector of an already terminated cycle. The scope of the prediction mechanism is to determine the vector components (i.e., the agent actions) that have a high probability of occurrence in the remainder of an ongoing operation cycle. This capability will effectively narrow the options of an agent to the most suitable ones and, thus, reduce the time required to compute its next step. The weight calculated for each action denotes the probability of its appearance in the corresponding operation cycle.

A mechanism for discovering common action patterns, which we call κ-Profile is employed to extract the recommendations. The κ-Profile involves a sequence of steps shown in Figure 2. It utilizes the Maximin [17] and K-Means [18] algorithms, in order to cluster the set of vectors B.

After clustering has been performed, a set of action bundle clusters, $BC = \{c_1, c_2, ..., c_k\}$ is extracted, where each c_i is a subset of B. For each action bundle cluster $c_i \in BC$, a representative vector is defined as the **cluster profile** cp_i. Vector cp_i is the vector closer to the cluster center. The components of cp_i that fall below a certain threshold μ are nullified. This way, only the most representative of the events in the cluster are taken into account. In the case of cluster c_i, for example, the profile cp_i is the set of $< action - weight >$ pairs, as defined by Equation 2:

$$cp_i = \{< p, weight(p, cp_i) > \mid p \in P \text{ and } weight(p, cp_i) \geq \mu\} \qquad (2)$$

The $weight(p, cp_i)$ of action p within profile cp_i is calculated using Equation 3:

$$weight(p, cp_i) = \frac{1}{|c_i|} \sum_{b \in c_i} w(p, b) \qquad (3)$$

where $w(p, b)$ is the weight of action p in action bundle $b \in c_i$. It is, therefore, obvious that each profile can be also represented as a vector of length n. Considering that the same representation mechanism is employed for the ongoing operation cycle vector, both profiles and action bundles can be manipulated as n-dimensional vectors in the action space. For example, a profile C, can be represented as:

$$C = \{w_1^C, w_2^C, ..., w_n^C\} \qquad (4)$$

where

$$w_i^C = \begin{cases} weight(p_i, C), \ p_i \in C \\ 0, \qquad\qquad otherwise \end{cases} \qquad (5)$$

Similarly, the ongoing operation cycle can be represented as a vector $S =< s_1, s_2, ..., s_n >$, where s_i is a weight denoting the significance of action p_i in the current cycle. The weighted values are calculated in the same manner as the weights for action vectors b are calculated (e.g. $s_i = 0$ if the agent has not taken action p_i). In both cases, a *Fuzzy Inference System* (FIS) is employed to produce the weights, which enables the incorporation of domain understanding into the prediction mechanism. The comparison of a certain profile with the vector representing the ongoing operation cycle is performed using the cosine coefficient, a metric widely used in information retrieval problems. $match(S, C)$, defined in Equation 6, calculates the cosine of the angle of the two vectors S and C, by normalizing their dot product with respect to their moduli.

$$match(S, C) = \frac{\sum_k w_k^C \cdot s_k}{\sqrt{\sum_k (s_k)^2 \times \sum_k (w_k^C)^2}} \qquad (6)$$

The actions that the prediction system recommends are determined through a *recommendation score*, defined for each action p_i in each of the already calculated profile vectors. This score is dependent on two factors:

1. The overall similarity of the current vector to the profile, and
2. The average weight of each action p_i in the profile

Given a profile C and an operation cycle vector S, the recommendation score $Rec(S, p_i)$ is calculated for each action p_i, according to Equation 7.

$$Rec(S, p_i) = \sqrt{weight(p_i, C) \cdot match(S, C)} \qquad (7)$$

Finally, a Next Action Recommendation set, $NAR(S)$, is compiled for the current action bundle S, containing only actions with recommendation scores that exceed a certain threshold, ρ, for all profiles. That is:

$$NAR(S) = \left\{ p_i \mid Rec(s, w_i^C) \geq \rho \right\} \qquad (8)$$

For each action appearing in more than one vectors, the maximum recommendation score is selected, from the corresponding profile. This way optimal coverage is achieved. Table 1 illustrates an example of a recommendation on action vector S, based on profile C. Recommendation is produced only on vector components that have a null value on S and a non-null value on C. For action p_2, for example, a recommendation score on S is calculated, according to Equation 7. In this case, $Rec(S, p_i) = \sqrt{0.375 \cdot match(S, C)}$, where $match(S, C) = 0.52$. Finally, $Rec(S, p_2) = 0.442$.

2.2   Applying κ-Profile on MAS

The κ-Profile mechanism aims to predict future agent actions within an operation cycle, based on knowledge of prior actions of this and/or similar agents. For the ongoing operation cycle, a z-size window is employed. That is, only the last z actions of the agent can influence the outcome of the recommendation process. κ-Profile can be easily adapted to predict agent behavior, mapping the vector elements to agent actions.

Table 1. Recommending the next action

Actions P	Profile Vector C	Vector S	$Rec(S, p_i)$
p_1	0	0	0
p_2	0.375	0	0.442
p_3	0	0	0
p_4	0.3	0.6	0.395
p_5	0	0.4	0

Let us consider an agent authorized to execute a number of functions on files, as determined by its action space $P = \{Select, Open, Modify, Save, Close\}$. Binary weights are assigned to the elements of the action vectors. Let us consider a profile $C = \{Open, Modify, Save\}$. The corresponding profile vector is, thus, $cp_C = [0\ 1\ 1\ 1\ 0]$. In case actions $\{Open\}$ and $\{Modify\}$ are executed during the current cycle and the prediction window has been set to $z = 2$, action $\{Save\}$ will be recommended, according to profile C (Table 2).

Table 2. An example on predicting the next action

Action	Profile	Recent History
Select	0	0
Open	1	1
Change	1	1
Save	1	0
Close	0	0

Although excluding the two actions $\{Select\}$ and $\{Close\}$ from a set of five possible actions does not seem interesting, an equivalent reduction of the candidate space in a system with a large number ($n \geq 100$) of options would be rather significant. κ-Profile provides this pruning mechanism through the grouping of action bundles into clusters and the identification of actions that are likely to occur next. These actions are determined by their degree of participation into the profile(s) taken into account, and by the similarity of the ongoing operation cycle vector to it(them).

In our example, the participation degree of action $\{Save\}$ is 1. This action is proposed to be the next action for the ongoing operation cycle vector with an $1 \times \{vector\, similarity\}$ similarity measure. The similarity measure is always < 1, since the current action bundle is generally different from the profile used for prediction. It should be denoted that the quality of the prediction is also related to the size of the historical dataset (the bigger the historical dataset, the better the prediction). A bigger dataset offers more training options, often leading to more accurate predictions.

In a sense, κ-Profile produces a type of association rules. For the current example, the rule would be:

$$\{Open\} \wedge \{Change\} \longrightarrow \{Save\} \tag{9}$$

Nevertheless, in the case of association rules, their participation degree (confidence) could be equal to 1, expressing certainty on the occurrence of the action.

The representation mechanism in our example is quite simple, since the weighted values are either 0s or 1s (the action has not/has been taken). In general, the mechanism is much more complicated and several parameters need to be considered (i.e., action frequency, action timing, etc.). The major advantage of κ-Profile is that it can manipulate vectors with fuzzy constituent values (fuzzy degrees of participation). In that case, the representation mechanism assigns values within the specified fuzzy interval, a flexibility that makes the κ-Profile mechanism suitable for a wide area of applications. Important issues that deserve further study include the agent action model and the specification of the operation cycle goal. These issues are discussed next.

2.3   Modeling Agent Actions in an Operation Cycle

Let us consider some multi-agent application and let $P = \{p_1, p_2, \ldots, p_n\}$ be a finite set of possible agent actions. In general, agent actions are asynchronous events occurring at times T_i. The time interval between two actions is, in most cases, of great importance. In the case of a web application, for example, the time interval between two successive page visits is the time the user spent on the first site (possibly exposed to electronic advertising). In order to monitor an agent operation cycle we use an ordered, variable-length vector Π, whose elements are pairs of the form $< action, executiontime >$. The time intervals between consecutive actions can be easily calculated. In fact, proper processing of Π can produce useful information for the operation cycle.

As an example, let us consider a system where the set of possible actions is $P = \{p_1, p_2, p_3\}$. Figure is a representation of an operation cycle with five agent actions occurring at times T_0 to T_4. Table 3 shows vector Π for this example.

Table 3. A vector representing the operation cycle

Vector Π
$< p_1, T_0 >$
$< p_3, T_1 >$
$< p_2, T_2 >$
$< p_3, T_3 >$
$< p_1, T_4 >$

According to the previous analysis, two things have to be determined, as far as the operation goal is concerned: a) the goal itself and, b) a terminating condition for the operation cycle. For an internet-based MAS, the operation goal

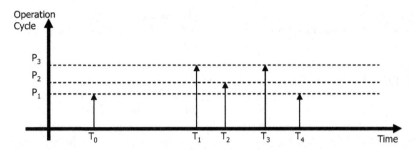

Fig. 3. The evolution of an operation cycle

would be the transition of an agent to one of the available web pages of the site (each transition is considered to be an action). In this case, the prediction mechanism can be quite straightforward, because the operation cycle itself has to be predicted and no terminating condition needs to be specified. During the online process, only an action window (z) is needed for the system to predict. This is not the case, though, for the offline process. where operation cycle vectors must be created and stored. Since the profile vectors must be of equal length, a terminating condition is needed. This condition can be related to either time or change of application status, or even both. Thorough analysis has led to the decision that the optimal choice in such systems with "predicting" capabilities would be the definition of an agent action signaling the end of the current operation cycle. In the web traversing example, the terminating action could be the end of the user's web navigation.

2.4 Mapping Agent Actions to Vectors

Another important issue for the prediction mechanism is the transformation of the operation cycles to agent action vectors. κ-Profile mechanism requires equal-size vectors, with their elements (weights) valued in the [0,1] interval (Table 4). Binary weights could be assigned in the simplest of cases, merely denoting the execution or not of an action in a specific operation cycle. This approach is not suitable, however, for the cases when the same action is executed more than once within the same operation cycle.

Table 4. Mapping agent actions to vectors

Vector π	Weighted Vector
$< p_1, T_0 >$	β_1
$< p_3, T_1 > \longrightarrow$	β_2
$< p_2, T_2 >$	β_3
$< p_3, T_3 >$	β_4

It should be emphasized that the representation mechanism is closely related to the scope of the specific MAS. In a MAS focused on the analysis of consumer behavior, for example, the items and their quantities purchased within the same transaction would be of interest. In other types of applications, the time interval between actions is important (e.g. the browsing duration of a specific web page). It is, therefore, obvious that thorough analysis is is required in order to achieve the proper modeling of the problem at hand.

The κ-Profile has been designed to recommend only actions of high importance. The mechanism perceives the importance of an action within the operation cycle through its weight (the corresponding element's weight). The action weights are calculated by the use of a FIS, that deals successfully with the issue of incorporating domain understanding. During fuzzification, the related parameters have to be defined and tuned, while the fuzzy rule base has to be created.

If the prediction system is developed following the methodology presented in Chapter 5, the only parameters that have to be defined are:

– The finite set of actions P
– The goal of the operation cycle and the terminating condition, and
– The parameters of the FIS, and their influence on the MAS performance.

3   Evaluating Efficiency

The efficiency of improving agent intelligence through data mining on agent behavior data can be measured at two levels:

a) the profile level, and
b) the prediction level

The behavior profiles extracted by the κ-Profile have to undoubtedly represent related behaviors among agents acting within the same application. If the profiles are successful, then **information personalization** can be achieved, which is of great importance to the performance of the system.

3.1   Profile Efficiency Evaluation

In order to evaluate profile efficiency, we can follow the analysis proposed by Perkowitz and Etzioni [5]. According to this analysis, an agent that has taken an action of the profile, will also take another action of the same profile, within the ongoing operation cycle. That is, if B is the set of profile vectors and cp_i is a profile, then B_{cp_i} is a subset of B, whose elements (b_j) contain at least one of the actions in cp_i. First, we must calculate the *average visit percentage* (AVP) for extracted profiles. The AVP of profile cp_i with respect to all the profile vectors is in this case given by Equation 10.

$$AVP = \sum_{b \in B_{cp_i}} \frac{(\overrightarrow{b} \cdot \overrightarrow{cp_i})}{|b|} \tag{10}$$

The *weighted average visit percentage, WAVP* metric is then calculated by dividing AVP with the sum of all profile pr elements' weights (Equation 11).

$$WAVP = \frac{\left(\sum_{b \in B_{cpi}} \frac{\vec{b} \cdot \vec{cp_i}}{|\vec{b}|}\right)}{\left(\sum_{p \in cp_i} weight(p, cp_i)\right)} \tag{11}$$

Values of $WAVP$ closer to 1 indicate better profile efficiency.

3.2   Prediction System Efficiency Evaluation

Several different approaches can be followed, in order to evaluate the efficiency of a prediction system. Nevertheless, the primitives of a MAS impose an approach that is somewhat different to the ones used for estimation and classification systems. A recommendation engine, like the one described, does not require the rigidity of such systems. More than one suggestions, equally important, can be produced. Therefore, the prediction itself cannot be considered as a valid evaluation metric, and this the reason for not employing the classic evaluation metrics, *precision* and *coverage*.

Instead, the following approach has been adopted:

Let $AS = s_1, s_2, ..., s_n$ be the test set, i.e. a set of action vectors that were not used during the application of the prediction mechanism on the initial data (training set). Let R be the set of actions proposed by the prediction system for action s. In the case $R \cap s \neq 0$, then we consider the recommendation to be a success. The metric for evaluating the efficiency of the recommendation system is then $PSSR$ (Prediction System Success Rate), which is defined as the percentage of successful recommendations ($SRec$) to the sum of recommendations made ($ORec$):

$$PSSR = \frac{SRec}{ORec} \tag{12}$$

Values of $PSSR$ closer to 1 indicate a better prediction efficiency.

4   Experimental Results

In order to demonstrate the added-value of the developed prediction mechanism and the diffusion of knowledge extracted by the use of DM techniques on agent behavior data, we have incorporated κ-Profile into the DM module[2] of the Agent Academy [20], a platform for building multi-agent systems and for enhancing their intelligence by the use of data mining techniques. The dataset used contained web traversing data, provided by a large web site. In our demonstrator, the action was defined as the transition to one of the available pages

---

[2] Data Miner [19] is one of the core components of the Agent Academy platform. It can also operate as a stand-alone DM suite, incorporating domain knowledge and supporting semantics. Available at: http://sourceforge.net/projects/aadataminer.

in the web site, while the parameters that were considered of importance (*time and frequency*)were defined appropriately.

Each one of the web site pages mapped to an agent action. The web site used has 142 discrete web pages, i.e. 142 possible agent actions. The set of action bundle vectors, B, contained 208 elements (b vectors). This set was provided as the training set to the κ-Profile mechanism. At first the *maximin* algorithm identified $K = 8$ clusters, and along with the most representative vectors of each cluster, the $K - Means$ algorithm was applied. The resulting clusters, along with the corresponding set percentage, are illustrated in Table 5. As can be easily seen, some of the produced clusters have very low vector membership. This is a result of the layout of the specific web site.

Table 5. The resulting vector clusters and their percentage distribution

Cluster	Vector
Cluster 1	56.73%
Cluster 2	4.33%
Cluster 3	~2%
Cluster 4	~3%
Cluster 5	24.5%
Cluster 6	2.4%
Cluster 7	1.44%
Cluster 8	4.33%

Using the resulting clusters, κ-Profile has identified the most representative actions, therefore constructing eight action clusters, which in fact comprise the agent profile set. Based on these profiles, the recommendation engine produced, in real-time, the agent suggestions. Table 6 illustrates the actions that comprise the profile of cluster 4, along with their normalized weights within the cluster.

The $WAVP$ metric was applied on the extracted profiles, in order to identify their efficiency. The $WAVP$ metric was calculated to be 78% for the first of the eight profiles extracted, 72.5% for the second profile, while for the rest of the profiles it stayed above a respectable 67%.

As far as the efficiency of the prediction mechanism is concerned, the *PSSR* metric was calculated to be 72.14%, a success rate that was considered satisfactory, since the action space was $n = 142$, while the maximum profile size was $m = 8$ (8 actions maximum). Taking under consideration the fact that the recommendation window was set to $z = 3$ (last three actions of the agent), in almost three out of four cases, the prediction mechanism proposed an action that the agent subsequently followed (a web page that the user chose to visit).

Table 6. The actions that comprise the profile of cluster 4

Action	Vector
p_{67}	0.9998
p_{86}	0.9999
p_{15}	0.8352
p_{82}	0.7827
p_{13}	1.0
p_{11}	0.9788
p_{10}	0.7273
p_9	0.8992
p_{100}	0.8264
p_{77}	0.7892
p_8	0.9999
p_{76}	1.0
p_7	0.9999
p_4	0.8307

5   Conclusions and Future Work

The main objective of this paper was the analysis of all issues involved in the development (through the methodology presented) of a system that exploits the results of data mining on agent behavior data, in order to predict their posterior actions. Through the analysis conducted, we have shown that data mining techniques can, indeed, be exploited for discovering common behavioral patterns between agents, as long as the problem is modeled appropriately and the system infrastructure entails the features presented in section 1. This way data preprocessing is possible and a suitable DM mechanism can be applied, for agent behavior profiles to be extracted. From that point on, agent behavior can be predicted.

References

1. Konstan, J.A., Miller, B.N., Maltz, D, Herlocker, J.L., Gordon, L.R., Riedl, J: GroupLens: Applying Collaborative Filtering to Usenet News. Communications of the ACM. **40** (1997) 77–87
2. Herlocker, J.L., Konstan, J.A., Borchers, B., Riedl, J.: An Algorithmic Framework for Performing Collaborative Filtering. In: Proceedings of the 22nd Annual International ACM SIGIR Conference on Research and Development in Information Retrieval. Theoretical Models (1999) 230–237
3. Nasraoui, O., Frigui, H., Joshi, A., Krishnapuram, R.: Mining Web Access Logs Using Relational Competitive Fuzzy Clustering. In: Proceedings of the Eight International Fuzzy Systems Association World Congress. (1999)
4. Spiliopoulou, M., Pohle, C., Faulstich, L.: Improving the Effectiveness of a Web Site with Web Usage Mining. In: WEBKDD. (1999) 142–162

5. Perkowitz, M., Etzioni, O.: Adaptive Web Sites: Automatically Synthesizing Web Pages. In: AAAI/IAAI. (1998) 727–732
6. Cooley, R., Mobasher, B., Srivastava, J.: Data Preparation for Mining World Wide Web Browsing Patterns. Knowledge and Information Systems **1** (1999) 5–32
7. Zaïane, O.R., Xin, M., Han, J.: Discovering Web Access Patterns and Trends by Applying OLAP and Data Mining Technology on Web Logs. In: Advances in Digital Libraries. (1998) 19–29
8. Mobasher, B., Dai, H., Luo, T., Nakagawa, M., Witshire, J.: Discovery of aggregate usage profiles for web personalization. In: Proceedings of the WebKDD Workshop. (2000)
9. Shahabi, C., Zarkesh, A.M., Adibi, J., Shah, V.: Knowledge Discovery from Users Web-Page Navigation. In: RIDE. (1997)
10. Schechter, S., Krishnan, M., Smith, S.: Using path profiles to predict HTTP requests. Computer Networks and ISDN Systems. **30** (1998) 457–467
11. Banerjee, A., Ghosh, J.: Clickstream Clustering using Weighted Longest Common Subsequences. (2001)
12. Agrawal, R., Srikant, R.: Fast Algorithms for Mining Association Rules. In Bocca, J.B., Jarke, M., Zaniolo, C., eds.: Proc. 20th Int. Conf. Very Large Data Bases, VLDB, Morgan Kaufmann (1994) 487–499
13. Agarwal, R.C., Aggarwal, C.C., Prasad, V. V. V.: A Tree Projection Algorithm for Generation of Frequent Item Sets. Journal of Parallel and Distributed Computing **61** (2001) 350–371
14. Mobasher, B.: A Web personalization engine based on user transaction clustering. In: Proceedings of the 9th Workshop on Information Technologies and Systems. (1999)
15. Mobasher, B., Srivastava, J., Cooley, C.: Creating Adaptive Web Sites Through Usage-Based Clustering of URLs. (1999)
16. Mobasher, B., Cooley, R., Srivastava, J.: Automatic personalization based on Web usage mining. Communications of the ACM. **43** (2000) 142–151
17. Looney, C. G.: Pattern Recognition Using Neural Networks: Theory and Algorithms for Engineers and Scientists. Oxford University Press (1997)
18. McQueen, J.B.: Some Methods of Classification and Analysis of Multivariate Observations. In Cam, L.M.L., Neyman, J., eds.: Proceedings of Fifth Berkeley Symposium on Mathematical Statistics and Probability. (1967) 281–297
19. Symeonidis, A.L., Mitkas, P.A., Kehagias, D.: Mining patterns and rules for improving agent intelligence through an integrated multi-agent platform. In: Proceedings of the 6th IASTED International Conference on Artificial Intelligence and Soft Computing. (2002)
20. Mitkas, P.A., Kehagias, D., Symeonidis, A.L., Athanasiadis, I.: A Framework for Constructing Multi-Agent Applications and Training Intelligent Agents. In: Proceedings of the 4th International Workshop on Agent-Oriented Software Engineering, Springer-Verlag (2003) 1–16

Topic-Specific Text Filtering Based
on Multiple Reducts

Qiang Li and Jianhua Li

Modern Communication Institute, Shanghai Jiaotong univ.,
Shanghai 200030, P.R. China
sjtuliqiang@163.com

Abstract. Feature selection is a very important step in text preprocessing, a
good selected feature subset can get the same performance than using full features, at the same time, it reduced the learning time. To make our system fit for
the application and to embed this model gateway for real-time text filtering, we
need to further select more accurate features. In this paper, we proposed a new
feature selection method based on Rough set theory. It generate several reducts,
but the special point is that between these reducts there are no common attributes, so these attributes have more powerfully capability to classify new objects,
especially for real data set in application. We choose two data sets to evaluate
our feature selection method, one is a benchmark data set from UCI machine
learning archive, and another is captured from Web. We use statistical classification methods to classify these objects, in the benchmark testing set, we get
good precision with a single reduct, but in real date set, we get good precision
with several reducts, and the data set is used in our system for topic-specific
text filtering. Thus we conclude our method is very effective in application. In
addition, we also conclude that SVM and VSM methods get better performance,
while Naïve Bayes method get poor performance with the same selected features on non-balance data set.

Keywords: Text Filtering; Content security; Rough Set; Feature Selection; Statistical Classification Methods.

1 Introduction

With the proliferation of harmful Internet content such as pornography, violence, and
hate messages, effective content-filtering systems are essential. An increasing number
of statistical classification methods and machine learning algorithms have been explored to build automatically a classifier by learning from previously labeled documents. These algorithms include vector space model [1,2], naive Bayes [3,4], k-
nearest neighbor [5], support vector machines [6,7], neural network [8] and decision
trees [9].

Feature selection is a very important step in text preprocessing, because irrelevant
and redundant words often degrade the performance of classification algorithms both
in speed and classification accuracy, and a good selected feature subset can even get

V. Gorodetsky, J. Liu, and V.A. Skormin (Eds.): AIS-ADM 2005, LNAI 3505, pp. 175 – 183, 2005.

better result than using full features. Exiting feature selection algorithms fall into two categories [10,11]: *the filter approach* and *the wrapper approach*. In filter approach, the feature subset selection is performed as a preprocessing step to induction algorithms. But the filter approach is ineffective in dealing with the feature redundancy. In wrapper approach, the feature subset selection is "wrapped around" an induction algorithm, so its running time would make the wrapper approach infeasible in practice, especially for text data, because the wrapper approach keeps running the induction algorithm on different subsets from the entire attributes set until a desired subset is identified.

With Rough sets theory proposed by Pawlak in 1982 [12,13], it has been successfully applied to many domains. This is due to the following aspects of the theory: Only the facts hidden in a data are analyzed; No addition information about the data is required such as expert knowledge or arbitrary thresholds; As a tool to discover data dependencies and reduce the number of attributes contained in a data set, these reduced attributes have the same power to classify objects as the full attributes.

Two main approaches to finding attribute reducts with Rough set theory are categorized as *discernibility functions-based* [14,15,16] and *attribute dependency-based* [17,18,19].

In paper [17,18,19], authors used Rough set in text classification. In this method, a single reduct base is generated to classify examples, and this single reduct base is not a minimal reduct, it is close to a minimal reduct. Good classification precision can be gotten in training datasets under this reduct, but to classify new examples may lead to low precision, because attributes acquired in only a single reduct are more sensitive to noise and there are may be some alternative attributes exit when classifying new examples. In paper [16], authors generated several reduct bases instead of a single reduct base to enhance the classification accuracy, and they used *Discernibility Matrix* to generate these multiple reduct bases, then to classify new examples by further generating rules. In our experiments, to generate several reducts using *Discernibility Matrix* for a medium-sized data set is even impossible to compute because a required memory is often insufficient. At the same time, many attributes are common between these reducts. Thirdly, there are many generated rules, which are hard to organize and implement in classifying new objects, that is to say, it is a hard work to match these rules when to classify new examples. In paper [20], authors proposed a new feature subset selection base on relative dependency between attributes, but the two algorithms are all based on backward elimination, so a required memory is sometimes insufficient for these algorithms in dealing with text data.

In this paper, we proposed a new feature selection method based on QUICKREDUCT Algorithm [17][18]. We generate several reducts, but the special point is that between these reducts there are no common attributes, so these attributes have more powerfully capability to classify new objects. And we use statistical classification methods to classify new objects, it is much easy to organize and implement than to classify with rules, and we get better results.

The paper is organized as follows: the basic concept for Rough sets theory is briefly introduced in Section 2. Section 3 presents the architecture of our proposed system. Section 4 describes experimental data sets and presents the experimental steps and results. Finally the conclusions are summarized in Section 5.

2   Basic Concept About Rough Sets

Rough Set theory is a formal mathematical tool that can be applied to reduce the dimensionality of datasets. Rough Set Attribute Reduction removes redundant conditional attributes from nominal datasets, retaining the information content intact whilst reducing the mount of knowledge involved. The main advantage of rough set analysis is that it requires no additional parameters to operate, and it makes use of the granularity of the supplied data only.

2.1   Decision System

A decision table is represented as a 4-tuple $S = (U, A, V_a, f_a)$, where U is the universe which consists of a finite set of objects, A is a finite set of attributes, for each $a \in A$, V_a is the value set of a and $f_a : U \to V_a$ is the information function such that $f_a(x) \in V_a$ for every $a \in A$ and $x \in U$. And $A = C \cup D$, $C \cap D = \Phi$, $C, D \subset A$ is the set of condition attributes and the set of decision attributes respectively. In general, there is only one decision attribute in a decision table such that $D = \{d\}$ and D can be simply written as d.

Indiscernibility is one of the most important concepts in Rough sets theory. For any $P \subseteq A$ ($P \neq \Phi$), an indiscernibility relation of P is defined with:

$$IND(P) = \{(x, y) \mid x, y \in U, \forall a \in P, f_a(x, a) = f_a(y, a)\}$$

$\forall x \in U, [x]_P = \{y \in U : xIND(P)y\}$ is the equivalence class containing x of the indiscernibility relation $IND(P)$. The collection $\{C_1, \cdots, C_s\}$ of classes of the indiscernibility relation $IND(P)$ constitutes a partition $U / IND(P)$. In Rough sets theory, the granulation of information contained by U can be described by the partition. This leads to the definitions of the lower and upper approximations. Let $X \subseteq U$, $P \subseteq A$, the lower and upper of set Y can be defined as $\underline{P}X = \{x \mid x \in U, [x]_P \subseteq X\}$ and $\overline{P}X = \{x \mid x \in U, [x]_P \cap X \neq \Phi\}$ respectively.

2.2   Attributes Reduction

Assuming P and Q are equivalence relations in U, the positive region $POS_P(Q)$ is defined as

$$POS_P(Q) = \bigcup_{X \in U/Q} \underline{P}X$$

A positive region contains all objects in U that can be classified in attributes Q using the information in attributes P. Intuitively, a set of attributes Q depends totally on a set of attributes P, if all attributes values from Q are uniquely determined by values of attributes from P. Q depends on P in a degree of $\gamma_P(Q)$ $(0 \leq \gamma_P(Q) \leq 1)$, if

$$\gamma_P(Q) = \frac{|POS_P(Q)|}{|U|}$$

Where $|U|$ denotes the cardinality of set U. the degree of dependency provides a measure of how important P is in mapping the dataset examples into Q.

Attributes are removed so that the reduced set provides the same quality of classification as the original. A *reduct* is defined as a subset R of the conditional attribute set C such that $\gamma_R(D) = \gamma_C(D)$, where D is the set of decision attributes. A dataset may have many attribute reduce sets, so the set R of all reduces is defined as:

$$R = \{X \mid X \subseteq C, \gamma_X(D) = \gamma_C(D)\}$$

The intersection of all the sets in R is called the *core*, the elements of which are those attributes that cannot be eliminated without introducing more contradictions to the data set. For Rough Set Attribute Reduction, the minimal reduce $R_{min} \subseteq R$ is defined as the set of any reduce searched in R with minimum cardinality:

$$R_{min} = \{X \mid X \in R, \ \forall Y \in R, |X| \leq |Y|\}$$

These minimal subsets can discern decision classes with the same discriminating power as the entire condition attributes.

2.3 Attributes Reduction Algorithms

In paper [17,18], a feature subset selection algorithm named QUICKREDUCT Algorithm is proposed base on the attribute dependency. The Algorithm only produces one possible minimum reduct. Good classification precision can be gotten in training datasets under this reduct, but to classify future examples may lead to low precision, because attributes acquired in only one reduct are more sensitive to noise and there are may be some alternative attributes exit when classifying new examples. So we proposed a new algorithm which produce m *reducts*, the number m needed to be given by the designer. Compared with using *Discernibility Matrix* to generate these multiple reducts, the special point is that between these reducts there are no common attributes, so these attributes have more powerfully capability to classify new objects. This Attributes Reduction algorithm is extended from the QUICKREDUCT Algorithm.

```
Input: C, the set of all feature attributes;
       D, the set of class attributes.
Output:  the unit of m reducts MR, MR ⊆ C
  (1)  MR= Φ
  (2)  for i=1 to m
  (3)      R:= Φ ,
  (4)      do
  (3)              T:=R,
  (4)              for each x∈ C − R
  (5)              if γ_{R∪{x}}(D) > γ_T(D)   T:= R∪{x} ,
  (6)              R:=T,
  (7)      until γ_R(D) = γ_C(D) ,
  (8)      C = C − R ,
  (9)      MR = MR∪R ,
  (10) end for
  (11) return MR
```

3   The Proposed Feature Selection Architecture

The architecture of our topic-specific text feature selection architecture is shown in Figure 1.

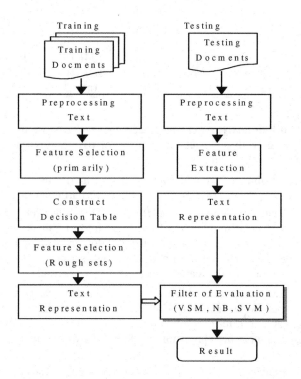

Fig. 1. The Proposed Feature Selection Architecture

In pre-processing documents, we first separate text into words, then prune infrequent words and high frequency words, and delete stop words. Next, we use CHI statistic methods to acquire keywords. And then, we use the rough set method to further reduce the number of the features. Thus more accurate and few features are extracted. At last we use *naïve Bayes model, vector space model, support vector machine model* to evaluate our feature selection method, respectively.

4   Experiment

4.1   Date Sets One

We choose two more relevant class: comp.sys.ibm.pc.hardware (abbr. as ibm) and comp.sys.mac.hardware (abbr. as mac) from mini-Newsgroup dataset [21] as our dataset for training, and we make *ibm* as positive data set, while *mac* as negative data set, which include 100 documents respectively. For testing, we use their full dataset: Newsgroup from UCI machine learning archive [22], which includes 1000 documents respectively. The information of data sets one is shown in Table 1.We primarily use white space and punctuation to separate words, then prune infrequent words and high frequency words, and translate upper to lower case. Thus we get a vocabulary of about 6000 after pre-processing.

Table 1. The information of data sets one

	Data Sets	Numbers	Sum Size	Average Size
Training	Positive Sets	100	154KB	1.54KB
	Negative Sets	100	164KB	1.65KB
Testing Sets		2000	3.08MB	3.08KB

Feature Selection Primarily. After pre-processing of words, we use CHI statistic to select features primarily, thus we get a vocabulary of 1077 in this phase. And next, we use rough set to reduce those attributes.

Feature Selection Using Rough Set Theory. We primarily use the term frequency-inverse document frequency (TF-IDF) to establish the particular degree of important of term in a document. We denote $w = value$ (TF-IDF). Since rough sets is suited to nominal datasets, we quantize the normalized space into 11 values calculated by floor (10w). Next we construct decision table for the 200 documents based on these primarily selected words. Then we use the improved rough set attribute reduct method to further reduce the number of the features.

Evaluation and Result. We use *naïve Bayes model, vector space model, and support vector machine model* to evaluate our feature selection method, respectively. As seen from Table 2 to Table 3, it reaches a high precision by the two-step feature selection. Especially, it reaches more high precision in testing sets with a single reduct.

Table 2. F1 Value in Training Sets A with different m

Classifier		original	number of reducts		
			m=1	m=2	m=3
Numbers of Attributes		1077	15	33	60
F1 Value in Training Sets A	Naïve Bayes	.965	.95	.945	.935
	VSM	.9706	.8064	.8138	.8824
	SVM-Linear	.985	.88	.89	.91
	SVM-RBF	.995	.90	.92	.94

Table 3. F1 Value in Testing Sets A with different m

Classifier		original	number of reducts		
			m=1	m=2	m=3
Numbers of Attributes		1077	15	33	60
F1 Value in Testing Sets A	Naïve Bayes	.81	.938	.9385	.9075
	VSM	.8045	.7869	.7365	.8738
	SVM-Linear	.8305	.8605	.859	.8445
	SVM-RBF	.8275	.9105	.901	.88

4.2 Data Sets Two

We choose a Chinese data set as our datasets, which is captured from Web. This dataset, which are relevant to some topic, includes two classes. One class is positive for the topic, which includes 949 documents; the other class is about objectionable content for the topic as negative, which includes 1464 documents. The information of data sets two is shown in Table 4. We firstly separate Chinese text into words, then prune infrequent words and high frequency words, and delete preposition, pronoun, auxiliary words, measure words, etc, and we only hold the noun, verb, adjective and some phrases. Thus we get a vocabulary of about 5139 words in this phase.

Table 4. The information of data sets two

	Data Sets	Numbers	Sum Size	Average Size
Training	Positive Sets	949	2.68MB	2.89KB
	Negative Sets	1464	57.2MB	40.01KB
	Testing Sets	343	23.8MB	70.65KB

Feature Selection Primarily. we use CHI statistic to select features primarily, thus we get a vocabulary of 1384 words in this phase. To make our system fit for the application and to embed this model gateway for real-time text filtering, we need to further select more accurate features. So next we use rough set to further reduce those attributes, and rough set have this function in nature.

Feature Selection Using Rough Set Theory. We primarily use the term frequency-inverse document frequency (TF-IDF) to establish the particular degree of important of term in a document. We denote $w = value$ (TF-IDF). Since rough set is suited to nominal datasets, we quantize the normalized space into 11 values calculated by floor ($10w$). Next we construct decision table for the 2413 documents based on these 1384 selected words. Then we use the rough set method we proposed to further reduce the number of the features.

Evaluation and Result. We use *naïve Bayes model, vector space model, and support vector machine model* to evaluate our feature selection method, respectively. And we get 343 negative documents for testing, which are got from other objectionable Web Sites. As seen from Table 5 to Table 6, when m is 3, the performance gives same almost accuracy as in unreduced training data set or testing data set. In this phase, 129 words are found, and we find these words are all more relevant to the positive and negative documents, moreover, underlying semantics between these words is preserved.

Table 5. F1 Value in Training Sets B with different m

	Classifier	original	number of reducts		
			m=1	m=2	m=3
Numbers of Attributes		1384	18	67	129
F1 Value in Training Sets B	Naïve Bayes	.9276	.889	.91	.9223
	VSM	.9569	.9641	.9631	.9599
	SVM-Linear	.9954	.9730	.9796	.9846
	SVM-RBF	.9987	.9656	.9859	.9904

Table 6. F1 Value in Testing Sets B with different m

Classifier		original	number of reducts		
			m=1	m=2	m=3
Numbers of Attributes		1384	18	67	129
F1 Value in Testing Sets B	Naïve Bayes	.309	.827	.7464	.7872
	VSM	.9942	.9101	.9768	.9884
	SVM-Linear	.9941	.8425	.9621	.9825
	SVM-RBF	.9970	.8775	.9446	.9737

5 Conclusions

In this paper, we got good result with vector space model, support vector machines and Naive Bayes Model in the benchmark data set one. Data set two is a non-balance data set, we also get good result with vector space model, support vector machines, but we got poor result with Naive Bayes Model in this data set, especially in the testing data set. The reason is due to the different text expressing methods, which different filter based. Vector space model and support vector machines are based on bag of words to express document, and normalization technique is used, while Naive Bayes Model is based on the probability of terms and class. Data set two is a non-balance data set, it is difficult for Naive Bayes Model with the probability of selected terms to map all the feature space, and so it has a poor precision to filter unseen non-balance data set. And in our experiment, we concluded the normalization technique is very important to improve the precision than not to normalize a document.

In addition, we proposed a novel method to select features methods based on rough set. We primarily use CHI statistic methods to select features primarily, and next, to further select features using rough set, which produce m reducts. And between these reducts there are no common attributes, so these attributes have more powerfully capability to classify new objects. Thus more accurate and few features are extracted. At last we use naïve Bayes model, vector space model, support vector machine model to evaluate our feature selection method, respectively, the result shows our method is very effective.

The future work is that we will consider relevant feedback technique to improve the capability to adapt to the rapid penetration of the Web.

Acknowledgements

This work is funded by the National Natural Science Foundation of China under NO.60402019, and the National 863 High-Tech Research Plan of China under NO.2003AA142160.

References

1. Salton, G., Lesk, M.E.: Computer evaluation of indexing and text processing. Journal of the ACM **15**(1) (January 1968) 8–36
2. Salton, G., Wong, A., Yang, C.S.: A vector space model for automatic indexing, Comm. ACM 18 (11) (1975) 613–620
3. Lewis, D.D.: Naïve Bayes at forty: The independence assumption in information retrieval. In Proceedings of ECML-98, 10th European Conference on Machine Learning (Chemnitz, Germany, 1998) 4–15
4. JanZizka, Ales Bourek, Ludek Frey,TEA: A Text Analysis Tool for the Intelligent Text Document Filtering, TSD 2000, LNAI (1902) 151–156
5. Mitchell, T., Machine Learning, McGraw-Hill, New York (1997)
6. Burges, C.: A tutorial on support vector machines for pattern recognition. Data Mining and Knowledge Discovery, (2):121–167, (1998) 284
7. Joachims, T.: Text categorization with support vector machines. In Proceedings of the European Conference on Machine Learning. Springer Verlag (1998)
8. Pui Y.Lee, Siu C.Hui, Alvis Cheuk M.Fong. Neural Networks for Web Content Filtering. IEEE Intelligent Systems **17** (2002) 48–57
9. Zhou, Z.-H., Jiang, Y.: Medical diagnosis with C4.5 rule preceded by artificial neural network ensemble. IEEE Transactions on Information Technology in Biomedicine (2003) 7(1): 37–42
10. John, G., Kohavi, R., Pfleger,K.: Irrelevant Features and the Subset Selection Problem, Proc. ICML (1994) 121–129
11. Yiming Yang An evaluation of statistical approaches to text categorization. Journal of Information Retrieval, **1** No. 1 (1999) 67–88
12. Pawlak, Z.: "Rough sets", International Journal of Information and computer Science, 11(5), (1982) 341–356
13. Pawlak, Z., Rough Sets: Theoretical Aspects of Reasoning About Data, Kluwer Academic Publishing, Dordrecht (1991)
14. Cercone, N., Ziarko, W., Hu, X.: Rule Discovery from Databases: A Decision Matrix Approach, Proc. of ISMIS, Zakopane, Poland (1996) 653–662
15. Skowron, A., Rauszer C.: The Discernibility Matrices and Functions in Information Systems, Intelligent Decision Support - Handbook of Applications and Advances of the Rough Sets Theory, K. Slowinski (ed), Kluwer, Dordrecht (1992) 331–362
16. Yongguang Bao, Daisuke Asai, Xiaoyong Du, Kazutaka Yamada, and Naohiro Ishii: An Effective Rough Set-Based Method for Text Classification. IDEAL 2003, LNCS 2690, pp.545-552,2003. Springer-Verlag Berlin Heidelberg 2003
17. Chouchoulas, A., Shen, Q.: Rough Set-Aided Keyword Reduction for Text Categorisation. Journal of Applied Artificial Intelligence **15**(9) (2001) 843-873
18. Chouchoulas, A., Shen, Q.: A Rough Set-Based Approach to Text Classification. Proceedings of the 7th International Workshop on Rough Sets (Lecture Notes in Artificial Intelligence, No. 1711) (1999) 118–127
19. Chouchoulas, A., Halliwell, J., Shen, Q.: On the implementation of rough set attribute reduction, Proc. 2002 UK Workshop on Computational Intelligence (2002) 18–23
20. Jianchao Han, Xiaohua Hu, Tsao Young Lin: Feature Subset Selection Based on Relative Dependency between Attributes, Rough Sets and Current Trends in Computing: 4th International Conference, RSCTC (2004) 176–185
21. http://www-2.cs.cmu.edu/afs/cs/project/theo-11/www/naive-bayes.html
22. http://kdd.ics.uci.edu/summary.data.application.html

Parallel Algorithm for Mining Frequent Closed Sequences

Chuanxiang Ma[1,2] and Qinghua Li[1]

[1] School of computer science, Huazhong University of science and technology,
430074, China
[2] School of mathematics and computer science, Hubei University, 430062, China
mcx838@yahoo.com

Abstract. Previous studies have presented convincing arguments that a frequent sequence mining algorithm should not mine all frequent sequences but only the closed ones because the latter leads to not only more compact yet complete result set but also better efficiency. However, frequent closed sequence mining is still challenging on stand-alone for its large size and high dimension. In this paper, an algorithm, PFCSeq, is presented for mining frequent closed sequence based on distributed-memory parallel machine, in which each processor mines local frequent closed sequence set independently using task parallelism with data parallelism approach, and only two communications are needed except that imbalance is detected. Therefore, time spent in communications is significantly reduced. In order to ensure good load balance among processors, a dynamic workload balance strategy is proposed. Experiments show that it is linearly scalable in terms of database size and the number of processors.

1 Introduction

Frequent sequential pattern mining, since it is introduced in [1], plays an important role in data mining task, with broad applications, such as discovery of motifs and tandem repeats in DAN sequences, analysis of customer shopping sequences and mining XML query access patterns for caching, and so on. Efficient mining methods have been studied extensively, including the general sequential pattern mining, constraint-based sequential pattern mining, frequent episode mining, temporal relation mining, and long sequential pattern mining in noisy environment.

In recent years a new argument has been presented that for mining frequent sequential patterns, one should not mine all frequent sequential patterns but the closed ones because the latter leads to not only more compact yet complete result set but also better efficiency [6][7].

However, the task of finding frequent closed sequence in large database is still challenging. The search space is still extremely large. Given search complexity, serial algorithms cannot provide scalability, in terms of the data size and the performance for large databases. Because there is always this limit to the performance of a single processor, we must rely on parallel multiprocessor systems to fulfill this role.

There are two kinds of parallel algorithms for mining sequential patterns according to the architecture they used in current research. The first is shared memory [3], in

V. Gorodetsky, J. Liu, and V.A. Skormin (Eds.): AIS-ADM 2005, LNAI 3505, pp. 184 – 192, 2005.
© Springer-Verlag Berlin Heidelberg 2005

which all processors access common memory, and each processor has direct and equal access to the common memory in the system, but the finite bandwidth of common bus can limit scalability; the other is distributed memory, in which each processor has a private memory that can only be accessed directly by itself and a message passing programming paradigm is utilized when a processor need to access to the data in the local memory of another processor. It may bring high communication overheads. In [4], three parallel algorithms, NPSPM, HPSPM and SPSPM based on GSP, are presented. The main limitation of all these parallel algorithms is that they make repeated passes over the disk-resident database partition, incurring high I/O overheads. Furthermore, the schemes involve exchanging the remote database partitions during each iteration; which resulting in high communication and synchronization overheads. They also use complicated hash structures, which entail additional overhead in maintenance and search and typically also have poor cache locality.

In this paper, we propose a parallel algorithm, PFCSeq, for mining frequent closed sequences on distributed memory machines. PFCSeq is an asynchronous algorithm in that it requires no synchronization among processors, except that at the beginning and the end of the program. And the database scanned decreases gradually in the algorithm. At the same time, a dynamic load balance scheme to ensure good load balance among processors is presented. Therefore, smaller communication and I/O overheads are needed in PFCSeq. Experiments show that it is successful for overcoming the above problems.

The rest of this paper is organized as follows: we describe related concepts and properties about frequent closed sequence mining in section 2; Section 3 describes frequent sequent tree generating; section 4 is the parallel algorithm for mining frequent closed sequences on distributed machine; Experiment result is given in section 5; and we conclude in Section 6.

2 Related Concepts and Properties

The problem of mining frequent closed sequence can be stated as follows: Let $I = \{i_1, i_2, ..., i_n\}$ be a set of n distinct items. An itemset is a non-empty unordered collection of items (without loss of generality, we assume that items in an itemset are sorted in increasing order). An itemset is denoted as $(i_1 i_2 ... i_k)$, where i_j is an item. A sequence is an ordered list of itemsets and denoted as $S = <s_1, s_2, ..., s_m>$, where s_i ($i=1,2,...,m$) is an itemset, i.e., $s_i \subseteq I$. The length of a sequence S is denoted as $|S| = \sum_{1 \le i \le m} |s_i|$. A sequence $S_a = <a_1, a_2, ..., a_n>$ is a subsequence of another sequence $S_b = <b_1, b_2, ..., b_m>$ (denoted as $S_a \subseteq S_b$), if the value of the expression $\exists (1 \le i_1 < i_2 < ... < i_n \le m) \wedge (a_1 \subseteq b_{i1}, a_2 \subseteq b_{i2}, ..., a_n \subseteq b_{in})$ is true, where S_a is the subsequence of S_b, and S_b is the supersequence of S_a. At the same time, we call S_a is the proper subsequence of S_b, and S_b is the proper supersequence of S_a if $|S_a| \neq |S_b|$, and denoted as $S_a \subset S_b$. A sequence database(denoted as SDB) is a set of tuples, which has the form $<Sid,S>$, where Sid is the identifier of sequence S. Table 1 is the sample dataset. The number of tuples is the size of SDB, denoted as $|SDB|$. A tuple

<Sid,S> contains a sequence s if and only if $s \subseteq S$. The absolute support of a sequence s, denoted as $sup(s)$, is the total number of tuples that contain this sequence in *SDB*. The relative support of a sequence is defined as $sup(S_a)/|SDB|$. Given a threshold *minsup* defined by user, a sequence is frequent if its support is no less than *minsup*. The set of the frequent sequence is denoted as *FS*.

Definition 1. For any sequence $s \in FS$, if $\neg \exists s'(s' \in FS \land s' \supset s \land \sup(s) = \sup(s'))$ is true, then s is called a frequent closed sequence.

Definition 2. Given a sequence $s = <t_1, t_2, ..., t_m>$ and an item α, $s \infty \alpha$ means that s concatenates with α. It can be I-step extension, $s \infty_i \alpha = <t_1, t_2, ..., t_m \cup \{\alpha\}>$ if $\forall k \in t_m, k < \alpha$; or S-step extension, $s \infty_s \alpha = <t_1, t_2, ..., t_m, \{\alpha\}>$. For example, <(af)> is an I-step extension of <(a)>, and <(a)(b)>is a S-step extension of <(a)> in the sample database *SDB*.

Definition 3. A sequence $S_a = <a_1, a_2, ..., a_n>$ is a prefix of another sequence $S_b = <b_1, b_2, ..., b_m>$, if and only if: ① $a_i = b_i$ ($i \leq m-1$); ② $a_m \subseteq b_m$; ③ all the items in $(a_m - b_m)$ are alphabetically after those in b_m.

Definition 4. Given a sequence S_a and one of its subsequence S_b, another subsequence S' of S_a is the projection corresponding to the prefix sequence S_b, if and only if: ① S' has got prefix S_b; ② there exists no supersequence S'', such that $S'' \subseteq S_a$, and has got prefix S_b. The remainder part after projection is called the postfix sequence corresponding to S_b in S_a. For example, sequence <(f)(d)>is a subsequence of the sequence <(af)(d)(e)(a)>, then <(af)(d)> is the projection corresponding to prefix <(f)(d)>, and <(e)(a)> is the postfix sequence corresponding to <(f)(d)> in <(af)(d)(e)(a)>.

Definition 5. Frequent sequence tree is a lexicographic sequence tree, denoted as PT= (V,E), where V is the set of nodes in tree, each node representing a frequent sequence, which is denoted as <sequence>:<d>, where d is support E is the set of edges in the tree. Let S_a be the child of sequence S_b, then $|S_a| = |S_b| + 1$. **Fig.1** is a projected tree corresponding to the sample sequence database (see **Table 1**). The sequences in elliptical node are frequent closed sequences.

Table 1. A Sample Sequence Database

Sid	Sequence
1	<(af) (d) (e)(a)>
2	<(e) (a) (b)>
3	<(e)(abf)(bde)>

Property 1. For two nodes s and s', if s is the child of s' and $sup(s)=sup(s')$, then s' is not a frequent closed sequence.

Property 2. Given two sequences s and s', if $sup(s)=sup(s')$ and $|s|=|s'|$, then $s \not\subset s'$ or $s' \not\subset s$.

3 Generating Frequent Sequence Tree

For a given sequence database (for instance, **Table 1**), frequent items are obtained firstly according to minimum support, and these items form initialization nodes in frequent sequence tree. Then these nodes are extended on I-Step extension or S-Step extension level by level. And the frequent extension items are obtained by scanning database consisted of postfix sequences corresponding to its parent node in original database. For the same item, we define that I-step extension is prior to S-step extension.

For example, sequence $<(a)>$:2 (see **Fig.1**) is one of the initialization nodes, then $<(\_f)(d)(e)(a)>$, $<(b)>$, $<(\_bf)(bde)>$ are the postfix sequences corresponding to the parent node $<(a)>$:2. We can get frequent items $<(\_f)>$, $<(b)>$, $<(d)>$ and $<(e)>$ using these postfix sequences. Then children, $<(af)>$:2, $<(a)(b)>$:2, $<(a)(d)>$:2 and $<(a)(e)>$:2, are obtained according to **definition 2**.

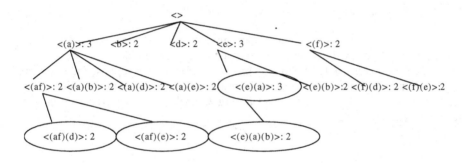

Fig. 1. Frequent sequence tree

For each node in frequent sequence tree, we check it whether it is frequent closed sequence according to **definition1, property 1** and **property 2**.

4 Parallel Mining Frequent Closed Sequence on Distributed Memory Machine

In this section we present a parallel algorithm, PFCSeq, for mining frequent closed sequences based on projected tree on distributed-memory parallel machine. The target is to obtain good speedup, which may be simply defined as follows:

$$S_p = \frac{T_s}{T_p} \tag{1}$$

Where T_s is the time spent by the best serial algorithm, and T_p is the time spent by parallel machine with p processors.

The key features of this algorithm are as follows: (1) each processor generates local frequent closed sequence independently by depth-first search; (2) the size of database scanned decreases as projection goes on; (3) only two communications are needed except that imbalance is detected; (4) a dynamic load balance strategy is adopted.

Theorem 1. Local non-frequent closed sequence is anything but globally frequent closed sequence; globally frequent closed sequence is local frequent closed sequence by all means.

4.1 Data Partition

At the beginning of the algorithm the original database is equally partitioned into p blocks, where p is the number of processors in the system. Each processor counts the local support for local items, exchanges the support among the processors, and computes the global frequent sequences set FS_1 with length of 1. Then FS_1 and the corresponding postfix sequence databases are distributed into the p processors equally.

4.2 Task Parallelism

In PFCSeq, each processor generates local frequent closed sequence independently based on local frequent 1-sequence set and postfix sequence databases by depth-first, no synchronization is needed during the process. For example, suppose there are three processors named P_1, P_2, P_3 respectively in the system, the task for mining sample database (**Table 1**) can be partitioned as **Fig.2**. Each processor processes an independently sub-tree.

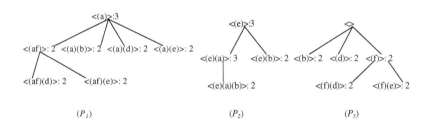

Fig. 2. Task in processor P_1, P_2 and P_3

4.3 Load Balance Method

The work on each processor consists of three processes. The first is PROJECT process which projects database into a smaller one. The second is SCAN process which scans postfix sequence database generated by PROJECT process to count frequent 1-items. The third is CHECK process which checks each node whether it is a frequent closed sequence.

If the time required by processor P_i for PROJECT, SCAN and CHECK process is expressed by PT_i, ST_i, and CT_i respectively, the overall processing time for that processor can be formulated by:

$$\Delta T_i = \Delta PT_i + \Delta ST_i + \Delta CT_i \qquad (2)$$

Where Δ is the time-interval.

Let n_i is the number of nodes on processor P_i, then $PT_i = \alpha n_i$, $ST_i = \beta n_i$, $CT_i = \chi n_i$. Coefficients α, β and χ are determined using statistical information collected during previous interval.

So the remaining time required by that processor can be estimated by the following expression:

$$restT_i = restPT_i + restST_i + restCT \qquad (3)$$

When projection goes in-depth gradually, load among processors may become imbalance. In order to have all processors complete their job at the same time, we use dynamic balance method to reallocate the load for each processor so that each processor has the same $restT_i$.

The skew is defined as follows:

$$skew = \frac{\max(restTi) - \min(restTi)}{avg(restTi)} \qquad (4)$$

We can judge the load control is needed if *skew* exceeds some certain threshold. Here we use a coordinator to run this plan. That is, the coordinator monitors the load on each processor, and computes the *skew*, if *skew* is more than the threshold given, then run the plan that migrates superfluous load from the processor with maximal load to the one with minimal load.

4.4 Parallel Algorithm Describing-PFCSeq

Parallel algorithm comprises three parts including initialization phase, asynchronism phase and collection phase. And each part is described as follows:

Initialization:

1) Partition original sequence database (*SDB*) equally into processors in the system, and the database in processor P_i is denoted by SDB^i;
2) Each processor scans local database, count supports for local 1-items;
3) Exchange local supports among processors, count global support for 1-items, generate frequent 1-items set FS_1, form the initial nodes;
4) Build projected database for each frequent 1-item in FS_1, divide frequent 1-items (initial nodes) and corresponding postfix sequence database into the processors in the system.

Asynchronism Phase:

For each node in processor P_i do

1) Scan database, and count frequent I-Step extension items and S-Step extension items;
2) Generate frequent k-sequence set FS_k, (k>=2), and form the new nodes;

3) For each new node, check whether it is frequent closed sequence according to the definition of frequent closed sequence and property 1 and property 2, and generate local frequent closed sequence set FCS^i;
4) Build postfix sequence database for each new node;
5) Repeat 1)~4), until there is no new node is generated.

Collection:
1) Compute candidate frequent closed sequence set $FCS=FCS^1 \cup FCS^2 \cup \ldots \cup FCS^p$ according to theorem 1;
2) Delete the non-frequent closed sequences in FCS, obtain globally frequent closed sequence set.

This algorithm uses task partition with data partition approach to compute frequent closed sequence independently, and only two communications are needed unless the coordinator detects imbalance. Communication overhead is reduced significantly. Moreover, the size of postfix sequence database decreases rapidly, so I/O overhead is also reduced. Therefore, the algorithm obtains good performance.

5   Experiments

5.1   Experimental Environment

In order to test the performance of algorithm PFCSeq, we do several experiments on dawning 3000 parallel machine which is a distributed-memory machine with 3 nodes. These nodes are connected by internal communication network, and in each node there are common main memory with capacity 2GB and HD with 9GB shared by 4 CPUs with 375MHZ. At most 12 processors are permitted in the system. Aggregation memory is 6GB.

5.2   Experiment Dataset

We generate three datasets by using a synthetic dataset generator provided by IBM which can be retrieved from an IBM website, http://www.almaden.ibm.com/cs/quest. They are

C10T5N10S4I1.25D1M,C20T5N10S4I1.25D1M and
C20T2.5N10S8I1.25D1M respectively. Where the parameters is explained as Table 2:

Table 2. Parameters for IBM Quest data generator

Abbr.	Meaning
D	Number of sequences in 000s
C	Average itemsets per sequence
T	Average items per itemset
N	Number of different items in 000s
S	Average itemsets in maximal sequences
I	Average items in maximal sequences

Let *minsup* = IDI*0.25%, we do the following experiments:
1) runtime as the number of processors increases in the system;
speedup as the number of processors increases in the system.

5.3 Experiment Results

Fig.3 shows the total execution time and the speedup charts for each dataset using the minimum support values given by **5.2**. We obtain near linear speedup in terms of the number of processors and the size of dataset.

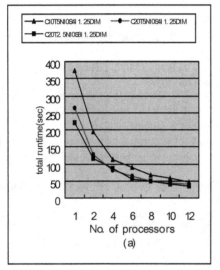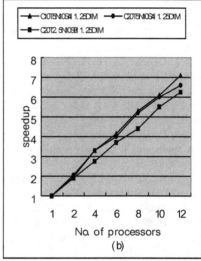

Fig. 3. Performance test for algorithm PFSCeq

6 Conclusions

Many studies have elaborated that frequent closed sequence mining has the same expressive power as that of all frequent sequence mining yet leads to more compact result set and significantly better efficiency. However, the task of finding frequent closed sequence in large database is still challenging. The search space is still extremely large. Given search complexity, serial algorithms cannot provide scalability, in terms of the data size and the performance for large databases. Because there is always this limit to the performance of a single processor, we must rely on parallel multiprocessor systems to fulfill this role. In this paper, we propose a parallel algorithm, PFCSeq, mining frequent closed sequence based on distributed-memory parallel machine. In this algorithm, each processor generates local frequent closed sequence independently, and only two communications are needed except that imbalance in the system is detected. Experiments results show that the algorithm PFCSeq has linear scalability in terms of the size of database and the number of processors in the system.

Acknowledgement

This research is supported by National Nature Science Foundation of China (No:602730075).

References

1. Agrawal, R., Srikant, R.: Mining Sequential patterns[C]. In ICDE'95, Taipei, Taiwan, Mar. (1995)
2. Ayres, J., Gehuke, J., Yiu, T., Flannick, J.: Sequential Pattern Mining using a Bitmap Representation[C]. In SIGKDD'02, Edmonton, Canada (July 2002)
3. Mohammed J. Zaki: Parallel sequence mining on smp machines[C]. In Workshop On Large-Scale Paralle KDD System(in conjunction 5th ACM SIGKDD International Conference on Konwledge Discovery and Data Mining), san Diego,CA (august 1999) 57–65
4. Shintani, T., Kitsuregawa, M.: Mining algorithms for sequential patterns in parallel: Hash based approach[C], In 2nd Pacific-Asia Conf. on Knowledge Discovery and Data Mining (April 1998)
5. Agrawal, R., Shafer, J.C.: Parallel Mining of Association Rules[J]□IEEE Trans.on knowledge and Data Engineering, Vol.8, No.6 (1996)
6. Yan, X., Han, J., AFSHAR, R.: CloSpan: Mining Closed Sequential Patterns in Large Databases[C]. In SDM'03, San Franciso, CA (May 2003)
7. Wang, J., Han, J.: BIDE: Efficient Mining of Frequent Closed Sequences[C]. In ICDE'04 , Boston, USA (2004)
8. Agarwall, R.C., Aggarwal, C. et al.: A tree projection algorithm for generation for frequent itemsets[J]. Journal of Parallel and Distributed Computing (2000)

Decision Trees Capacity
and Probability of Misclassification

Victor Nedel'ko

Institute of Mathematics SB RAS, Laboratory of Data Analysis,
660090 Novosibirsk, Russia
nedelko@math.nsc.ru
http://math.nsc.ru/LBRT/i1/nedelko/index.html

Abstract. Deciding functions statistical robustness problem is considered. The goal is to estimate misclassification probability for decision function by training sample. The paper contains results of investigation an empirical risk bias for decision tree classifier in comparison with a linear classifiers and with exact bias estimates for a discrete case. This allows to find out how far Vapnik–Chervonenkis risk estimates are off for considered decision function classes and to choose optimal complexity parameters for constructed decision functions. For heuristic algorithms those do not perform exhaustive search there was proposed a method for estimating an effective capacity.

1   Introduction

An overtraining problem consists in that decision function quality being evaluated by the training sample appears much better than its real quality. To get true risk estimation in data mining one uses a validation set or leave-one-out method. But these methods have some disadvantages. The first one decreases a sample available for building a decision function. The second one takes extra computational resources and is unable to estimate risk volatility.

So, one needs a method that allows estimating a risk by training sample directly, i. e. by an empirical risk. This requires estimating first an empirical risk bias, because an empirical risk is usually much lower than a risk (misclassification probability), i. e. it is a biased risk estimate.

The problem was solved by Vapnik and Chervonenkis [1]. They introduced a concept of capacity (growth function) of a decision rules set. This approach is quite powerful, but known decision quality estimates are pessimistic and not precise. There are several issues of its inaccuracy, the most significant one is a probabilistic approximation like: $P\left(\sum A_i\right) \le \sum P\left(A_i\right)$.

For a case of discrete features, there were exact estimates of an empirical risk bias obtained [4].

The goal of this paper is to extrapolate that result on continuous case and to evaluate an accuracy of VC–estimations for decision tree classifier.

V. Gorodetsky, J. Liu, and V.A. Skormin (Eds.): AIS-ADM 2005, LNAI 3505, pp. 193–199, 2005.

2 Formal Problem Definition

Let deciding function be a correspondence $f : X \to Y$, where X – a features values space and Y – a forecasting values space.

For the determination of deciding functions quality we need to assign a function of losses: $L : Y^2 \to [0, \infty)$.

By a risk we shall understand an average loss:

$$R(c, f) = \int L(y, f(x)) dP_c[D].$$

Here C is a set of probabilistic measures on $D = X \times Y$ and $c \in C$ is a measure $P_c[D]$. The set C contains all the measures for those a conditional measure $P_c[Y/x]$ exists $\forall x \in X$.

Hereinafter square parentheses will hold a set that a probabilistic space is defined on.

For building a deciding function there is a random independent sample $v_c = \left\{ (x^i, y^i) \in D \mid i = \overline{1, N} \right\}$ from distribution $P_c[D]$ used.

An empirical risk will mean a sample risk estimation: $\tilde{R}(v, f) = \frac{1}{N} \sum_{i=1}^{N} L(y^i, f(x^i))$.

For the all practically used algorithms building deciding functions an empirical risk appears a biased risk estimation, being always lowered, as far as algorithms minimize an empirical risk.

So, estimating this bias is actual.

Enter indications:

$$F(c, Q) = ER(c, f_{Q,v}), \qquad \tilde{F}(c, Q) = E\tilde{R}(c, f_{Q,v}).$$

Here $Q : \{v\} \to \{f\}$ is an algorithm building deciding functions, and $f_{Q,v}$ – a deciding function built on the sample v by algorithm Q.

Expectation is calculated over the all samples of volume N.

Introduce an extreme bias function:

$$S_Q(\tilde{F}_0) = \hat{F}_Q(\tilde{F}_0) - \tilde{F}_0, \tag{1}$$

where $\hat{F}_Q(\tilde{F}_0) = \sup\limits_{c : \tilde{F}(c, Q) = \tilde{F}_0} F(c, Q)$.

We shall consider a problem of classification i. e. $Y = \{1, 2\}$ with the loss function:

$$L(y, y') = \begin{cases} 0, & y = y' \\ 1, & y \neq y' \end{cases}.$$

3 Multinomial Case

In [4] there is reported the dependency $S_Q\left(\tilde{F}_0\right)$ for the multinomial case when X is discrete, i. e. $X = \{1,\ldots,n\}$, and Q minimizes an empirical risk in each $x \in X$.

For the further comparison let's remember a dependency $S_Q\left(\tilde{F}_0\right)$ in asymptotic case: $\dfrac{N}{n} = M = \text{const}, \quad N \to \infty,$

$n \to \infty$.

This asymptotic approximation is wholly acceptable already by $n = 10$, herewith it has only one input parameter M.

Now we can calculate an accuracy of Vapnik–Chervonenkis evaluations for the considered case of discrete X, as far as we know an exact dependency of average risk on the empirical risk for the "worst" strategy of nature.

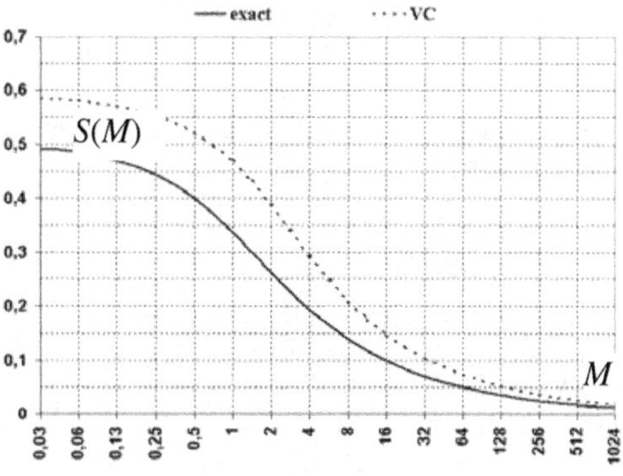

For $S\left(\tilde{F}_0\right)$ in [1] there is reported an estimation $S_V'\left(\tilde{F}_0\right) = \tau$, as well as an improved estimation:

Fig. 1. Risk bias and VC–estimation. Multinomial case, $ER = 0.5$

$$S_V'\left(\tilde{F}_0\right) = \tau^2\left(1 + \sqrt{1 + \frac{2\tilde{F}_0}{\tau^2}}\right), \quad \text{where} \quad \tau \quad \text{asymptotically tends to} \quad \sqrt{\frac{\ln 2}{2M'}},$$

$$M' = M \big/ \left(1 - e^{-M}\right).$$

On figure 1 there are drawn the dependency $S(M) = \max\limits_{\tilde{F}_0} S\left(\tilde{F}_0\right)_M$ and its estimation $S_V(M) = \max\limits_{\tilde{F}_0} S_V\left(\tilde{F}_0\right)_M$. Plots demonstrate significant greatness of the last.

Note that the accuracy of Vapnik–Chervonenkis estimation falls since $\tilde{F}_0$ decreases. For example, in "deterministic case" when $\tilde{F}_0 = 0$ we have:

$$\frac{S_V'(0)}{S_Q(0)} = \frac{2Me\left(1 - e^{-M}\right)\ln 2}{M} \xrightarrow[M \to \infty]{} 2e\ln 2 \approx 3,77 .$$

By $M \le 1$ the "worst" distribution (that provides maximal bias) is uniform on X and the results obtained is consistent with results for multinomial case reported in [2]. By $M > 1$ and restricted $\tilde{F}_0$ the "worst" distribution is not uniform on X.

4 Linear Decision Functions

Let us compare risk bias values for discrete case with bias for linear decision functions.

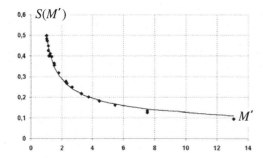

Fig. 2. Risk biases for multinomial and linear decision functions

Table 1. Risk bias for linear decision functions

d	N	M'	S
1	3	1.16	0.4
1	10	2.31	0.27
1	20	3.75	0.20
1	50	7.53	0.13
1	100	13.08	0.095
2	4	1.05	0.47
2	10	1.53	0.357
2	20	2.33	0.27
2	50	4.44	0.18
2	100	7.53	0.13
3	5	1.019	0.48
3	10	1.247	0.41
3	20	1.79	0.32
3	50	3.28	0.22
3	100	5.46	0.162
4	10	1.111	0.45
4	20	1.5	0.355
4	50	2.66	0.249
5	10	1.044	0.476
5	20	1.33	0.398
5	50	2.27	0.275

For simplifying there was considered uniform distribution on features for both classes. For such c misclassification probability equals to 0.5 for every decision function, but empirical risk appears to be much lower.

To find a dependence $S(M)$ for linear deciding functions in $X = [0,1]^d$ a statistical modeling was used. By the modeling there was for each combination of parameters a hundred of samples drawn from uniform distribution on D, for each sample the best linear classifier built by exhaustive search. Note that the uniform distribution on D provides maximum of empirical risk bias since we put no restrictions on $\tilde{F}_0$.

A table 1 shows the result of modeling. Here d – features space X dimensionality, N – sample size, $M' = \dfrac{N}{\log_2 \mathbf{C}}$ – sample size divided by VC-capacity of linear functions class ($\mathbf{C}$ is a total number of possible decision assignments to sample points by using linear decision functions), S – risk bias.

The same results are shown (by markers) on fig. 2 in comparison with $S(M')$ for discrete case (solid line).

Obtained results show that bias dependence on M' for linear functions is close to dependence for discrete (multinomial) case.

5   Decision Tree Classifier

The goal now is to evaluate a risk bias for decision functions in form of binary decision trees [3].

Decision tree is a binary tree with terminal nodes marked by goal class (certain value y) and non-terminal nodes marked by predicates in form: $X_j < \alpha$, where α is a value. Two arcs starting from each non-terminal node correspond to true and false predicate values.

Each decision tree forms certain sequential partitioning in X.

There was the exhaustive search algorithm implemented. The search is performed over the all decision trees with L terminal nodes and the best tree minimizing an empirical risk is founded.

While searching, the algorithm counts $\mathbf{C}$ – the number of different assignments y to sample objects.

Table 2. Risk bias for tree decision functions

d	N	L	M'	S
1	2	1	2	0.26
1	2	2	1	0.5
1	5	2	1.51	0.36
1	5	3	1.12	0.44
1	10	2	2.31	0.27
1	10	3	1.53	0.34
1	20	2	3.76	0.19
1	20	3	2.33	0.26
1	20	5	1.50	0.34
2	5	2	1.26	0.40
2	5	3	1.02	0.49
2	10	2	1.92	0.30
2	10	3	1.28	0.40
2	20	2	3.19	0.23
2	20	3	1.94	0.31
2	20	4	1.46	0.37
3	5	2	1.17	0.42
3	20	2	2.92	0.24
3	20	3	1.77	0.34
3	20	5	1.12	0.45
4	20	2	2.76	0.25
5	10	2	1.57	0.35
10	10	2	1.39	0.38

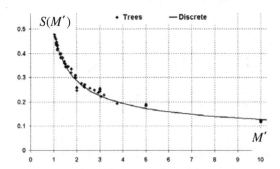

Fig. 3. Risk biases for multinomial and tree decision functions

Since $\mathbf{C}$ essentially differs on different samples one need to evaluate an entropy $H = \mathrm{E} \log_2 \mathbf{C}$.

Then $M' = \dfrac{N}{H}$.

Table 2 shows statistical robustness of decision trees by different parameters while uniform distribution on D assumed. The same result is shown on figure 3 in comparison with multinomial case.

One can see again that risk bias is caused and determined by M' (sample size per complexity) rather than any other factor.

6 Relevant Capacities

Let's compare complexities (capacities) of decision trees and linear classifier.

Table 3 shows linear classifier dimensionality d' that provides the same entropy (average number of different assignments y to sample objects) like decision trees with L terminal nodes in d-dimensional space.

Non-integer values of d' appears because of interpolation performed.

Though decision trees seem to be simple they have essential capacity. For example if $L = d$ decision trees capacity exceeds capacity of linear classifier.

Column d'' corresponds to a case of a gradient search.

The most of practical algorithms do not perform exhaustive search, but make some kind of gradient one. Hence their capacity should be essentially lower than decision functions class capacity (that is the same as the capacity of exhaustive search algorithm).

Note that if an algorithm does not try all the functions, but always finds the best one, then its capacity is equal to whole class capacity. So, an effective capacity depends not on the number of decisions tested, but on the distance between the decision obtained and the best one.

Table 3. Correspondent dimensionality for tree and linear decision functions. Non-integer values of d' appears because of interpolation performed

d	N	L	d'	d''	d	N	L	d'	d''
1	5	2	1	1.07	2	5	2	1.56	1.5
2	10	2	1.4	1.47	2	20	2	1.3	1.43
3	2	2	1	1	3	5	2	1.83	1.74
3	10	2	1.64	1.71	3	20	2	1.47	1.59
4	5	2	2.09	1.89	4	20	2	1.59	1.79
5	10	2	1.93	2.02	10	10	2	2.45	2.58
1	5	3	2	1.39	2	5	3	2.95	2.01
2	10	3	2.86	2.4	2	20	3	2.66	2.55
3	5	3	3.76	2.54	3	10	3	3.48	3.1
3	20	3	3.07	3.18	4	5	3	3.99	3.36
4	10	3	3.94	3.21	2	5	4	3.99	2.04
2	20	4	4.26	3.31	3	5	4	4	2.47
3	10	4	5.82	3.65	3	20	4	5.1	4.1
4	10	4	6.77	4.33	1	10	5	4	1.82
2	10	5	6.45	2.83	3	15	5	7.77	4.41

To estimate an algorithm effective capacity we suggest the following method.

First, by generating random samples from the uniform distribution on D an expectation of empirical risk is estimated. Since a risk for any decision is equal to 0,5 a risk bias is known too.

Then, having risk bias a correspondent value M' that delivers the same bias in discrete case may be found.

Finally, a value $\frac{N}{M'}$ may be considered as an effective capacity. Note that the reported method for calculation an effective capacity is, in fact, the definition of the last.

Value d'' in the table 3 is an effective capacity of gradient algorithm that performs sequential construction a tree, adding on each step a node providing biggest increment of criterion.

7   Conclusion

It is known that risk estimations by Vapnik and Chervonenkis may increase an expected risk up to several times from its true maximum. For the multinomial case (a discrete feature) these estimations was essentially improved and the exact maximum of empirical risk bias was found.

This work shows that such improvement is applicable also for continuous space, e.g. linear decision functions and decision trees.

Practical use of the result consists in that one can apply obtained scaling of VC-estimations to real tasks. The results obtained for multinomial case may be propagated on continuous one by using VC-capacity of decision function class instead of n.

Comparison of linear classifier and decision trees capacities is also performed.

For algorithms those do not perform exhaustive search (but use heuristics) there was proposed a method for estimating an effective capacity.

Acknowledgement

The work is supported by RFBR, grant 04-01-00858-a.

References

1. Vapnik, V.N., Chervonenkis, A. Ja.: Theory of pattern recognition. Moscow "Nauka" (1974) 415 (in Russian)
2. Raudys, S.: Statistical and neural classifiers, Springer (2001)
3. Lbov, G.S., Startseva, N.G.: Logical deciding functions and questions of statistical stability of decisions. Novosibirsk: Institute of mathematics (1999) 211 (in Russian)
4. Nedel'ko, V.M.: Estimating a Quality of Decision Function by Empirical Risk // LNAI 2734. Machine Learning and Data Mining, MLDM 2003, Leipzig. Proceedings. Springer-Verlag. (2003) 182–187

Querying Dynamic and Context-Sensitive Metadata in Semantic Web

Sergiy Nikitin, Vagan Terziyan, Yaroslav Tsaruk, and Andriy Zharko

Industrial Ontologies Group, Agora Center, University of Jyväskylä,
P.O. Box 35, FIN-40014 Jyväskylä, Finland
`senikiti@cc.jyu.fi`

Abstract. RDF (core Semantic Web standard) is not originally appropriate for context representation, because of its initial focus on the ordinary Web resources, such as web pages, files, databases, services, etc., which structure and content are more or less stable. However, on the other hand, emerging industrial applications consider e.g. machines, processes, personnel, services for condition monitoring, remote diagnostics and maintenance, etc. to be specific classes of Web resources and thus a subject for semantic annotation. Such resources are naturally dynamic, not only from the point of view of changing values for some attributes (state of resource), but also from the point of view of changing "status-labels" (condition of the resource). Thus, context-awareness and dynamism appear to be new requirements to the existing RDF. This paper discusses the issues of representing the contexts in RDF and constructions coming with context representation. We discover certain representation patterns and their classification towards development of the general approach of querying dynamic and context-sensitive metadata in Semantic Web by autonomous agents.

1 Introduction

Emerging Semantic Web technology offers a Resource Description Framework (RDF) as a standard for semantic annotation of Web resources. It is expected that Web content with RDF-based metadata layer and ontological basis for it will be enough to enable interoperable and automated processing of Web data by various applications. RDF-based tools, e.g. Hewlett-Packard's Jena [14] and Stanford's Protégé [15] provide a base for reasoning about metadata and about situated data (entities situated in time and space) that is superior to alternatives such as relational databases or object-oriented databases. However, according e.g. to [10] essential representational ability is missing from the current generation of Semantic Web tools and languages. When that ability is added, the resulting capabilities offer a combination of novelty and flexibility that may usher in a wave of commercial Semantic Web tool-based applications. Evidently the existing RDF tools should be extended to support contexts to enable querying a set of RDF statements having common temporal, spatial or other metadata attributes. In [10] it was concluded that the "clear winners" for possible solution can be quads (i.e. adding a fourth field of type 'context' to each RDF triple) and a context mechanism that references individuals instead of state-

V. Gorodetsky, J. Liu, and V.A. Skormin (Eds.): AIS-ADM 2005, LNAI 3505, pp. 200 – 214, 2005.

ments. Another attempt has been made recently to add C-OWL (Context OWL), an extended language with an enriched semantics which allows us to contextualize ontologies, namely, to localize their contents (and, therefore, to make them not visible to the outside) and to allow for explicit mappings (bridge rules). The core open issue is the tension between how much knowledge should be shared and globalized (via ontologies) and how much should be localized with limited and controlled forms of globalization (via contexts) [11]. In [12] the usage of context- and content-based trust mechanisms have been proposed and the cRDF trust architecture was presented which allows the formulation of subjective and task-specific trust policies as a combination of reputation-, context- and content-based trust mechanisms. There exist different ways how to understand and use context information for RDF data. In [13] these different ways have been summarized and the RDF-Source related Storage System (RDF-S3) has been proposed. RDF-S3 aimed to keep track of the source information for each stored RDF triple. On top the RDF-S3 has an extended version of *easy RQL* (eRQL) that makes use of the source information supported by RDF-S3. Therefore queries can be restricted to trusted sources and results can be viewed inside their RDF graph context. Two main arguments are stated in [13] for using context nodes instead of quads. First, quads are not compatible with the RDF model and second, the distinction between the given RDF information and information that is given in addition, like external context information, is much more complicated when using quads, whereas additional context nodes can be easily distinct from RDF triples. Therefore context nodes were used instead of context parts (quads).

There is not yet clear vision, which way is better (triples or quads) for representing contextual metadata in RDF. Another issue is for what kind of resources such descriptions will be required. On one hand the ordinary Web resources, such as web pages, files, databases, services, etc., which structure and content are more or less stable, probably do not need a specific way of context representation. However, on the other hand, emerging industrial applications consider e.g. machines, processes, personnel, services for condition monitoring, remote diagnostics and maintenance, etc. represent specific classes of Web resources and thus a subject for semantic annotation. Such resources are naturally dynamic, not only from the point of view of changing values for some attributes (state of resource) but also from the point of view of changing "status-labels" (condition of the resource). In our former effort within SmartResource project [16] we presented Resource State/Condition Description Framework (RscDF), as an extension to RDF, which introduces upper-ontology for describing such characteristics of resources as states and corresponding conditions, dynamics of state changes, target conditions and historical data about previous states. These descriptions are supposed to be used by external Web-services (e.g. condition monitoring, remote diagnostics and predictive maintenance of the resources). We presented RscDF as temporal and contextual extensions of RDF and discussed a State-Symptom-Diagnosis-Decision-Maintenance model as the basis for RscDF schema.

RSCDF is a unified representation format for resource state and condition description (encoding). RscDF-language formalizes context definition structure. RscDF-Schema defines main concepts and structure of the language. The structure is highly flexible, thus allowing definition of different complex constructions over the basic statements. Different definitions being used for resource description must refer to or define instances of classes from Industrial Maintenance Ontology. Detailed description of RscDF-language is not in a scope of this paper, so we refer to [17]. Figure 1 shows the key element of RscDF – "SR_Statement".

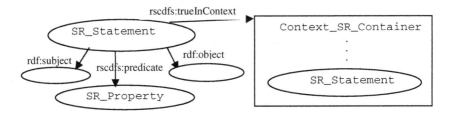

Fig. 1. SR_Statement structure

The SR_Statement defines the basic structure of statements being used in RscDF. The combinations of statements and references to statements and statement containers may form highly structured semantic description. The important semantics are represented by SR_Property class and its subproperties. The property in the rscdfs:predicate container defines the type and structure of rdf:object of current SR_Statement. However, the property specification defines only domain and range. So to know the structure of the statement, we have to attach some pattern description to SR_Property.

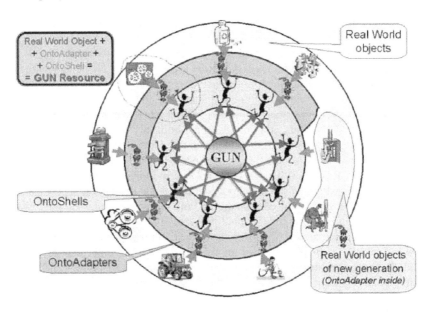

Fig. 2. GUN concept illustrated (adopted from [1])

The RscDF language was designed to serve the concept of a Global Understanding Environment [1]. GUN concept utilises Semantic Web approach for resource annota-

tion and ontology-based semantic representation and describes communities of interacting Smart Resources. GUN provides a framework for making resources smart, for
interaction, collaboration, coordination of these resources and resource discovery
support. Types of resources are not restricted to traditional web content, but can be
physical resources from real world, such as humans and devices (see Figure 2).

GUN paradigm provides every participant with common structured data representation format, allowing explicit and unambiguous knowledge sharing. In order to
become GUN participant certain steps of adaptation should be taken. In GUN development our research group focuses on industrial case study that is concerned with
large-scale platforms for automated management of industrial objects. The adaptation
process to GUN environment is described in General Adaptation Framework [18].
"General adaptation" assumes a design of a sufficient framework for an integration of
different (by structure and nature) resources into the GUN environment. This environment will provide a mutual interaction between heterogeneous resources. Adaptation assumes elaboration of a common mechanism for new resource integration, and
its provision with a unified way of interaction. The main idea of adaptation is based
on a concept of "adapter", which plays role of a bridge between an internal representation of resource and a unified environment.

Adapter is a software component, which provides a bidirectional link between a resource interface and an interface of the environment. GUN assumes interoperability
of Smart Resources. Smart Resource is a conjunction of Real World Resource
(RWR), Adapter and Agent. By extending RWR within Adapter and Agent we make
it GUN compatible. General Adaptation includes development of Adapter for RWR.
Adaptation to GUN is not just syntactical transformation from one representation
format to another. The key element of adaptation is mapping of concepts being used
by "Real-World-Resource" to Industrial Maintenance Ontology (IMO) elements. The
role of IMO lies in unification and structuring of data being represented in such way
that every resource description taking part in GUN must refer to it.

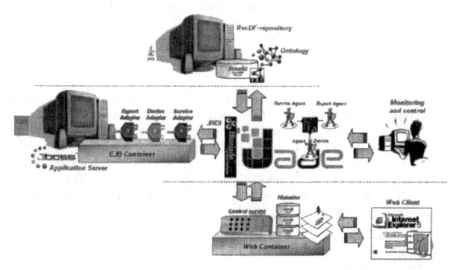

Fig. 3. SmartResource as a Multi-Agent System

Semantic Web standards are not yet supporting semantic descriptions of resources with proactive behavior. However, as the research within the SmartResource project shows [16], to enable effective and predictive maintenance of an industrial device in distributed and open environment, it will be necessary to have autonomous agent based monitoring over device state and condition and also support from remote diagnostics Web-Services (see Figure 3).

This means that the description of a device as a resource will require also the description of proactive behavior of autonomous condition monitoring applications (agents, services) towards effective and predictive maintenance of the device. For that we plan to develop in 2005 another extension of RDF, which is Resource Goal/Behavior Description Framework (RGBDF) to enable explicit specification of maintenance goals and possible actions towards faults monitoring, diagnostics and maintenance. Based on RSCDF and RGBDF and appropriate ontological support, we also plan to design RSCDF/RGBDF platforms for smart resources (devices, Web-services and human experts) equipped by adapters and agents for proactivity, and then to apply several scenarios of communication between the platforms towards learning Web-services based on device data and expert diagnostics to enable automated remote diagnostics of devices by Web-services.

In this paper we present our solution how to manage (according to the structure of the paper Section 2 describes about storing and Section 3 is dedicated to querying) the context-sensitive metadata for applications compatible with Semantic Web and GUN concepts by utilising existing technologies and tools. Some examples with industrial metadata are also provided.

2   Storing RDF-Based Metadata

Nowadays there are a lot of proposals related to storing RDF data in RDF databases, each with different client-server protocols and different client APIs. For our purposes we surveyed a number of most popular RDF-storages (Kowari[1], Sesame[2], Joseki[3]) and selected Joseki storage as most suitable allowing access to RDF-data through HTTP.

2.1   Joseki

Joseki has been proposed and maintained by Semantic Web group at HP Labs. Joseki is a web application for publishing RDF models on the web and realized useful access to models through HTTP protocol. This allows getting easy access to model from anywhere you want. It is built on Jena and, via its flexible configuration, allows a Model to be made available on a specified URL and queried using a number of languages. Results can be returned as RDF/XML, RDF/N3, or NTriples. The query languages, result formats, and model sources can be extended to produce new alternatives tailored to the user's needs.

---

[1] http://www.kowari.org/
[2] http://www.openrdf.org/
[3] http://www.joseki.org/

2.2 Storing and Extracting Data in Joseki

Information stored in Joseki are presented in a format of models. The client application has an access to a specified model and executes operation on this model. Operations that can be done upon the remote model:

- add new model or statement
- remove model or statement
- extract data from storage

New model can be appended to already existing model on the Joseki server. This operation also allows appending new statement to the predefined model. Each model or statement can be removed from the storage by using the remove operation.

Data extraction from Joseki storage can be implemented by using different mechanisms:

- fetch the whole model
- SPO query (single triple match language)
- RDQL query

Information from the storage can be extracted partly or as a whole model. To extract the whole model the fetch mechanism is used. For extracting just specified information, SPO and RDQL queries are available. SPO (also known as "Triples") is an experimental minimal query language. An SPO query is a single triple pattern, with optional subject (parameter "s"), predicate (parameter "p"), and object (parameter "o", if an URIref or parameter "v" for a string literal). Absence of the parameter implies "any" for matching that slot of the triple pattern.

RDQL is a query language, which is similar to SQL (Structured Query Language) and allows specifying the set of conditions, which should suite the extracted set of statements.

The architecture of Joseki is presented in Figure 4.

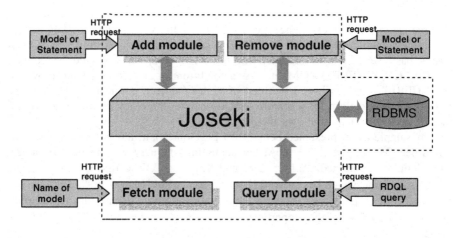

Fig. 4. Architecture of Joseki storage

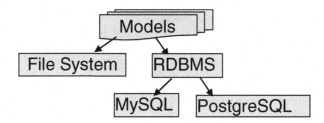

Fig. 5. Types of storing models in Joseki

It consists of the core module and modules, which execute specialized functions on the remote model (fetching, adding, removing, querying). Interaction between the client and the Joseki server is implemented through HTTP query. The type of the query depends on the length of the query. It could be GET if query is not longer then 200 characters, otherwise POST method is used. Each model in Joseki server has a predefined set of operations, which could be executed upon it. When server gets query to one of the defined models, it checks the list of operations which could be executed and if the operation is not specified it responds by a fail message. Each operation is executed by a specified module. As an input each module requires special parameters. For example, Addition and Remove modules need as an input model or statement, which have to be added or removed. As a response Joseki sends empty model, if the operation was successful.

One more optional component is RDBMS assigned for storing models in a persistent storage. The models in Joseki can be saved in two ways (See Figure 5):

- to a file
- to a RDBMS.

The target RDBMS is specified in the configuration file **joseki-db.n3**.

2.3 RDQL

Resource Description Query Language (RDQL) is a query language for RDF. RDQL is an implementation of the SquishQL RDF query language and is similar to SQL. It borrows basic set of words for specifying the set of data, which should be returned (e.g. SELECT, WHERE, FROM, etc). As a condition for extracting, RDQL provides, the "WHERE" clause followed by a list of triples (subject, predicate, object). These triples define the pattern for a search. RDQL has one more key word for defining a space of URI identifiers. It allows avoiding long names.

In the sample query presented below (SELECT-query), as a result, two values will be returned: Matthew and Jones. At the beginning of query we specify the values, which should be returned: "?family" and "?given". The first condition determines a statement, which has vcard:FN property value "Matt Jones". Then we extract data from property vcard:N to the variable "name". Basing on this information, we extract values of the property vcard:Family and vcard:Given.

```
SELECT ?family, ?given
WHERE (?vcard vcard:FN "Matt Jones")
```

```
(?vcard vcard:N ?name)
(?name vcard:Family ?family)
(?name vcard:Given ?given)
USING vcard FOR <http://www.w3.org/2001/vcard-rdf/3.0#>
```

Scheme on Figure 6 shows the steps of the query execution. The names of nodes are presented as names of variables to make picture clearer. The values of variables "vcard" and "name" are used as an input to the next condition statements.

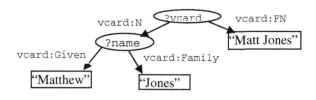

Fig. 6. Query description scheme

3 RscDF Data Management in GUN

The capabilities GUN provides rely on the common data representation format (RSCDF) and the common understanding of domain (Industrial Maintenance Ontology). As far as RSCDF is RDF-compatible, we reuse already existing RDF-databases to store RSCDF data.

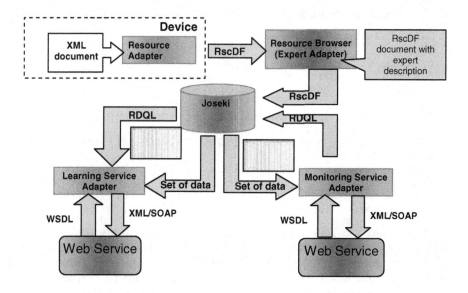

Fig. 7. Presentation scenario

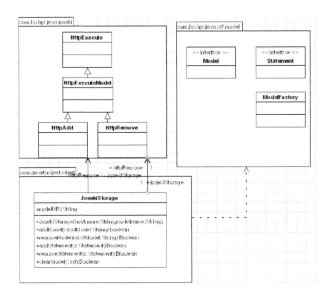

Fig. 8. Class diagram showing classes needed for interaction with the Joseki server

3.1 Applying RDQL to RscDF Querying

When querying RscDF data we deal with Statement objects that has the additional property `rscdfs:trueInContext`. When selecting a Statement about an object having certain property, we have to consequently apply queries, specifying the rdf:object, rscdfs:predicate or rdf:subject property values, so the query may look like:

```
SELECT ?stmts
WHERE
(?stmts,<rdf:subject>,<papmDescr:123456XZ24>),
(?stmts,<rscdfs:predicate>,<measureOnt:surfacelevel>)
USING
papmDescr FOR
<http://www.cc.jyu.fi/~olkhriye/rscdfs/resource/resourc
eInstanceDescription#>,
rdf FOR <http://www.w3.org/1999/02/22-rdf-syntax-ns#>,
rscdfs FOR
<http://www.cc.jyu.fi/~olkhriye/rscdfs/0.3/rscdfs#>,
measureOnt FOR
<http://www.cc.jyu.fi/~olkhriye/rscdfs/0.3/ontologies/m
easurementOntology#>
```

The resulting variable `stmts` will contain the set of Statements, whose subject and predicate properties satisfy the condition presented in Figure 9 in a form of a graph.

However, when the query contains context-related parts, we meet a problem of representing it in the RDQL language. The query becomes difficult to read, because of additional constructions. For example, when the statements describing different object properties at the certain moment of time, should be selected, we have to specify the value of time-statement lying in the context container.

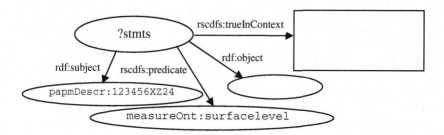

Fig. 9. Visual query representation

3.2 Querying Patterns

RscDF language provides a facility to select Statements by a certain template. The template Statement is put to the context container of Statement, wrapping the Statements selected according to the template. Figure 10 shows the structure of Statement, being created as a result of data collection according to a certain template.

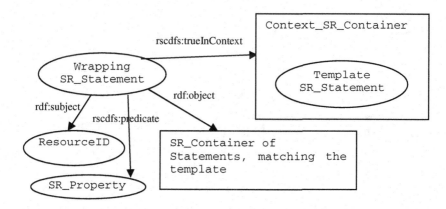

Fig. 10. Data Collection Statement selecting data according to a template

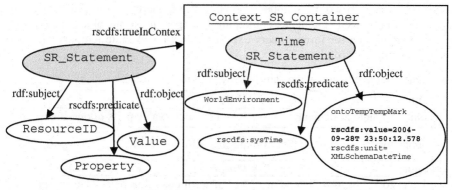

Fig. 11. Statement with time context

The most vivid example of the template context-dependent data collection is State-template data collection. For example, we have a certain resource, logging a track of its states. Different Statements about resource states are marked with time. So, the Statements will contain Statement about time in context container (Figure 11).

Figure 12 shows the data collection (subhistory) statement. The `rdf:object` property contains reference to container with Statements, matching the data collection template. The data collection template Statement is placed to the Context_SR_Container of the State Statement.

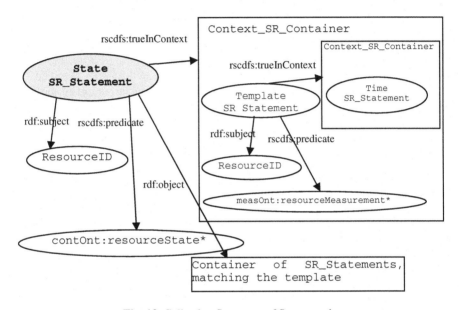

Fig. 12. Collecting Statement of State template

All the names marked with (*) are not actually present in Industrial Maintenance Ontology, but mean more generic classes or properties.

To apply the query, to data collection structures residing in RDF storage via RDQL language we have to write a number of routine triple queries, so it is reasonable to discover certain RDQL templates combining the operations into blocks and asking only start input data for further query execution. In case of State template we have discovered following routines:

– State RscDF-Statement To "attribute-value pairs" Routine:

Input	Output
Pointer to State Statement	Set of attribute-value pairs of one state

– Subhistory Statement to "Set of State Records"

Input	Output
Pointer to Subhistory Statement	Set of attribute-value pairs of correspondent states

Further on we omit namespaces definition and USING clause. For the first case the RDQL query looks like:

```
SELECT ?ValueStatements, ?NumUnits, ?NumValues
WHERE
(<StateStmtID>, <rdf:object>, ?StateContainer),
(?StateContainer, <rscdfs:member>, ?ValueStatements),
(?ValueStatements, <rdf:object>, ?NumValueInstances),
(?NumValueInstances, <rscdfs:value>,?NumValues),
(?NumValueInstances, <rscdfs:unit>, ?NumUnits)
```

The output of the query is a plain 3-column table with a set of rows. It is implied that every record in the table belongs to State, hence here we have 3 output variables, but in cases, when this routine is used as a subroutine, we have to return also the State Statement identifiers in order to be able to identify then relationships of values to states. Table 1 illustrates a possible output of the query:

Table 1. RDQL Query output

Statement ID	Units	Value
somens:valueStatementID_1	measureUnitsOnt:temperatureCelsius	70
somens:valueStatementID_2	measureUnitsOnt:roundsPerMinute	1500

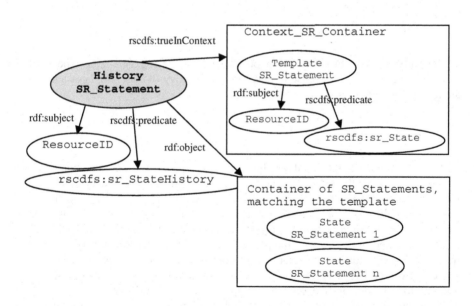

Fig. 13. History Statement

We put Statement ID to query output, because it uniquely identifies the belonging of values and units and allows further inference upon received results. As far as

RDQL query result is displayed in one non-normalized table, we store redundant data, but save the semantics.

The routine logic can be wrapped as a method, whose input is the name of Statement and output - RDQL subroutine. Example in Figure 13 shows more complex logic. It reuses previous example of State data selection, but provides a Set of States.

Below is the RDQL query:

```
SELECT?StateStmts,?ValueStatements,?NumUnits, ?NumVaues
WHERE
(<HistoryStmtID>, <rdf:object>, ?StatesCont),
(?StatesCont, <rscdfs:member>, ?StateStmts),
(?StateStmts, <rdf:object>, ?StateContainers),
(?StateContainers, <rscdfs:member>, ?ValueStatements),
(?ValueStatements, <rdf:object>, ?NumValueInsts),
(?NumValueInsts, <rscdfs:value>,?NumValues),
(?NumValueInsts, <rscdfs:unit>, ?NumUnits)
```

The five last strings of the query above are almost equivalent to the State query template. The only difference is presence of variable ?StateStmts instead of static given value StateStmtID. Query doesn't contain any references to types of properties being used in statements because we know beforehand what kind of data we deal with. In general, when the statement's ID is not known, we should first look for it, specifying as a search criteria Resource's ID and property type, for example:

```
SELECT ?stmts
WHERE
(?stmts,<rdf:subject>,<resourceID>),
(?stmts,<rscdfs:predicate>,<rscdfs:sr_StateHistory>)
```

Basically, the SR_Property being pointed by rscdfs:predicate, specifies the data template. So it makes sense to develop the ontology of data templates and associate it with SR_Properties.

4   Conclusions

In this paper we tried to analyze the problems of storing and managing context-enabled data via RDF storages. Finally, Joseki RDF storage and querying engine has been chosen as the most appropriate for integration to the prototype platform for adaptation of industrial resources to Semantic Web – pilot system, result of the Adaptation Stage of the SmartResource project. The approach based on the RDQL-patterns has been applied in the logic of the part of General Semantic Adapter, responsible for querying RscDF storages – dynamic and context-sensitive histories of industrial resources (experts, web services and devices). The flexibility of the RDQL-patterns has allowed to design a unified semantic adapter – a mediator between software agents (which implement proactive goal-driven behavior of originally passive industrial resources) and RDF-based storage of the history data of the corresponding industrial resources.

Further, it is planned to apply the developed method based on the RDQL-patterns in the design of querying mechanism for goal/behavior rule storages, which will utilize RGBDF – Resource Goal/Behavior Description Framework. The latter will be designed during the Proactivity Stage of the SmartResource activities as a part of the Pro-GAF – General Proactivity Framework.

Acknowledgements

This research has been performed as part of the SmartResource ("Proactive Self-Maintained Resources in Semantic Web") project in Agora Center (University of Jyväskylä, Finland) and funded by TEKES and industrial consortium of following companies: Metso Automation, TeliaSonera, TietoEnator and Science Park of Jyväskylä.

References

1. Terziyan, V.: Semantic Web Services for Smart Devices in a "Global Understanding Environment", In: R. Meersman and Z. Tari (eds.), *On the Move to Meaningful Internet Systems 2003: OTM 2003 Workshops*, Lecture Notes in Computer Science, Vol. 2889, Springer-Verlag (2003) 279–291
2. Online Jena API tutorial by B. McBride, "An Introduction to RDF and the Jena RDF API", August 2003, http://jena.sourceforge.net/tutorial/RDF_API/
3. Online Jena tutorial by A. Seaborne, Hewlett Packard, "Jena Tutorial. A Programmer's Introduction to RDQL", April 2002, http://www.hpl.hp.com/semweb/doc/tutorial/RDQL/
4. Kevin Wilkinson, Craig Sayers, Harumi A. Kuno, and Dave Reynolds: Efficient RDF Storage and Retrieval in Jena2, In: I. F. Cruz, V. Kashyap, S. Decker, R. Eckstein (Eds.): Proceedings of SWDB'03, The first International Workshop on Semantic Web and Databases, Co-located with VLDB 2003, Humboldt-Universität, Berlin, Germany, September 7–8 (2003) 131–150
5. Barnell, A.: RDF Objects, Technical Report, Semantic Web Applications Group, Hewlett Packard Laboratories Bristol, Avon, England, November 2002
6. Webpage of Jena on the official website of B. McBride, Hewlett Packard, "Jena, An RDF API in Java", http://www.uk.hpl.hp.com/people/bwm/rdf/jena
7. Lee, R.: Scalability Report on Triple Store Applications, Technical Report, SIMILE project (2004)
8. Beckett, D.: Semantic Web scalability and storage: survey of free software/open source RDF storage systems, Deliverable 10.1 report, SWAD-Europe project (IST-2001-34732) (2002)
9. B. McBride, Jena: Implementing the RDF Model and Syntax Specification, HP Labs in proceedings of the Second International Workshop on the Semantic Web, WWW10, Hong Kong, 1st May 2001
10. MacGregor, R.: In-Young Ko, Representing Contextualized Data using Semantic Web Tools, In Proceedings of the 1st International Workshop on Practical and Scalable Semantic Systems, ISWC 2003, October 2003, Sanibal Island, Florida, USA
11. Bouquet, P., Giunchiglia, F., Harmelen, F., Serafini, L. and Stuckenschmidt, H.: Contextualizing Ontologies, *Journal of Web Semantics* 26 (2004) 1–19
12. Bizer, C., Oldakowski, R.: Using Context- and Content-Based Trust Policies on the Semantic Web. In 13th World Wide Web Conference, WWW2004 (Poster) (2004)
13. Official website of RDF-S3 — RDF Source related Storage System, http://www.dbis.informatik.uni-frankfurt.de/~tolle/RDF/RDFS3/

14. Official website of JENA – a Semantic Web Framework for Java, http://jena.source-forge.net/
15. Official website of the Protégé ontology management tool, http://protege.stanford.edu/
16. Webpage of the SmartResource project, http://www.cs.jyu.fi/ai/OntoGroup/SmartRe-source_details.htm
17. Kaykova, O., Khriyenko, O., Naumenko, A., Terziyan, V., Zharko, A.: "RSCDF: Resource State/Condition Description Framework", Deliverable 1.1 report, September 2004, SmartResource project, (http://www.cs.jyu.fi/ai/IJWGS-2004_v2.doc)
18. Kaykova, O., Khriyenko, O., Kovtun, D., Naumenko, A., Terziyan, V., Zharko, A.: "GAF: General Adaptation Framework", Deliverable 1.2 report, October 2004, SmartResource project (http://www.cs.jyu.fi/ai/SJIS-2005.doc)

Ontology Issue in Multi-agent Distributed Learning

Vladimir Samoylov and Vladimir Gorodetsky

SPIIRAS, 39, 14-th Liniya, St. Petersburg, 199178, Russia
{samovl, gor}@mail.iias.spb.su

Abstract. Integration of the multi-agent and data mining technologies is one of the noticeable trends in the modern information technology. This integration contributes to the further progress in both above areas and provides practitioners with a new kind of technology of distributed intelligent systems. However, this integration generates a number of new non-typical problems both in areas, data mining and multi-agent systems. This fact is explicitly confirmed by the tasks of multi-agent distributed learning where new problems are mostly caused by the fact that data mining and learning procedures are always interactive and if learning data are distributed and private then multiple humans supported by distributed software should be involved in these procedures. Therefore, special means are needed to coordinate their activities in order to achieve consistency and integrity of the final solutions. The paper considers one of the key problems of the multi-agent distributed learning: development of the distributed classification systems' ontology. The paper analyzes the basic aspects of this weakly studied though important and challenging problem and proposes several solutions capable to constitute a basis for ontology design technology as applied to distributed data mining, learning and classification.

1 Introduction

Currently distributed intelligent information technologies integrating recent advances in various fields of artificial intelligence have acquired special significance in many application areas. One of the noticeable trends is an integration of the multi-agent and data mining technologies. This integration contributes to the further progress in both areas and provides practitioners with a qualitatively new level of distributed intelligent technology. Due to this integration new classes of the applications have become real. A class of applications where the distributed decision making, e.g., distributed classification, is the central problem provides for an example of the kind. In these applications decisions are produced using multiple distributed data sources and efforts of many entities: humans, interacting software and hardware components, visualization means, etc. Examples of such applications can be found in such domains as monitoring and forecasting of natural and man–made disasters and catastrophes [9], management and joint processing of information received by distributed sensor networks, computer network security [1], supply chain management [6], etc.

Multi-agent technology provides an advantageous framework for the distributed decision making systems. On the other hand, it is well known that the key problem of any distributed decision making system is a design of its distributed knowledge base.

V. Gorodetsky, J. Liu, and V.A. Skormin (Eds.): AIS-ADM 2005, LNAI 3505, pp. 215 – 230, 2005.
© Springer-Verlag Berlin Heidelberg 2005

Knowledge required for effective and efficient operation of decision making systems are developed using data mining technology aiming at learning of classification. If a system that is the subject of learning is distributed then the data mining problem becomes much more difficult and complex and brings to light new challenges which up to recent days have been either unknown or not studied in depth. Unfortunately, an experience has proved [4] that the above challenges are manifold, diverse and difficult.

The paper considers distributed ontology design that is one of the key problems of the *multi-agent distributed learning* as applied to Distributed Classification Systems (DCS). Section 2 describes the ontology's role in DCS, its structure and components. Sections 3 and 4 discuss the ontology design issue with regard to the problem domain ontology and application ontology respectively. Section 5 outlines the experience in ontology software implementation. Conclusion summarizes the paper contribution and outlines some other distributed ontology design aspects.

2 Ontology Issue

Distributed classification is a process where many distributed entities, e.g., sensors, preprocessing procedures, hardware, classifiers, humans, etc. are participating. Each such entity operates with a fragment of available data and information: a subset of data, observed facts, private and shared knowledge. These data and information are either received from some sources, or results from processing of input data arriving from several sources or represented in the DCS. Distributed entities participating in distributed classification produce decisions using available data and own knowledge fragments composing what is called a distributed knowledge base. Providing integrity and consistency of the distributed data and knowledge bases is one of the most important and difficult tasks in the development of any distributed intelligent system including DCS.

According to the modern understanding, integrity and consistency of the distributed and shared data and knowledge may be effectively provided by the ontology-based approach. In any multi-agent system (MAS), including multi-agent DCS (DCS MAS), the ontology shared by all entities of the system plays the topmost role. Indeed, ontology provides distributed entities (agents, humans) with a certain common thesaurus used for specification of the messages they exchange with; it

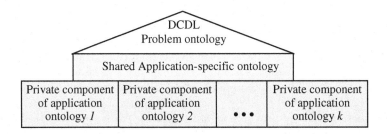

Fig. 1. Structure of the ontology used in DCS MAS

supports identical interpretation and consistent use of the notions in whose terms the agent's private knowledge is specified; it allows to automatically support relations existing between the above notions; the ontology can be provided with reusable components convenient for the use in other applications of the same problem domain. In this research the shared ontology is used as the top level and core of the distributed knowledge base of DCS MAS.

The shared ontology is composed of two components: problem domain ontology (hereinafter, problem ontology) and application ontology (Fig.1).

Problem ontology is a component of the shared ontology presenting the top-level component of the ontology independent of the particular application of the given problem domain. In the paper it is Distributed Classification and Distributed Learning problems ontology, DCDL ontology. This component of the entire ontology is considered briefly in *section 3*.

Application ontology is a component of the shared ontology inheriting the DCDL problem ontology, representing basic notion and relations of an application of the problem domain in question. Some important aspects of the shared application ontology design are considered in *section 5*.

Knowledge of each entity of a multi-agent application is specified by the notions of the shared ontology and can be also used (and as a rule, are used) by private notions inheriting the properties of the shared ontology and possessing peculiar properties (Fig.1). These components are called *Private components of application ontology* (private ontology, for brevity). In DCS MASs considered in the paper private ontology of an agent specifies *particular characteristics of data sources*.

An important component of ontology-based intelligent systems is a so-called *Task ontology*. Task ontology is defined as "a system/theory of vocabulary for describing inherent problem solving structure of all the existing tasks domain-independently. It is obtained by analyzing task structures of real world problems. ... Design of task ontology is done in order to overcome the shortcomings of generic tasks while preserving their basic philosophies" [7]. Task ontology is also considered as a component of the entire ontology of DCS MAS. Its correlation with the shared problem and application ontology is highlighted in Fig.1. Task ontology mostly determines the architecture of the system being designed. DCS MAS Task ontology is described in *section 4*.

3   DCDL Problem Ontology

DCDL problem ontology specifies key notions (concepts) and their relations peculiar for any problem related applications. In some publications this ontology is also called Meta–ontology.

The basis of this ontology is formed by KDD domain ontology proposed in [10]. DCDL ontology extends the above ontology by specific notions reflecting the distributed nature of the decision making procedure in the problem in question. This ontology introduces such notions as *Application domain, Basic data, Data dictionary, Object* (to be classified), *Attribute, Attribute type, Attribute domain, Relation, Interpretation function, Sample Set Local Discovery Task, Basic Knowledge and some other*. The strict definition of these notions and their relations can be found in [10].

The list of the Problem ontology notions introduced specifically for the distributed data mining tasks is as follows:

Local data source: Geographically, physically, or logically separates data source with its own data storage structure and mechanism.

Basic data: Real data residing in local data sources in the form they are usually gathered. Some local sources may be stored in data warehouses with pre-processed and cleaned data; others may contain raw sensor readings not ready for immediate use.

Base classifier: A decision support system (classifier) based on rules derived from the single source of data and aiming at making decision (classification) using corresponding inference mechanism.

Object domain entity identifier: Entity identifier is an analog of the first key for a flat table defined for an object of the application domain. For each such identifier, in the application ontology, a rule is defined, to be used to calculate the key value. E.g., a unique combination of several attributes of a specific entity could be such a rule.

Base classifier: A decision support system (classifier) based on a mechanism derived from the single source of data and aiming at making decision (classification) using corresponding inference mechanism.

Meta-data: Tuple of the decisions produced by base classifiers regarding classes of an object specified in terms of local data sources.

Meta-classifier: Base classifier using meta-data as input to be classified.

Source meta-characteristics: Statistical characteristics of the data source in terms of the private ontology. Such characteristics could be, for instance, quantity of objects of such a class of the object domain ontology (determined by the quantity of unique values of *entity identifiers*), percentage of missed values of object domain object class attribute (determined through the local source interpretation functions), etc.

4 Task Ontology

Task ontology contains the notions presenting types of tasks to be solved by the system being designed, whereas the relations of this ontology, as a rule, specify decomposition of the system tasks into subtasks. Let us emphasize that the Task ontology practically determines the architecture of the system and system users' roles and interfaces, i.e. mostly influences upon the organization of the software implementing the system.

When developing a system it is important to define types of its users. The main users of the DCS MAS are (1) analysts, i.e. the users experienced in the analysis methodology as well as in management and monitoring of the learning processes and (2) application domain experts possessing deep and thorough knowledge about the application domain and formulating the task in the application terms. Other users of the system can be local source experts: administrators and developers of local source databases knowledgeable in the structure of the stored information and authorized to process data of the respective local sources. Let us outline the *basic* task (functions) of the DCS MAS design at the learning stage.

Task setting. This tasks results in determining the system goals and corresponding tasks in the application terms.

Meta-data description. The aim of this function is to create the list of the application (shared) ontology notions. Application domain experts both of the meta-level and source level are involved in this design.

Data description. The task aims to describe the interpretation functions of the application ontology notions at data source level. For each data source the same is also done for entity identifiers introduced in the ontology.

Meta-learning. This is one of the main system's functions: it formulates the learning tasks for the local sources, knowledge generalization scheme, and supports meta-classifier learning procedure.

Base classifier learning. The aim of this function is to mine patterns in the data of the source to be used in classification mechanism.

Base level decision-making. This function is performed either by a person making decisions based on the decisions produced by the base classifier or automatically using the mechanism designed by function *Base classifier learning.*

Let us elaborate in detail the *basic* Task ontology represented by the above listed notions in terms of their sub–tasks (sub–notions), relations between them and also relations between the tasks and the above users and represent the resulting Task ontology in terms of the use case diagram of the UML language (Fig.2). This diagram forms more detailed representation of the Task ontology that constitutes the contents of the distributed classification system. Let us outline the Task ontology presented in Fig.2.

Task setting
- *Meta-learning task formulation.* It is the task resulting in specification of the learning task in terms of the application domain, training data and classes of desired patterns to be determined.

Meta-data description
- *Development of the application ontology.* This task is to describe terms, notions, and relations existing in the application domain. It creates the data vocabulary, thus, describing the application domain.
- *Computation of data source meta-properties.* This is a function computing statistical and other properties of the data sources in terms of the application ontology notions.

Data description
- *Design of the local ontology.* The task aims to describe the subset of the application ontology notions corresponding to the data sources. Besides, the notions of this part of ontology may enlarge the shared application ontology by adding objects and attributes of the application domain that are relevant to the respective source.
- *Adjusting the gateway to the source data base providing access from the ontology.* This task is solved by the local source experts and aims at adjusting the data base gateway providing for the objects' attributes and the local ontology notions interpretation functions.

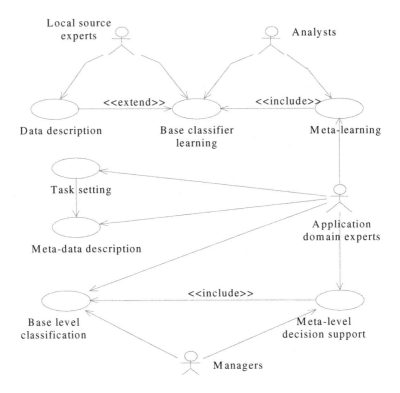

Fig. 2. Relations between basic Task ontology notions, and between them and main system's users

Meta-learning
- *Computation of the meta-data.* The process essence is to gather and to compose the decisions produced by the base classifiers of the data sources. Composition of the above decisions is done using entity identifiers providing filtering the inputs of the base classifiers.
- *Design of the decision combining structure.* This task aims to design the structure determining how decisions produced by base classifiers are combined at the meta-level. It also determines how the meta-data are computed. Meta-characteristics of the data sources are used by this task as an input.
- *Data preparation.* This task aims to generate the meta-data sample having certain characteristics using data of the sources as input.
- *Base classifier decision making.* This task implements classification of an object specified as assumed by the corresponding classifier.
- *Training of the meta-classifier.* The task consists of two subtasks: (1) training based on meta–data sample, (2) design of a meta-classification mechanism.

Base classifier learning
- *Setting of the base classifier learning task.* This task has to determine the settings of the learning task that are training and testing datasets, and type of patterns desired to further design the classification mechanism.

- *Learning procedure.* This task is a conventional training and testing procedure resulting in a set of patterns (e.g., rules) used for classification mechanism.
- *Classification procedure.* This task is a basic function of any classifier.
- *Scales transformation.* This task is solved in the cases if the same attributes are measured in different sources in various measurement scales. Its goal is to transform such attributes to a common scale.
- *Design of the classification mechanism of the base classifier.* The essence of this task is to design the classification mechanism based on the extracted patterns and test it. The testing procedure uses the above introduced *Classification procedure.*
- *Base classifier evaluation.* This is a base classifier tested via the subsequent computation of the selected evaluation criteria values.

5 Shared Application Ontology Design: Conceptual Issues

The key peculiarities of the DCS MAS shared application ontology design are caused by the fact that data sources are distributed, heterogeneous and can contain private data. As a rule, data sources are spatially distributed or, at least, they are represented in several databases located on different hosts. Heterogeneity is entailed by the diversity of possible data structures, variety of data specification languages, differences in data natures (geographical, statistical, images, etc.) and so on. As a rule, this data are of large scale. The above data peculiarities put several challenging problems in design DCS MAS application ontology. Let us analyze them.

The first step of the shared application ontology design is to designate identifiers to the ontology notions constituting *the shared thesaurus* of distributed DCS MAS entities (agents). Since the local data contents and structures can be unavailable for meta–level expert, the source data experts if they independently develop local thesauruses can assign different domain entities the same names and vice versa, assign the identical entities different names what should lead to the misunderstanding of the messages the agents exchange with. Therefore, special collaborative procedure (protocol) has to be used in the shared thesaurus design [3].

Other problem, non-coherency of data measurement scales, is caused by the fact that the identical data attributes may be differently specified in different sources, e.g., in various measurement scales, and at the meta-level, in learning and classification, they have to be used identically. Thus, a procedure is needed to provide for the distributed data consistent specification.

The next problem, "entity instance identification" [2] is conditioned by distributed specification of the objects that are the subjects of classification. The fragments of data specifying such an object are represented in several data sources and while computing meta-data and in meta-classification all object specification fragments should be used commonly. Therefore, a mechanism to identify an object's fragments stored in various data bases is needed. It is important to note that some such fragments of the object in question can be missing in some sources. Fig.2 provides for a graphical representation of the entity instance identification problem.

Let us outline how the last two problems are solved in DCS MAS.

The *entity identification problem* is solved as follows. In the shared application ontology, the notion of entity identifier ("*ID entity*") is introduced for each entity.

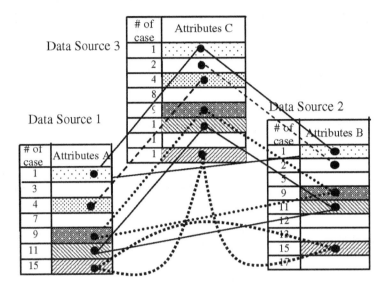

Fig. 3. Illustration of the essence of the "*entity instance identification problem*"

This entity identifier plays the role of the entity primary key (by analogy with the primary key of a database table). For each such an identifier, a rule is defined within the shared application ontology, which is used to calculate the key value. E.g., a unique combination of a subset of this entity attributes can be used as an argument of a rule. A specific rule is defined for each data source that uniquely associates the entity identifier and the source primary key. In some cases it may simply be a list of pairs "value of entity identifier"–"value of local key". When such rules have been introduced for data sources, a list of all the instances of entities stored in the sources can be determined at the meta-level, thus, identifying instances stored in several sources.

The next problem, "*non-coherency of data measurement scales*", is solved as shown further. Let us designate the attribute measured differently in different sources as X. In the shared application ontology the type and the unit of X measurement are determined by the meta–level expert. Then in all the sources where attribute X is presented, for this attribute, the meta–level introduces algorithms to be used for transformation of the attribute from the primary scale into the one used at the meta–level. This allows using the values of attributes at the meta-level regardless the data source where they are originated from. The entire procedure is also realized as a protocol according to which the meta–level and local experts are negotiating.

A specific problem called for brevity "*providing gateway to access from ontology to the source data*" is described hereafter. Actually, the agents handle ontology notions. However, the data interpreting these notions are represented in database structures other than the structures adopted in the ontology. Therefore, a gateway transforming the queries specified in the ontology language into queries understandable for DBMS is needed.

In the developed DCDL technology, this problem is solved trough creation of a set of *VIEW* objects of the database at the stage of definition of the DB functions interpretation. In this set, each shared application ontology entity is associated with a *VIEW* object having fields of corresponding types allocated to each attribute.

In this approach, the client (agent) side is enabled to create the application entity attribute queries that may be processed by the DBMS kernel at the DB side. This is very important. Indeed, firstly, in this approach, transformation of the data represented in the DB internal structure into the structure adopted in the ontology is performed by the DB server kernel, what noticeably speeds up the query processing. Secondly, this approach allows formulating queries in terms of application ontology even if the queried data are distributed over different tables. Thirdly, this approach enables the DB administrator to supply queried information according to the adopted security policy, since the *VIEW* object contains information deliberately available for outside access, and the access rights to the *VIEW* object itself may be set up in the same manner as for any DB object.

To provide access of the DCDL software components to the created *VIEW* objects, it is necessary to determine mapping of the names of the entities specified in the shared application ontology and their attributes, on the one hand, and the names of the *VIEW* objects and their fields respectively, on the other hand. For this purpose, in the application ontology, the notions *"Data source entity properties"* and *"Data source attribute properties"* are introduced, which are "projections" of the application ontology onto the particular data sources. In these notions, the attributes *NameVIEW*

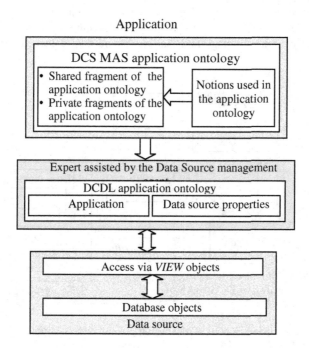

Fig. 4. Three-level hierarchy of database objects access

and *NameField* take values of names and attributes of the data source entities respectively. In fact, here a three-level access to the DB objects is used (Fig.4).

Because the queries originating from other agents are always represented in terms of the application ontology, it is necessary to have a software component providing a gateway for an access to databases. In the developed DCDL architecture this role is assigned to the *Data source management agent* (DSM). The access of the DSM agent to the external data source is performed through the standard ODBC gateway. Each agent of the DSM type provides access to a single data source whose name is stored in the ODBC manager of the agent's knowledge base.

In the developed DCS MAS architecture that includes DCDL software, application ontology design procedure supports solution of the above problems. Several agents participating in design of the application ontology implement the corresponding functionalities (roles).

6 DCS MAS Architecture

Let us outline the multi-agent architecture of a software tool aimed to support the DCS MAS design, including support of the DCS MAS learning technology. This architecture is not oriented to particular application of the DCS scope and rather considered as a generic one. In development of such generic-like architecture, Task ontology plays the topmost role. The tasks of this ontology determine the basic roles of the MAS in question and their allocation to particular classes of agents.

The proposed architecture includes the agents handling data of sources and the agents implementing the meta-level functionalities. It is important to note that the components of the architecture supporting distributed learning technology can be used only at the DCS MAS design stage and that is why may be detached from it at the

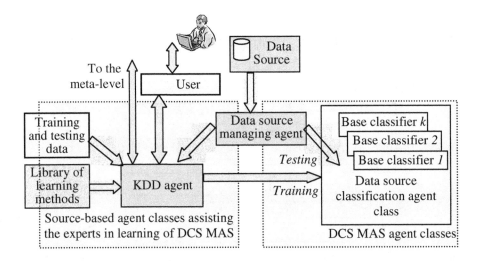

Fig. 5. Architecture and interaction of the learning (left) and classification (right) agent classes of the source-based DCS MAS

operation stage. On the other hand, if, during the maintenance resulting DCS MAS, modification of the classifiers or classifiers' structure assumes that these components may be preserved and used later.

The architecture of the DCS MAS source-based component is presented in Fig.5 while Fig.6 presents the architecture of its meta–level component. Let us outline functions of DCS MAS components. The source-based classes of the DCS MAS agents and their functions (Fig.5) are described below.

Data source managing agent
- Participates in the distributed design of the shared components of the application ontology;
- Collaborates with meta-level agents in management of training and testing of particular source-based classifiers and in computing the meta-data needed for meta-classifier learning.
- Supports gateway to data bases through transformation of the queries from ontology language into SQL language.

KDD agent of data source
This agent class performs training of the base classifiers of the data source classification agents and evaluation of their performance quality. It uses library of the learning procedures, accesses shared and private application ontology components and training and testing datasets.

Data source classification agent
The agent of this class performs classification of the objects specified in data source It can contain several classifiers working with the same data source, e.g., operating in different feature spaces and/or using various classification algorithms. These classifiers are trained and tested by the KDD agent.

Let us describe the meta-level agent classes (Fig.6) and their roles (Fig.6).

Meta-Learning agent ("KDD Master")
- Assists in distributed design of the shared application ontology;
- Computes the training and testing meta-data samples;
- Assists in the design of the classification structure.

Meta-level KDD agent
This agent class assists the meta-level expert in training of the *Meta-level classification agent* and in assessing its performance quality.

Agent-classifier of meta-level
This agent class performs combining of the data source classifiers using meta-data. It is trained and tested by the Meta-level KDD agent class.

Decision combining management agent
This agent class coordinates operation of the *Agent-classifier of meta-level* and *Meta-level KDD* agent both in training and decision combining modes.

Both at the source-based level and meta-level *library of the software classes* implementing particular KDD methods, metrics, etc. is available.

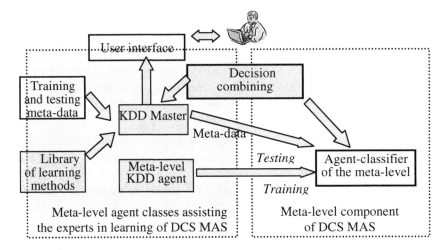

Fig. 6. Architecture and interaction of the learning (left) and decision combining (right) agent classes of the DCS MAS meta-level

Below we shall consider specific examples of realization of some tasks related to ontology development and use, through the example of users' interfaces of these classes of agents.

7 DCS MAS Implementation Issues

The design of the shared application ontology starts the process of the applied DS MAS development. Distributed experts participating in this design communicate through special protocol. In the current prototype of the design supporting software the simplest of the developed protocols, "top-down", (see [3], where this protocol is formally specified) is implemented. It is quite essential that this protocol based on the shared application ontology is designed by the meta-level designer ("expert of the meta–level") with the subsequent dialog with other (distributed) source experts with the mediation of the *KDD Master* agent. The application ontology designed by the expert of the meta–level is forwarded to the instances of *Data Source Manager* agents that enable the interface with particular experts, thus, mediating the ontology design. Then the data sources experts tune the interpretation functions to the corresponding fragments of the shared application ontology in the data sources databases.

To support the shared application ontology design, the ontology editor implemented as a function of the *KDD Master* agent is used (Fig.7). The editor is intended for solving the following subtasks:

Design and editing of the shared application ontology. This procedure results in the formal specification of the application ontology notions, their attributes, and the corresponding value domains of the attributes.

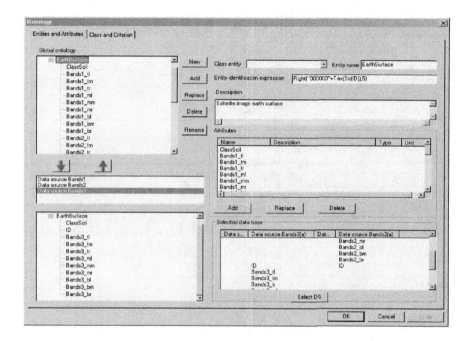

Fig. 7. Shared application ontology editor

Specification of data of data sources in terms of the shared application ontology. This activity results in formal specification of these data in terms of shared application ontology.

Creation and specification of the secondary properties of the ontology notions. The result of this design activity is the list of secondary properties of the notions specified in terms of their attributes.

Creation and specification of the list of the data classes. The result of this design activity is the list of classes to be used for classification of the input data in terms of the labels of the object classes.

The ontology editor is called up from user interface *of the KDD Master* agent. The template used for invocation of the ontology editor is shown in Fig.7. The support for solving the remaining two subtasks out of the four mentioned in section 5 is provided by the user's interface shown in Fig.8.

Let us outline *DSM-agent* user interface. The tuning of the ontology of the application ontology notions of the *DSM-agents* is conducted by the database administrator whose task is to create the *VIEW* objects in the database with the fields corresponding to the attributes of the notion (notions) of the application ontology, and the notion instance identifier field. Corresponding user interface is shown in Fig.9. The dialog is initiated by the user command *Open DB Gateway editor* that supports the expert's activity intended for tuning up the agent's interface to the external database.

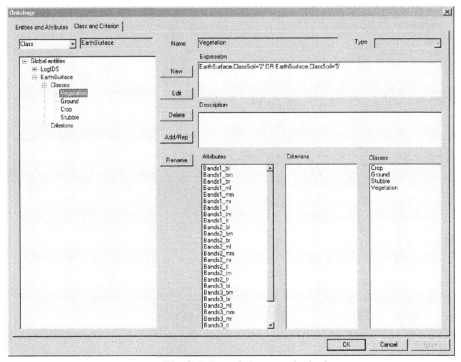

Fig. 8. Editor of classes and criteria

8 Conclusion

Ontology is one of the most important components of a multi-agent distributed classification system. In this class of applications, the ontology role is manifold: it provides distributed entities (agents, humans) with common thesaurus for specification of the messages they exchange with; it supports identical interpretation and consistent use of the notions in whose terms the agent's knowledge is specified; ontology allows to automatically support consistency of the relations existing between the above notions, etc. In this paper the shared ontology is used as the top level and essential for the distributed knowledge base of DCS MAS. That is why ontology design thorough technology is an important prerequisite in the successful design of any distributed classification system.

The paper contribution concerns various aspects of the development of the ontology design technology applied to distributed classification systems:

1. Analyses of the general structure of the DCS MAS ontology and functions of its components: Problem ontology ("Meta-ontology"), Shared application ontology, Private components of the application ontology and Task ontology.

2. Extension of the existing data mining and learning Problem ontology: new notions involved in the distributed data mining and learning as well as relations existing between them are introduced.

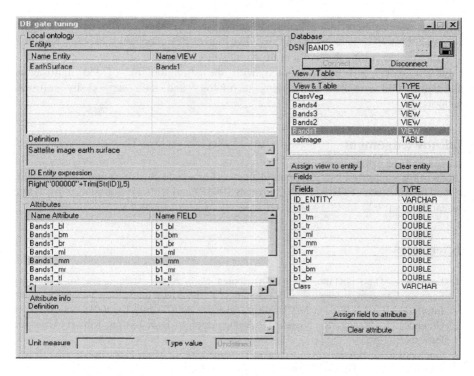

Fig. 9. Dialog for tuning of the DB gateway

3. Task ontology of generic DCS MAS, specified as a structured set of the tasks to be solved at the stage of DCS MAS distributed learning and at the stage of its operation as multi-agent distributed classification system. This result has allowed proposing a generic multi-agent architecture designated for solution of both aforementioned tasks.

4. Technology of the distributed design of the shared and private components of the application ontology supported by special coordination mechanisms implemented in terms of agents assisting the distributed experts in development of the ontology provided with the consistency and the integrity properties.

The main results presented in the paper were implemented as a software extending the reusable components of the standard multi-agent software tool, MASDK [4] in order to prototype a specialized multi-agent software tool specifically designated to support the analysis, design, implementation and deployment of applied multi-agent distributed classification systems.

In the more general sense the proposed technology of the distributed ontology design can be considered as a prototype of a multi-agent technology with a number of novel properties, in particular:

i. It involves agents assisting the designers in the development of a multi-agent application. Such kind of the multi-agent technology can be called "*agent mediated software engineering*" technology.

ii. The development of distributed ontology is a novel type of multi-agent technology: it is carried out by distributed designers and experts who use distributed components of a multi-agent software tool.

Further work will be associated with the strengthening of the multi-agent distributed data mining and learning technology and their support by software components.

Acknowledgement

This work is supported by European Office of Aerospace Research and Development of the US Air Force (EOARD-ISTC Project 1993P) and Russian Foundation for Basic Research (grant #04-01-00494a).

References

1. Engelhardt, D., Anderson, M.: A Distributed Multi-Agent Architecture for Computer Security Situational Awareness. Proceedings of the Sixth International Conference on Information Fusion (Fusion 2003), Cairns, Australia, July 7 - July 10 (2003) 193–200
2. Goodman, I., Mahler, R., Nguen, H.: Mathematics of Data Fusion. Kluwer Academic Publishers (1997)
3. Gorodetski, V., Karsayev, O., Kotenko, I., Samoilov, V.: Multi-agent information fusion: methodology, architecture and software tool for learning of object and situation assessment. Proceedings of the Seventh International Conference on Information Fusion (FUSION 2004), Stockholm, Sweden, 28 June – 1 July (2004) 346–353
4. Gorodetski, V., Karsayev, O., Samoilov, V.: Multi-agent Data Fusion Systems: Design and Implementation Issues. Proceedings of the 10th International Conference on Telecommunication Systems - Modeling and Analysis, Monterey, CA, October 3-6, Vol. 2. (2002) 762–774
5. Gorodetski, V., Skormin, V., Popyack, L., Karsayev. O.: Distributed Learning in a Data Fusion System. Proceedings of the Conference of the World Computer Congress (WCC-2000) "Intelligent Information Processing" (IIP2000) (2000) 147–154
6. Guo, Y., Muller, J.: Multiagent Collaborative Learning for Distributed Business Systems. Proceedings of the Third International Joint Conference on Autonomous Agents and Multi Agent Systems (AAMAS 2004), New York, NY, USA, July 19-23 (2004) 1154–1161
7. Mizoguchi, R., Sinitsa, K.: Task Ontology Design for Intelligent Educational & Training Systems. Proceedings of the Workshop on Architectures and Methods for Designing Cost-Effective and Reusable ITSs (ITS'96), Montreal, June 10 (1996)
8. Samoilov, V.: Data Fusion Systems: Principles and Architecture for Data Processing in Decision Making System Learning. Transactions of SPIIRAS, Vol. 1. (2002) (In Russian)
9. Scott, P., Rogova, G.: Crisis Management in a Data Fusion Synthetic Task Environment. Proceedings of the Seventh International Conference on Information Fusion (FUSION 2004), Stockholm, Sweden, 28 June– 1 July (2004) 330–337
10. Zytkov, J., Klosgen, W.: Machine Discovery Terminology.http://orgwis.gmd.de/projects/explora/terms.html

Ontology-Based Users and Requests Clustering in Customer Service Management System

Alexander Smirnov, Mikhail Pashkin, Nikolai Chilov, Tatiana Levashova, Andrew Krizhanovsky, and Alexey Kashevnik

St. Petersburg Institute for Informatics and Automation of the Russian Academy of Sciences, 39, 14th Line, St Petersburg, 199178, Russia
{Smir, Michael, Nick, Oleg, Aka, Alexey}@iias.spb.su

Abstract. Customer Service Management is one of major business activities to better serve company customers through the introduction of reliable processes and procedures. Today this kind of activities is implemented through e-services to directly involve customers into business processes. Traditionally Customer Service Management involves application of data mining techniques to discover usage patterns from the company knowledge memory. Hence grouping of customers/requests to clusters is one of major technique to improve the level of company customization. The goal of this paper is to present an efficient for implementation approach for clustering users and their requests. The approach uses ontology as knowledge representation model to improve the semantic interoperability between units of the company and customers. Some fragments of the approach tested in an industrial company are also presented in the paper.

Keywords: Text Mining, Clustering, Ontology, Agent.

1 Introduction

Many research efforts have been undertaken in the area of Customer Service Management (CSM) to perform a shift from "product-centric" production to "customer-centric" production. CSM has the following main functions: searching for information about company's products by the customers (with clustering, ranking, etc. to organize found results); storing, organizing and processing information about the users and their contacts by the system administrators and managers [1].

Developed by the authors CSM system is referred to as "Intelligent Access to Catalogue and Documents" (IACD) and has the following major features: (i) intelligence of the system in providing interface forms: static templates for special structured inputs and precise results for specific tasks, free text inputs for knowledge sources search, and learning-based intelligent adviser; and (ii) customizability: from unknown unspecified customer to building and supporting target groups (e.g., by job titles, area of interests etc.), and to personalized profile-based support. Structured customer requests represent templates (specially designed forms for searching within a limited group of products/solutions) that allow achieving high relevance of the found results but miss universality. Free text requests have maximal universality but achieving high

V. Gorodetsky, J. Liu, and V.A. Skormin (Eds.): AIS-ADM 2005, LNAI 3505, pp. 231–246, 2005.

levels of the result relevance is a challenging task. Described here CSM system does this by setting some syntactical constraints on the free text requests and by using a part of the shared ontology of the company. To further improve free text request processing it is reasonable to accumulate information about customers' interests by grouping based on user profiles (with request history information) and using text mining techniques. These are the topics the paper concentrates on.

Grouping can show similarities between different customers that would make it possible to better serve them, to provide interesting for them information "just-in-time" or even "just-before-time". Besides, producing "good" groups can provide additional useful benefits (e.g., better filtering of results corresponding to customers' interests). For this purpose clustering of the customers into a number of distinct segments or groups in an effective and efficient manner is required. Text clustering (direction of text mining [2]) helps in customer problems (interests or preferences) identification and classification.

There are the following ontology-based clustering scenarios suitable for CRM:

First, *requests clustering for one user*. The goal of this clustering is to define prevalent user interests (e.g. product category, preferred brand name, level of quality). This is important to foresee user's needs and satisfy it just in time.

Second, *users clustering*. This scenario identifies users groups. Without information about customer groups the CSM system administrator should treat each user separately. On the contrary, treating only of each group (after the clustering) will be less time-consuming, because number of groups is much smaller than number of users.

Third, *requests clustering*. This scenario groups together similar requests. This clustering is used in order identify categories of users' interests. Another goal of requests' clustering is to perform text analysis to get 1) common types of user request, 2) common misspellings, 3) customer/user lexicons, 4) frequency / popularity of used term, 5) bottleneck requests (requests that return too many / few results), 6) promising request (i.e. potential customers/new market/direction of future work), 7) recommendations for request templates development, etc.

Agents are very promising technology for distributed data / text mining [3], [4].

The paper is structured as follows: section 2 describes research efforts related to the system IACD and implemented scenarios. In section 3 a description of the clustering algorithm is presented. Experiments and future work discussions conclude the paper.

2   The System IACD: The Concept and Functions

2.1   KSNet-Based Customer Service Management

Recently, there has been an increased interest in developing CSM systems that incorporate knowledge management and data & text mining techniques [1].

Proposed by the authors KSNet-approach considers knowledge logistics (a direction of knowledge management) as a problem of a knowledge source network (KSNet) configuration that includes as network units - end-users / customers, loosely

coupled knowledge sources / resources, and a set of tools and methods for information / knowledge processing [5]. A multi-agent system architecture based on FIPA
Reference Model was chosen as a technological basis for the KSNet-approach. FIPA-
based technological kernel agents used in the system are: wrapper (interaction with
knowledge sources), facilitator ("yellow pages" directory service for the agents),
mediator (task execution control), and user agent (interaction with users).

The KSNet approach is selected as a kernel for creation a distributed CSM system
which provides the global company's face to the customer through a single point of
information access [6]. Major motivation of this solution was that the agent-based
technology is a good basis for CSM in the global companies since agents can operate
in a distributed environment independently from the user and apply ontologies to
knowledge representation, sharing and exchange.

Ontology could be specified as a set of concepts with informal definitions, a set of
relations holding among these concepts not limited to hierarchical ones (*is-a* and *part-
of*), and a set of axioms to formalize the definitions and relations [7]. Here ontology
plays very important role as a common vocabulary (language) in agent community
and the company, and as a model which supports semantic interoperability of company units (customers, users, departments, plants, etc.). User profiles are used during
interactions to provide for an efficient personalized service.

The system is considered as an Internet-based support system where customers initiate a real-time "electronic dialog" with the customer support agent. For each dialog
session, the dialog between agent and customer interaction is recorded and stored in
the customer / user profile. The structured elements of this session log include information about the customer (who, what, where, when, etc.). The unstructured data is
the verbatim (free-form text) of the customer/agent dialog itself. Timely and accurate
customer & request group identification is critical for the support agents as well as the
product engineers and service managers. The system is an example of deriving value
from the integration of free-form text (dialogs and user requests) and structured data
(electronic product catalogues, etc.).

The aim of text mining is similar to data mining in that it attempts to analyze texts
to discover interesting patterns such as clusters, associations, deviations, similarities,
and differences in sets of text [8].Text mining process consists of six steps — source
selection, information retrieval from text collection, information extraction to obtain
data from individual texts, data warehousing for the extracted data, data mining to
discover useful pattern in the data, and visualization of the resulting pattern [9]. Here
major techniques include clustering and classification methods, such as nearest
neighbor, relational learning models, and genetic algorithms, and dependency models,
including graph-theoretic link analysis, linear regression, decision trees, nonlinear
regression, and neural networks [10].

Ontology-based CSM systems could help to determine characteristics of the customer / user data and of the desired mining results, and to enumerate the knowledge
discovery processes that are valid for producing the desired results from the given
company data / text sets. The ontology-based approach was developed for CSM and
implemented in the system IACD. Current version of the system provides for customers a common way to search for products and solutions and presents information

about different applications: (i) technical data of company's products, (ii) project-specific solutions based on tasks' conditions given by customers and (iii) corporate documents and available Web sites taking into account customers' interests and constraints stored in the corporate ontology. It helps to easily find solutions for planning simple methods and for alternative comparison. Especially ontology implementation is useful when prediction of customers' interests is required but customers use different languages, different terms, different levels of abstraction and different units of measures, have different areas of interests and different levels of customizability, and make decisions on different levels.

User profiles are used heavily in clustering (customer & request grouping). For better customer serving, the approach assumes creation of user profiles correlating with the ontology. User profile, besides other information and knowledge characterizing the user and the user activity, stores the history of the user requests. The user requests are grouping on the basis of the similarity metrics and hierarchical relations of ontology classes.

Referring to text mining steps some related to CSM activities problems could find solution based on the ontology-driven approach. The first problem is that the results may differ from the real user needs. The second problem is that the description of the sources is not uniform – there are different formats such as sentences, items and tables.

It is difficult to extract the information by conventional methods of information extraction [11]. Filtering agent / service based on domain expert knowledge is needed (ontology could be useful here too). Current methods in text mining use keywords, term weighting, or association rules to present text context. It can be implemented by means of *context filtering*.

The following classical text mining techniques are also used in the system IACD: text processing and clustering [Fig. 1]. *Text processing* includes a sequence of steps: tokenization, stop-words finding, spelling, stemming, search for units of measures (e.g. "kg", "mm"), etc. [12]. The following problem-oriented agents specific for KSNet, and scenarios for their collaboration were developed and adapted for text mining problems: (i) text processing — translation agent (terms translation between different vocabularies) and ontology management agent (ontology operations performance) and (ii) clustering — monitoring agent (verification of knowledge sources).

Input for clustering algorithm would be user requests and the ontology. In [2] the following categorization of major clustering methods is proposed: partitioning methods, hierarchical methods, density-based methods, grid-based methods, model-based methods. The hierarchical method is used in the proposed approach that is described in detail in sec. 3. Since user requests and instances of ontology classes can be tied with context information (e.g., time, location, language), input data could be filtered in order to mine data about products which are geographically located near customer, delivered in time, have appropriate level of quality.

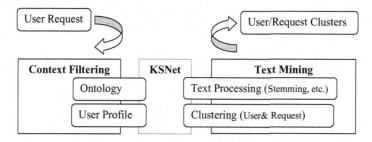

Fig. 1. Application of the KSNet-approach to ontology-based CSM

2.2   The System IACD Functional Specification

The system IACD has been developed for a company producing manufacturing equipment that has more than 300.000 customers in 176 countries supported by more than 50 companies worldwide with more than 250 branch offices and authorized agencies in further 36 countries.

The main goal of the presented here CSM system based on the KSNet-approach is to provide information about solutions to customers in addition to existing product catalogue and to find products and solutions. Therefore, besides company's documents two other applications were selected as knowledge sources: (i) the product catalogue containing information about 20'000 items produced by the company: technical data, price, etc. for different languages, and (ii) an application containing a set of rules for configuration of handling system projects, structured data for industry segment and automation function description, and technical data of carried out products. These 1st and 2nd applications are oriented to industrial engineers and designers. Extension of these target groups with new ones allows increasing the number of potential clients and providing additional benefits to the company. Based on this information a part of the shared ontology of the company is built. The ontology uses frame-based knowledge representation model and includes classes and attributes.

Usually, it is proposed to have a shared ontology for a global company. However, the practice shows that this is not always possible due to the large number and heterogeneity of company members. Sometimes it is enough to build a smaller shared ontology for one aspect of the company activities or one company member only (later in the paper referred to as "ontology"), but this ontology should also support synonyms that might be used by its customers to provide for interoperability. This is how it was implemented in the presented approach.

The developed CRM system uses the company ontology consisting of more than 240 classes, 355 attributes from different sources [12]. The ontology currently is based on six taxonomies: VDMA (association of German machine and plant construction companies), industry segments (with basic functions as attributes – Workpiece, Handling, Assembly, Light assembly, Packaging, Automotive processes, Process automation, Food manufacturing, etc.), automation functions (with basic functions as attributes), handling system projects classification, technical data of industrial applications, and user-defined taxonomy.

The following scenario of the customer access to corporate information was developed: the customer passes authentication procedure, selects an appropriate interface form and enters a request into the system. The system recognizes the request and defines which data the customer needs. If the customer needs to solve a problem the system defines load conditions (parameters describing a certain problem: e.g. mass to be moved, direction of the transportation, environmental conditions etc.) and looks for handling system projects. If no certain problem is defined by the customer the system checks information in product catalogue, database storing technical data of standard handling systems and in company's documents.

Implemented approach for the user and request clustering scenarios (see 1st, 2nd and 3rd scenarios in the introduction) has the following steps:

1. Extract words / phrases from the request;
2. Calculate *similarity metrics* between the request and ontology (i.e. compare text strings extracted from the request and the name of the class or attribute);
3. Ontology-based algorithm of users & requests clustering

Step 1: Construct weighted graph consisting of nodes: classes, attributes, and users. Weights of arcs are calculated on the basis of 1) similarity metrics (i.e. they are different for different user requests) and 2) taxonomic relations in ontology;

Step 2: Construct weighted graph consisting of user / customers (when classes and attributes are removed, arcs weights are recalculated).

Step 3: Hierarchical clustering of users (customers) graph.

3   Ontology-Based Algorithm of Users and Requests Clustering

3.1   Similarity Metrics

Calculation of similarity between the user request and the corporate ontology is based on the similarity of the names for classes and attributes of the ontology and strings (concepts, phrases) of the request.

Request-Class Similarity. The essence of this task is to find classes in the ontology corresponding to the user request. This is done by comparing names of the classes (text strings) with stemmed and corrected (when misspelled) words extracted from the user request (names of classes, which are not numbers, misspelled words or units of measures).

The algorithm of *fuzzy string comparison* is used for this purpose. It calculates occurrence of substrings of one string in the other string. The algorithm can be illustrated by comparing strings "motor" and "mortar".

The first string "motor" has 5 different substrings (m, o, t, r, mo) contained in the second string "mortar". The total number of different substrings in "motor" is the following 13 strings: ((m, o, t, r), (mo, ot, to, or), (mot, oto, tor), (moto, otor)). The result is the following string "motor" corresponds to the string "mortar" with the similarity of 5/13 or 38%.

Request-Attribute Similarity. Attributes (corresponding to the user request) are searched within the names of the ontology elements. Regular expressions [13] are used for text processing. Below, *Entries* denotes a part of attribute name (one or several words) found in the request:

Request: "Pay load 5 kg, *Stroke X* 100 mm, *Stroke* Y 200 mm"
Attribute: "Stroke X"
Entries (parts of user requests): "Stroke X", "Stroke"

In this example the attribute name "Stroke X" (from the ontology) is found in the request once entirely ("Stroke X") and once partially ("Stroke").

For each attribute the following parameters are defined: N_{Words} — number of words in the attribute name; $AttrName_{Rest}[0..N_{Words}]$ — array of words forming the attribute name; $Word_{Attr}$ — an element of the array $AttrName_{Rest}[]$; $Position_{UserRequest}$ — point to the current position in the user request.

The algorithm of calculating *the similarity of the attribute to the request* is the following:

```
N_Entries = 0;
Position_UserRequest = 0;
Initialize AttrName_Rest[];
Similarity = 0;
FOREACH Word_Attr IN (AttrName_Rest[]) {
   FOREACH (Position_New =
   strpos(Word_Attr, UserRequest, Position_UserRequest))
   {
      Position_UserRequest += Position_New;
      remove Word_Attr from AttrName_Rest[];
      Similarity = max (
         Similarity,
         CalcSimilarity(Position_UserRequest, AttrName_Rest[]));
   }
}
```

Similarity for each part of the request (entry) to the attribute is calculated by the function *CalcSimilarity()* with the following properties. First, the more words from a name of the attribute are found in the request, the greater similarity. For example, *CalcSimilarity()* is greater for the entry "Stroke X" than for the entry "Stroke". Second, the longer the *Entry* the greater the similarity, e.g. similarity of "Stroke" is greater than that of "X".

Function *strpos* in the algorithm above returns the position of the attribute substring $Word_{Attr}$ in the string UserRequest, starting at the position "$Position_{UserRequest}$". So, the variable $Position_{UserRequest}$ takes values (starting from zero) through all the positions of the *attribute* substring in the text of the *user request*.

Thus, the similarity metric shows the degree of the correspondence of user requests to classes and attributes of the ontology. Similarity is a real number in the range [0, 1]. After processing the user requests, extracting terms, calculating similarity metrics, an XML structure is filled. It consists of the tags (i) related to classes (<CID> — the ontology class ID (unique identifier), <CWeight> — similarity of the class to the user request) and (ii) the tags related to attributes (<AID> — ID of an attribute from the ontology, <AWeight> — similarity of the attribute to the user request). These data are the input for the clustering algorithm described in the next section.

3.2   Users and Requests Clustering

This section describes proposed ontology-based clustering algorithm related to agglomerative hierarchical methods. The hierarchical method creates a decomposition of the given set of data objects. The agglomerative approach, also called the *bottom-up* approach, starts with each object forming a separate group. It successively merges the objects or groups close to one another, until all of the groups are merged into one (the topmost level of the hierarchy), or until a termination condition holds. More information about hierarchical methods see in [2].

The proposed algorithm relies on user profiles consisting of: (i) personal data (user name, country, etc.); (ii) list of classes (found in the ontology using requests of the user) and their similarity to the user/request CU_{sim}; (iii) list of attributes (found in the ontology using requests of the user) and their similarity to the user/request AU_{sim}.

It is needed to group the users by their requests. A groups should not consist of all the users or (another extreme case) of only one user.

The user in this task is presented via a set of his/her requests. Therefore it is possible to turn from "request" relations (class-request and attribute-request) to "user" relations (class-user (CU) and attribute-user (AU)).

A weighted user-ontology graph G_0=<N, E>=<(C, A, U), (CA, CC, CU, AU)> is considered. N represents three types of nodes: C — class, A — attribute and U — user. Since arcs E=(CA, CC, CU, AU) of the graph G_0 are marked with numbers (weights) then graph G_0 can be presented as *weight matrix*:

$$G_0[i, j] = \begin{cases} 0, & if\ i = j \\ c_{ij}, & \text{finite quantity, if there is an arc from node i to j} \\ \infty, & \text{if there is no arc from i to j} \end{cases} \tag{1}$$

User-ontology graph G_0 consists of two types of arcs. The type I of arcs (! " , ! !) is defined by the hierarchy of classes and belonging to them attributes in the ontology. The type II of arcs (CU, AU) is defined by the set of relations between use requests and classes/attributes (Fig. 2).

Weights of arcs between the nodes representing classes and users CU_{weight}, and attributes and users AU_{weight} are defined via the similarity CU_{sim} and AU_{sim} (values of XML tags <CWeight> and <AWeight>) as follows:

$$\begin{aligned} CU_{weight} &= 1 - CU_{sim} \\ AU_{weight} &= 1 - AU_{sim} \end{aligned} \tag{2}$$

All arcs CA and CC tying together classes and attributes have CA_{weight}, CC_{weight} $\in (\varepsilon, 1)$ defined by the IACD system administrator (see experiment results in sec. 4). CC_{weight} denotes arcs' weight of linked classes in the ontology. CA_{weight} — arcs' weight of linked attributes and classes.

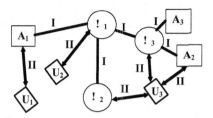

Fig. 2. User-ontology graph G_0

Step 1: Weight Assignment. The weight of the arc CU (class–user/request) is considered in the graph G_0. The class C can be encountered several times in different requests of user U in this graph. This should be taken into account in the weight of the arc CU. If class C is encountered in N requests of user U, then the *weight of arc* CU-_{weight} between class C and user U can be defined as follows:

$$CU_{weight} = 1 - \underset{i=1}{\overset{N}{\%}} \frac{1 - CU^i_{weight}}{N_{max}}, \tag{3}$$

where N_{max} is the maximum number of instances of the same class for all requests.

If similarity CU_{sim} is equal to 1 then the weight of arcs CU (AU) will be equal to 0 (see (2)) and the user with several similar requests will not have priority. So, in order to take into account the number of requests which coincide with the same class (attribute) several times, weight CU_{weight} and AU_{weight} should be assigned to ε instead of 0. ε should be close enough to 0 and defined in the range (0,1).

Step 2: User Graph Constructing. Usually Floyd algorithm [14] is used to find the shortest path between every pair of the graph nodes. In the considered case it is enough to know the weight of the *shortest path* between every pair of users. Therefore the *modified Floyd algorithm* is proposed and used. The table T of relations between users and classes is defined by the user-ontology graph:

– T[i, j] is the weight between nodes i and j,
– T[i, j] = ∞, if there is no path from node i to j.

The variable p in the algorithm is the number of nodes in the graph G_1.

Algorithm to calculate the weight of the shortest path between every pair of users in the graph G_1:

```
for i from 1 to p do
  for j from 1 to p do
    for k from 1 to p do
      if i<>j and T[i,j]<>∞ and
         i<>k and T[i,k]<>∞ and
               (T[j,k] = ∞ or
                T[j,k]>T[j,i]+T[i,k])
```

```
    then
                    T[j,k]  :=  T[j,i]+T[i,k]
      end if
    end for
  end for
end for
```

As a result the matrix T is created (i.e. users' graph G_2). Thus the weight of arc between every pair of users in G_2 is equal to the weight of the shortest path in G_1, or ∞ if such path does not exist.

Step 3: User Graph Clustering. Now in order to group users to clusters it is enough to divide the graph G_2 to subgraphs G^i, i=1,n, where n – is the number of clusters. Cluster mass G^i is the sum of weights of all arcs in the subgraph G^i.

The optimal clustering is proposed to be defined as follows:
a) n# min, i.e. minimize number of user groups,
b) $D_{max} > D[G^i]$, i=1,n, i.e. the maximum cluster mass for every subgraph is less than some (defined in advance by the IACD system administrator) constant D_{max}.

Hierarchical clustering algorithm:

```
1. D[Ui]=0, i=1,n. At the beginning of the algorithm
   every node corresponds to a subgraph. The value of
   subgraph mass D[Ui] is zero.
2. Fill vector A: A[z] = ARCweight + D[Ui] + D[Uj]; i.e.
   element ![z] of vector A equals to the sum of weight
   of the arc between Ui and Uj nodes of the graph and
   cluster mass D[Ui] + D[Uj] of these nodes.
3. Take the element A[z] from the vector A with the mini-
   mum value (sum of weight of the arc and the cluster
   mass).
4. If A[z] > DMax then terminate algorithm.
5. Join nodes Ui, Uj; result mass of Ui, Uj is D[Ui] =
   ARCweight[i,j] + D[Ui] + D[Uj]; remove D[Uj] from vec-
   tor D and the minimal element from A.
6. Update values in the vector A for arcs of adjacent
   nodes Ui (e.g. if node Uk is an adjacent node to Ui
   then A[ik] = ARCweight[i,k] + D[Ui] + D[Uk])
7. Go to line 3.
```

Due to the testing of inequality $D < D_{max}$ (line number 4), the second condition of the optimal clustering (b) will be satisfied.

Algorithm time complexity uses three parameters (N – sum of classes and users (class-user graph size); n — number of users (user graph); L – number of classes related to a request) and has three constituents. First, time complexity of creating class-user graph is $o(N \cdot L)$, because every L classes/attributes are retrieved from a database for each N requests. Second, modified Floyd algorithm uses three nested loops to calculate the shortest paths between nodes in graph, so its complexity is $o(N^3)$.

Third, time complexity of hierarchical clustering algorithm has two parts: outside of the cycle (steps 1-2) and of the cycle itself (steps 3-7). Complexity of step 1 is $o(1)$ and step 2 is $o(n^2)$ in case of building vector A for fully connected graph. The cycle: step 3 (searching minimal element in vector A) is $o(n)$, step 4 and step 5 has complexity $o(1)$, step 6 is $o(n)$ for fully connected graph (vector A is updating for adjacent arcs). Number of maximum cycle iterations is n in the worse case (one cluster includes all users). So, time complexity of the cycle is $o(n^2)$. Thus, complexity of hierarchical clustering algorithm is $o(n^2) + o(n^2) = o(n^2)$.

So, total time complexity of the three constituents is $o(N \cdot L) + o(N^3) + o(n^2)$. It is $o(N \cdot L) + o(N^3)$ when N $ n. Usually number of requests N is greater then number of classes L related to a request due to user requests are short enough (L % N), so $o(N^2) + o(N^3) = o(N^3)$.

4 Experiments

The goal of these experiments is to study the clustering approach and to evaluate how user clusterization depends on variables D_{Max} and CC_{weight}. The IACD system administrator can use this dependence to determine parameters of the clusterization (D_{Max} and CC_{weight}).

The graph (Fig. 3) demonstrates automatically generated set of two request clusters using the Graphviz tool [15]. The following parameters are used for this clustering: number of classes = 10, number of users = 5, CC_{Weight} = 0.2 for all the classes in the ontology and D_{Max}.(maximal cluster mass) = 0.6. For illustrative purpose user requests are shown instead of users. Classes in Fig. 3 are marked with ovals and requests are marked with rectangles. Clusters are marked with rectangles enclosing requests' rectangles. The magnified part of the graph includes: classes: "Pick & place" and "Projects", and requests: "Pick & place" and "Pick & place pay load > 0 and Stroke = 5". The exact name of the class "Pick & Place" is presented in both requests, so arc weight between the request and the class "Pick & Place" is ε =0,001 (Fig. 3) in both cases (two arcs from class Pick & Place to these requests). CC_{Weight} = 0.2, hence the weight of arc between the class "Pick & place" and the class "Projects" is 0.2.

It can be seen (Fig. 4) that for $D_{Max} < \varepsilon$ = 0,0001 the number of groups is equal to the number of users for all values CC_{Weight} (AB in Fig. 4). Increasing D_{Max} causes the number of groups to decrease down to two (BC_i in Fig. 4). Then, the steady level of the group number (C_1D_1 and C_2D_2 in Fig. 4) can be seen. At this interval the groups remain unchanged though D_{Max} increases. Given $CC_{Weight} = \varepsilon$ the interval C_3D_3 is lacking. This can be explained as follows. If the value of CC_{Weight} is low, to add a new user to the cluster, D_{Max} has to increase by the value equal to the weight between that user and the nearest to him/her class. In this case weight between C_2 and C_5 can be neglected because it is significantly lower than weight between that user and the class nearest to him/her. Area D_iE describes a low number of groups (tending to one group consisting of all users). It can be concluded that the IACD system administrator has to define D_{Max} from within C_iD_i interval.

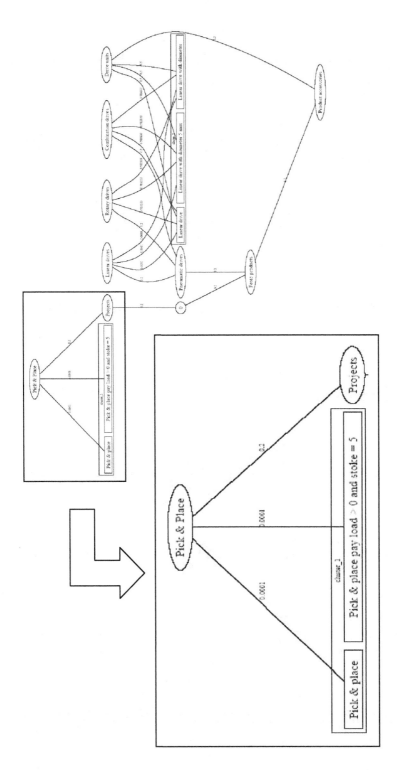

Fig. 3. The user graph consists of two clusters which are marked by rectangles. A part of this graph is zoomed in for convenient reading

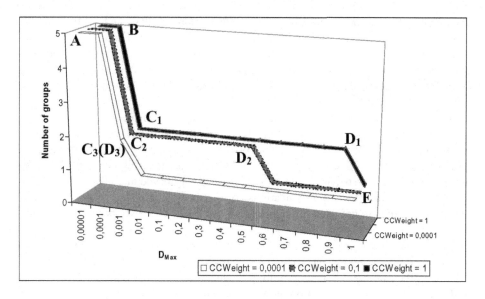

Fig. 4. Number of clusters depending on D_{Max} and CC_{weight}

5   Discussion and Conclusion

Ontology-based clustering is used to group related users and request information. Difference of this approach and other approaches are discussed below.

In [16] the ROCK hierarchical clustering algorithm for categorical attributes is proposed and implemented. In ROCK concept of links to measure the similarity/proximity between a pair of data points is presented. The feature of the ROCK algorithm is that the merging clusters/points with the most number of links is performed in the first order during the clustering. In contrast, the clustering algorithm proposed in this article merges clusters/points which are nearest in the graph. Another distinctive feature of the algorithm proposed in this article is that text processing and ontology data are used to form input data for clustering.

In [17] COSA (Concept Selection and Aggregation) the approach uses a simple, core, domain-specific ontology for restricting a set of relevant document features to cluster documents by K-Means algorithm. The definition of clustering quality metric is one of the benefits of this work. The user may decide to prefer one over another clustering result based on the actual concepts used for clustering as well as on standard quality measures (such as the silhouette measure). Unlike proposed here approach considering relatively short user requests, in [17] clustered data are text documents. Another difference is that the quality of the result is estimated by the administrator in the proposed approach.

Human-based and computer based clustering methods is one more classification of clustering. For example, in [18] an integration of the technical domain experts work with the data mining tools is presented. In this integration the following step is done to cluster science documents: (1) defining of words frequency (to identify topic of document), (2) determination of the relationships among themes, and (3) tracking the evolution of these themes and their relationships through time. The first and the second step are designed and implemented (see [18]). Since in this paper the definition of parameters of ontology-based clustering algorithm by the system administrator is very crucial for the algorithm (sec. 0), it can be concluded that the approach presented here is integrated (human-based & computer based).

In [19] the web-users clustering algorithm (based on K-means clustering and genetic algorithm) is proposed, implemented, and tested. The web-users clustering algorithm uses the integration of a neural network and self-organized maps (SOM) to cope with insufficient information about users. In [4] ideas about distributed data clustering are presented. This distributed data clustering is density-based and takes into account the issues of privacy and communications costs. Since genetic algorithms, SOM, and density methodic are not used in the proposed approach, these works can not be compared with.

Possible improving of the implemented in the system IACD clustering approach can be achieved by taking into account probability relations between classes and attributes in the ontology. It is an ontology engineering task that requires involvement of domain experts. This type of ontology can be very suitable for semantic relations in text mining area, because complex semantic relations can not be reduced to simple present/absent relations (like in ontology taxonomy). This is believed to increase the efficiency of context-aware CSM system especially for learning and predicting customer actions and interests, better recognition of their requests, etc.

The system IACD has the following properties of modern applications [Chen, 2001] related to free text processing (which is necessary for customer request recognition): (i) *multi-language support*, currently the system IACD supports three languages: English, Russian, German; (ii) *automatic taxonomy creation*, the company ontology (taxonomy) is built automatically in the system IACD based on the available knowledge sources; (iii) *domain-specific knowledge filter* (using vocabularies or ontologies), four level ontology is used in IACD; (iv) *indexer*: all documents are indexed for rapid access; (v) *multi-document format support*, the system IACD supports MSOffice documents, RTF documents, web pages, Adobe PDF files, ASCII text files; (vi) *natural or statistical language processing*; in IACD natural language processing consists of tokenization, spelling, stemming, etc.; (vii) *term extraction*, in IACD names of ontology classes and attributes, units of measures (e.g. "kg" and "mm") are extracted from customer requests.

Acknowledgment

Some parts of the research were done by the Contract titled "Intelligent Access to Catalogues and Documents" between Festo and SPIIRAS and as parts of the project # 16.2.44 of the research program "Mathematical Modelling and Intelligent Systems" and the project # 1.9 of the research program "Fundamental Basics of Information Technologies and Computer Systems" of the Russian Academy of Sciences.

References

1. Chen, Hsinchun: Knowledge Management Systems: A Text Mining Perspective, in Knowledge Computing Corporation. (2001) URL http://dlist.sir.arizona.edu/archive/00000483/01/chenKMSi.pdf
2. Han, J., and Kamber, M. Data Mining: Concepts and Techniques. San Francisco: Morgan Kaufmann Publishers (2001)
3. Gorodetsky, V., Karsaev, O., Samoilov, V.: Multi-Agent Technology for Distributed Data Mining and Classification. In the 2003 International Conference on Intelligent Agent Technology (IAT'2003), IEEE Computer Society press, Halifax, Canada October (2003) 438-441
4. Klusch, M., Lodi, S., Moro, G-L.: The Role of Agents in Distributed Data Mining. In the 2003 International Conference on Intelligent Agent Technology (IAT'2003), IEEE Computer Society press, Halifax, Canada October 2003. – Pp.211-217
5. Smirnov, A., Pashkin, M., Chilov, N., Levashova, T.: Agents-based Knowledge Logistics. In R. Khosla, N. Ichalkaranje, L.C. Jain (eds.) Design of Intelligent Multi-Agent Systems, Springer, 2005, 63—101
6. Smirnov, A., Pashkin, M., Chilov, N., Levashova, T., Haritatos, F.: Knowledge Source Network Configuration Approach to Knowledge Logistics. Int. J. of General Systems. Vol. 32, No. 3. Taylor & Francis Group (2003) 251–269
7. Kitamura, Y., Mizoguchi, R.: Ontology-based systematization of functional knowledge. Journal of Engineering Design, Taylor & Francis, Vol. 15, Number 4, (2004) 327-351. URL http://www.ei.sanken.osaka-u.ac.jp/pub/kita/
8. Hidalgo, J.: Text Mining and Internet Content Filtering (2002) URL http://www.esi.uem.es/~jmgomez/tutorials/ecmlpkdd02
9. Losiewicz, P., Oard, D., Kostoff, R.: Text Data Mining to Support Science and technology management // Journal of Intelligent Information Systems, vol.15, N2 sept/oct (2000) 99-119
10. Kostoff, D., Losiewicz, P., Oard, D.: Since and Technolohy Text Mining Basic Concepts. Technical Report A688514. AFRL, Rome NY (2003) 28 URL http://www.stormingmedia.us/68/6885/A688514.html
11. Kuhlins, S., Tredwell, R.: Toolkits for generating Wrappers – A Survey of Software Toolkits for Automated Data Extraction from Websites (2005) http://www.netobjectdays.org/pdf/02/papers/node/0188.pdf
12. Hinselmann, T., Smirnov, A., Pashkin, M., Chilov, N., Krizhanovsky, A.: Implementation of Customer Service Management System for Corporate Knowledge Utilization. Proceedings of the 5th International Conference on Practical Aspects of Knowledge Management (PAKM 2004), Vienna, Austria, LNAI 3336 (2004) 475–486
13. Friedl, J.E.F.: Mastering Regular Expressions, O'REILLY (2003)
14. Novikov, F.A.: Discrete mathematics for programmers, Piter, St Petersburg, (2004)
15. Graphviz — Graph Visualization Software (2005) URL http://graphviz.org
16. Guha, S., Rastogi, R., Shim, K.: ROCK: A Clustering Algorithm for Categorical Attributes. Information System Journal 25(5):, Elsevier Science Ltd (2000) URL http://ee.snu.ac.kr/~shim/is-rock.pdf
17. Hotho, A., Maedche, A., & Staab, S.: Ontology-based text clustering. In Proceedings of the IJCAI-001 Workshop "Text Learning: Beyond Supervision", August, Seattle, USA, (2001) URL http://www.fzi.de/KCMS/kcms_file.php?action=link&id=54

18. Kostoff, R., N., Braun, T., Schubert, A., Toothman, D., R. & Humenik, J.: Fullerene road-maps using bibliometrics and database tomography. Journal of Chemical Information and Computer Science. 40(1). 19-39 (2000) URL http://www.onr.navy.mil/sci_tech/special/354/technowatch/textmine.asp

19. Lingras, P.J., Hogo, M., Snorek, M.: Interval Set Clustering of Web Users using Modified Kohonen Self-Organizing Maps based on the Properties of Rough Sets, Web Intelligence and Agent Systems: An International Journal, Vol. 2, Number 3 (2004)

Multi-agent Approach for Community Clustering Based on Individual Ontology Annotations

Dmitri Soshnikov

Moscow Aviation Institute (Technical University),
Dept. of Numerical Mathematics and Programming,
Artificial Intelligence Group
dsh@mailabs.ru,
http://www.soshnikov.com

Abstract. The paper presents peer-to-peer multi-agent framework for community clustering based on contact propagation in the global network of contacts with individual ontology-based descriptions. The framework allows people to meet interested parties by specifying flexible ontology-based requests and/or proposals and relaying them between the nodes of the system along the most ontologically-prominent directions, thus covering wide yet very targeted audience. It also supports ad hoc meeting using mobile devices such as PDAs, SmartPhones, etc.

The system works over standard means of communication such as e-mail/ICQ, and provides user with personalized relaying assistant that can automatically process ontologically-annotated messages, relaying and/ or responding to them. It can also collect user's knowledge about his contact base, thus acting as a personalized assistant in the certain area of communication.

Keywords: Ontology-Based Community Clustering, Multi-Agent Peer-To-Peer System.

1 Introduction

In our everyday life, we tend to use more and more electronic devices (such as cell phones, PDAa, Tablet PCs, etc.) and software systems, which potentially can be or already are equipped with intelligent, AI-based functionality [1]. Such devices potentially could learn from the user, resulting in more and more personal knowledge being stored in some formalized electronic form, suitable for automated usage and processing. Many activities we perform are based on our knowledge, and automating those activities to larger extent would greatly empower our computing experience, eventually leading to the concept of **cybernetic immortality** [2], when enough human personal knowledge is extracted for the computer system to be able to act intelligently on human's behalf, without human supervision. Thus, a person may be eventually replaced by his digital

V. Gorodetsky, J. Liu, and V.A. Skormin (Eds.): AIS-ADM 2005, LNAI 3505, pp. 247–262, 2005.

assistant that would carry out many external activities much in the same way as the original person. In fact, cybernetic immortality can be considered to be one of the goals of contemporary AI, replacing to a certain extent the idea of creating intelligent self-conscious systems.

Cybernetic immortality can be achieved by automating almost all areas of human activity. One area of activity that can be automated in this manner is communication. Often we find ourselves in the situation when we help our friends and acquaintances to get in touch with the right people by suggesting transitive contacts. Our contact base, being properly annotated by our knowledge about them, does encompass certain area of our expertise that can be used for helping other people in finding the right contacts. This would be one of the main objectives described in this paper, which is achieved by using expressive ontology and distributed knowledge repository for describing contacts, and multi-agent environment for automated communication.

Exchanging information on relevant contacts between interested parties would lead to **community clustering** according to some ontologically-formulated criteria. Initially, the network of contacts would be clustered somehow according to the existing friend-of relation that would to a certain extent correspond to interests. Proposed multi-agent system would allow this network of contacts to evolve in the direction of further multi-dimensional clustering around ontological concepts. Further on, we propose the use of ad hoc networks to augment building additional randomly-distributed friend-of relations, that would later on be clustered around interests.

In this paper, we propose the architecture of the software system named MAORIE (Multi-Agent Ontology-Relevance Interconnection Engine) that uses ontologically annotated contact list to handle transitive requests for contacts and self-descriptions. To some extent annotation of friend lists and personal profile information using simple meta-data has been proposed in the FOAF (Friend Of A Friend) Project [3]. In this paper we propose to extend FOAF descriptions with proper ontological semantically strict annotations, and also describe an architecture of multi-agent system that would perform actual community clustering over the set of extended FOAF descriptions by exchanging requests and proposals in the directions defined by ontology relevance metrics. The action of finding relevant contacts would be performed automatically using digital software assistant operating with ontologically-formalized messages.

There are many people we see around us in the everyday life that we will never get a chance to talk to and to know if they share the same interests. Proposed technology empowers our ability to spot potentially interesting contacts by delegating the first part of communication to personal agents. Those agents are able to help us in many ways: not only see if the person standing next to us in the bus is relevant to our search goals or shares some of our interests, but also in exposing information about our contact base and allowing transitive meeting requests to be relayed in the meaningful manner. We would be able to express both the description of ourselves and the criteria for people we are interested in using very flexible ontology-based mechanism, and then use all means of communication (e-mail, MSN Messenger, wireless technologies, etc.) to find the right contacts.

2   Ontology-Based Community Clustering

2.1   Existing Community Clustering Techniques

One of the emerging phenomena in the contemporary world is the formation of user communities according to some criteria, which is empowered by various flexible means of communication. We can consider the following basic community-building techniques:

- **Explicit community formation** (e.g. community web-sites, mailing lists, yahoo groups, etc.), where users express their interest to join a specific community
- **Implicit community formation**, where users are made part of a community by performing certain actions (e.g. visiting a web site, making a purchase, writing a message to the USENET group, etc.)

Recently, more complex community building techniques appeared. In particular, we can identify the following:

- **Simple interest-based clustering** (an example being [4]), where users can chose to participate in different communities based on their interests, and then enjoy combined community services like joint blogs, news, etc.
- **Simple friend-relation clustering** (used in [5] and similar communities), where users define a set of other users as friends, thus defining a graph of contacts, in which certain implicit clusters arise. While the basis of the community building is only friendly relation, assuming people tend to chose friends based on their interests we can argue that clusters in such a graph have strong relation to people's interests.
- **Complex Transitive Friend-Relation Clustering** (seen in [6]), where people maintain a set of their contacts, and then have access to certain partial transitive closure of contact relation (typically up to certain degree of transitivity).

In general, community structure can be defined by the **acquaintance relation** $R \subseteq I \times I$, where I is a set of all community members. For each member x, we can define his **social atom** as $A(x) = \{z \in I | R(x, z)\}$.

2.2   Transitive Community Restructuring

In real life, when we need to acquire some specific contacts, we typically ask our friends if they know someone relevant to our needs — thus we obtains some additional contact that belongs to the transitive closure R^+. However, this closure in itself is not really interesting, because as indicated by many sociological studies it is likely to include the whole community I, except for maybe some very asocial individuals. To find individuals relevant to our needs, we introduce the notion of **directed transitive closure** that takes relevancy into account.

Suppose we define relevancy of any person to our goal by some **utility function** $\mu : I \rightarrow [0,1]$, and we want to find contacts with relevancy higher than certain threshold τ. While the set $A_\mu(x) = \{z \in I | R^+(x,z) \wedge (\mu(z) < \tau)\}$ would look like a reasonable answer, computing such a set in reality is a complex task, because it involves traversing through almost all the community members. In real life, our friends typically pass the request to some of their friends with similar interests, thus we actually end up with the set

$$A_\mu^\infty(x) = \bigcup_{i=1}^\infty A_\mu^{(i)}(x)$$

where

$$A_\mu^{(i+1)}(x) = \bigcup_{\xi \in A_\mu^{(i)}(x)} \{z \in I | R(\xi, z) \wedge (\mu(z) < \tau)\}$$

where τ in this case is the propagation threshold. Because $A_\mu^\infty(x) \subset A_\mu(x)$, we will lose some potentially interesting contacts, but on the other hand in this process at any given point we deal with relatively small number of contacts and requests, which is why in the real life we are likely to use this kind of procedure for the propagation of acquaintance relation.

Now suppose we have a set of interests $\{\mu_1, \ldots, \mu_n\}$. We might want to expand our initial social atom to include all potentially interesting contacts from $A_{\mu_i}^\infty(x)$, which would lead to a new acquaintance relation $R^{(1)}$. For this new relation, the procedure might be repeated, and so on. Since this process in ideal case is monotonous, and the number of community members is limited, it is bound to reach some fixpoint, which would correspond to **interest-based community clustering**. In fact, even starting from some random uniform distribution of contacts, this process is likely to converge to some stable clusters of contacts centered around specific interests defined by utility functions μ_i.

2.3   Ontology-Based Contact Description

For the process above to work, we need some way to define utility function μ. In this paper we present a way of community clustering based on ontological annotation of contacts. In the existing communities [4,5,6] it is possible for people to annotate their user profiles with a list of interests specified in the form of keywords (LiveJournal), or provide more sophisticated annotations yet still based on some fixed schema (LinkedIn). In each case, those annotations allow us to see how close our interests are to potential contacts, i.e. they implicitly define the utility function.

We propose to use ontology-based annotations, where person can define his/her profile by binding to certain existing well-known ontologies. This method has the following advantages:

- Very flexible annotations are possible. For example, it is possible to describe that someone is male, born in 1974, has Ph.D. degree from certain university, is interested in multi-agent systems and tennis (all the terms above taken from the standard MAORIE ontology) and presented a paper on AIS-ADM-2005 workshop in 2005 (the later terms being taken from some specific ontology developed by people interested in AI).
- It is possible to develop new domain ontologies for specific areas of expertise, thus overcoming the fixed schema and making the annotation technology open to new concepts.
- Search in such annotations can be inference-based, e.g. it would be possible to infer that a person interested in multi-agent systems is also interested in artificial intelligence (subsumption inference), and that the person born in 1974 is 30 years old as of December 2004 (rule-based inference).
- Annotation is still pretty simple for the end-users, because they are only binding to the existing ontology terms, and ontology development is left to more advanced users or knowledge engineers.
- All systems mentioned above allow statements to be made by users about their own interests. In the ontology-based system it is possible for other users to make statements about their contacts, for example a person can specify that his friend John cooks well (according to his own judgment), and this annotation can also be taken into account.

In this case, the function μ would correspond to the notion of **ontological relevance**, discussed later in this paper.

2.4   Peer-to-Peer Contact Propagation

All existing communities with clustering techniques are implemented as centralized web-based systems, which is an enormous limitation to

- **scalability**, because as the number of contacts grow it results in more and more load on the single server or web farm
- **security**, because most people do not consider it secure to place the list of their contacts on a public server
- **accessibility**, because we can only access information through the internet, and we are not using the real-life opportunities of meeting people and acquiring new contacts.

What we propose in this paper is a multi-agent distributed framework that works by **contact propagation**, using algorithms typical for peer-to-peer systems such as Gnutella [7]. The idea of using peer-to-peer model for ontology-based information retrieval is not new (see [8], for example); in this paper we suggest enhancing it with the notion of **ontological relevance** to proceed with contact propagation in the most prominent directions.

Each node in the system (which we can call an agent, or **macro-agent**) represents a certain person with his/her list of contacts, annotated by binding to a set of well-known ontologies[1]. Each user also creates a personal **profile** by specifying his relation to some ontologies, including standard MAORIE ontology and possibly some third-party ontologies created by any user interest groups and placed on the web. In the global network of contacts, each user is identified by an URI that can also be used as the URL allowing contacting users personal agent.

In the similar manner to profile annotation, the user is able to issue **queries** describing people he is looking for (for example, someone older than 18, interested in AI and who has attended at least one AI conference).

Communities are implicitly formed in real-time when people start looking for new contacts. This can happen in two ways:

– User personal profiles can be (if user specifies so) pushed into the multi-agent peer-to-peer network in terms of **proposals**, i.e. the profile is forwarded to some people from user's contact list who have high ontological relevance to the proposal. Direct contacts, having received the proposal, can forward it further along most ontologically prominent (gradient) directions, and so on.
– User queries are pushed into the network in the form of **requests** that travel along the same ontological directions.

At some node in the network it can happen that certain proposal matches a request (i.e. they have high ontological relevance) – in which case this node sends notification messages to originators of both the proposal and the request, containing the URI of the other party.

The process of request and proposal propagation is similar to the wave propagation, only it takes into account the most prominent directions. However, the effectiveness of this approach is based on the assumption that people tend to get acquainted according to their interests expressed in ontological form, which is not always the case. Thus, it still makes sense to distribute the requests along other directions as well, but somehow limiting this distribution.

To take this idea into account, we propose to use the fuzzy wave attenuation mechanism that takes ontological relevance into account. Upon each forward the weight of proposal or request is decreased by multiplying it by ontology relevance (which is assumed to be between 0 and 1), and at some point when it is lower than the threshold, the proposal or request is discarded. Thus, the proposal or request would travel longer along ontologically promising directions, and would stop after a few forwards along directions that are not relevant.

2.5   Ad Hoc Propagation

The proposed approach can work over any communication means that are able to deliver requests and proposals from one node to another. In addition to the usual communication means such as e-mail or specialized web services, it is possible

---

[1] By well-known we mean that those ontologies are widely available on the internet, and can be easily downloaded by all agents in the system.

to use the same approach in ad hoc networks of mobile devices such as PDAs or smartphones. This would allow taking the community clustering process from the cyberspace to the dimension of the real world.

In the ad hoc peer-to-peer network, proposed mechanism is enhanced by the **negotiation phase**, in which the macro-agent running on the mobile device discovers all neighbouring agents and exchanges public profile information with them. Those contacts are added to the contact list and automatically marked as ad hoc contacts by binding to special architectural ontology. On the next phase, normal proposal/request exchange takes place, which takes newly acquainted contacts into account, and can relay some of queued requests and proposals to them. Introducing new ad hoc contacts into the contact list plays an important role of creating some initial random distribution of the acquaintance relation, which is later on re-structured into stable interest-based communities by the process of contact propagation.

Ad hoc contacts are assigned **time to live** value that is decreased with time, until contacts are deleted. This allows freeing up the contact base, unless some ad hoc contact does not turn out to be interesting ontologically — in which case it can be moved to the normal contact base by being properly annotated.

In addition, in the ad hoc network, when the agent notices that some user in the physical vicinity is relevant to one of user's requests, **physical identification** phase is initiated, in which case the user hears an immediate audible notification and is allowed to contact another party via instant messaging or exchange profile photographs, which helps to identify the other person and immediately meet in real life.

2.6   Flood, SPAM and Security Issues

One of the problems with the proposed approach is the issue of floods and SPAM requests, because it would be theoretically possible to issue such a request that would catch all contacts on the way, thus making it simple for the intruder to collect the list of users' addresses.

It has to be noted that request weight attenuation algorithm can be adjusted in such a way that the total weight of the outgoing messages distributed as a result of one incoming message will be limited. Thus, if the incoming request is very broad and has high ontological relevance to many contacts, it will be distributed further with significantly decreased weight. Even though it would be possible for an intruder to design a system that passes requests along without decreasing their weight, this anomaly would be compensated by the system having all other agents forwarding requests properly.

Further on, it is possible to use some fee-based or bonus-based policy for message exchange and distribution, where some bonus points are awarded for helping other people to meet, and some are deduced for sending out queries/proposals. The determination of the exact bonus policy is still the issue of further investigation, which can be done by performing a series of simulation experiments on some real-life community data.

Also, an important issue that has not yet been dealt with is security, i.e. making it impossible for the intruder to pretend to be someone else. To rectify this it is possible to use cryptographic methods with public/private keys, or some public authentication mechanism such as Microsoft Passport — the details would be determined at the stage when the system goes beyond the experimental prototype.

3   Ontology-Based Description and Routing

3.1   Semantic Web Annotation Standards

The general idea behind community clustering does not rely on any specific technology for ontology knowledge representation, as long as we are able to compute ontology relevance metrics between any two concepts annotated using the ontology. However, it is very convenient to use Semantic Web technologies, in particular extended version of FOAF [3] for the actual contact list and contact descriptions that are bound to ontologies defined in OWL [9].

Using this approach, all ontological concepts are identified by the URI[2], and in order to introduce a new ontology it is enough to create an OWL file, place it somewhere on the Internet and start referring to the corresponding URL. Also, using FOAF standard for defining the acquaintance relation allows using third-party FOAF-based tools over the MAORIE network for exploring the community structure.

3.2   Classification of Ontologies

In the MAORIE system, we distinguish between the following types of ontologies:

- **Core ontology** is the main ontology used in describing contacts; it is sufficient for most non-demanding applications. Core ontology is intended to be distributed together with the MAORIE software, and can be periodically updated from the web. It includes the generic concepts $\top$ and $\bot$, and such common entities as person, human being, male, female, etc.
- **Architecture ontology** is built into the software suite and is used for internal purposes. In particular, it contains concepts for classifying contacts based on the type of acquaintance (ad hoc contact, direct contact, transitive contact, etc.), and concepts for most common types of contact groups (friends, acquaintances, business contacts, etc.).
- **Domain-specific ontologies** can be developed by any community or individual, placed on the web, and then used in annotating contacts. However, as with any ontology development, domain-specific ontologies only become useful when there is sufficient number of users that refer to them.
- **Personal ontology** can be easily developed by an individual user, and used for classifying contacts into arbitrary groups for presentation purposes.

---

[2] We actually require URI to be a valid URL that can be used to retrieve the corresponding ontology.

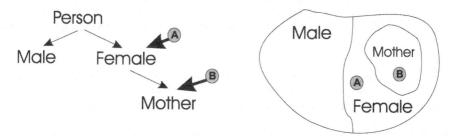

Fig. 1. Subsumption-based (left) and Interpretation-based (right) Ontological Relevance

3.3 Ontological Relevance

An important notion used in the propagation algorithm is **ontological relevance** between two concepts, described by a metric function μ that returns a relevance number for any two concepts[3] bound to the given ontology.

By **ontology** we mean some Description Logic (DL) T-Box that provides a set $\{C_i\}$ of named concepts that are naturally organized into a hierarchy by subsumption relation $\sqsubseteq$. A concept bound to an ontology in this case is specified by DL formula of the form

$$C_{i_1} \sqcap \ldots \sqcap C_{i_n} \tag{1}$$

Definition 1. *An* **ontology relevance** *is a function* $\mu : \{C_i\} \to [0,1]$ *that has the following properties (for all concepts* C, C_a, C_b, C_c*):*

$$
\begin{aligned}
\mu(C, C) &= 1 & \text{(reflexivity)} \\
\mu(C_a, C_b) &= \mu(C_b, C_a) & \text{(symmetry)} \\
\mu(C_a, C_c) &> \tfrac{\mu(C_a, C_b)\mu(C_b, C_c)}{\mu(C_a, C_b) + \mu(C_b, C_c)} & \text{(metric inequality)}
\end{aligned}
\tag{2}
$$

Two methods of computing ontological relevance are proposed:

- **Interpretation-Based Relevance** (Fig.1, right), where relevance is computed according to the number of individuals in the sets corresponding to given concepts under an interpretation $\mathcal{I}$. More precisely, for two concepts A and B, such that $A \sqsubseteq B$:

$$\mu_{\mathcal{I}}(A, B) = \frac{\#A^{\mathcal{I}}}{\#B^{\mathcal{I}}} \tag{3}$$

  In more general case,

$$\mu_{\mathcal{I}}(A, B) = \frac{\#(A^{\mathcal{I}} \cap B^{\mathcal{I}})}{\#(A^{\mathcal{I}} \cup B^{\mathcal{I}})} \tag{4}$$

---

[3] Utility function μ introduced in section 2.2 in our case is the ontological relevance function with one argument fixed to be the query.

- **Subsumption-Based Relevance** (Fig.1, left), which is similar to the way proposed in [10], and is based on computing the distance between concepts in the ontology hierarchy.

While interpretation-based relevance may appear to be more precise, in most cases the exact number of individuals in a given class is not known. Thus we have to use some variants of subsumption-based relevance, defined below.

Definition 2. *Let $\mathcal{O} = \{\mathcal{C}_i\}$ be an ontology, and $\mathcal{C}_a, \mathcal{C}_b \in \mathcal{O}$ — two concepts, such that $\mathcal{C}_a \sqsubseteq \mathcal{C}_b$. In finite ontologies it is always possible to effectively construct a chain $\mathcal{C}_a = \mathcal{C}_{i_0} \sqsubseteq \mathcal{C}_{i_1} \sqsubseteq \ldots \sqsubseteq \mathcal{C}_{i_k} = \mathcal{C}_b$. We would call $k = \mathrm{dist}(\mathcal{C}_a, \mathcal{C}_b)$* **subsumption distance** *between $\mathcal{C}_a$ and $\mathcal{C}_b$.*

We can also extend the notion of subsumption distance on arbitrary concepts in the following manner:

Definition 3. *A* **least common subsumer** *for concepts $\mathcal{C}_a$ and $\mathcal{C}_b$ is $\mathrm{lcs}(\mathcal{C}_a, \mathcal{C}_b)$ $= \inf\{\mathcal{C} | \mathcal{C}_a \sqsubseteq \mathcal{C}, \mathcal{C}_b \sqsubseteq \mathcal{C}\}$ (where $\inf$ is meant with respect to subsumption relation).*

Definition 4. **Generalized subsumption distance** *between two arbitrary concepts $\mathcal{C}_a$ and $\mathcal{C}_b$ is defined as $\mathrm{dist}(\mathcal{C}_a, \mathcal{C}_b) = \mathrm{dist}(\mathcal{C}_a, \mathrm{lcs}(\mathcal{C}_a, \mathcal{C}_b)) + \mathrm{dist}(\mathrm{lcs}(\mathcal{C}_a, \mathcal{C}_b), \mathcal{C}_b)$.*

Definition 5. *Let $A = A_1 \sqcap \ldots \sqcap A_n$ and $B = B_1 \sqcap \ldots \sqcap B_m$ be two concepts bound to ontology $\mathcal{O} = \{\mathcal{C}_i\}$. We would define* **strong asymmetrical distance** *between A and B as follows:*

$$\mathrm{ldist}(A, B) = \frac{\sum_{j=1}^{n} \sum_{\mathcal{C} \in \mathcal{Z}(A_j)} \mathrm{dist}(A_j, \mathcal{C})}{\# \cup_{j=1}^{n} \mathcal{Z}(A_j)} \tag{5}$$

where

$$\mathcal{Z}(A_j) = \{\mathcal{C} \in \{B_1, \ldots, B_m\} | \mathcal{C} \sqsubseteq A_j \vee A_j \sqsubseteq \mathcal{C}\} \tag{6}$$

In this definition, we take each atomic concept A_i from A, and compute average ontological distance to those atomic concepts B_i, that either subsume or are subsumed by A_i. Repeating this for each atomic concepts from A_1 to A_n, we obtain the desired distance.

This definition only takes into account pairs of concepts from ontology that are in subsumption relation. We can also compare the distances between all concepts, as described in.

Definition 6. *In the notation given in definition 5,* **weak asymmetrical distance** *between A and B is*

$$\mathrm{wdist}(A, B) = \frac{1}{mn} \sum_{i=1}^{n} \sum_{j=1}^{m} \mathrm{dist}(A_i, B_j) \tag{7}$$

Definition 7. *Strong / weak ontological relevance* between concepts A and B is defined as

$$\mu_s(A, B) = 1/(1 + \mathrm{ldist}(A, B) + \mathrm{ldist}(B, A))$$
$$\mu_w(A, B) = 1/(1 + \mathrm{wdist}(A, B) + \mathrm{wdist}(B, A)) \tag{8}$$

In the contact propagation algorithm, we use either strong or weak ontological relevance (or their weighted average) to compare requests and proposals. Because our definition of relevance is symmetric, a person looking for someone interested in AI and another person interested in Neural Networks would have the same relevance to each other as person looking for someone interested in Neural Networks and another person interested in AI. This probably does make sense, but it is also possible to enhance the definition of ontological relevance by adding coefficients taking the direction of subsumption into account.

3.4   Propagation Algorithm

Suppose at some node of the global peer-to-peer network we have a set of contacts $\{\mathcal{C}_i \sqcap \mathcal{P}_i\}$, where $\mathcal{C}_i$ is the personal profile of i-th contact, and $\mathcal{P}_i$ is our own description of the contact, both being some DL-formulae of the form (1).

When some request or proposal $\mathcal{R}$ with weight w is received, it has to be forwarded further, modifying the weight w according to ontological relevance. This process is controlled by the following parameters:

– **Discard threshold** T_d that specifies the weight below which the request is discarded and not forwarded
– **Relevance threshold** T_r, which controls when the request is considered relevant, and notifications should be sent to both parties
– **Forwarding Limit** L limiting the cumulative weight of all outgoing requests.

The following propagation routing algorithm is used:

1. From all contacts $\{\mathcal{C}_i \cap \mathcal{P}_i\}$ select the set of hits $\mathcal{H} = \{\mathcal{C}_i \cap \mathcal{P}_i | \mu(\mathcal{C}_i \cap \mathcal{P}_i, \mathcal{R}) > T_r\}$, and send notifications to the originator of the request $\mathcal{R}$ and to each contact from $\mathcal{H}$
2. From all contacts $\{\mathcal{C}_i \cap \mathcal{P}_i\}$ select the set of candidate contacts $\mathcal{S} = \{\mathcal{C}_i \cap \mathcal{P}_i | w \times \mu(\mathcal{C}_i \cap \mathcal{P}_i, \mathcal{R}) > T_d\}$.
3. Compute the normalization factor $f = \min(1, L \times (\sum_{x \in \mathcal{S}} w \times \mu(x, \mathcal{R}))^{-1})$
4. For each contact $x \in \mathcal{S}$, forward the request $\mathcal{R}$ with weight $f \times w \times \mu(x, \mathcal{R})$.

4   System Architecture

4.1   Agent Configuration

Global MAORIE peer-to-peer network consists of a number of individual nodes, or **macro-agents**. Those nodes run a number of smaller components responsible for different aspects of system operation that we call **micro-agents**. In some configurations it is possible that one micro-agent serves a number of nodes — for example, in the local area network of an enterprise one ontology broker can be responsible for maintaining centralized ontology cache.

Depending on the configuration of micro-agents, we can generally distinguish two types of macro-agents: **ad hoc macro-agents** that are capable of establishing wireless network communication sessions and typically run on PDAs, SmartPhones, Tablet PCs and Notebooks, which might not have dedicated Internet connection, and **desktop macro-agents** that run on desktop computers without ad hoc capabilities. This distinction is actually not very strict, as a desktop computer can play the role of an ad hoc agent provided it has wireless network card — for example, it makes sense to provide such "meeting stations" at conference locations, or any other public places.

One user can have more than one macro-agent acting on his behalf. In a typical situation, a user would have a desktop computer and a PDA that is synchronized to that desktop computer. Upon each synchronization, contact base is synchronized, and the ontology cache is updated[4].

MAORIE automated communication framework is built on top of the existing communication protocols such as e-mail, MSN/ICQ, Web Services, etc. Thus the framework does not require any specific centralized authentication mechanisms — it is the responsibility of a user to ensure that his identifying URI is unique and correctly corresponds to the means of communication monitored by personal communication agent (e.g. to a valid e-mail address, ICQ number, etc.).

4.2   Macro-agent Architecture

Each macro-agent consists of a set of individual micro-agents, which differ depending on computer configuration (e.g. whether we are installing on a wireless terminal such as PDA or Tablet PC, or desktop computer). Main components of the system are:

- **Routing micro-agent** carries out most of the systems activities. When an automated message is received, routing agent computes ontological relevance of the message against the existing contact base and forwards it along the most prominent directions, decreasing the current "weight" of the message. Messages with low weight are discarded.
- **Ontology broker** keeps track of used ontologies, caches and downloads ontologies from the Internet if required.
- **Communication micro-agents** are responsible for sending / receiving formalized messages. For example, Microsoft Outlook communication agent is a plug-in that monitors incoming mail, detects special automated messages

---

[4] This is important for mobile computers that do not have permanent Internet connectivity. When certain ontology was requested during the previous session, it is retrieved from the web upon the next synchronization.

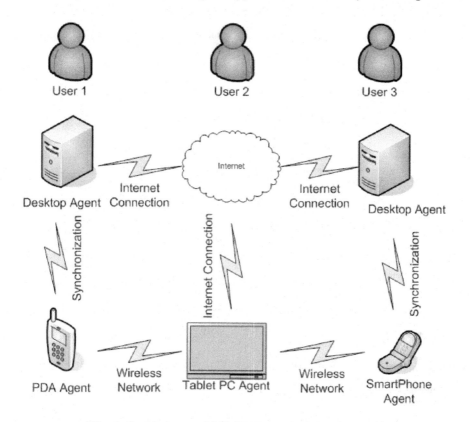

Fig. 2. Architecture of MAORIE Macro-Agent Network

and passes them to routing agent. It is also responsible for delivery of outgoing messages. There is a special class of communication agents for ad hoc
networking (Wi-Fi, Bluetooth) that are capable of discovering MAORIE-
empowered devices in the neighbourhood, adding them to the ad hoc contact
list, and then forcing exchange of queries and proposals.

- **User interface micro-agents** provide the user interface to the system,
  allowing to see the contact list, current set of requests, as well as formulating
  new request, annotating contacts and our own ontology-based description.
  There are different types of UI micro-agents designed for desktop computers
  and mobile platforms.

Architecture of typical MAORIE installation is presented on Fig. 3. All micro-
agents are separate software components communicating with each other using
Web Services — thus it is possible to run certain micro-agents on centralized
nodes on the network, and also to easily provide different means of communications for the given macro-agent.

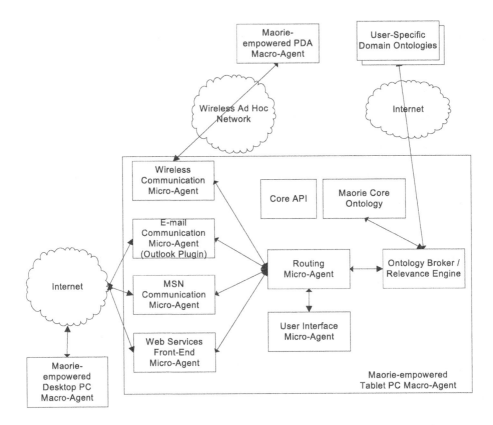

Fig. 3. Architecture of MAORIE Macro-Agent and its Relations to Other Agents

4.3   Agent Dissemination

Since the social impact of such a project would only be observable when it is widely adopted, the convenient means for technology dissemination are essential. Technically, agent dissemination is incorporated into the product, because automated messages sent out by the client include textual introduction intended to explain to the uninitiated user what the project is all about. Thus, if we send meeting requests, queries or proposals to some of our contacts without MAORIE agents installed, they are provided with an explanation and a link they can use to download and install the software in order to be able to process those requests automatically.

5   Implementation

At the present stage of development a prototype system has been created that works on both standard desktop and mobile computers (Tablet PCs, notebooks,

PDAs, SmartPhones). The system is implemented using Microsoft .NET platform, with Web Services Enhancements (WSE) 2.0 for communication between micro-agents. On mobile platforms such as PDAa it is possible to link different micro-agents together to produce single executable file. Web Services are also used for communication between some of the macro-agents, in addition to such open communication protocols as e-mail and ICQ.

6   Future Work

To study the behaviour of the complex multi-agent system it would be helpful to perform a series of simulation experiments on the modeling environment. This environment should simulate some realistic spatial distribution of agents in real and cyber-space and allow exchanging sample messages between them using the same routing algorithms as in the actual application. As a result of simulation, we would be able to fine-tune routing parameters to optimize routing behaviour in real-life situations, and develop effective bonus-based policies to prevent spam and flood issues in the network.

7   Conclusion

Proposed approach to automated communication allows clustering people according to their interests distribution in multi-dimensional space, thus automatically creating natural dynamic communities of people with the same interests, without the need to promote or center them around certain web resource – communities exist in the decentralized virtual manner. Similarly, networks of contacts are distributed and very dynamic, unlike the presently emerging contact network building sites such as [6]. The use of Semantic Web standards eventually would allow seamless integration of the proposed contact network together with propagation framework into emerging knowledge-based environments [11].

Using personal communication agent for routing requests should greatly impact the effectiveness of some areas of human communication by delegating tasks to software agents. In particular, we would no longer need any efforts to act as a liaison when introducing people to each other and when dispatching certain typical messages to interested direct or transitive friends. Wireless modules allow us to automatically monitor the people crowd for potentially interesting contacts, spot them in real time and exchange ontology-based messages, thus bridging the gap between the world of Internet contacts and real-life acquaintances. Proposed multi-agent framework would be among the first ones to explore the combined physical- and cyber-space around us using wireless consumer devices.

Acknowledgement. The material presented in this paper is based on research supported by the grant of President of Russian Federation No. MK-2569.2004.9.

References

1. Narinyani, A.: eHomo — Two in One, In Proc. of Intl. Conf. Dialog-2004, Russia. 457–464 (In Russian)
2. Heylighen, F., Joslyn, C., Turchin, V.: Cybernetic Immortality. In Principia Cybernetica Web (Principia Cybernetica, Brussels), URL: `http://pespmc1.vub.ac.be/CYBIMM.html`.
3. FOAF Project, `http://www.foaf-project.org`
4. TheSpoke, `http://www.thespoke.net`
5. Live Journal, `http://www.livejournal.com`
6. LinkedIn, `http://www.linkedin.com`
7. Ripeanu, M.: Peer-to-Peer Architecture Case Study: Gnutella Network. In Proc. 1st Intl. Conf. on Peer-to-Peer Computing, Lingköping, Sweden (2001) 99–101
8. Nejdl, W., Wolf, B. et.al.: EDUTELLA: a P2P Networking Infrastructure based on RDF. In Proc. of 11th World Wide Web Conference, Hawaii, USA, May 2002
9. OWL Web Ontology Language Overview, D.L. McGuinness and Frank van Harmelen, eds. W3C Recommendation 10 February 2004. – `http://www.w3.org/TR/owl-features`
10. Ehrig, M., Maedche, A.: Ontology-focused crawling of Web documents. In Proc.of the 2003 ACM symposium on Applied computing, Melbourne, Florida (2003)
11. Zhuge, H.: China's E-Science Knowledge Grid Environment, IEEE Intelligent Systems **19**(1) (2004) 13–17

Effective Discovery of Intrusion Protection Strategies

Edward Pogossian, Arsen Javadyan, and Edgar Ivanyan

State Engineering University of Armenia, Academy of Science of Armenia,
Institute for Informatics and Automation Problems
epogossi@aua.am, ajavadyan@gmail.com, edgar@ycrdi.am

Abstract. Effectiveness of discovery of strategy knowledge is studied for problems where the space of hypothesis of solutions is specified by game trees and target solutions are discovered by methods capable of systematic acquisition of expert knowledge about them. A version of Botvinnik's Intermediate Goals At First algorithm is developed for strategy formation based on common knowledge planning and dynamic testing of the plans in the corresponding game tree. Applied to the intrusion protection problem the algorithm for a range of types of knowledge in form of goals and rules demonstrates strong tendency to increasing the efficiency of strategy formation with an increase in the amount of knowledge available to the system.

1 Introduction

Our starting idea about the nature of knowledge states that solutions of problems, components of the solutions or any of their descriptions, as well as any procedure or record acquired by systems in a way that improves their performance, are knowledge.

In the framework of that idea, solutions of problems with human independent formal specifications, such as problems of mathematical optimization, program synthesis, improvement, etc., may deliver knowledge of various kind but say little about the nature of human knowledge.

That is why we associate further progress in understanding human knowledge with studying the problems where the quality of target solutions is determined by the adequacy of models of human knowledge imbedded in those solutions and being inseparable from them. The corresponding class of problems, named Solvable by Adequate Models of Human Knowledge, includes, in particular, problems where solutions have to be learned by systematic acquisition of human knowledge in a given application area.

A pioneer research of strengthening the performance of chess programs simulating the process of chess masters decisions by systematic acquisition of human knowledge was studied in [2,3,4] and developed in [24].

A significant advances in ontology of the security domain, ontology-based representation of distributed knowledge of agents, formal grammar of attacks and their application to the network intrusion protection systems as well as a comprehensive review of ontology studying in the field are presented in [6], [8].

In [15] an attempt was undertaken to study viability of a decision making system with a variety of chess knowledge, including the ontology of about 300 concepts. For

V. Gorodetsky, J. Liu, and V.A. Skormin (Eds.): AIS-ADM 2005, LNAI 3505, pp. 263–276, 2005.

problems of that class hypothesis about solutions are *strategies* and *space* of their search is specified by *game trees* (SSGT) and target solutions have to be discovered by methods able to systematic acquisition of knowledge about them. Many security and competition problems, belong to the SHGT class, particularly, networks intrusion protection, management in oligopoly competitions as well as disaster forecast, computer terrorism countermeasures and prevention, information security and medical countermeasures announced by NATO may be reduced to the SSGT class (www.nato.int/science/e/newinitiative. htm).

To solve the SSGT problems we define a class of combating agents, based on the following models and procedures:

- a game tree model for the target competition, including the sub-models of the states, actions and contractions, the rules to apply (contra)actions to the states and transform them to the new ones, descriptors of the goal states
- the optimal strategy search procedure, including the strategy planning unit, aimed to narrow the search area in the game tree, the plans quantification, their game tree based dynamic testing and the best actions selection units.

A Common Planning and Dynamic Testing methodology for combating agents is developed allowing to construct agents with the best, in the framework of corresponding game tree models, strategies. The methodology in its Botvinnik's approach version - Intermediate Goals At First (IGAF1), was successfully probed in the network intrusion protection (IP) and some other SSGT problems. For example, for the IP problem it was outperforming system administrators and known standard protection systems in about 60% in experiments on fighting against 12 different types of known network attacks [16,17].

To increase the efficiency of the IGAF1 algorithm we suggest its more advanced version able to acquire a range of expert knowledge in form of goals or rules and to increase the efficiency of strategy formation with increasing the amount of expert knowledge available to the algorithm.

A viability of the IGAF2 algorithm was tested against representatives of four classes of attacks. There is not comprehensive classification of the variety of network attacks [6], [5], [10], because of widely distribution of mechanisms of attacks, their distribution in time, influence on different types of resources, dynamic increase of their number, possible damage and many other reasons. That is why the attacks for our experiments only approximate the coverage of a few known classes of attacks.

A Linux version of the IGAF2 algorithm is now realized for intrusion protecting system of the ArmCluster [1].

Compared with [20,22,23], where network-vulnerability analysis is based on finding critical paths in the graphs of attack , in our game tree based model we search counteraction strategies comprised from elementary and universal units – elementary procedures, an alphabet, that intruder or administrator use to combine either attacks or defense procedures, correspondingly. Some of those procedures can coincide, particularly, with elementary attacks of the [20,22,23]. But the aim is to find procedures enough elementary to cover diversity of intruders and defenders behaviors but nevertheless being meaningful for human understanding and operations. Alphabetic approach to representation of attacks and defense operations causes game tree size explosion which we try to overcome using computer chess successful experience.

IGAF based agent combats against other ones (one or more) where the game tree integrates their all possible behaviors – strategies. The agent have to discover new knowledge - the optimal strategy, analyzing enormous amount of mainly useless data. These intersections make strategy discovery interesting for traditional DM and multi agents researchers to use experience gained in many years studying of strategy discovery.

Development of IP agents can directly contribute to other SSGT problems what is confirmed by our experience in computer chess [15] as well as in management support systems for oligopoly competitions [14,19]. That is why we restrain to specify control problems impossible to reduce to the SSGT class and are ready to share experience with enthusiasts studying other representatives of the SSGT class.

The paper is structured as follows. Section 2 outlines game tree model for intrusion protection, defines expert goals and rules and the IGAF algorithm for game tree knowledge based strategy formation. Section 3 describes the strategy evaluation methodology and Section 4 presents the experiments in strategy discovery. The Conclusion outlines the main results of the research.

2   Game Tree Knowledge Based Strategy Discovery for Intrusion Protection

2.1   Game Tree Model for Intrusion Protection

The game tree model for Intrusion Protection is presented in [16,17]. In brief it is a game between two playing in turn sides with opposite interests - the attacker (A) and the defender (D), described by a set of states and a collection of conversion procedures from one position to another defined as the following.

System resources are particularly processor time, the size of TCP buffer, and a number of incoming packages. Let $R = \{r\}$ is a non-empty set of the system resources and Q is a set of resource parameters. Different measuring scales, such as seconds, bytes, numbers of incorrect logins or incoming packages, etc., are used to measure different parameters. Each $r \in R$ is associated with a pair <q; w> - a real system resource, where $q \in Q$, $w \in W$ and W is a set of possible scales.

A criterion function is an arbitrary function f with the range of values $Z = [0, 1]$ and F is the set of such functions f.

A local system resource state on a non-empty set $R` \subseteq R$ is called the value $e \in Z$ of the criterion function $f \in F$ on this set: $e = f(r1, r2, ..., rk)$, where $R` = (r1, r2, ..., rk)$ & $\varnothing \neq R` \subseteq R$.

The *local state* is called *normal* if $e = 0$ and *critical* if $e = 1$, and L will denote the set of local states e. Intuitively, by criterion functions are measuring "distance" of current states from those that are considered as normal. A system state on a non-empty set $L` \subseteq L$ is called the value $s \in Z$ of the criterion function $g \in F$ on this set: $s = g(e1, e2, ..., en)$, where $L` = (e1, e2, ..., en)$ & $\varnothing \neq L` \subseteq L$ The *state* is called *normal* if $s = 0$ and *critical* if $s = 1$, and S will denote the set of states s.

The main goals of the attackers and defenders are to bring the system in the critical states and avoid them, correspondingly.

Let us call an arbitrary function p(si, sj), the ranges of definition and values of which are subsets of R, *a conversion procedure* of system from the state si to sj:

p(si, sj) : {{r1, r2, ..., rk}} → {{r`1, r`2, ..., r`k}}, where {r1, r2, ..., rk} ⊆ R & {r`1, r`2, ..., r`k} ⊆ R.

Let P is the set of conversion procedures, Pa and Pd are its subsets for the attacking and the counteracting sides, pa(si, sj) ∈ Pa and pd(si, sj) ∈ Pd are the conversion procedures from the state si ∈ S to sj ∈ S for the attacking and the counteracting sides, correspondingly.

The counteraction game model is represented by "AND/OR" tree G(S, P), where S and P are finite, non-empty sets of all states (nodes, vertices) and all possible conversion procedures (edges, ribs), correspondingly (Fig. 1).

At first the attacker moves from the initial state s0 ∈ S then the defender replies in turn. Thus, the initial node s0 is an "AND" type. The terminal nodes correspond to the winning states of the defender.

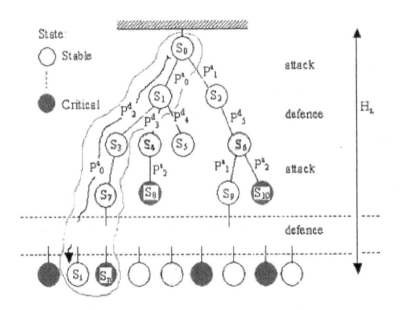

Fig. 1. A game tree model for the Intrusion Protection problem

2.2 Expert Goals and Rules Based Strategy Discovery

2.2.1. Using the above game tree model we experiment with a variety of algorithms to counteract to intrusions. Our Intermediate Goals At First algorithm (IGAF1) is similar to Botvinnik's chess tree cutting-down algorithm. The last is based on the natural hierarchies of goals in control problems and the assertion that search algorithms become more efficient if try to achieve subordinate goals before fighting for the main ones. The trajectories of confronting parties to those subgoals are chained in order to construct around them the zones of the most likelihood actions and counteractions.

As the result of comparative experiments with the minmax and IGAF1 algorithms in [16, 17] we state the following:

- the model, which is using the minimax algorithm, is compatible with experts (the system administrators or specialized programs) against intrusions or other forms of perturbations of the base system
- the IGAF1 cutting-down tree algorithm along with being compatible with the minimax one can work enough efficient to be used for real IP problems.

Here we suggest more advanced version 2 of the algorithm – IGAF2, which is able

- to acquire a range of expert knowledge in form of goals or rules
- to increase the efficiency of strategy formation with increasing the amount of expert knowledge available to the algorithm.

Let us describe the types of that knowledge and their inclusion into the IGAF algorithm.

2.2.2. We rely on the following concepts of "trajectory of an attack" and "zone of counteraction".

The trajectory of an attack is a subtree $Ga(S', P')$ (Fig.2), where S' is a subset of the system states $S' \subseteq S$ and P' is a subset of the actions, consisted of an offensive's conversion procedures Pa and a defender's normal conversion procedures Pdn, i.e. $P'=Pa \cup Pdn$, $P' \subseteq P$, $P' \neq \varnothing$.

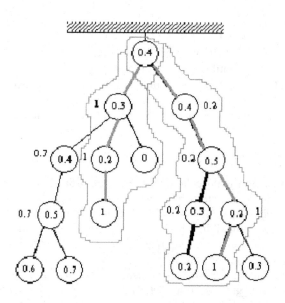

Fig. 2. Two trajectories of attack with zones of counteractions

The zone of counteraction is a subtree $Gz(S'', P'')$ built around the graph of the trajectory of an attack $Ga(S', P')$, i.e. $Ga \subseteq Gz$, where S'' is a subset of the system states

S" $\subseteq$ S, which belong to the trajectory of an attack, hence S' $\subseteq$ S", and P" is a subset of the actions, which consist of the conversion procedures, defined on the trajectory of an attack, P' and the defender's special conversion procedures Pds, i.e. P"= P'$\cup$ Pds, P"$\subseteq$P, P" $\neq \emptyset$, hence P'$\subseteq$ P".

2.2.3. The following expert goals and rules have been embedded into the IGAF2 algorithm:

The goals:

1. the *critical vs. normal states* are determined by a range of values of the states of the system; for example, any state of the system with a value of corresponding criterion function, that is more or equal to some threshold, may be determined as a critical goal.
2. the *suspicious vs. normal resources* are determined by a range of states of the classificators of the resources; combinations of values of the classificators identified as suspicious or normal induce signals for appropriate actions.

The rules:

1. Identify the suspicious resources by the classifiers and narrow the search to corresponding game subtree.
2. Avoid critical states and tend to the normal ones.
3. Normalize the state of the system. First, try such actions of the defender that influence on the resources caused current change of its state and if they don't help try other ones.
4. In building game subtree for suspicious resources use
   - defending actions able to influence on such resources.
   - use normal actions until there is no critical states.
   - if some defensive actions were used on previous steps decrease their usage priority.
5. Balance the parameters of resources by keeping them in the given ranges of permitted changes.

2.2.4. The IGAF2 algorithm is composed using the following instructions:

1. We use standard min max technique with alpha-beta pruning [21] based on the range of critical/normal state values introduced as the goal 1. Current node is created and the value of its local state calculated. If the node is terminal, the local state value is compared with sibling nodes, and their max (either min) value is sent to the parent node. C++ program level realization of it is described in [16,17] .
2. Determine all suspicious resources.
3. Build the game subtree for suspicious resources starting from the root state of the tree and using the 4th group of rules determine the trajectories of attacks (Fig.3).
4. Calculate the values of the terminal states of the tree, find the values of others by minmax procedure and determine the best minmax action from the root state (the green branch on the Fig.4).
5. Determine the trajectories of attacks induced by the best action from the root of the tree to its critical states and consider them as targets (Fig 5).

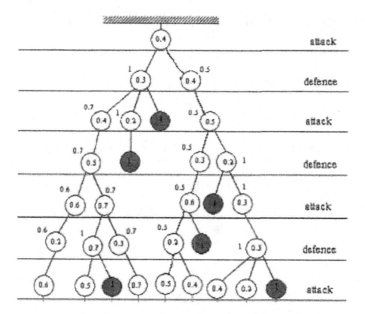

Fig. 3. The game subtree

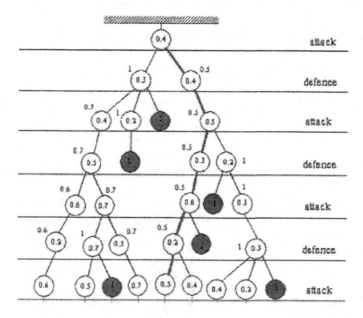

Fig. 4. The best minmax action

6. Build the zones of counteractions for the target trajectories using the 4th group of rules and rule 5th, then calculate the values of the states of the corresponding subtree using the minmax (Fig.6).

7. Choose the defender's action from the root as the one leading to the state with min value, i.e. to the most stable state estimated by the minmax.
8. End the defense analysis and wait for the attacker's actions.

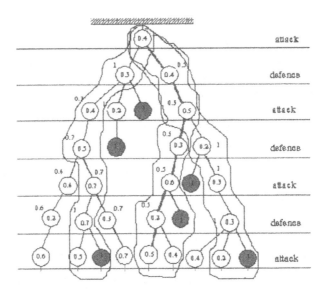

Fig. 5. The trajectories of attacks

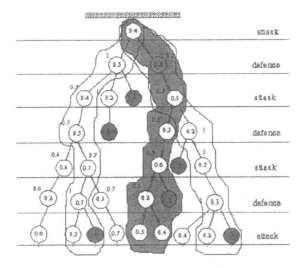

Fig. 6. The zones of counteractions

3 Strategy Evaluation Methodology

3.1. The criteria for comparing the IP algorithms estimate the 'distance" of current states of protected systems from the normal ones and the level of performance that the IP algorithms can preserve for them. They are:

1. *Distance to Safety (DtS)* estimates in the scale [0,1] the distance of the current state of the system from the safe or normal ones.
2. *Productivity (P)* is the number of performance units preserved in a unit of time for the system in average in process of an experiment. The performance units are defined in the context of current focus of interests of the users and may be measured, for example, by number of packages or files the system processes, by number of served of users , etc.

3.2. A special tool is developed to estimate the quality of protection against unauthorized access [18]. The tool allows to vary the component parts of the experiments, such as estimated criteria, the types of attacks, and the parameters of the IP systems.

Each experiment includes the imitation of the work of the base system with/without suspicion of an attack (or any other perturbation in the system), during which the IP algorithm makes a decision about the best strategy and chooses the best action according to the strategy. The data of the experiments of any attacks contain the system state's safety estimate for each step, the actions taken by each side, the system's performance.

3.3. The experimented attacks have to be representative for the variety of possible ones. We assume combinatorial, individual nature of the attacks that are unified in the classes of similar ones. Experimenting with a few representatives of the classes we hope to approximate a coverage of their variety. We chose the following groups of criteria to classify them:

1. Denial of Service
   a. Remote DoS
   b. Local DoS
2. Scanner
   a. Network scanner
   b. Vulnerability scanner
3. Penetration
   a. Remote penetration
   b. Local penetration
4. Information gathering
5. Password cracker
6. Sniffer
7. Suspicious activity
8. Unauthorized access
9. Code errors

In the experiments we choused representatives of four classes of attacks described in [10][11]. The criteria they satisfy by the groups are listed in the (Table 1).

Table 1. Classes of attacks

	Attack Name	By groups
1	SYN-Flood	1.a,1.b
2	Smurf	4, 3.b, 1.b
3	Fraggle	8, 1.b
4	Login-bomb	5

3.4. Each protecting system was tested against all attacks and corresponding vectors of the results were compared and analyzed for each attack separately and by all attacks in average.

The performance of a protection system against any attack was estimated by the means of corresponding distributions of measurements by each of two criteria in the series of offense –defense pairs of actions.

Any series were including about 200 pairs of those actions.

For each series the sampling means for 200 values measured by the criteria – Distance to Safety and Productivity, were calculated and identified with the means of the distributions. That identification is consistent with the Central Limit Theorem applied to a large sample of measurements with unknown distribution.

4 Experiments in Strategy Discovery

4.1. The experiments were aimed to proving that the IGAF2 cutting-down tree algorithm along with being compatible with the minimax one is working more efficient increasing the efficiency with embedding the amount of expert knowledge.

The investigated version of the algorithm was using the following components:

- Over twelve single-level and multilevel solver-classifiers of the local system states.
- 6 actions-procedures of the attacking side
- 8 "normal" actions/procedures of the system
- 22 known counteractions against actions/procedures of attacks (the database of counteractions).

It was tested in experiments against four attacks with a depth of the game tree search up to 13 and the following controlled and measured criteria and parameters: distance to safety, productivity, working time and number of searched in the game tree nodes, new queue of incoming packages, TCP connection queue, number of processed packages, RAM, HD, unauthorized access to the files and login into the system.

The results of experiments below are presented mainly for the SYN-Flood attack because they are typical for all of them.

Table 2. Sampling means for Distance to Safety (with Standard deviation) and Productivity of the IGAF2 and minmax algorithms against   attacks SYN-Flood, Fraggle, Smurf and Login-bomb attacks are compatible

Attacks	Distance to Safety		Standard .Deviation		Productivity	
	Min-Max	IGAF2	Min-Max	IGAF2	Min-Max	IGAF2
SYN-Flood	0,7575	0,7897	0,0888	0,0925	3,14	3,6
Fraggle	0,7254	0,6445	0,1332	0,2068	2,1	2,2
Smurf	0,584	0,7004	0,1861	0,1417	3,9	4,2
Login-bomb	0,4662	0,5416	0,2483	0,2275	6,8	7,2

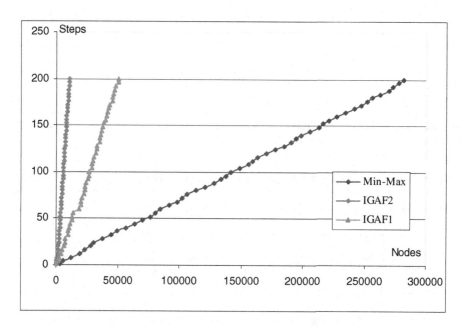

Fig. 7. Number of nodes searched by the IGAF2 algorithm with all expert rules and subgoals are decreasing compared with the IGAF1 algorithm or the minimax one. [experiments against SYN- Flood attack with the depth of search 5 and 200 steps of the defense actions]

5   Conclusion

A version of Botvinnik's Intermediate Goals At First (IGAF2) algorithm is developed able to acquire a range of expert knowledge in form of goals or rules and to increase the efficiency of strategy formation with increasing the amount of expert knowledge available to the algorithm.

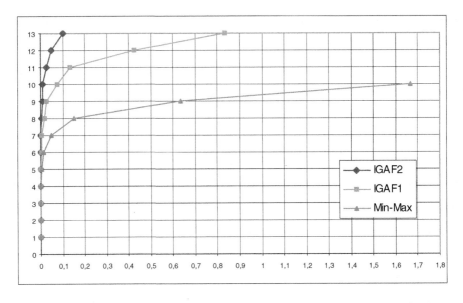

Fig. 8. Number of nodes searched by the IGAF2 algorithm with all expert rules and subgoals is the smallest compared with the IGAF1 algorithm or the minimax one when the depth of search is increasing up to 13 in experiments against the SYN- Flood attack

Table 3. Number of nodes searched by the IGAF2 algorithm and time spent (in milliseconds) with all expert rules and subgoals is the smallest with the IGAF1 algorithm or the minimax one when the depth of search is increasing up to 13 in experiments against the SYN- Flood attack

Depth of search	IGAF2		IGAF1		Min-Max	
	Node Count	Time	Node Count	Time	Node Count	Time
1	19	269	19	270	21	480
2	42	271	42	290	64	490
3	70	300	70	305	388	580
4	254	529	406	570	1162	771
5	562	561	1030	750	4231	1541
6	943	921	3580	1692	11512	3473
7	1775	1060	5083	1982	50797	13717
8	2987	1611	16493	5636	150096	43365
9	7389	2994	24502	8110	631960	172436
10	9503	4546	77573	25192	1668643	590242
11	27076	10822	133448	43655	--	--
12	48428	20675	427218	141689	--	--
13	101905	41932	833876	284948	--	--

A viability of the IGAF2 algorithm was successfully tested in the network intrusion protection problems against representatives of four classes of attacks: SYN-Flood, Fraggle, Smurf and Login-bomb, allowing to formulate the following statements:

- Sampling means for Distance to Safety and Productivity of the IGAF2 and min-max algorithms are compatible.
- Number of nodes searched by the IGAF2 algorithm with all expert rules and sub-goals are decreasing compared with the IGAF1 algorithm or with the minimax one.
- Number of nodes searched by the IGAF2 algorithm with all expert rules and sub-goals is the smallest compared with the IGAF1 algorithm or with the minimax one when the depth of search is increasing up to 13.
- The time spent by the IGAF2 algorithm with all expert rules and subgoals is the smallest compared with the IGAF1 algorithm or with the minimax one when the depth of search is increasing up to 13.
- The recommended version of the IGAF2 algorithm with all expert rules and sub-goals, for the depth of search 5 and 200 defending steps is overperforming the Productivity of minmax algorithm in 14% , using for that 6 times less computing time and searching 27 times less nodes of the tree.

The future plans include, particularly, the following lines:

1. Expanding the alphabet of attack and defense actions including hidden ones.
2. Developing our approach to increase the strength of the IGAF algorithms by systematic enrichment their knowledge base by new IP goals and rules .
3. Developing on the job performance versions of the IGAF algorithm for actual applications, particularly completing its Cluster IP implementation [1].

References

1. Astsatryan, H. V., Shoukourian, Yu. H., Sahakyan, V. G.: The ArmCluster1 Project: Creation of High-Performance Computation Cluster and Databases in Armenia Proceedings of Conference. Computer Science and Information Technologies (2001) 376–379
2. Botvinnik, M.M.: About solving approximate problems, S. Radio, Moscow (1979) (Russian)
3. Botvinnik, M.M.: Computers in Chess: Solving Inexact Search Problems. Springer Series in Symbolic Computation, with Appendixes, Springer-Verlag: New York (1984)
4. Botvinnik, M. M., Stilman, B., Yudin, A. D., Reznitskiy , A. I., Tsfasman, M.A.: Thinking of Man and Computer, Proc. of the Second International Meeting on Artificial Intelligence, Repino, Leningrad, Russia (Oct. 1980) 1–9
5. Chi, S.-D., Park, J.S., Jung, K.-C., Lee, J.-S.: Network Security Modeling and Cyber Attack Simulation Methodology. Lecture Notes in Computer Science, Vol.2119 (2001)
6. Gorodetski, V., Kotenko, I.: Attacks against Computer Network: Formal Grammar Based Framework and Simulation Tool. Proc. of the 5 Intern. Conf. "Recent Advances in Intrusion Detection", Lecture Notes in Computer Science, v.2516, Springer Verlag (2002) 219–238
7. Gorodetski, V. Kotenko, I., Karsaev, O.: Framework for ontology-based representation of distributed knowledge in multiagent network security system. Proc. of the 4-th World Multi-conf. on Systems, Cybernetics and Informatics (SCI-2000), vol. III, "Virtual Engineering and Emergent Computing", Orlando, USA (July 2000) 52–58

8. Kotenko, I., A. Alexeev E., Man'kov: Formal Framework for Modeling and Simulation of DDoS Attacks Based on Teamwork of Hackers-Agents. Proc. of 2003 IEEE/WIC Intern. Conf. on Intelligent Agent Technology, Halifax, Canada, Oct. 13-16, 2003, IEEE Computer Society (2003) 507–510

9. Lindqvist, U., Porras, P.A.: Detecting Computer and Network Misuse with the Production-Based Expert System Toolset, IEEE Symp. Security and Privacy, IEEE CS Press, Los Alamitos, Calif. (1999)

10. Lukacki, A.: Attack Detection, BXB-Petersburg, St. Petersburg (2001) (in Russian)

11. Miloslavskaya, N. G., Tolstoj, A. I.: Intranetwork: Intrusion Detection ,Unity, Moscow, (2001) (in Russian)

12. Ilgun, K., Kemmerer, R.A. , Porras, P.A.: State Transition Analysis: A Rule-Based Intrusion Detection System, IEEE Trans. Software Eng. 21, no. 3 (Mar. 1995)

13. V. Paxson, Bro: A System for Detecting Network Intruders in Real-Time, Proc. Seventh Usenix Security Symp., Usenix Assoc., Berkeley

14. Pogossian, E, Baghdasaryan T.: Cutting Time of Strategy Search By Sequential Quatification of Management Plans, Proceedings of the CSIT2003, 4th International Conference in Computer Science and Information Technologies, Yerevan (2003) 8

15. Pogossian, E.: Adaptation of Combinatorial Algorithms.(inRussian), Yerevan (1983) 293

16. Pogossian, E., Javadyan, A. A.: Game Model And Effective Counteraction Strategies Against Network Intrusion. 4th International Conference in Computer Science and Information Technologies, CSIT2003, Yerevan (2003) 5

17. Pogossian, E., Javadyan, A. A.: Game Model For Effective Counteraction Against Computer Attacks In Intrusion Detection Systems, NATO ASI 2003, Data Fusion for Situation Monitoring, Incident Detection, Alert and Response Management", Tsahkadzor, Armenia, August 19-30, 30

18. Pogossian, E., Javadyan, A., Ivanyan, E.: Toward a Toolkit for Modeling Attacks and Evaluation Methods of Intrusion Protection, Annual Conference of the State Engineering University of Armenia (2004) 5 (in Russian).

19. Pogossian, E.: Focusing Management Strategy Provision Simulation. Proceedings of the CSIT2001, 3d International Conference in Computer Science and Information Technologies, Yerevan (2001) 5

20. Phillips, C., Swiler, L.: A Graph-Based System for Network-Vulnerability Analysis, New Security Paradigms Workshop ,Proceedings of the 1998 workshop on New security paradigm

21. Russell, S., Norvig, P.: Artificial Intelligence: A Modern Approach. Prentice-Hall, Englewood Cliffs, NJ (2002)

22. Sheyner, O., Jha, S., Haines, J., Lippmann, R., Wing, J.: Automated Generation and Analysis of Attack Graphs .Proceed. of the IEEE Symposium on Security and Privacy, Oakland, (2002)

23. Sheyner, O., Wing, J.: Tools for Generating and Analyzing Attack Graphs, to appear in Proceed. of Formal Methods for Components and Objects, Lecture Notes in Computer Science (2005)

24. Stilman, B.: Linguistic Geometry: From Search to Construction, Kluwer Academic Publishers, (Feb.2000) 416

Integrating Knowledge Through Cooperative Negotiation – A Case Study in Bioinformatics

Cassia T. dos Santos and Ana L.C. Bazzan

Instituto de Informática, Universidade Federal do Rio Grande do Sul,
Caixa Postal 15064, 90.501-970, Porto Alegre, RS, Brazil
{ctsantos, bazzan}@inf.ufrgs.br

Abstract. Data Mining techniques have been used for knowledge extraction from large volumes of data. A recent practice is to combine Data Mining and Multi-Agent Systems approaches. In this paper we propose the use of cooperative negotiation to construct an integrated and coherent domain model from several sources. Agents encapsule different symbolic machine learning algorithms to induce their individual models. After this, a global model yields from the interaction via cooperative negotiation of these agents. The results shows that the proposed approach improves the accuracy of the individual models, integrating the best representations of each one.

1 Introduction

Knowledge discovery and data mining are concerned with the use of machine learning techniques for knowledge extraction from large volumes of data. A recent practice is to combine data mining and multi-agent systems approaches [16, 18]. In these systems, a group of agents are responsible for applying different machine learning algorithms and/or using subsets of the data to be mined, and are able to cooperate to discover knowledge from these subsets. This approach has shown high potential for many applications and it is opening interesting research questions. An important one is how to integrate the discovered knowledge by agents into a globally coherent model.

In this paper we propose the use of cooperative negotiation to construct an integrated domain model from several sources. In our approach, agents encapsulate different symbolic machine learning algorithms to induce their individual models. After this, a global model results from the interaction of these agents via cooperative negotiation.

To demonstrate the application of this approach, we use a scenario from bioinformatics, which is related to automated annotation of proteins' keywords. However, any domain can be used, provided the problem can be stated as a set of attribute-value pairs, as it is the standard practice in machine learning. This is so because the agents do not use any domain dependent information as they just encapsulate data and machine learning algorithms.

In the case of bioinformatics, the machine learning algorithms are used to induce models to predict the annotation, using data from biological databases.

V. Gorodetsky, J. Liu, and V.A. Skormin (Eds.): AIS-ADM 2005, LNAI 3505, pp. 277–288, 2005.

Since these databases are very large, both in number of records and in number of attributes, using all available data for symbolic machine learning algorithms is prohibitive. Our approach can be used to solve this problem, allowing several agents to cooperate to induce a global classifier, from subsets of the data to be mined.

This paper is structured as follows. The next section briefly reviews some issues in cooperative negotiation. Section 3 introduces our approach to integrate knowledge of learning agents, while Section 4 presents its use in the automated annotation of proteins. Section 5 describes some related work regarding multi-agent systems and data mining. Section 6 presents the final remarks and the future works.

2   Cooperative Negotiation

Negotiation is a process in which two or more parties make a joint decision. It is a key form of interaction that enables groups of agents to arrive to mutual agreement regarding some belief, goal or plan [2]. Hence the basic idea behind negotiation is reaching a consensus [9].

According to [12], a negotiation model is composed by two basic components: the negotiation protocol and the negotiation strategies. The protocol specifies the rule of encounter between the negotiation participants. That is, it defines the circumstances under which the interaction between agents take place, what deals can be made and what sequences of actions are allowed [6]. An strategy is the specification of the sequence of actions the agent plans to make during the negotiation.

Negotiation usually proceeds in a series of rounds, with every agent making a proposal at each round. According to [11], the process can be described as follow. One agent generates a proposal and other agents review it. If some other agent does not like the proposal, it rejects and may generate a counter-proposal. If so, the others agents (including the agent that generated the first proposal) then review the counter-proposal and the process repeats. It assumes that a proposal becomes a solution when it is accepted by all agents.

Cooperative negotiation is a particular kind of negotiation where agents co-operate and collaborate to achieve a common objective, in the best interest of the system as a whole [2, 9]. In cooperative negotiation, each agent has a partial view of the problem and the results are put together via negotiation trying to solve the conflicts posed by having only partial views [8]. According to [10], cooperative negotiations can be described as the decision-making process of resolving a conflict involving two or more parties over multiple independent, but non-mutually exclusive goals.

This kind of negotiation has been currently adopted in resource and task allocation fields [3, 13, 20]. In these approaches, the agents try to reach the maximum global utility that takes into account the worth of all their activities. In our case, we view cooperative negotiation as a way to achieve knowledge integration, in order to remove redundancy or conflict between the partial views.

3   Approach

In our distributed learning system, the agents encapsulate different symbolic machine learning algorithms and use subsets of the data to be mined. Individual models are integrated using cooperative negotiation. This approach has the following advantages. First, each agent is responsible for a subset of considerably smaller size and dimensionality, improving the accuracy and performance of the algorithms. Second, the cooperative negotiation allows us to deal with redundancy and conflicts. Finally, no algorithm can be the best choice in all possible domains. Each algorithm contains an explicit or implicit bias that leads it to prefer certain generalizations over others: the strength of one can be the other's weakness [5]. Therefore, different machine learning techniques applied to the same data set hardly generate the same results [18]. An algorithm A can construct an accurate model for concept X and a weak description for concept Y, while the algorithm B constructs an accurate model for concept Y and a weak model for concept X. The combination of different learning algorithms can lead to more accurate models.

Basically, the process involves the following phases: (1) preparation of the data, (2) generation and evaluation of the individual models, and (3) construction of the integrated model through cooperative negotiation.

In the phase (1) the data to be mined is split into training, validation, and test subsets. The training subset is divided equally among the agents in the systems, creating views of it. The validation and test subsets are not divided. The former is used to evaluate the individual models (all agents use the same subset). The latter is reserved for the final evaluation of the integrated model.

In the phase (2), the agents work in an independent manner, and as a result they produce their individual models. Each agent constructs its own model based on its own subset of data, using one symbolic machine learning algorithm (here we use C4.5 [15] or CN2 [4]). The individual models are evaluated using the validation subset and each rule accuracy is estimated applying the Laplace expected error estimate (Equation 1). The formula depends on TP (number of true positives which means the number of examples correctly covered by the rule), FP (the false positives or the number of examples wrongly covered by the rule), and K (the number of classes in the domain).

$$LaplaceAccuracy = (TP + 1)/(TP + FP + K) \qquad (1)$$

Phase (3) is dedicated to constructing an integrated model based on the results obtained in phase (2). Considering that each learning algorithm uses a proper syntax to describe the induced model, it is necessary to have the models represented in the same format. The PBM [14] format is adopted, which generates sets of propositional rules of the form: *if <condition> then <class=C>*. The representation process takes place after the agents applies their learning algorithms to induce its models, before the negotiation process starts.

The negotiation process involves two types of agents: learning agents and mediator agent. The learning agents encapsule the machine learning algorithms

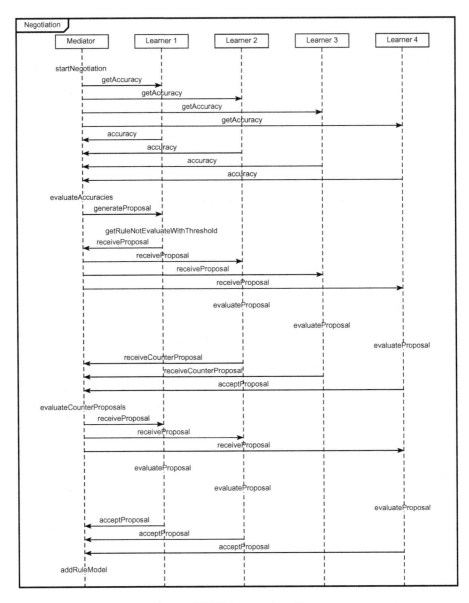

Fig. 1. AUML interaction diagram

and the mediator agent is responsible for controlling the communication among the learning agents and finalize the negotiation.

Figure 1 shows an AUML interaction diagram with the messages exchanged between the agents during a negotiation round. We use an extension of AUML-2 standard to represent agents' actions (e.g. startNegotiation, getAccuracy, etc.).

The negotiation process starts with the mediator agent asking the learning agents to send their overall accuracies. The first learning agent to generate a proposal is the one that has the poorest overall accuracy (learner 1, in the specific example). The proposal contains the first rule in the rule set of this agent, which has not yet been evaluated, and which has an accuracy equal or better than a threshold. Rules which do not satisfy the threshold are not considered. This proposal is then sent to the mediator agent, which repasses it to others agents. Each agent then evaluates the proposal, searching for a equivalent rule with better accuracy.

This evaluation requires comparison of rules and, therefore, it is necessary to establish equivalences for them. One rule is equivalent to another one when both describe the same concept and at least one attribute overlaps. If an equivalent rule is not found, or an equivalent one does not have better accuracy, then the agent accepts the proposal (in the example in Figure 1, learner 4 has accepted the first proposal). Otherwise, if the agent has a rule with a better accuracy than the proposed rule, then its rule is sent as a counter-proposal to the mediator agent, which evaluates the several counter-proposals received. This is so because several agents can send a counter-proposal. In our example, learners 2 and 3 have both generated counter-proposals. The one which has the best accuracy is selected. Here, this is the case for learner 3's rule. The selected counter-proposal is then sent to the other agents (including the agent that generated the first proposal). These review it, and the process is repeated. When a proposal or a counter-proposal is accepted by all agents, the mediator adds the corresponding rule in the integrated model and the learning agents mark its equivalent one as evaluated. The negotiation ends when all rules were evaluated.

4   Case Study in Automated Annotation of Proteins

We apply the proposed approach to induce a model for annotation of proteins, regarding specifically the field called *Keywords* in Swiss-Prot[1] [7]. Swiss-Prot is a curated database which provides a high level of annotation for each protein, including a description of its function, its domain structure, etc. It has also extensive links to others databases. The *Keyword* field gives several hints to experts as to what regards proteins functions and structure.

4.1   Methods

We used proteins from the model organism *Arabidopsis thaliana*, which are available in public databases such as Swiss-Prot. The data used comes from a local version of the Swiss-Prot database downloaded in November of 2004. Using it, 3038 proteins were found which relates to *A. thaliana*. 347 keywords appeared in the data but we focus here on those whose number of instances is higher than 100. The number of keywords satisfying this criterion is 29.

---

[1] http://www.expasy.ch/sprot

The attributes which appeared in this data are only the *accession numbers* (a sort of protein family classification) for all attributes related to the Interpro[2] [1], which appear in Swiss-Prot as a cross-referenced database. The number of attributes of this domain is 1496.

For each keyword, the collected data was split in three subsets: training (80% – 2430 instances), validation (10% – 304 instances) and test (10% – 304 instances). The training set was split in four subsets, each one with approximately 607 examples. The data was split according to the appearance order in the database. For instance, the first 2430 instances were used in the training set. Since there is no ordering in the original database, the split is not biased.

Each subset of the training set was assigned to one of the learning agents A, B, C, and D. Besides, two agents encapsulate the C4.5 algorithm (agents A and C) and the other two (agents B and D) use the CN2 algorithm. These subsets were organized in input files, respecting the specific syntax of the C4.5 and CN2.

Using the input data, the four learning agents induce rules for each keyword (target class). Figure 2 (a) shows the output of the agent A (C4.5) for the keyword "Iron". Due to lack of space, we do not show all induced rules for this keyword. The rule 3 in Figure 2 suggests the annotation of the keyword "Iron" for a given protein if it belongs to the IPR002226 family of proteins. According to the rule 4, the protein must be annotated with the "Iron" keyword if it belongs to the IPR001199. Similar boolean tests are performed in the rule 5, here suggesting that the keyword should not be annotated if it does not belong to the Interpro families IPR002680, IPR006186, IPR002226, and IPR001199.

Figure 2 (b) shows the output of the agent B (CN2) for the same keyword. The rules are read as follows. If the protein belongs to Interpro family IPR005708 (first rule) or IPR005956 (second rule), then it shall be annotated with the keyword "Iron". According to the third rule, if the protein does not belong to the Interpro families IPR005123, IPR000181, IPR006057, IPR008331, IPR001260, IPR005708, IPR001015, and IPR005956 then "Iron" shall not be annotated.

Once the rules were generated, they were transformed into the PBM format. Figures 3 (a) and 3 (b) respectively show the rules presented in the Figures 2 (a) and 2 (b) in the PBM format.

After the rule transformation process, the rules of the four agents are evaluated using the validation subset. For each rule of the model, its accuracy was estimated by applying the Laplace expected error measure (Equation 1). Only rules with accuracy equal or better than a threshold are considered. The overall accuracy of the agent is obtained from the average accuracy of its rules that satisfied the threshold.

Once the evaluation of the individual models was made, the negotiation process starts. As said above, the negotiation process (Figure 1) starts with the mediator agent asking to the four learning agents for their overall accuracies. The first learning agent to generate a proposal is the one that has the poorest overall accuracy. This then selects the first rule in its rule set that satisfies the

---

[2] http://www.ebi.ac.uk/interpro

```
Rule 3:                                       IF     IPR005708 = y
     .    IPR002226 = y                        THEN   class = Iron   [1 0]
          -> class Iron   [63.0%]
     .                                         IF     IPR005956 = y
Rule 4:                                        THEN   class = Iron   [1 0]
     .    IPR001199 = y
          -> class Iron   [50.0%]              IF     IPR005123 = n
                                               AND IPR000181 = n
Rule 5:                                        AND IPR006057 = n
     .    IPR002680 = n                        AND IPR008331 = n
     .    IPR006186 = n                        AND IPR001260 = n
     .    IPR002226 = n                        AND IPR005708 = n
     .    IPR001199 = n                        AND IPR001015 = n
     .    -> class n   [99.0%]                 AND IPR005956 = n
                                               THEN   class = n   [0 590]
          (a)                                            (b)
```

Fig. 2. (a) Output of the C4.5; (b) output of the CN2

```
                                         R0007.   IF IPR005708 = y
                                           .      THEN CLASS = Iron

                                         R0008.   IF IPR005956 = y
R0003.   IF IPR002226 = y                  .      THEN CLASS = Iron
  .      THEN CLASS =  Iron
                                         R0009.   IF IPR005123 = n
R0004.   IF IPR001199 = y                  .         .     AND IPR000181 = n
  .      THEN CLASS =  Iron                .         .     AND IPR006057 = n
                                           .         .     AND IPR008331 = n
R0005.   IF IPR002680 = n                  .         .     AND IPR001260 = n
  .         .     AND IPR006186 = n         .         .     AND IPR005708 = n
  .         .     AND IPR002226 = n         .         .     AND IPR001015 = n
  .         .     AND IPR001199 = n         .         .     AND IPR005956 = n
  .      THEN CLASS =  n                     .      THEN CLASS = n
          (a)                                            (b)
```

Fig. 3. (a) C4.5 rules in the PBM format; (b) CN2 rules in the PBM format

threshold and sends it to the mediator agent, which repasses the rule to the others learning agents. These agents evaluate the rule, searching for an equivalent one, with better accuracy. If an equivalent rule with better accuracy than the proposed rule is not found, the agent that is evaluating the proposal accepts the proposed rule. Otherwise, if it has an equivalent rule with better accuracy, it sends it as a counter-proposal to the mediator agent, which evaluates the several rules received and selects the one that has the best accuracy. The selected rule is then sent to other agents which review it.

A rule is added to the integrated model if it is accepted by all agents. This rule and its equivalent one are marked as evaluated by the corresponding agent during the evaluating rules process. The negotiation process is repeated until there are no more rules to evaluate. This process was done for each keyword (i.e. the agents negotiate integrated models for each keyword).

4.2   Results and Discussion

The integrated model generated through cooperative negotiation was evaluated using the test subset. For comparative purposes, the individual models were also evaluated using this subset. Table 1 shows the overall accuracies obtained for each individual model (agents A, B, C and D) and for the integrated model, for each keyword. In these experiments, a threshold equal to 0.5 was used and only rules with accuracy equal or superior than this threshold were considered in the negotiation process.

As shown in Table 1, the integrated model has a better overall accuracy than the individual models. This result was obtained for all keywords.

Regarding the individual learning agents, those that encapsulated the C4.5 algorithm obtained better results than those with the CN2 algorithm. For in-

Table 1. Overall accuracies obtained using validation subset

Keyword	Agent A C4.5	Agent B CN2	Agent C C4.5	Agent D CN2	Integrated model
Alternative-splicing	0.72	0.51	0.94	0.51	0.94
ATP-binding	0.55	0.52	0.54	0.53	0.96
Calcium	0.98	0.66	0.62	0.62	0.98
Cell-wall	0.88	0.55	0.88	0.55	0.88
Chloroplast	0.53	0.50	0.54	0.50	0.93
Coiled-coil	0.60	0.52	0.60	0.53	0.91
DNA-binding	0.53	0.51	0.52	0.51	0.73
Glycoprotein	0.55	0.52	0.61	0.54	0.96
Heme	0.64	0.51	0.69	0.62	0.74
Hydrolase	0.52	0.51	0.53	0.52	0.82
Iron	0.58	0.54	0.59	0.56	0.99
Membrane	0.55	0.59	0.61	0.52	0.65
Metal-binding	0.55	0.53	0.56	0.52	0.96
Mitochondrion	0.55	0.51	0.65	0.51	0.96
Nuclear-protein	0.51	0.50	0.52	0.50	0.70
Oxidoreductase	0.55	0.51	0.52	0.53	0.98
Phosphorylation	0.57	0.54	0.58	0.53	0.99
Plant-defense	0.66	0.58	0.59	0.58	0.98
Protein-transport	0.58	0.60	0.56	0.60	0.92
Repeat	0.53	0.51	0.53	0.51	0.89
Ribosomal-protein	0.66	0.99	0.56	0.50	0.99
Signal	0.52	0.51	0.53	0.52	0.81
Transcription-regulation	0.53	0.51	0.54	0.52	0.73
Transferase	0.53	0.51	0.52	0.51	0.85
Transit-peptide	0.53	0.50	0.53	0.50	0.94
Transmembrane	0.51	0.51	0.52	0.51	0.86
Transport	0.53	0.56	0.53	0.55	0.89
Zinc	0.56	0.54	0.65	0.53	0.99
Zinc-finger	0.61	0.55	0.96	0.54	0.96
Average	0.59	0.54	0.60	0.53	0.89

stance, considering the keyword "Iron", agent B (CN2) has the poorest overall accuracy and generated the first proposal. The proposed rule has an accuracy equal to 0.58 and suggests the non annotation of the keyword "Iron". This rule was then evaluated by the agents A (C4.5), C (C4.5), and D (CN2). Agents C and D do not find an equivalent rule with better accuracy and they accept the proposed rule. However, agent A found an equivalent one with accuracy equal to 0.99, thus it generated a counter-proposal. Then, agents B, C, and D evaluate the counter-proposal and accepted it. Finally, each agent mark the equivalent rules as evaluated. This way, in each round, the best rule that satisfied the threshold is added to the integrated model.

Also experiments with only two agents, each using all training data, were performed. In this case, each agent encapsulates one of the machine learning algorithms – C4.5 and CN2. Both used all 2430 instances of the training set to induce its model. The validation was performed using the instances of the validation set. The C4.5 agent obtained an overall accuracy (for all keywords) equal to 0.52 and the CN2 agent produced an accuracy of 0.50. For both agents, the quality of rules was poor when compared to the results obtained by the integrated model (0.89 – overall accuracy for all keywords). In one specific case, considering only the keyword "Iron", the C4.5 agent had an accuracy equal to 0.51 and CN2 agent presented an accuracy of 0.53, while the integrated model obtained an accuracy of 0.99. This happens because the amount of data is very high, thus the algorithms do not induce good models. Also, this task is time-consuming.

These results show that the proposed approach can be applied to improve the accuracy of the individual models, integrating the better representations of each one.

5   Related Work

A multi-agent system for mining distributed data is presented in [17]. There are two types of agents: the learner and the meta-learner. The learner has a machine learning algorithm, and each learner applies its technique separately and brings the results to be combined by the meta-learner.

The CILT system [18, 19] is based on agents with different machine learning algorithms that collaborate with each other to improve the classification task. Due to this collaboration, the agents generate new data and add it to the training file, which is further presented to the agents for the sake of classification improvement. In [16] an architecture for an environment is proposed, which combines different machine learning algorithms encapsulated in agents that collaborate to improve their knowledge. The learning process happens in two stages: individual and cooperative. The objective of the first stage is to create an individual domain model, based on different classifiers. In the cooperative learning stage, agents cooperate to improve their knowledge by sharing it with others to achieve better results. The data is not divided among the agents, i.e. all agents use the same dataset.

In general, the above mentioned approaches are based on selecting the best rules to compose a global domain model. The main contribution of the approach proposed here is a model of cooperative negotiation to solve conflicts and redundancies among the several models, hold by different learning agents having different views of the data set.

6   Final Remarks and Future Work

The application of a multi-agent system for improving symbolic learning through knowledge integration has shown high potential for many applications and it is opening important and interesting research questions. The possibility of combining different machine learning algorithms can lead to better results and using subsets of considerably smaller size and dimensionality improves the accuracy and performance of these algorithms.

This paper describes an approach based on cooperative negotiation to construct an integrated domain model from several sources. Several agents encapsule different symbolic machine learning algorithms to induce their individual models and the global model results from the cooperative negotiation of these agents.

The main achievement of this approach is to integrate knowledge from models which are generated by different machine learning agents, using different views of the training data, thus improving the accuracy of the individual models.

We have described an application in bioinformatics, namely the automated annotation of proteins, with data obtained from the Swiss-Prot database regarding the model organism *A. thaliana*. In our initial experiments, we obtained an integrated model which presents good classification rates on the validation data. The best representations of each learning agent were added to the integrated model, improving the performance of the annotation.

Cooperative negotiation to solve the conflicts posed by the partial views is still little explored in the process of knowledge integration. This work is a step towards an effective use of agents in knowledge integration and data mining. The negotiation process presented here is a basic one, which depends on a mediator. Further improvements can be done towards agents anticipating other proposals and counter-proposals, as well as learning from past deals among them. Possibly, this will require domain knowledge so that there will be a trade-off between better negotiation protocols and domain-independence. This issue will be investigated in the near future.

Acknowledgement

Authors partially supported by CNPq; the project is partially supported by CNPq and by FAPERGS.

References

1. Apweiler, R., Attwood, T. K., Bairoch, A., Bateman, A., Birney, E., Biswas, M., Bucher, P., Cerutti, L., Corpet, F., Croning, M. D. R., Durbin, R., Falquet, L., Fleischmann, W., Gouzy, J., Hermjakob, H., Hulo, N., Jonassen, I., Kahn, D., Kanapin, A., Karavidopoulou, Y., Lopez, R., Marx, B., Mulder, N. J., Oinn, T. M., Pagni, M., Servant, F., Sigrist, C. J. A., Zdobnov, E. M.: The InterPro database, an integrated documentation resource for protein families, domains and functional sites. *Nucleic Acids Research* **29**(1) (2001) 37–40

2. Beer, M., d'Inverno, M., Luck, M., Jennings, N., Preist, C., Schroeder, M.: Negotiation in multi-agent systems. In *Workshop of the UK Special Interest Group on Multi-Agent Systems* (1998)

3. Bigham, J., Du, L.: Cooperative negotiation in a multi-agent system for real-time load balancing of a mobile cellular network. In *Proceedings of the Second International Joint Conference on Autonomous Agents and Multiagent Systems*, ACM Press (2003) 568–575

4. Clark, P., Niblett, T.: The CN2 induction algorithm. *Machine Learning* **3** (1989) 261–283

5. Dietterich, T.: Limitations on inductive learning. In *Proceedings of the Sixth International Workshop on Machine Learning* (1989) 124–128

6. Fatima, S., Wooldridge, M., Jennings, N.: An agenda-based framework for multi-issue negotiation. *Artificial Intelligence* **152** (2004) 1–45

7. Gasteiger, E., Jung, E., Bairoch, A.: Swiss-prot: Connecting biological knowledge via a protein database. *Curr. Issues Mol. Biol.* **3** (2001) 47–55

8. Gatti, N., Amigoni, F.: A cooperative negotiation protocol for physiological model combination. In *Proceedings of the Third Internation Joint Conference on Automomous Agents and Multi-Agent Systems* (2004) 655–662

9. Green, S., Hurst, L., Nangle, B., Cunningham, P., Somers, F., Evans, R.: Software agents: A review. Technical report, Trinity College (1997)

10. Guttman, R. H., Maes, P.: Cooperative vs. competitive multi-agent negotiations in retail electronic commerce. *Lecture Notes in Computer Science* **1435** (1998) 135–147

11. Lander, S., Lesser, V.: Understanding the role of negotiation in distributed search among heterogeneous agents. In *Proceedings of the International Joint Conference on Artificial Intelligence* (January 1993)

12. Lomuscio, A. R., Wooldridge, M., Jennings, N.: A classification scheme for negotiation in electronic commerce. *Agent-Mediated Electronic Commerce: A European Agent Link Perspective* (2001) 19–33

13. Mailler, M., Lesser, V., Horling, B.: Cooperative negotiation for soft real-time distributed resource allocation. In *Proceedings of the second international joint conference on Autonomous agents and multiagent systems*. ACM Press (2003) 576–583

14. Prati, R. C., Baranauskas, J. A., Monard, M. C.: Uma proposta de unificação da linguagem de representao de conceitos de algoritmos de aprendizado de máquina simbólicos. Technical Report 137, ICMC-USP (2001)

15. Quinlan, J. R.: *C4.5: Programs for Machine Learning*. Morgan Kaufmann (1993)

16. Schroeder, L. F., Bazzan, A. L. C.: A multi-agent system to facilitate knowledge discovery: an application to bioinformatics. In *Proceedings of the Workshop on Bioinformatics and Multi-Agent Systems*, Bologna, Italy (2002) 44–50

17. Stolfo, S., Prodromidis, A., Tselepis, S., Lee, W., Fan, D.: Jam: Java agents for meta-learning over distributed databases. In *Proceedings of the Third Internation Conference on Knowledge Discovery and Data Mining.* AAAI Press (1997)
18. Viktor, H., Arndt, H.: Combining data mining and human expertise for making decisions, sense and policies. *Journal of Systems and Information Technology* 4(2) (2000) 33–56
19. Viktor, H., Arndt, H.: Data mining in practice: From data to knowledge using hybrid mining approach. *The International Journal of Computers, Systems and Signal,* 1(2) (2000) 139–153
20. Zhang, X., Lesser, V., Podorozhny, R.: Multi-dimensional, multistep negoriation for task allocation in a cooperative system. *Autonomous Agents and Multi-Agent Systems* 10 (2005) 5–40

Data Mining Techniques for RoboCup Soccer Agents

Lev Stankevich[1], Sergey Serebryakov[2], and Anton Ivanov[3]

[1] Saint Petersburg State Technical University,
29, Politechnicheskaya, St. Petersburg, 195251, Russia
stank@phtf.stu.neva.ru
[2] Saint Petersburg Institute for Informatics and Automation of the
Russian Academy of Science,
39, 14-th liniya of Vasilievskii Island, St. Petersburg, 199178, Russia
sergey_s@iias.spb.su
[3] Dr. Web Ltd,
80, Nevsky av, St. Petersburg, 195248, Russia
ai@drweb.com

Abstract. The paper describes an application of the data mining components with learning for RoboCup soccer agents. Data mining modules capable of on-line learning in dynamically changing environment are suggested. These modules provide for adaptive agent behavior in the form of the cognitive control systems that are able to self-tune in non-deterministic environment. Reinforcement learning is considered as the basic method for forming an agent behavior. A cognitive soccer agent for RoboCup Simulation League competitions capable of on-line learning has been developed and studied. Examples of shooting and teamwork are considered. The STEP team based on the cognitive agent succeeded in RoboCup German Open 2004 and was the winner of the RoboCup-2004 World Championship in simulation league.

1 Introduction

Using data mining techniques based on machine learning makes it possible to develop information and control systems able to learn from and adapt to their environment. The data mining techniques can be used for creating intelligent systems that may be able to solve complex control problems in adaptive manner based on a cognitive approach.

The cognitive approach in artificial intelligence has been a subject of discussion for a long time, e.g. [1]. It has resulted in creating some powerful cognitive systems that can be defined as intelligent systems able to learn and implement mental reasoning for decision making support in non-deterministic, dynamically changing environments. In such systems, the cognition is achieved through implementing the cognitive functions providing the systems with the learning capability and intelligent (proactive) behavior.

During the last twenty years various architectures for cognitive systems design have been developed. Multi-level, reactive and BDI (Belief-Desire-Intention) architectures [2] are well known. The last mentioned architecture is based on practical

V. Gorodetsky, J. Liu, and V.A. Skormin (Eds.): AIS-ADM 2005, LNAI 3505, pp. 289–301, 2005.

(human-like) reasoning. Lately, the BDI architecture has been used extensively for distributed control systems design based on the multi-agent system technology.

According to the multi-agent systems technology, the distributed control is implemented as a set of cooperating agents [3]. The agents implemented as cognitive systems coordinating their behavior are called "cognitive agents". Each particular cognitive agent performs a set of cognitive functions implementing individual or group behavior. The most sophisticated cognitive BDI agents are able to achieve human-similar behavior.

The cognitive agents must be able to learn and/or self-learn using various machine learning methods. A good example of implementation of a cognitive agent with learning is Theo (4], [5]). Theo was designed as a framework to support the "next generation" of the machine learning algorithms. These algorithms allow for an agent to adequately respond to environment changes. At present, on-line machine learning approach based on data mining techniques is used in cognitive agents design. It allows for processing raw data acquired directly from the environment in order to work out the behavior rules required for fast adaptation to the environment changes.

The interaction of a cognitive agent with the other ones is determined by its functions of upper level (group behavior). Special cognitive functions implementing the coordination mechanisms must be used for the cooperation between the agents. They have to provide the agents with an ability to learn how to co-operate and/or compete. Among the other methods of this kind, the reinforcement learning is viewed as the prime method of forming the group behavior of a cognitive agent.

In this paper we are showing how the cognitive agents and uniform learning components implementing the cognitive functions realizing the individual and group behavior of the adaptive agents can be built. The developed uniform data mining components can be specialized and adapted by means of tuning. Using a case study from the Robocup framework, we will also show, that the on-line adaptive cooperation of the cognitive soccer agents built on the basis of combining the multi-level and reactive architectures with the BDI architecture in combination with using the data mining components, can provide for high efficiency of the distributed control.

The work is based on the authors' experience in designing a multi-agent cognitive system intended for industrial and socio-technical object control [6] and specific cognitive soccer agents designed for the RoboCup Simulation League competitions [7], and cognitive control systems for intelligent robotics ([8], [9]).

The rest of the paper is organized as follows. Section 2 contains brief description of the agent's architecture, section 3 describes agent's learning components, section 4 presents experiments with data-mining learning components. Conclusion summarizes the paper results.

2 Architecture of Cognitive Agents

For a cognitive agent to be provided with a sophisticated adaptive individual and group behavior, it must be built using a combination of multilevel and layered architectures. Several versions of three-level cognitive agents [10] have been developed.

The low level of the agent has a layered reactive architecture. It includes several executive layers. Each of them has its own priority. It reacts to the current situation and responses to it corresponding actions. A set of such reactions defines a certain primitive executive behavior called agent's skills. A sequence of the reactions corresponds to the current intentions of the agent.

The middle level of the agent in supplied with some elements of the BDI architecture. It consists of modules built according to cognitive concepts of beliefs, desires and intentions defining an individual agent's behavior. The agent's beliefs correspond to the data, facts, and situations that are known to the agent. The desires are defined as the goals or plans. They are also known to the agent. The intentions include the sequences of actions that must be performed by the agent according to its plan. The upper level of the agent is also supplied with some elements of the BDI architecture that are responsible for the corresponding group behavior of the agent. This level uses the potential intentions of the agent produced by the middle level, and coordinates them with the intentions of the other agents. In case of conflicts, the common beliefs of agents are formed. A conflict is supposed to be solved when the agent's intentions and beliefs have been satisfied. Afterwards, each agent corrects its individual intentions according to the common intentions of the agent community.

One of the versions of the cognitive agent having the described architecture was used for development of the soccer agents. A set of modules of all levels was implemented using rule-based and neuro-logical components. The agent achieved good results at the World Championship RoboCup-2004: STEP (Soccer Team of ElectroPult) team of agents that had been built according to the above described architecture was the winner in Simulation Soccer 2D league.

3 Learning Components of the Cognitive Agents

The main structural components of the cognitive soccer agent are modules capable of on-line learning. Well-known formal neuron and neural network modules can be used for implementing the cognitive functions. However, these modules have significant restrictions in terms of the variety of the functions they are able to implement and of the learning rate. To get over these restrictions, special data mining modules based on the fast adaptive functional approximation were developed and studied. One of them, the cluster module based on the neuro- and fuzzy-logic approach was selected for practical usage [10].

3.1 The Neuro-Logical Module

This module includes two components: Activator and Learner. Unlike standard fuzzy-logical systems, it does not require a preliminary set of input terms since they are formed dynamically via training the examples. Besides, the Activator of the module calculates a precise output vector directly, i.e. without fuzzification. In this approach, we lose accuracy of transformation but decrease the volume of the resources consumed.

Let $\mu_j(x_i)$ be the value of the j-th term function of the i-th input signal. Then, the function being realized by the Activator can be represented as follows:

$$Y = sign(w_k) \bigcup_{i=1}^{m} \left| w_i \bigcap_{j=1}^{n} \mu_{ij}(X_j) \right| , \tag{1}$$

where n stands for the number of inputs; m stands for the number of learning examples; w_i stands for the weight coefficient corresponding to the i-th term; and k stands for the number of a defining term.

The Learner implements tuning of the weights of the individual terms and coordinates their boundaries and center. The process of learning consists of two phases. At the beginning, for each example, an n-dimensional term is generated, the top of which lies at the point where this example is defined. The boundaries of each term are shaped as an n-dimensional hyper rectangle in the space of the object's inputs. In the first phase, the boundaries of all terms coincide with the boundaries of the input space. In the second phase, the term's boundaries are normalized in such a way that all the examples could be calculated correctly. Having processed all the examples, the correction of the term boundaries is performed. The purpose of this correction consists in fixing the common constraints superimposed by the terms to each other. Thus, the fast learning process is achieved.

3.2   The Data Mining Module with Reinforcement Learning

Reinforcement learning (RL) problem implies learning through interaction with the environment to achieve a given goal (fig. 1). The learner is viewed as an agent. It interacts with the environment that includes everything outside of the agent. They interact continuously – the agent chooses actions and the environment submits new situations to the agent:

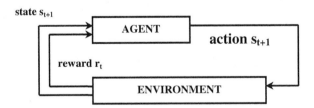

Fig. 1. Agent-environment interface

More specifically, the agent and its environment interact sequentially at each discrete time instant t_k, $k = 0,1,2,3,...$. At given time instant, t , the agent receives a representation of the environment's *state*, $s_t \in S$, where S is the set of all possible states, and based on this information selects an *action*, $a_t \in A(s_t)$, where $A(s_t)$ is the set of actions available in state s_t. At the next time instant, the agent receives a numerical *reward*, $r_{t+1} \in R$, and finds out a new state, s_{t+1}. At each time instant, the agent implements a mapping from state representations to the probability space determining the probability distribution of the possible action choices. This mapping is called the agent's *policy* and denoted π_t, where $\pi_t(s,a)$ is the probability that $a_t = a$ if $s_t = s$. Reinforcement learning methods specify how the agent changes its policy as a result of its experience accumulated. Roughly speaking, the agent's goal is to maximize the total amount of rewards it receives over a long run.

3.3 Algorithm of Multi-agent Learning

The basic RL algorithms can be found in [11]. In this paper we will describe only a modification of this algorithm [12].

There exists an assumption in the reinforcement learning theory, that an agent is able to call the environment to obtain the next state. A reward is also given to the agent by the environment. However, in the soccer a server controls the environment and informs the agent about its state at non-deterministic time instants. To cope with this uncertainty three additional routines are used:

BeginEpisode() –the agent calls for this routine at the very beginning of each episode; *DoEpisodeStep*() –the agent calls for this routine to process the non-terminal step of the current episode;

EndEpisode(bool success) –this routine is called for if the current episode reaches a terminal state, which is to be processed in some special way. *Success* – the parameter determining the successfulness of the episode (*true* – success, *false* - failure). In the Fig.2 the modified *Sarsa* (λ) algorithm is presented.

The neuro-logical module is used for value function approximation. Any input vector (state) falls within the range of some of the local receptive fields (the excited receptive fields), and falls outside of the range of most of the receptive fields. The response of the neuro-logical module to a given input is the average of the responses of the receptive fields, excited by that input, and is not affected by the other receptive fields. Similarly, a neural network trained for a given input vector affects the adjustable parameters of the excited receptive fields, but does not affect the parameters of the remaining majority of receptive fields. Lines 3, 10, 17, 26 of the algorithm presented in Fig.2, 3 reflect the above fact. Lines 5 and 19 point out the technique of the action selection. In most cases, the action with the highest value function is chosen. This strategy is called "exploitation". But sometimes other, non-optimal, action having law probability may be chosen, the strategy being called "exploration" – in this way, the estimate of a non-optimal action's value is improved.

BeginEpisode ()

1. $currentStep \leftarrow 1$

2. $\vec{e} = 0$

3. $T \leftarrow$ set of active tiles for new (current) state s

4. $\vec{Q}_a \leftarrow \{\sum_{i \in T} \theta(i)\}_j, j = \overline{1, n}, n -$ number of possible actions

5. $lastOption \leftarrow \begin{cases} \arg\max_a \vec{Q}_a & \text{with probability } 1 - \varepsilon \\ random(\arg \vec{Q}_a) & \text{with probability } \varepsilon \end{cases}$

7. $Q_{lastOption} \leftarrow \vec{Q}_{lastOption}$

DoEpisodeStep ()

8. $currentStep \leftarrow currentStep + 1$

9. $if\,(stepLimit\,\&\,\&currentStep > MAX\_STEPS)\,return\,false$

10. $T \leftarrow$ set of active tiles for previous state S

11. for all a

12.   for all $i \in T$

13.   if $a == lastOption$

14. $e(i) = 1$

15.   else

16. $e(i) = 0$

17. $T \leftarrow$ set of active tiles for new (current) state s'

18. $\vec{Q}_a \leftarrow \{\sum_{i \in T} \theta(i)\}_j, j = \overline{1, n}, n -$ number of possible actions

19. $newOption \leftarrow \begin{cases} \arg\max_a \vec{Q}_a & \text{with probability } 1 - \varepsilon \\ random(\arg \vec{Q}_a) & \text{with probability } \varepsilon \end{cases}$

20. $Q_{newOption} \leftarrow \vec{Q}_{newOption}$

21. $\delta \leftarrow rewardForStep + \gamma Q_{newOption} - Q_{oldOption}$

22. $\vec{\theta} \leftarrow \vec{\theta} + \alpha \delta \vec{e}$

23. $Q_{lastOption} = Q_{newOption}$

24. $\vec{e} \leftarrow \lambda \vec{e}$

EndEpisode (bool success)

25. $numberOfPlayedEpisodes \leftarrow numberOfPlayedEpisodes + 1$

26. $T \leftarrow$ set of active tiles for previous state S

27. for all a

28.   for all $i \in T$

29.   if $a == lastOption$

30. $e(i) = 1$

31.   else

32. $e(i) = 0$

33. if $success == true$

34. $reward \leftarrow rewardForSuccess$

35. else

36. $reward \leftarrow rewardForFailure$

37. $\delta \leftarrow reward - Q_{oldOption}$

38. $\vec{\theta} \leftarrow \vec{\theta} + \alpha \delta \vec{e}$

39. $SaveEpisode()$ - saving information about the episode.

Fig. 2. Modified $Sarsa(\lambda)$ algorithm

4 Study of the Cognitive Soccer Agent Using Data Mining Modules

4.1 Simple Cognitive Shoot Function

Let's consider the following situation: an agent (shooter) tries to kick the ball in a way that prevents it being intercepted by another agent (e.g., by the goalkeeper). The first possible approach to achieving the above aim consists in the interception point calculation. Using this method, the agent calculates the interception point of the goalkeeper. If this point is out of the pitch and beyond the line of goal, the shot is assessed as a success; otherwise it is assessed as a failure. The disadvantages of this method are as follows:

- The approach is not able to compute the probability of success or failure, i.e. that information would be very useful for the agent;
- This is a time consuming method. Indeed, the full time of the calculation may be too long (agent has to try many values of kick angle and speed to choose the optimum ones).

Better results are achieved based on the approach using the above described neuro-logic module that can be trained an examples and performs well enough even in "unseen" situations, i.e., in the situations that are not presented in the training data set. So, the task under consideration consists in constructing the function

$$p = F(s), p \in R^1, s \in S,\tag{2}$$

transforming a specification of the current situation s into the probability p of non-successful performance of the goalkeeper. In the formula (2), S stands for the set of all possible states.

In the above task, there exist several ways to represent formally the world state s. One of them is given below in the equation (3)

$$s = < A_p, G_p, G_v, K_v >,\tag{3}$$

where A_p stands for the position of the shooting player(shooter), G_p stands for the goalkeeper's position relatively to the shooter's one, G_v stands for the goalkeeper's velocity vector, K_v stands for the kick speed.

The problem to be solved in this case consists in searching for the optimal shoot angle:

$$\alpha_{opt} = \alpha_i : p_{\alpha_i} = \max_{K_v} F(s), \alpha_i \in \alpha,\tag{4}$$

where K_v is the set of all possible kick angles, p_{α_i} - the probability of the kick along i-th angle.

Experiment

The experiment described below aims at collecting the examples constituting the training and testing data set, including the examples of successful and unsuccessful kicks. In the experiment, the following situation was analyzed: the shooter is standing at 15 meters facing the goal. The ball is placed near the player in front of him. The position of the goalkeeper is chosen randomly between the shooter and the goal line inside the rectangle, as shown in Fig. 1. The shooter waits 10 simulation cycles to give the goalkeeper time to localize himself and to detect where the ball is. After this technical delay, the shooter kicks the ball with the speed of 2.0 meters per cycles straight to the goal. The episode is considered to be success if the ball moves out of the pitch (and beyond the line of goal), otherwise it is assumed that the goalkeeper intercepts the ball and, consequently, the episode is assessed as a failure.

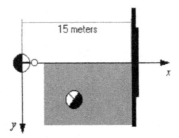

Fig. 3. Shoot training episode

Any episode is described by the following parameters:

- the distance from the shooter to the point of intersection of the ball path line and the field edge;
- the kick speed;
- the distance between the goalkeeper and the ball trajectory;
- the distance between the shooter and the goalkeeper's projection point onto the ball trajectory.

For the whole period the first two parameters remain constant, and the rest ones vary randomly. It's supposed that the goalkeeper begins to intercept the moving ball in the cycle following the shooter's kick; the initial goalkeeper's speed is zero, his body is positioned facing the ball. For this case, the world state is represented by the tuple:

$$s =< d, K_v, G_p >,\qquad(5)$$

where d stands for the distance between the shooter and the point formed by intersection of the ball path and field edge, K_v – the shoot speed (absolute value), G_p – goalkeeper position (G_x, G_y) in the coordinates depicted in Fig.4.

Having played a large number of episodes, the following set of examples was collected:

The number of played episodes –11638;

The number of goals – 8710;

The number of successful ball interceptions by the goalkeeper - 2928;

Later, the data processing intended at getting the examples required for training and testing of the fuzzy-logic system from given data set was performed. For this data processing, the area, in which the goalkeeper had been placed during the training was divided into 100 sub-areas.

The shooter's position is represented by the vector having coordinates (0, 0). The line with x=15 is considered as the edge line. Each sub–area is specified by the following parameters:

- values of x and y of the center in the coordinates depicted in Fig. 4;
- the number of the episodes in which the coordinates of the initial goalkeeper's position belong to this particular sub-area;
- the numbers of the successful and non-successful shooter's kicks.

Each area is characterized by the pair:

$$a_i =< C_i, p_i >, i = \overline{1, N}, \qquad (6)$$

where N - the number of areas, C_i is the center of the i-th area, p_i is the frequency of successful shots for the i-th area.

Thus, the set A of learning examples is represented as follows:

$$A = \{a_i\}_{i=1}^{N}. \qquad (7)$$

Experimental results

Based on the above data, the following calculations have been performed.

The input of the fuzzy-logic system is represented as an array of the coordinates of the sub-area centers. The output specifies the frequency of successful kicks. Table 1 presents the sample of the examples.

Table 1. Experimental results

Coordi-nates	0,75	2,25	3,75	5,25	6,75	8,25	9,75	11,25	12,75	14,25
0,75	0.1	0.069	0.053	0.062	0.062	0.044	0.023	0.0076	0	0.006
2,25	0.54	0.45	0.39	0.43	0.4	0.31	0.2	0.063	0.0052	0.048
3,75	0.97	0.96	0.96	0.96	0.9	0.79	0.51	0.22	0.082	0.16
5,25	1	1	1	1	0.99	0.93	0.73	0.57	0.34	0.37
6,75	1	1	1	1	1	0.99	0.96	0.9	0.73	0.71
8,25	1	1	1	1	1	1	1	1	0.99	0.96
9,75	1	1	1	1	1	1	1	1	1	1
11,25	1	1	1	1	1	1	1	1	1	1
12,75	1	1	1	1	1	1	1	1	1	1
14,25	1	1	1	1	1	1	1	1	1	1

It can be seen from the table that the number of the examples can be reduced by removing superfluous examples. After that, 53 examples were obtained. Thus, while using these results, the agent can forecast the probability of successful shooting even in the situations, which are not presented by the training examples.

The mentioned above covers the situations in which the distance between the shooter and the goal is 15 meters and the kick speed is 2 meters per cycle. In the same way fuzzy-logic systems can be trained for other situations, e.g. if the distances are 0, 15 and 20 meters, and the speed value is chosen from the sequence of values 1.5, 2.0, 2.5 meters per cycle. In a real game, the agent can use the best suitable learned system.

The developed cognitive function possesses the following advantages:

– While exploring the kick angle aspect, the agent gets not only the information whether a shoot was or was not a success, but also learns a number from the interval [0, 1] which is the measure of this success;
– In some cases, this method outperforms the one based on interception point calculations, while working approximately 7 times faster than the latter.

4.2 Cognitive Function for Multi-agent Scenario Control

Acquiring the skill of acting in a multi-agent environment is being studied in the context of scenarios. Formally, a scenario consists of two parts – conditions of initialization, and a control system, i.e. a policy (the rules for acting within the scenario). In this paragraph, the experiment in which the original rule-based control system was replaced by the proposed system is described.

It is well known that using scenarios in the opponent's penalty area is of great importance, that why a scenario of this kind was considered. It is assumed that three players are involved in such scenarios – two teammates trying to score a goal, and one opponent, the goalkeeper, defending the goal. The learning task consists in finding a policy allowing the agents to score a goal as fast as possible:

$$\pi^* = \arg\min_{\forall \pi \in \Pi} K \tag{8}$$

where $K = K(\pi)$ stands for the function determining duration of an episode if the agent follows policy π; Π stands for the set of all possible policies and π^* is the optimal one.

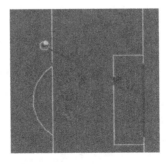

Fig. 4. State representation

Denotations:

d_1 - the distance between teammate with the ball and the opponent; d_2 - the distance between teammate with the ball and its partner; d_3 - the distance between teammate with the ball and the center of the goal; β - angle between d_1 and d_2; $s = (d_1, d_2, d_3, \beta)^T$;

It is assumed that only one agent learns to act i.e. an agent, possessing the ball (the first teammate). This agent initiates the scenario. It must learn how to act at every stage of any episode: either to dribble to goal or to pass ball directly to a teammate. The second teammate, when having received the ball, just kicks it into the goal along the optimal kicking line. The episode is assessed as a success if a goal is scored or as failure if the goalkeeper catches the ball. All other possible terminal states are considered as errors, and are not processed.

According to the time minimization criteria, the following rewards are used: for each episode step the reward $r_{forEpisodeStep} = -0.001$; for a success the reward is $r_{forSuccessEnd} = 1$, and, if the result is a failure, the reward is $r_{forFailureEnd} = -1$. In Fig. 4 a typical snapshot of the episode containing information about the state representation is depicted.

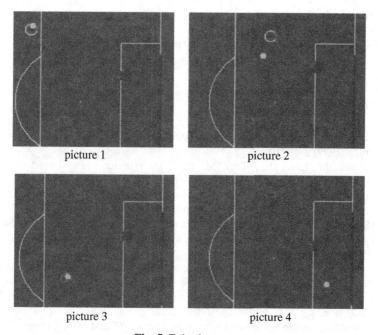

picture 1   picture 2

picture 3   picture 4

Fig. 5. Episode steps

Fig. 5 presents four steps of the played episode. The first (left upper) picture corresponds to the beginning of the episode. The agent has chosen to dribble. In the picture 2 (right upper) one can see that the agent has passed the ball to its partner. The next picture (left lower) shows that the second agent has received the ball, and is going to try to score the goal. At that moment, the goalkeeper is changing its defending position trying to prevent the goal. The situation before the end of the episode is shown in the last picture. The second agent has scored the goal, and goalkeeper, having being outplayed, is not able to get the ball. The episode in about two simulation cycles will be ended successfully.

5   Conclusion

A cognitive soccer agent for RoboCup Simulation League competitions based on the proposed combined architecture and new data mining modules intended for on-line learning has been developed and studied. The proposed cognitive functions based on the data mining modules provide a noticeable increase of efficiency and effectiveness of the teammate shoot skill and team-play scenario for 2 players attacking the opponent's goal. The STEP team successfully participated in the RoboCup German Open 2004 in Paderborn, Germany and in the RoboCup-2004 World Championship in Lisbon, Portugal was the winner. Future work intends to study the capabilities of the proposed data mining module in other agent coordination applications.

Acknowledgement

This work was supported by EOARD of the US Air Force (ISTC Project 1992P) and Joint-Stock Company Electropult Plant.

References

1. Hayes-Roth, B., Hayes-Roth, F.: A Cognitive Model of Planning. In Cognitive Science. Vol. 3 (1979) 275–310
2. Bratman, M., Israel D., Pollack, M.: Plans and resource-bounded practical reasoning. In Computational Intelligence, #4 (1988) 349–355
3. Gorodetski, V., Lebedev, A.: Multi-agent Technology for Planning, Scheduling, and Resource Allocation. Proc. of 3d Int. Conf. on Multi-Agent Systems, Paris, France (1998)
4. Mitchell, T., Allen, J., Chalasani, P., Cheng, J., Etzioni, O., Ringuette, M., Schlimmer, J.: Theo: A framework for self-improving systems. K. VanLehn (ed.), In Architectures for Intelligence (1991) 323–355
5. Mitchell, T.: Plan-then-compile Architectures. In SIGART Bulletin 2 (1991) 136–139
6. Nurulin, Y., Stankevich, L.: Cognitive modeling and management of socio-technical systems. Proceeding of ICIL'99, S-Petersburg, Russia, Univ. of Southampton, UK (1999)
7. Stankevich, L.: A cognitive agent for soccer game. Proceeding of First Workshop of Central and Eastern Europe on Multi-agent Systems (CEEMAC'99), Printed by "Anatolyi", S-Petersburg (1999)
8. Stankevich, L.: Multiagent technology in cognitive control systems for autonomous robots. «Extreme robotics. Proc. of 10-th Conference, St. Petersburg», STUPress (1999)
9. Stankevich, L.: Cognitive robotics. «Extreme robotics. Proceeding of XII-th Conference, St. Petersburg», St. Petersburg STUPress (2002)

10. Stankevich, L.: Cognitive structures and agents in intellectual robot control systems. AI News #1 (2004) 41–55

11. Sutton, R., Barto, A.: Reinforcement Learning: An introduction. MIT Press, Cambridge, MA (1998)

12. Serebryakov, S., Ivanov, A., Stankevich, L.: Robotic soccer, reinforcement learning and teamwork. X International Student Olympiad on Automatic Control (Baltic Olympiad). Preprints. Saint-Petersburg, Saint-Petersburg State University of Information Technologies, Mechanics And Optics (2004) 123–128

Author Index

Lecture Notes in Artificial Intelligence (LNAI)

Vol. 3518: T.B. Ho, D. Cheung, H. Li (Eds.), Advances in Knowledge Discovery and Data Mining. XXI, 864 pages. 2005.

Vol. 3508: P. Bresciani, P. Giorgini, B. Henderson-Sellers, G. Low, M. Winikoff (Eds.), Agent-Oriented Information Systems II. X, 227 pages. 2005.

Vol. 3505: V. Gorodetsky, J. Liu, V. A. Skormin (Eds.), Autonomous Intelligent Systems: Agents and Data Mining. XIII, 303 pages. 2005.

Vol. 3501: B. Kégl, G. Lapalme (Eds.), Advances in Artificial Intelligence. XV, 458 pages. 2005.

Vol. 3492: P. Blache, E. Stabler, J. Busquets, R. Moot (Eds.), Logical Aspects of Computational Linguistics. X, 363 pages. 2005.

Vol. 3488: M.-S. Hacid, N.V. Murray, Z.W. Raś, S. Tsumoto (Eds.), Foundations of Intelligent Systems. XIII, 700 pages. 2005.

Vol. 3452: F. Baader, A. Voronkov (Eds.), Logic for Programming, Artificial Intelligence, and Reasoning. XI, 562 pages. 2005.

Vol. 3419: B. Faltings, A. Petcu, F. Fages, F. Rossi (Eds.), Constraint Satisfaction and Constraint Logic Programming. X, 217 pages. 2005.

Vol. 3416: M. Böhlen, J. Gamper, W. Polasek, M.A. Wimmer (Eds.), E-Government: Towards Electronic Democracy. XIII, 311 pages. 2005.

Vol. 3415: P. Davidsson, B. Logan, K. Takadama (Eds.), Multi-Agent and Multi-Agent-Based Simulation. X, 265 pages. 2005.

Vol. 3403: B. Ganter, R. Godin (Eds.), Formal Concept Analysis. XI, 419 pages. 2005.

Vol. 3398: D.-K. Baik (Ed.), Systems Modeling and Simulation: Theory and Applications. XIV, 733 pages. 2005.

Vol. 3397: T.G. Kim (Ed.), Artificial Intelligence and Simulation. XV, 711 pages. 2005.

Vol. 3396: R.M. van Eijk, M.-P. Huget, F. Dignum (Eds.), Agent Communication. X, 261 pages. 2005.

Vol. 3394: D. Kudenko, D. Kazakov, E. Alonso (Eds.), Adaptive Agents and Multi-Agent Systems II. VIII, 313 pages. 2005.

Vol. 3392: D. Seipel, M. Hanus, U. Geske, O. Bartenstein (Eds.), Applications of Declarative Programming and Knowledge Management. X, 309 pages. 2005.

Vol. 3374: D. Weyns, H.V.D. Parunak, F. Michel (Eds.), Environments for Multi-Agent Systems. X, 279 pages. 2005.

Vol. 3371: M.W. Barley, N. Kasabov (Eds.), Intelligent Agents and Multi-Agent Systems. X, 329 pages. 2005.

Vol. 3369: V.R. Benjamins, P. Casanovas, J. Breuker, A. Gangemi (Eds.), Law and the Semantic Web. XII, 249 pages. 2005.

Vol. 3366: I. Rahwan, P. Moraitis, C. Reed (Eds.), Argumentation in Multi-Agent Systems. XII, 263 pages. 2005.

Vol. 3359: G. Grieser, Y. Tanaka (Eds.), Intuitive Human Interfaces for Organizing and Accessing Intellectual Assets. XIV, 257 pages. 2005.

Vol. 3346: R.H. Bordini, M. Dastani, J. Dix, A.E.F. Seghrouchni (Eds.), Programming Multi-Agent Systems. XIV, 249 pages. 2005.

Vol. 3345: Y. Cai (Ed.), Ambient Intelligence for Scientific Discovery. XII, 311 pages. 2005.

Vol. 3343: C. Freksa, M. Knauff, B. Krieg-Brückner, B. Nebel, T. Barkowsky (Eds.), Spatial Cognition IV. XIII, 519 pages. 2005.

Vol. 3339: G.I. Webb, X. Yu (Eds.), AI 2004: Advances in Artificial Intelligence. XXII, 1272 pages. 2004.

Vol. 3336: D. Karagiannis, U. Reimer (Eds.), Practical Aspects of Knowledge Management. X, 523 pages. 2004.

Vol. 3327: Y. Shi, W. Xu, Z. Chen (Eds.), Data Mining and Knowledge Management. XIII, 263 pages. 2005.

Vol. 3315: C. Lemaître, C.A. Reyes, J.A. González (Eds.), Advances in Artificial Intelligence – IBERAMIA 2004. XX, 987 pages. 2004.

Vol. 3303: J.A. López, E. Benfenati, W. Dubitzky (Eds.), Knowledge Exploration in Life Science Informatics. X, 249 pages. 2004.

Vol. 3301: G. Kern-Isberner, W. Rödder, F. Kulmann (Eds.), Conditionals, Information, and Inference. XII, 219 pages. 2005.

Vol. 3276: D. Nardi, M. Riedmiller, C. Sammut, J. Santos-Victor (Eds.), RoboCup 2004: Robot Soccer World Cup VIII. XVIII, 678 pages. 2005.

Vol. 3275: P. Perner (Ed.), Advances in Data Mining. VIII, 173 pages. 2004.

Vol. 3265: R.E. Frederking, K.B. Taylor (Eds.), Machine Translation: From Real Users to Research. XI, 392 pages. 2004.

Vol. 3264: G. Paliouras, Y. Sakakibara (Eds.), Grammatical Inference: Algorithms and Applications. XI, 291 pages. 2004.

Vol. 3259: J. Dix, J. Leite (Eds.), Computational Logic in Multi-Agent Systems. XII, 251 pages. 2004.

Vol. 3257: E. Motta, N.R. Shadbolt, A. Stutt, N. Gibbins (Eds.), Engineering Knowledge in the Age of the Semantic Web. XVII, 517 pages. 2004.

Vol. 3249: B. Buchberger, J.A. Campbell (Eds.), Artificial Intelligence and Symbolic Computation. X, 285 pages. 2004.

Vol. 3248: K.-Y. Su, J. Tsujii, J.-H. Lee, O.Y. Kwong (Eds.), Natural Language Processing – IJCNLP 2004. XVIII, 817 pages. 2005.

Vol. 3245: E. Suzuki, S. Arikawa (Eds.), Discovery Science. XIV, 430 pages. 2004.

Vol. 3244: S. Ben-David, J. Case, A. Maruoka (Eds.), Algorithmic Learning Theory. XIV, 505 pages. 2004.

Vol. 3238: S. Biundo, T. Frühwirth, G. Palm (Eds.), KI 2004: Advances in Artificial Intelligence. XI, 467 pages. 2004.

Vol. 3230: J.L. Vicedo, P. Martínez-Barco, R. Muñoz, M. Saiz Noeda (Eds.), Advances in Natural Language Processing. XII, 488 pages. 2004.

Vol. 3229: J.J. Alferes, J. Leite (Eds.), Logics in Artificial Intelligence. XIV, 744 pages. 2004.

Vol. 3228: M.G. Hinchey, J.L. Rash, W.F. Truszkowski, C.A. Rouff (Eds.), Formal Approaches to Agent-Based Systems. VIII, 290 pages. 2004.

Vol. 3215: M.G.. Negoita, R.J. Howlett, L.C. Jain (Eds.), Knowledge-Based Intelligent Information and Engineering Systems, Part III. LVII, 906 pages. 2004.

Vol. 3214: M.G.. Negoita, R.J. Howlett, L.C. Jain (Eds.), Knowledge-Based Intelligent Information and Engineering Systems, Part II. LVIII, 1302 pages. 2004.

Vol. 3213: M.G.. Negoita, R.J. Howlett, L.C. Jain (Eds.), Knowledge-Based Intelligent Information and Engineering Systems, Part I. LVIII, 1280 pages. 2004.

Vol. 3209: B. Berendt, A. Hotho, D. Mladenic, M. van Someren, M. Spiliopoulou, G. Stumme (Eds.), Web Mining: From Web to Semantic Web. IX, 201 pages. 2004.

Vol. 3206: P. Sojka, I. Kopecek, K. Pala (Eds.), Text, Speech and Dialogue. XIII, 667 pages. 2004.

Vol. 3202: J.-F. Boulicaut, F. Esposito, F. Giannotti, D. Pedreschi (Eds.), Knowledge Discovery in Databases: PKDD 2004. XIX, 560 pages. 2004.

Vol. 3201: J.-F. Boulicaut, F. Esposito, F. Giannotti, D. Pedreschi (Eds.), Machine Learning: ECML 2004. XVIII, 580 pages. 2004.

Vol. 3194: R. Camacho, R. King, A. Srinivasan (Eds.), Inductive Logic Programming. XI, 361 pages. 2004.

Vol. 3192: C. Bussler, D. Fensel (Eds.), Artificial Intelligence: Methodology, Systems, and Applications. XIII, 522 pages. 2004.

Vol. 3191: M. Klusch, S. Ossowski, V. Kashyap, R. Unland (Eds.), Cooperative Information Agents VIII. XI, 303 pages. 2004.

Vol. 3187: G. Lindemann, J. Denzinger, I.J. Timm, R. Unland (Eds.), Multiagent System Technologies. XIII, 341 pages. 2004.

Vol. 3176: O. Bousquet, U. von Luxburg, G. Rätsch (Eds.), Advanced Lectures on Machine Learning. IX, 241 pages. 2004.

Vol. 3171: A.L.C. Bazzan, S. Labidi (Eds.), Advances in Artificial Intelligence – SBIA 2004. XVII, 548 pages. 2004.

Vol. 3159: U. Visser, Intelligent Information Integration for the Semantic Web. XIV, 150 pages. 2004.

Vol. 3157: C. Zhang, H. W. Guesgen, W.K. Yeap (Eds.), PRICAI 2004: Trends in Artificial Intelligence. XX, 1023 pages. 2004.

Vol. 3155: P. Funk, P.A. González Calero (Eds.), Advances in Case-Based Reasoning. XIII, 822 pages. 2004.

Vol. 3139: F. Iida, R. Pfeifer, L. Steels, Y. Kuniyoshi (Eds.), Embodied Artificial Intelligence. IX, 331 pages. 2004.

Vol. 3131: V. Torra, Y. Narukawa (Eds.), Modeling Decisions for Artificial Intelligence. XI, 327 pages. 2004.

Vol. 3127: K.E. Wolff, H.D. Pfeiffer, H.S. Delugach (Eds.), Conceptual Structures at Work. XI, 403 pages. 2004.

Vol. 3123: A. Belz, R. Evans, P. Piwek (Eds.), Natural Language Generation. X, 219 pages. 2004.

Vol. 3120: J. Shawe-Taylor, Y. Singer (Eds.), Learning Theory. X, 648 pages. 2004.

Vol. 3097: D. Basin, M. Rusinowitch (Eds.), Automated Reasoning. XII, 493 pages. 2004.

Vol. 3071: A. Omicini, P. Petta, J. Pitt (Eds.), Engineering Societies in the Agents World. XIII, 409 pages. 2004.

Vol. 3070: L. Rutkowski, J. Siekmann, R. Tadeusiewicz, L.A. Zadeh (Eds.), Artificial Intelligence and Soft Computing - ICAISC 2004. XXV, 1208 pages. 2004.

Vol. 3068: E. André, L. Dybkjær, W. Minker, P. Heisterkamp (Eds.), Affective Dialogue Systems. XII, 324 pages. 2004.

Vol. 3067: M. Dastani, J. Dix, A. El Fallah-Seghrouchni (Eds.), Programming Multi-Agent Systems. X, 221 pages. 2004.

Vol. 3066: S. Tsumoto, R. Słowiński, J. Komorowski, J.W. Grzymała-Busse (Eds.), Rough Sets and Current Trends in Computing. XX, 853 pages. 2004.

Vol. 3065: A. Lomuscio, D. Nute (Eds.), Deontic Logic in Computer Science. X, 275 pages. 2004.

Vol. 3060: A.Y. Tawfik, S.D. Goodwin (Eds.), Advances in Artificial Intelligence. XIII, 582 pages. 2004.

Vol. 3056: H. Dai, R. Srikant, C. Zhang (Eds.), Advances in Knowledge Discovery and Data Mining. XIX, 713 pages. 2004.

Vol. 3055: H. Christiansen, M.-S. Hacid, T. Andreasen, H.L. Larsen (Eds.), Flexible Query Answering Systems. X, 500 pages. 2004.

Vol. 3048: P. Faratin, D.C. Parkes, J.A. Rodríguez-Aguilar, W.E. Walsh (Eds.), Agent-Mediated Electronic Commerce V. XI, 155 pages. 2004.

Vol. 3040: R. Conejo, M. Urretavizcaya, J.-L. Pérez-de-la-Cruz (Eds.), Current Topics in Artificial Intelligence. XIV, 689 pages. 2004.

Vol. 3035: M.A. Wimmer (Ed.), Knowledge Management in Electronic Government. XII, 326 pages. 2004.

Vol. 3034: J. Favela, E. Menasalvas, E. Chávez (Eds.), Advances in Web Intelligence. XIII, 227 pages. 2004.

Vol. 3030: P. Giorgini, B. Henderson-Sellers, M. Winikoff (Eds.), Agent-Oriented Information Systems. XIV, 207 pages. 2004.

Vol. 3029: B. Orchard, C. Yang, M. Ali (Eds.), Innovations in Applied Artificial Intelligence. XXI, 1272 pages. 2004.